D0090676

Praise for *Empty Hands, Open Arms*

"We are about to lose one of our closest cousins, like us a primate. How many more cousins can we afford to lose before we are alone? And when we're alone will we still be human—or a diminished animal ourselves? This dramatic account of heroic conservation efforts to save the bonobo, 'our closest living relative alongside the chimpanzee,' is at once riveting, emotional, historical, and scientific, full of vignettes that disclose human and animal conflicts, sexuality, political and economic realities, psychological insight, and compassion. Into the Congo, this adventure reveals not a heart of darkness but a rich world of light, shade, and imperiled life, a connection between the human and the great circle of being, on whose circumference near us sits—if we help it—the bonobo, and the great rain forest it inhabits."

—James Engell, editor of *Environment: An Interdisciplinary Anthology* and Faculty Associate of the Harvard University Center for the Environment

"Reading *Empty Hands, Open Arms* brought me nearly to tears of despair for the desperate, desperate situation of bonobos, the world's most endearing and endangered great apes—and then again to tears of joyful admiration for the brave and smart people working to save them in the Democratic Republic of the Congo. Buy this book, and you will discover a seed of hope in our time's garden of despair."

—Dale Peterson, author of *The Moral Lives of Animals* and *Jane Goodall: The Woman Who Redefined Man*

"In this compelling and inspirational account, Béchard chronicles the visionary work being done to protect the bonobo and the world's second largest rainforest—the 'left lung' of the planet that produces much of the oxygen needed to sustain life on earth."

—Chip Comins, Founder, Chairman & CEO, American Renewable Energy Institute

"*Empty Hands, Open Arms* offers us a vision of a truly non-colonial approach to conservation, one that respects both the rights and knowledge of local people, and engages with them as equal partners in conservation. As we work toward the UN Millennium Development Goal of ensuring environmental sustainability, this book has much to teach us about how we can save the earth's wildlife and rainforests."

—Philip Bonn, Director-General of World of Hope International, Special Consultative Status to United Nations ECOSOC (Economic and Social Council)

"Béchard offers us an inspired, poignant, and seriously researched look at a subject of profound importance, the protection of bonobos and of the rainforest. He reveals the crucial role that local indigenous knowledge and traditions can play in addressing what is truly the greatest threat to humanity: the degradation and destruction of our ecosystems. In a story at once captivating and shocking, he shows us that Western scientific experts do not have all of the answers and cannot simply impose programs developed in the US and Europe, but that committed, visionary individuals who are ready to make sacrifices and listen to the voices of the forest can also have a profound and lasting impact."

—Wade Davis, National Geographic explorer-in-residence and author of *The Serpent and the Rainbow*, *One River: Explorations and Discoveries in the Amazon Rain Forest*, and *Into the Silence: The Great War, Mallory and the Conquest of Everest*

"We have poured billions into campaigns to protect iconic or charismatic species from extinction. As human numbers and economic demands continue to climb, we are well into a sixth great extinction episode and thus the conservation efforts become all the

more urgent. Nevertheless, money and human resources to protect nature pale beside the economic muscle-power of corporations and so conservation ventures must be more nimble, adaptable and efficient. Deni Béchard's riveting journey through the 'dark continent' provides a surprisingly uplifting story about a radically different and successful conservation program."
—David Suzuki, author of *The Sacred Balance: Rediscovering Our Place in Nature*

"Deni Béchard in *Empty Hands, Open Arms* has accomplished no less than a tour de force in recounting the improbable and inspiring efforts of a small non-governmental group, the Bonobo Conservation Initiative, that together with local indigenous leaders in the Democratic Republic of the Congo is working to save one of the world's most important rainforests and the living creature genetically closest to humankind, the bonobo. With literary flair, he offers a gripping account of the complicated and war-torn historical, political, and social context of conservation efforts in one of the most challenging places on earth—and makes a convincing case for hope. It is a story that movingly illuminates the time we live in, a tale of an emblematic struggle in which the fate of all of us and our future on this planet are at stake."
—Bruce Rich, Visiting Scholar, Environmental Law Institute, Washington, DC, and author of *Mortgaging the Earth: The World Bank, Environmental Impoverishment, and the Crisis of Development,* and *To Uphold the World: The Message of Ashoka and Kautilya for the 21st Century*

"*Empty Hands, Open Arms* is an emotionally-enthralling, nuanced voyage into the conundrums of bonobo conservation. Béchard evokes both the eye-popping culture of these peaceful great-apes and the inspiring community-conservationists collaborating in their survival. I highly recommend this absorbing, well-researched, and compassionate book to both environmentalists and general readers."
—William Powers, author of *Blue Clay People: Seasons on Africa's Fragile Edge*

"Readers of this book will be entertained and moved by Deni Béchard's stories about this remarkable endangered and irreplaceable species and those dedicating their lives to saving them. On top of this, they will be informed and enlightened about the Congo, its lush forests, its tragic history, and its peoples' struggle to build a sustainable future."
—Riane Eisler, author of *The Chalice and the Blade, Sacred Pleasure,* and *The Real Wealth of Nations*

"Deni Béchard's *Empty Hands, Open Arms* is the embodiment of the type of reporting that we dream of reading, but all too rarely encounter—intelligent, engaged, and above all, astonishingly perceptive. Here is a portrait of a nation and the conservationists trying to protect it, rendered with all the necessary complexity to make this book joyously alive."
—Dinaw Mengestu, MacArthur Fellow and author of *The Beautiful Things that Heaven Bears* and *How to Read the Air*

"'People are at once the problem and the solution,' says Sally Jewell Coxe, founder of the Bonobo Conservation Initiative, and Deni Béchard's masterful and moving history of BCI bears this out. In BCI, Béchard finds a brilliant example of how conservationists can work with communities to save not only their own immediate environments but also the world at large through courage, cooperation, and compassion."
—Grant Hayter-Menzies, author of *Imperial Masquerade* and *Shadow Woman*

Empty Hands, Open Arms

Also by Deni Béchard

Cures for Hunger
Vandal Love

Empty Hands,
Open Arms

The Race to Save
Bonobos in the Congo
and Make Conservation Go Viral

DENI BÉCHARD

milkweed
editions

© 2013, Text by Deni Béchard
All rights reserved. Except for brief quotations in critical articles or reviews, no part of this book may be reproduced in any manner without prior written permission from the publisher: Milkweed Editions, 1011 Washington Avenue South, Suite 300, Minneapolis, Minnesota 55415.
(800) 520-6455
www.milkweed.org

Published 2013 by Milkweed Editions
Printed in the United States of America
Cover design by Christian Fuenfhausen
Cover photos © Christian Ziegler and Getty Images
13 14 15 16 17   5 4 3 2 1
First Edition

Milkweed Editions, an independent nonprofit publisher, gratefully acknowledges sustaining support from the Bush Foundation; the Patrick and Aimee Butler Foundation; the Dougherty Family Foundation; the Driscoll Foundation; the Jerome Foundation; the Lindquist & Vennum Foundation; the McKnight Foundation; the voters of Minnesota through a Minnesota State Arts Board Operating Support grant, thanks to a legislative appropriation from the arts and cultural heritage fund, and a grant from the Wells Fargo Foundation Minnesota; the National Endowment for the Arts; the Target Foundation; and other generous contributions from foundations, corporations, and individuals. For a full listing of Milkweed Editions supporters, please visit www.milkweed.org.

Library of Congress Control Number: 2013944089

Milkweed Editions is committed to ecological stewardship. We strive to align our book production practices with this principle, and to reduce the impact of our operations in the environment. We are a member of the Green Press Initiative, a nonprofit coalition of publishers, manufacturers, and authors working to protect the world's endangered forests and conserve natural resources. *Empty Hands, Open Arms* was printed on acid-free 100% postconsumer-waste paper by Edwards Brothers Malloy.

Contents

I will take with me the emptiness of my hands
What you do not have you find everywhere

—W. S. Merwin

Prologue: February 2012

On a sweltering afternoon, I reached the border that separates Gisenyi, Rwanda, from the city of Goma in the Democratic Republic of the Congo. The sky was cloudless, the sun glaring on the dusty, broken roadway and the windless lake that stretched alongside it. After receiving the Rwandan exit stamp in my passport, I walked around a metal gate raised by a single soldier for passing cars, though there were none.

I approached the yellow building on the other side, where an agent sat at a counter, behind an open window. He suddenly appeared engrossed in organizing his desk. He thrust his jaw and furrowed his brow, gathered papers into a pile, then spread them like a stack of cards. He scanned the pages, moving his head back and forth, as if hunting the source of a grave injustice. I'd often seen officials do this, demonstrating self-importance, making travelers wait, creating an atmosphere of disapproval and difficulty, so that when they finally took the passport, it would seem natural for them to find fault and demand an additional payment.

Across the street from the yellow building, in what appeared to be a small guardhouse, a door opened, and another agent stepped out, perspiration beading on his round face. He hurried over, smiled at me, and reached for my passport. The first one grunted and shook his head, sat back in his chair and crossed his arms, staring off in anger.

The new agent stepped into the yellow building, behind the counter, and flipped open a book of smudged graph paper. He wrote my passport information, asking my profession and, when I said *écrivain*, "writer," what I would be writing.

"A book on conservation," I replied in French, "on tropical forests and natural resources, and endangered great apes." He listened, his eyebrows raised, nodding as if I were corroborating a view he had long held. Seeing his look of genuine interest, I offered more details: my planned visit to a community-based reserve in the Congo's Équateur Province, the importance of conservation not only for the wildlife, but also for the local people.

I showed him my letter of invitation, and he studied it, the page explaining that I would help "protect biodiversity by writing a book about the Bonobo Peace Forest . . . and raise up the image of the DRC in its conservation efforts." When I'd received it a month before, the ambitious statements surprised me. The letter was necessary for my visa, and I was beginning to understand that the Congolese who composed it must have thought it important to impress officials. Now, as this one read it, he nodded repeatedly. When he finished, he flashed me a broad smile and thanked me, with what sounded like earnestness, for having come to the Congo. He stamped my passport and said, "Bon voyage."

As I walked, jumbled concrete buildings and a few sprawling hotels cluttered the descending land between the road and the rocky shore of Lake Kivu, its waters reaching to a hazy blue line at the horizon. Five young men on motorcycles shadowed me, asking if I wanted a ride, though I could easily reach the hotels on foot. Where the road branched inland, the city appeared empty, a ghost town but for two white UN Land Cruisers racing in the distance, lifting plumes of dust.

It was hard not to be vigilant. From my readings, I had mixed impressions of Goma, a backpackers' haven that, in the almost two decades since the Rwandan genocide, had become the epicenter of a chronic warzone. To make matters worse, in 2002, about 40 percent of the city, then home to more than half a million people, was destroyed in the eruption of Mount Nyiragongo. A stream of lava at times two thirds of a mile wide had poured through. Even now, volcanic rock protruded from the dirt where the roads were unpaved, catching at the wheels of passing motorcycles.

I was most struck by how the Congolese looked at me. Rwandans and Ugandans were used to visitors, and even those who wanted to sell something gave no more than cursory attention, whereas the Congolese I passed studied me, as if to see who was before them, to know why I was there. They carried more scars, on foreheads and cheeks, or had missing teeth, a droop in the corner of an eyelid, hints of old injuries in the way they walked, positioned themselves to pick up a bag, or rode a motorcycle. They gazed at my eyes, narrowing their own, at once cautious and curious. But when I smiled, they smiled back quickly, as if relieved.

I spent that night in the only hotel I could find with a vacancy, the others filled with the personnel of NGOs. My room was more luxurious than I expected, with polished wood cabinets and shiny bathroom fixtures, though nothing quite worked. Electric sockets sizzled when I wiggled the plug, but gave no power; the shower head dripped, and none of the doors, bathroom or wardrobe, sat well on its hinges.

I was too tired to care, but after I lay in bed, I couldn't fall asleep. The next day, I'd fly to Kinshasa, one of Africa's most populous and chaotic cities. If all went to plan, a week later I would head into the forest, either by dugout canoe or bush plane. I'd looked at maps, at satellite images of the Congo basin rainforest, the second largest on earth after the Amazon, its hundreds of rivers the real highways, far more perceptible than the occasional yellow line of a dirt road. How would it feel when the only clear space was that surrounding a few huts, each village an island of sky? If you walked out, you traveled for weeks beneath the trees, barely seeing the sun.

But to experience this place and its people clearly would require a conscious decision to look beyond the stereotypes. The Western view of the Congo remained limited by colonial mythologies: the great river, the dark heart of Africa, notions that Cold War rivalries, mineral exploitation, and the recent wars had kept alive in our minds. The Congo had come to signify savagery, and hearing its name, many shuddered without quite knowing why. But for millions of Congolese who struggled to build ordinary lives, this shudder pushed them deeper into alienation, further from the global community. The shudder increased our blindness not only to the forest and its importance to life on earth, but to the very people whose actions were crucial to saving it.

Outside my window, Goma was silent but for the occasional passing vehicle and the brief, muted voice of the guard in the hotel's entrance.

Empty Hands, Open Arms

Part I
From Iowa to the Bonobos of Équateur

Naked Apes,
Furry Apes, Godlike Apes

In an age when the state of the planet preoccupies us—from climate change to deforestation, and from the extinction of species to the degradation of human habitat—it's hard not to wonder whether we are capable of working through lasting challenges. Do we have the cultural staying power, or will short attention spans, coupled with our love of instant gratification, doom our attempts to rehabilitate the environment, just as the naysayers have been predicting? Having read countless dismal news reports in recent years, I wanted to know about the sorts of people and projects that aren't dominating the headlines, those developing long-term solutions to environmental destruction, their work done year in, year out, in all its routine and tiresome glory.

The Congo caught my attention early on because its rainforests are so crucial to preventing climate change, and because the country itself was at a crossroads. In 2003, it emerged from possibly the world's most devastating conflict since World War II, and with increasing political stability, its massive forests and mineral wealth were again vulnerable to large-scale exploitation. Conservationists were rushing in, and of those working there, one group, the Bonobo Conservation Initiative (BCI), was fostering a surprising number of conservation areas in spite of its small size and limited funding. Two large community-based reserves had already been established and several others were in the works, all with the goal of protecting the habitat of the bonobo, a matriarchal great ape that, like the chimpanzee, has more than 98.6 percent of its DNA in common with humans.

When I contacted BCI's president, Sally Jewell Coxe, and explained my interest in writing about new approaches to conservation, she described how she and a few others started the organization in 1998, in the spirit of bonobo cohesiveness, its goal to build coalitions so as to use resources more sustainably. Unlike national parks, the reserves contained villages whose occupants were trained to manage and protect the natural resources and wildlife. BCI's model was inclusive, she said, inviting people in rainforest villages to participate and taking into account their histories, cultures, and needs in order to foster grassroots conservation movements.

This last detail caught my attention, that understanding another culture's values had allowed BCI to develop a self-replicating conservation model. They focused on creating forums to discuss different ways of thinking about natural resources, and encouraging the local people to take leadership roles in conservation projects. Given that populations and the global demand for raw materials were soaring, that millions of hungry people were eager to cut down the Congo's forest for farmland and hunt the remaining wildlife, a change of consciousness was as urgent as the application of environmental laws. The rainforest's importance for life on earth was undeniably clear: it protected watersheds while releasing oxygen and removing carbon from the atmosphere. As for bonobos, they were already on the verge of extinction, their habitat only in the DRC, to the south of the Congo River's curve, in an area where the national government's influence barely reached.

The portrait that Sally painted of effective conservation work was a mixture of anthropology and conservation biology, in which knowledge of the land, the people, the animals, and the country's history was essential. At the center of BCI's vision was the bonobo. As one of humanity's two closest living relatives, the bonobo was—Sally told me—important for our understanding of ourselves as humans: not only in terms of where we have come from and how we have evolved, but also in terms of what we can be.

Though I had read articles noting all that great apes might teach us about our evolution, none had said anything about how they could shed light on our future. They were often portrayed in simplistic terms. Bonobos were furry sex addicts that swung both ways, and chimpanzees waged war as best an ape could without modern weapons and the cold mathematics of organized armies. Gorillas were vegetarians, largely gentle despite gladiator physiques, and orangutans solitary forest creatures that paired up only for sex, a lifestyle that sounded uncomfortably similar to that of many writers. What those articles didn't lead me to expect was the degree to which my research on bonobos would in fact change how I understood myself. While I would learn that their social structure did offer lessons in the origins of human nature, it also said a great deal about our potential, both as individuals and as a species, and the paths we might choose.

Just seeing photos of bonobos made a strong impression on me. They have lustrous black skin and red lips, black hair neatly parted in the middle and descending like muttonchops, flaring out proudly in the style of Martin Van Buren. But it was the way they looked at the camera that I found unforgettable.

Empty Hands, Open Arms

The bonobos' eyes appeared curious and contemplative, unlike the often aggressive, guarded look I'd found common in chimpanzees. No doubt this was reductive and I had a lot to learn, but I saw in the gaze of the bonobo evidence of a deeply social being that, if it could speak, might have a number of questions for me.

Other photographs showed bonobos in a variety of familiar postures: lounging on their backs, one leg crossed over the other; or mating in the missionary position, muscles taut in their arms, the male grinning as if life couldn't be better; or a mother standing, staring off, holding sugarcane, head poised on a stretched neck. With their long, slender limbs, they appeared so human-like that, just to get a sense of proportion, I had to look up their weight: one hundred pounds for males—a little less than chimpanzees—and seventy for females. It was difficult to imagine such a close relative being hunted for the bushmeat trade, thousands slaughtered during the two Congo wars between 1996 and 2003, possibly as few as five thousand remaining.

Both because of their highly sexual nature and because one has never been witnessed killing another of its own kind, bonobos have recently become the stars of the great ape world. Even orangutan males, when battling over females, occasionally deliver fatal wounds, as do silverback gorillas. Gorillas sometimes kill infants, and for chimpanzees this can be a matter of course. Dominant chimpanzee mothers do away with the children of others, and males wage all-out wars, then slaughter the infants and take the females for their own, a description that reads like any of a million lines out of human history.

Bonobo society, however, is matriarchal. Females forge the alliances, and a male's rank depends on that of his mother. When groups meet, males hoot but stand back while females cross over to one another in what may end up resembling an orgy. As for infanticide, it has never been witnessed; all bonobos in the group care for the welfare of their young. They have been nicknamed the "hippies of the forest" and the "Left Bank ape," owing to where they live in relation to the Congo River. Unlike other great apes, they use a variety of sexual positions and often mate face-to-face, gazing into each other's eyes. They enjoy oral sex and French kissing, and they make love for pleasure, comfort, or closeness, as a means of greeting, or just because they love each other. Sex is their hug, their handshake, their massage, and their noon martini. Sometimes, it allows them to defuse social tension, minimize violence, and resolve conflicts over resources, the females rubbing one another's clitorises and the males penis-fencing—hardly solutions our leaders would try.

Whereas gorillas, chimpanzees, and orangutans have clear places in the popular imagination, bonobos are latecomers. Their resemblance to chimps and their home far from the coast, within one of the Congo's most daunting landscapes, have prolonged our ignorance. Chimpanzees first appeared in Western literature in the sixteenth century, orangutans in the seventeenth, and the gorilla's name dates back to a Carthaginian who, in 500 BC, traveled Africa's West Coast and returned with the skins of "wild men" that the locals called *gorillae*. Though records since the 1880s show apes at the heart of the Congo basin, bonobos were not recognized as a distinct species until the twentieth century. Yale primatologist Robert Yerkes owned a bonobo named Prince Chim in the mid-1920s but thought he was a chimpanzee, albeit an extraordinary one. He wrote: "In all my experience as a student of animal behavior I have never met an animal the equal of Prince Chim in approach to physical perfection, alertness, adaptability, and agreeableness of disposition. . . . Doubtless there are geniuses even among the anthro-poid apes."

Bonobos were not identified as distinct from chimpanzees until the late 1920s. Harvard zoologist Harold J. Coolidge Jr. wrote that he visited Tervuren, Belgium, in 1928, after a long university expedition to collect gorilla specimens in the Belgian Congo. "I shall never forget, late one afternoon in Tervuren, casually picking up from a storage tray what clearly looked like a juvenile chimp's skull from south of the Congo and finding, to my amazement, that the epiphyses were totally fused." This meant that, despite its size, the skull was that of an adult. He found four more similar skulls among those of the chimpanzees and planned to write a scientific paper on the subject, describing a new type of chimpanzee. However, two weeks later, the German anatomist Ernst Schwarz visited, and Henri Schouteden, the director of Tervuren's Royal Museum for Central Africa, showed him the skulls that had interested Coolidge. "In a flash Schwarz grabbed a pencil and paper, measured one small skull, wrote up a brief description, and named a new pygmy chimpanzee race: *Pan satyrus paniscus*," recalled Coolidge. "He asked Schouteden to have his brief account printed without delay in the *Revue Zoologique* of the Congo Museum. I had been taxonomically scooped." But reasonably enough, Schwarz had his own account: he'd been studying primates, he wrote, and had come to Tervuren specifically to examine the skulls, a recent shipment from the Congo.

Despite not receiving credit for being the first to identify the bonobo, in 1933 Coolidge published the paper that would establish it not as a subspecies of the chimpanzee, *Pan troglodytes,* but as a separate species, *Pan paniscus.* Having remarked the similarities in the torso-to-limb proportions of bonobos and humans, he wrote that the species, still known as the pygmy chimpanzee despite being marginally smaller than most chimpanzees, "may approach more closely to the common ancestor of chimpanzees and man than does any living chimpanzee hitherto discovered and described."

In 1954, German scientists Eduard Tratz and Heinz Heck proposed that, because of its marked differences from the chimpanzee, the pygmy chimpanzee should be classified under a different genus. They suggested *Bonobo paniscus,* as they believed *bonobo* to be the Congolese name for the species. Though the word *bonobo* wasn't found historically among the Bantu dialects, it may have been a misspelling on a crate shipped from Bolobo, a town on the Congo River from which bonobos were sent.

While Tratz and Heck's classification has been generally accepted by the scientific community, some argue that bonobos and chimpanzees are so close to humans that they should be classified in the *Homo* genus. Even Carl Linnaeus, who in the eighteenth century developed the system of Latin names that botanists and zoologists still use, called the orangutan *Homo nocturnus* or *Homo sylvestris orang-outang,* though he based his evaluation on the reports of travelers who claimed that the Indonesian great ape could speak.

Until recently, bonobos lacked public champions whereas the other great apes have had Jane Goodall, Dian Fossey, and Birutė Galdikas. But with a growing number of books, documentaries, and films now dedicated to them, bonobos are becoming media darlings even as they are being exterminated in the Congo. The attention they receive can be attributed to their peaceful disposition and their reputation as Kama Sutra apes—a reputation that is, of course, based on behavior seen through the lens of human sexuality.

The primatologist Frans de Waal writes in *Bonobo: The Forgotten Ape* of how bonobos use sex for both appeasement and affection, saying that the label *sex* might be inappropriate if perceived as a "behavioral category aimed at an orgasmic climax." A little later in his career, though, in response to an article questioning the sexual nature of bonobo behavior, he writes, "Fortunately, a United States court settled this monumental issue in the Paula Jones case against President Bill Clinton. It clarified that the term 'sex' includes any deliberate contact with the genitalia, anus, groin, breast, inner thigh, or buttocks." With bonobos, sex encompasses a number of tendencies—something, de Waal points out, that is also true for humans, though rarely acknowledged: "Our sexual urges are subject to such powerful moral constraints that it may have become hard to recognize how—as Sigmund Freud was the first to point out—they permeate all aspects of social life." De Waal suggests that bonobo society could teach us much about what human sexuality might look like without those constraints.

As I began to gain a better understanding of bonobos, of what traits they share with humans and how they might experience the world, I encountered the work of Dr. Sue Savage-Rumbaugh, an American primatologist. Since the 1970s, Savage-Rumbaugh has been working with great apes in captivity, investigating whether they have a capacity for language. She first studied chimpanzees at Georgia State University, then bonobos that had been brought from the Congo. She developed technology that enabled bonobos to communicate with humans by pushing a lexigram on a keyboard attached to a computer, which would log and articulate its corresponding word in English. The approach Savage-Rumbaugh developed wasn't clinical but holistic; she used the lexigrams in conjunction with activities that gave them immediate, relevant, even urgent meaning to the bonobos. But despite her creative approaches, her work remained challenging for years until Kanzi, a baby bonobo who observed the language lessons that his adoptive mother, Matata, suffered through, revealed his skills. On a day when Matata had been taken away for breeding and Kanzi was alone with Savage-Rumbaugh, he began using the keyboard to communicate, producing "120 separate utterances, using 12 different symbols." She hadn't realized that he'd been learning English naturally, the way human children do, just by "being exposed to it."

Kanzi has since become a celebrity, demonstrating his talents on CNN and *The Oprah Winfrey Show*. Given that a bonobo's vocal cords are not suited to human language, he has to communicate using his keyboard or a sheet printed with lexigrams. When a lexigram is lacking, he composes, asking for pizza by pointing to "cheese," "tomato," and "bread." He can also understand spoken language and has responded correctly to sentences such as "Could you carry the television outdoors, please?" and "Can you put your shirt in the refrigerator?" even though Savage-Rumbaugh made no gestures and had her face covered. He has also learned to make stone tools, build fires, and cook.

I spoke to Savage-Rumbaugh by Skype not long after she had been selected as one of *Time* magazine's one hundred most influential people for a body of work that spans questions of primatology, language acquisition in humans and apes, and cognitive science. I wanted to understand what had won her a place on the list, and I began with the question that I most often heard when I told others about the project I was embarking on.

"Why bonobos? What makes them interesting?"

At first, she answered simply: "In terms of anatomy, genetics, and personality, bonobos are the most humanlike of all apes. . . . They most closely touch the origins of humankind. . . . We still carry so much genetic heritage in common with the bonobo that only by studying them can we have any inkling of what might actually have happened in the past."

"And this is more true of bonobos than of chimpanzees?" I asked.

"When the data is fully in," she said, "I think it will be seen that bonobos are more fully related to humans in how their genes express themselves."

Much of what I had read about bonobos was based on scientists' field observations, but there's a line between what we can understand as researchers and what we learn by living with another creature, by sharing in its daily life. Savage-Rumbaugh had worked with bonobos for more than three decades, taking part in their culture while they studied hers, and I asked what this had taught her.

"Freeing oneself absolutely," she said, "from any thought or tendency toward aggression, and focusing on group love and cohesion—and I don't mean sex, I mean love—is the way of the bonobos. It's a message that humanity needs to try to understand."

"But don't they have conflict the way we do?" I asked. She acknowledged that they did, often behaving like humans by screaming at each other and showing off their strength.

"But," she added, "they tend to find ways not to actually harm each other. They search for that. . . . Working with bonobos has given me a perspective on humanity, a perspective on myself that I could never otherwise have had. . . . Jane Goodall changed humanity's view of itself when she revealed through her efforts with *National Geographic* that humankind shared a feeling world with chimpanzees. . . . With Kanzi, it has been shown that truly for the first time there are other animals on the planet that can share a language, an intellectual, thinking world with human beings. You put those two together, and you have to ask what is human. So Kanzi is stretching the definition of human. He's forcing a redefinition of what humanity means. And that for some is intriguing and fascinating. For others, it is very uncomfortable. In part, you can be influential because you upset the social system. Kanzi upsets the social norm."

If *Time* had acknowledged the importance of Savage-Rumbaugh's work, I realized, it was also because of what it says about our dynamic nature: that what we consider human can shift drastically, just as Kanzi is learning across cultures and expanding his notion of self.

"The important aspect of that message," Savage-Rumbaugh told me, "is that humanity isn't stuck in the current rut. . . . We might consider ourselves a naked ape, but we have the capacity to be, let's say, a godlike ape. We can do far more than we're doing. We have limited ourselves and our understanding of our biology—our understanding of how we must structure the world—by the past. And we don't have to continue to do that. If Kanzi can learn a language, what can human beings learn? We can certainly learn how to get along."

I was surprised when I heard the words *godlike ape*, but Savage-Rumbaugh's idea wasn't new; humans often admire and tell stories about those with transformative powers.

"We're just on the cusp," she said, "of really understanding how brains interact. . . . We have thought of ourselves as individual sacks of skin. We're far more connected than we've ever understood. And bonobos have almost a sixth sense. They have an understanding of their connectedness. And when we are able to finally grasp and measure that scientifically, I think we'll be able to know what it means when we say humans have vibes or humans react with each other. I don't think that's just a phrase. I think there's something going on that's really happening between us, but that linguistically we have, through our culture, shut out. And bonobos haven't shut that part of themselves out. I want people to realize that we're just on the cusp of understanding the most fascinating species on the planet—not that elephants and dolphins and others aren't—but we're on the cusp of understanding that species and we're about to decimate it in the Congo."

In her writings, Savage-Rumbaugh explores the question of bonobo cultures, whether they, like human cultures, exist and are taught, exerting an influence on the instinctive behavior of apes. She describes how bonobos and humans who live together come to share a hybrid culture, an observation that leads naturally to speculation as to how humans might learn a new way of being. Simply looking at the history of human culture reminds us of the degree to which it shapes us, leading us to select for certain genetic traits, the most obvious being the ideas of beauty that we might value at any given time. Culture may become the most significant element of the environment to which we adapt.

I was eager to meet bonobos, to understand what bond they could share with us, how we could interact, and how spending time with them might shift my views. Savage-Rumbaugh was living with bonobos on the outskirts of Des Moines, Iowa, at the Great Ape Trust, a research facility the philanthropist Ted Townsend had created.

It was April when I visited, the sun warm though the air was still cool, the land yet to bloom. A grove of leafless trees and a small lake separate the tall, electrified fence topped with barbed wire from the Trust's two concrete buildings. Tyler, the laboratory supervisor, a man in his twenties, showed me into the bonobo building and let me watch as he ran experiments with a fourteen-year-old female bonobo, Elykia ("hope" in Lingala, the lingua franca of the western Congo). He told me I'd have to sit in the hallway and stay still, that bonobos were generally shy. He went into a small room next to a glass-walled chamber with a computer touch screen.

A doorway in the back of the chamber opened into the area where the bonobos lived. Elykia entered through it on all fours, craned her neck, scanning the inside, then moved fluidly, rapidly, onto the platform near the touch screen. She gazed out and saw me, her large black eyes opening wide, before she fled in a black blur.

"She's just being dramatic," Tyler called to me. "She'll be flirting with you in no time."

She neared again, looking in, and made a high-pitched, birdlike sound before bounding to sit on the platform. Though I'd read Japanese primatologist Takayoshi Kano's description of hearing bonobos in the Congo, like "hornbills twittering in the distance," I was startled by how different their calls were from the barks and low hoots of the chimpanzees I had seen in zoos.

Elykia glanced around and settled in. Lexigrams appeared on the screen, and she hesitated before touching one with a fingertip. Her hands resembled my own but were long, with more distance between each knuckle. The muscles of her arms were finely shaped, like those of an athlete. She had somewhat less hair than the wild bonobos I had seen in pictures, since captive bonobos can become restless and overgroom. In zoos and sanctuaries, they are sometimes nearly naked, revealing how similar their musculature is to ours, or at least how some of us might like ours to be.

My expectations were high. I'd heard stories of human-bonobo interactions, of bonobos blowing kisses in zoos and staring into people's eyes. But Elykia forgot about me as she touched the screen, selecting one of several lexigrams, none of which I could understand. Each time, Tyler released a grape through a slot in the wall, near the floor, to reward her. She scooped it with speed and dexterity, barely pausing before refocusing on the screen. I couldn't imagine a human moving so immediately in response to a stimulus; it was almost as if Elykia's body were doing the thinking. She touched lexigrams a few more times, and then, hardly looking, she shot her arm out and captured a grape as it began to roll. If we humans have gained brainpower in our evolution, we've certainly lost physicality.

After the session with Elykia, Tyler took me through the hallway to the outdoor enclosures, a series of large cages attached by corridors of steel mesh to a yard of yellowed grass. Speaking as he would to a person, he introduced me to an eleven-year-old male, Maisha ("life" in Swahili), who, he explained, was basically a teenager. (Bonobos become sexually mature at nine but do not reach their full adult size until after the age of fifteen.) From watching TV, Tyler explained, Maisha had become obsessed with motorcycles. He didn't understand why he couldn't have one. In the same enclosure was Matata, "tough" or "trouble" in Lingala, the group's wild-born matriarch, now at least forty years old. She rested as Maisha ran back and forth, dragging his laminated sheet of lexigrams across the ground. Seeing me, he threw a paisley cloth over his head and swung along the cage's ceiling, playing the stooge, then raced out into the sunlit grass.

The differences among the bonobos—the distinctness of their personalities— was undeniable. In the way she held her body, Matata exuded a wild energy, as if her limbs remembered the rainforest. There was authority in her presence even as she dozed, like an old chieftain closing her eyes, barely interested in people like me. She glanced only once before lying on her belly in the sun and going to sleep. Finally, Maisha came over to greet me shyly, lowering his eyes, his fingers hooked in the mesh of the enclosure wall.

Kanzi and his half sister, Panbanisha, whose name meant "cleave together for the purpose of contrast" in Swahili, appeared more curious. As I spoke, I could sense Panbanisha studying me. Her dark eyes peered into my own with a mix of wariness and curiosity that I'd seen on first dates. Female bonobos have pink genital swellings that grow large and pillowlike as they mature, and Panbanisha's was infected. I asked her how she was, and she stood up and showed me the inflamed area, then sat and crossed her arms, staring at me, as if it might be my turn to reveal something intimate.

As for Kanzi, he was a handsome, well-built bonobo with a wide forehead and barrel chest. He was used to media attention, and when I walked in and he saw my camera, he flashed a photogenic grin and lifted a hand. I failed to snap him in time, and he sighed, appearing exasperated. He studied me, as if to determine just how interesting this encounter might be. After all, he'd played music with Paul McCartney and Peter Gabriel.

Despite their relatively peaceful nature, I wasn't allowed into the enclosures. Bonobos are significantly stronger than we are, and they can accidentally injure us. There is also confusion around their putative benevolence. The media describe them as sexy, peace-loving creatures, but like us, they can be violent. People are shocked to hear this, since there is a general tendency to simplify, as when we think of someone as "nice" and imagine her, therefore, without anger or jealousy. The same is true of the way we think of bonobos, though by human and chimp standards, they do display remarkable restraint.

My encounters with the bonobos were pleasant, all of them according me some time. They used frequent eye-contact, looking into my eyes as if trying to figure out why I was there. But they didn't react to me in any dramatic way, except for Elykia, who, as I walked through the building, hooted and peeked from every corner of her enclosure, finally flirting, excited to see a new male.

Kanzi pushed his belly against the mesh and motioned to Tyler, who crouched and tickled him. Kanzi picked up his laminated sheet of lexigrams. Each time he pointed to one, Tyler explained it to me. Kanzi was requesting grape Kool-Aid and celery now, but he was also pointing at lexigrams to indicate that he wanted strawberries before bedtime. Watching, I recalled words from a book Savage-Rumbaugh had co-written with two fellow researchers, Pär Segerdahl and William Fields: "That Kanzi lives in a world permeated with language is visible in his physiognomy. . . . The way his eyes meet your eyes, the way he glances at other persons or cultural objects, the way he gestures towards you or manipulates objects with his hands: everything bears witness to his language." As Tyler went to the kitchen to get Kool-Aid and celery, I sat on one side of the mesh, Kanzi on the other, a few inches between us. He glanced over and sighed, then just stared off, content with my company on this sleepy afternoon.

Even before my experiences here, my definition of humanity was larger than the one prevalent a few decades ago. Philosopher and anthropologist Raymond Corbey, in his essay "Ambiguous Apes," describes how, in the 1950s, Belgian cinemas showed a film in which a scientist kills a mother gorilla and skins her body as her infant, soon to be sent to a zoo, sits crying next to her. He writes, "Ten or fifteen years later, such a scene, in a film meant to be seen by Western families with their children, had become unthinkable." He reflects on French philosopher Emmanuel Lévinas's theory that the gaze of another "appeals directly, without mediation, to our moral awareness," and he asks whether this holds true when it is not the gaze of "a human child but that of a gorilla child or an orang-utan child?" However, human attitudes are changing, and if we were exposed to the suffering of hunted and imprisoned great apes rather than to glossy photos of wildlife beauty on NGO fundraising calendars—and if we understood the causes, frequency, and severity of this suffering—we might respond in greater numbers.

A firsthand experience, of course, has a different level of power, and for me, even during my short visit to the Great Ape Trust, there was no doubting the intelligence in the gazes of the bonobos. When we look into another's eyes, we can tell whether her mind is spacious, holding room to consider, to see things from different angles and evaluate them, or whether she is simply carrying through motions, confined, driven by instinct and habit.

How would the bonobos in the Congo appear to me? Kanzi and Panbanisha were used to humans, my own visit insignificant to them. They'd taken a step into our world despite the gap between us, a gap made clear by the steel mesh of the enclosures—one no doubt smaller for those who worked with them. Though I was curious to know how I would perceive bonobos in the abundant rainforest that had formed their bodies, instincts, and cultures, I also wanted to see how conservation efforts could protect them. I was only beginning to understand that bonobos lived in social groups not so different from those of humans, sharing many behavioral traits with us: playing games, daydreaming, teaching children, establishing friendships, caring for each other's injuries, or grieving for the loss of loved ones. It was hard to imagine their families broken apart, the adults shot, their bodies butchered or smoked, sold in bushmeat markets; the traumatized infants tied in baskets, starving for weeks as traders attempted to sell them. This, too, was part of the story, and I wondered if, when I saw the bonobos in the rainforest, it would affect the way they looked at me.

Kinshasa

For many Westerners, it would be hard to travel to the Congo without confronting the way our cultural narrative portrays it: through a media rap sheet of barbarism so long it predates Joseph Conrad's *Heart of Darkness*. But what our fear blinds us to is that these descriptions say less about how the Congolese traditionally lived, and still live, than about the result of their living in one of the most fertile, mineral-rich, and strategically important nations on earth.

Before Western colonization, the area that now constitutes the DRC was home to dozens of complex societies. Over four hundred years ago, the Kongo Kingdom had ambassadors in Portugal, Spain, and the papal courts, as well as organized and trained militaries. The slow rise of the Portuguese slave trade—in conjunction with the spread of cash crop plantations in the New World—eroded the kingdom. In the late nineteenth century, rather than export the Congolese, the Belgians enslaved them at home, further disintegrating the social fabric. From there, the story of the Congo is one of constant exploitation: of humans, rubber, ivory, lumber, cotton, coffee, copper, cobalt, gold, diamonds, and now coltan, used in computers and handheld electronics. Since the colonial period and all through the Cold War, the West has fed the country a steady flow of weapons and bought its raw materials, whether from the regime of Sese Seko Mobutu, its president from 1965 to 1997, or from Belgium, Uganda, and Rwanda, usually to the detriment of the Congo's people. Even the recent wars have had less to do with the Congolese than with the outside world, with Western industrial and military interests, rivalries between developed nations, and the increased global demand for minerals. And yet, though the ambitions and material needs of other nations have charted the Congo's decline, we often misread *Heart of Darkness*, telling ourselves that the darkness is in the Africans.

Being familiar with the West's fears, I tried to consider the situation from the African point of view and realized that the obvious question was, what are the Congolese afraid of? One answer—being exploited and manipulated by outsiders—makes clear the challenges of large-scale conservation here. Building trust is no easy task. Africa's most brutal colonial history and its most corrupt Cold War–era dictator have left the Congolese both wary and desperate. After the United States ceased to prop up Mobutu and he lost power in 1997, war killed as many as five and a half million people, the majority from disease and starvation. Soldiers, whether those of the Congo's government or the numerous rebel forces, pillaged and raped, often as a means of controlling local populations, and spread HIV into even the most remote areas. Villagers abandoned their fields and hid in forests to protect their families, hunting for survival and decimating the wildlife. By 2011, the DRC received the lowest rating on the UN Development Programme's Human Development Report, which tracks progress in health, education, and basic living standards.

For conservationists to work successfully here, they have to understand the people well enough to build trust and at the same time harness their desire for change. In our conversations, Sally Jewell Coxe of the Bonobo Conservation Initiative distinguished between two basic conservation approaches: one that the Congolese often see as colonial in attitude, whereby outsiders come with money and impose change, and the other whereby outsiders integrate with local communities, respecting their values and supporting their leaders in order to achieve shared goals. However, conservation often requires a quid pro quo: the local people taking the pressure off the forests and wildlife in exchange for new means of survival. Conservationists can foster trade, health care, education, even law enforcement, and yet if they want to build a deeper sense of community investment, they need insight not just into the problems that arise but into how those problems came to be. Part of finding a new way of relating to people, Sally suggested, lies in seeing how much damage was caused by the old way.

In telling me about BCI's projects, she spoke of the Bongandu, the Congolese ethnic group with whom she'd worked primarily. She described their respect for bonobos and their knowledge of the rainforest, emphasizing that we must not equate poverty with ignorance. As for bonobos, they served as a flagship species, a concept that elevates the profile of one animal to protect the biodiversity of its habitat. The bonobos' charismatic nature made it possible for BCI to rally support around them as a symbol of the rainforest.

Through 2010, I researched rainforest and bonobo conservation, and on several occasions, I interviewed Sally by Skype. I listened carefully, trying to determine if BCI's projects could create lasting change, and what could be learned from the solutions they were finding. In mid-2011, I proposed accompanying them on an expedition to a bonobo reserve. I wanted to understand how their model differed from those of other NGOs, and how building coalitions and social capital could make up for a lack of funds. Sally told me that such a trip could be a stunning experience, but she also emphasized that the reserve was set up with only the bare minimum, for the purpose of work. And she warned me to budget well. Just getting to Kinshasa would be expensive since so few airlines served it. Then we would have in-country flights, and because there was little infrastructure for trade, food and supplies would be costly.

BCI had been going through a difficult period, struggling to fund its operating costs. The continuing aftershocks of the global financial crisis had diminished the flow of charitable donations. The wars in Afghanistan and Iraq exhausted the US economy and political will, and with the Arab Spring, then the tsunami and nuclear meltdown in Japan, the media's attention wasn't on conservation. Not until late 2011 did BCI have the funds for its next expedition into the rainforest.

But in November, the DRC held its second free multi-party elections since not only the end of the Second Congo War in 2003 but the country's independence in 1960. The Congolese were dissatisfied with their current leaders, and the media anticipated violence and conflict over ballot rigging by each candidate's supporters. Given that we would be as far off the grid as possible, we needed to be careful not to get caught in the rainforests if conflicts reignited. BCI's contacts in the reserves said that the atmosphere was tense, with local politicians looking for ways to leverage power, and they warned us to postpone the trip.

I was already overseas, and I flew by way of Doha, Qatar, to East Africa. I took my time in Uganda and Rwanda, learning about conservation efforts there. Election results were announced in December, and Joseph Kabila, the incumbent president since January 2001, was reelected to a second term despite allegations of fraud. Though the DRC's security forces killed at least two dozen protesters, and residents of the capital stoned a Westerner's car, blaming the election results on foreign intervention, the peace held. The Congolese, it seemed, were sick of war.

Finally, on February 3, 2012, the day after my arrival in Goma, and after two trips to the offices of the Compagnie Africaine d'Aviation (CAA) to make sure my flight to Kinshasa would be departing, I took a taxi to the airport. One side of it was heaped with broken chunks of volcanic rock, and a few junked planes had been shoved off the runway, brown with dust, their noses to the sky.

Beyond security, a man at a desk again recorded the details of my passport. I noticed a single bullet hole in the top of the window behind him. He interrogated me on my reason for being in the Congo just as another agent would do when I arrived in Kinshasa, as if the sky above the DRC were a different country and each return to earth required a new visit to customs.

The plane was on time, and as it took off, I stared out the window: a military helicopter parked in the distance, khaki cargo planes, a cannon and a tank, both draped with dun tarp, set back in the trees. A narrow neighborhood of clustered homes with tin roofs passed beneath us, then the city of Goma with its wide avenues and desolate roundabouts, and the shore of Lake Kivu, the dark volcanoes of the Virungas to the east. Soon we were above hills, the unbroken thatch of the forest, before we lifted through a bank of clouds.

For a while, we glided just above them, working our way into a dense, otherworldly terrain. Dozens of cumulonimbus rose above the white plain, casting long clefts of shadow over it. All across the glowing horizon, at the luminous blue line between the clouds and the sky, further cumulonimbus soared, red at their edges, flattened by the cold air above, like mesas in a primeval vision of the American Southwest.

Though I fly often, I've never tired of cloudscapes, and I'd never seen one like this. It seemed an expression of the Congo basin, 695,000 square miles, approximately 20 percent of the planet's remaining tropical forest, spanning Gabon, Cameroon, Equatorial Guinea, the Central African Republic, the Democratic Republic of the Congo as well as its similarly named neighbor, the Republic of Congo. We were crossing over its edge, thousands of feet down, heat and humidity boiling up as it breathed dense air into the atmosphere.

It's hard to imagine forests like this vanishing, though farmland and plantations have replaced them in most of the world. What makes the impact of deforestation difficult to grasp is that it's at once gradual and rapid. Humans have cut down much of the world's forests, including the vast majority of old growth, and we can no longer fully comprehend how they influenced regional climates, regulating humidity, preventing drought, and protecting rivers, watersheds more likely to dry up if exposed to the sun. The vast quantity of carbon released from felled and burned trees escalates climate change and is absorbed into the oceans, gradually acidifying them.

Even now, massive swaths of forests are vanishing. In Southeast Asia, where the human population is booming, forests are being decimated for palm oil plantations, diminishing the orangutan habitat by 50 percent each decade. In Brazil, forests are being cleared for logging, cattle grazing, and soy. In the Congo, with the new political stability, logging companies are again seeking concessions. At a time when industrial powers are charting this forest's worth, a conservation plan for it is urgent.

For more than an hour, the plane flew above the clouds, larger cumulonimbus muscling up, the sun flaring at their edges, falling quickly now, a blinding disk edging against the white landscape. And then we passed beyond the clouds, into a clear sky, and in the twilight, we swooped low over Kinshasa, the nation's capital, the rolling savannah beyond it scattered with homesteads, before landing at N'Djili Airport.

Over the years, the articles and books I'd read about the DRC described aggressive people—pushing, shouting, asking for bribes, travelers shoving each other in airport lines. This wasn't my impression, neither here nor at the border crossing. People apologized for bumping into me, and even the security agents, notorious for extortion and made-up taxes, were courteous, one telling me he was a poet, adjusting his glasses as he explained that he wrote about AIDS, inequality, and handicapped children. Maybe the DRC was changing. Life here certainly used to be worse. But I'd traveled enough not to fixate on media reports, which rated Kinshasa as one of the most dangerous cities in Africa and described the Congo with a daily fare of spectacularly depressing statistics and stories of inhumanity—massacres, slavery, mass rapes, cannibalism, and brutal witchcraft. These reports, though necessary and true in certain regions, easily blind outsiders to the great majority of the country's people, who work hard to feed themselves and their families.

Eric Epheni Kandolo, a Congolese conservationist in his late twenties and BCI's communications coordinator, was waiting for me at the airport. Short and solidly built, he spoke as if we'd known each other for years. This immediate familiarity, I was soon to learn, is one of the most endearing qualities of the Congolese. Eric explained that his taxi had refused to wait, and he asked if I'd like a beer while he found another. I declined, but he led me to a beer stall anyway and said I should wait there since he needed to negotiate with taxi drivers.

"If they see a white man," he told me, "the price won't be very good."

He found one, a car of no discernible make, its windshield webbed as if hit by a brick, every panel a different color. When I opened the rear passenger door, the smell of the dark, musty, tattered interior cast me decades back to the rural Virgina junkyards I prospected in as a teenager, looking for parts to rebuild my car and motorcycle.

Beyond the airport, men gathered around booths selling Vodacom, Tigo, and Airtel phone cards, talking and laughing, money changing hands. In the shade of a concrete building, a teenage boy lounged on a swatch cut from a car rug next to a stack of used tires for sale. Women carried bundled market goods on their heads, their spines drawn long, necks as elegant as those of ballerinas.

We drove into the most densely populated neighborhoods of Kinshasa, the wide, uneven streets of broken asphalt littered with trash and rubble and crammed with vehicles. Many of these were also patched together, their varied panels so dented they appeared as if they'd been beaten into place with hammers. People ran through traffic that didn't slow or swerve. Huge unbranded trucks rumbled past, looking as if assembled from dozens of old vehicles, their engines half exposed. At least one hundred yellow jerry cans were tied to their sides and the cargo was lashed down beneath blue tarps, young men sitting on top.

Eric launched into a political discussion with the taxi driver, a rail-thin man with a weathered, angular head and veins so prominent that his forearms appeared twined with electrical wire. In excellent, mildly academic French, the driver debated President Kabila's merits, pointing out that though he wasn't popular in Kinshasa, he was gaining support. As he and Eric broached the topic of whether the president was promoting the country's development while protecting its national resources, a red passenger van with a rectangular opening in its side cut into our path. Our driver braked and swerved, and Eric told me that these vans, group taxis, were called *les esprits des morts,* "the spirits of the dead." They were the most salvaged-looking vehicles on the road, their headlights and grilles missing, people crammed into them, a few clutching the edges of the doorless openings.

Suddenly, our taxi hit a border of raised asphalt and we were in a different city, one of smooth, dark, wide avenues with fresh white crosswalks painted on them, symmetric lines of streetlamps, an immense lit-up hospital off to the left. Eric told me that it was the largest hospital in Central Africa, that all of this, the perfect boulevard and the hospital, was the work of the Chinese, who were opening mines and building highways into the continent's interior. The vehicles, though, remained dented, and the red or yellow vans, *les esprits des morts,* raced ahead, the eyes of their passengers shining through the open sides.

We finally stopped at a drab concrete building that looked uninhabited. It stood at a curve in the busy two-lane street where vendors sold grilled meat on sticks and men and women lined up to hail any car with an empty seat. But just past the metal gate, a flight of stairs climbed to BCI's offices. When I followed Eric inside, I expected to see the small operation they were when I began researching their work several years ago. At that time, BCI consisted of two or three people in the US and a few in the Congo. Now, I saw five Congolese, two women and three men, sitting at desks, working at computers. They introduced themselves: Evelyn Samu, BCI's national director; Dieudonné Mushagalusa, deputy national director; Richard Demondana, finance manager; Dominique Sakoy, accounting assistant; and Corinne Okitakula, legal officer. Two others, Bienvenu Mupenda, chief of operations, and Papy "Pitchen" Kapuya, program assistant and logistician, had flown to Équateur's capital, Mbandaka, a city 365 miles up the Congo River, to join BCI staff stationed there, and would soon be on boats, taking supplies upriver to the Kokolopori Bonobo Reserve.

Michael Hurley, BCI's executive director, left his computer and shook my hand. He pushed his glasses down to speak, pale indentations on the bridge of his nose where the skin had been damaged after many years in the sun. He was maybe six feet tall, with wavy gray-blond hair, and though fifty-nine, he had a boyish smile, his front teeth slightly overlapped.

"This week has been overwhelming," he told me. "Sally rushed here from DC for a meeting with the national government. Now we have deadlines with the African Development Bank, and we are working to meet their criteria."

Standing at a map, Michael pointed out fifteen conservation areas under development within the bonobo habitat, 193,000 square miles of dense forest to the south of the Congo River. BCI's goal, he explained, was to create a chain of protected areas that, linked by wildlife corridors, would become the Bonobo Peace Forest. Over a period of ten years, during which their annual budget had grown from about $100,000 to a million dollars, BCI had helped establish three times as much government-recognized protected area as all of the big NGOs in the DRC combined: the Kokolopori Bonobo Reserve (larger than Rhode Island at 1,847 square miles) and the immense Sankuru Nature Reserve (11,803 square miles, bigger than Massachusetts). A number of other reserves were under development and would eventually link up to Kokolopori and Sankuru, protecting a huge swath of the bonobo habitat.

Michael put his index finger on the area we would be visiting: the Kokolopori Bonobo Reserve at the upper reaches of the Maringa River, a tributary that flows northwest before curving south within the Congo's great riverine arc. The dark green of the Congo basin covers much of Central Africa, its many tributaries trending west as the Congo River flows north and then turns toward the Atlantic Ocean before veering south, picking up the tributaries and growing in size. I gradually charted our path within this labyrinth that, more than anything else, mapped out the uniform expanse of the rainforest.

From the office down the hall, Sally Jewell Coxe, whose voice I recognized from our numerous telephone conversations, called out a question I missed because part of it sounded like Lingala, or maybe someone's name. Michael crossed the room, shouting out information for a report she was about to deliver. He realized he left his coffee mug on his desk and, still talking, reached back for it even as he seemed to be moving forward.

Sally was fifty-one, eight years younger than Michael, with sandy hair and large green eyes that gave an impression of someone who loved observing the world. Like Michael, she got lost in her train of thought, and over the next few days I would see her checking budgets, writing grant applications, and contacting donors while fielding calls from Mbandaka to prepare the boats that would take supplies on the ten-day trip to the reserve, then following up with staff to make sure those supplies were ready: hand pumps and ultraviolet SteriPENs for drinking water; medicine for the reserve's clinic and for BCI's staff in case anyone got malaria; headlamps, machetes, and new rain ponchos for trackers and eco-guards; batteries for everything and everyone. The list went on.

Another concern was transporting fuel to the reserve. Because of its high price in the DRC, the fuel for the outboard motors and for a month in the reserve, where it would be needed to power generators, motocycles, as well as a Land Cruiser and a Land Rover, could cost $10,000. This was still cheaper than paying to take all cargo and passengers by bush plane, or buying fuel there, where it was marked up three times. The boats could bring more supplies and more people, but the time the trip would take depended on the water level. We were at the end of the dry season, when the boats often got caught on sandbars and had to stop at night.

As Sally spoke, I could barely keep up with all of the details. Skype beeped constantly on her computer, receiving messages from BCI's office in Washington, DC.

"I'm sorry," she said. "I just have to send a report. I'll be right back."

Both Sally and Michael worked the nine-to-five shift in two time zones, until the US office closed at 10:00 p.m. West Central Africa time, and when I said goodnight, they hurried back to their computers in different rooms, still calling out to each other. They had been a couple for ten years, BCI in its early stages when they met. Its current incarnation was in many ways the fruit of their relationship.

That evening, I stayed at the home of BCI's national director in the DRC, Evelyn Samu, a statuesque woman with a still, appraising gaze and a sudden, at times wary smile. She'd been in conservation for over fifteen years and lived with her younger brothers, her granddaughter, and her niece. Her father had been a successful businessman under Mobutu and built the sprawling home off Matadi Road. Its pipes were a less reliable source of water than the swimming pool where insects skimmed the surface, so the maids filled blue plastic buckets and carried them on their heads to the tiled bathrooms. When the power failed, they switched to another network, from a different hydroelectric plant, and when both grids went down, they waited until nightfall to start the generator. Well-kept gardens surrounded the grounds, and the terrace by the kitchen offered a view of the western horizon, its rolling blue hills speckled with buildings, the setting sun spectacular over the savannah.

The night was pleasantly warm. Normally, in the DRC, the dry season south of the equator lasts from April to October, the opposite of the seasons to the north of it. There is little variation in temperature, with a yearly average high of 86 degrees Fahrenheit and an average low of 70. Kinshasa usually has a particularly short dry season, from June through August, but there had been almost no rain that February, and the dust and the lingering, acrid smell of smoke from trash fires had the Congolese wondering when it would rain.

The next morning, before departing for the BCI offices with Evelyn, I waited at the front gate of her home as she prayed near a wall-size shrine to the Virgin Mary. Michael had told me how much energy it took to get around and shop for basic needs, how demanding life was for BCI's staff. Just traveling the four miles to BCI's offices gave me a sense of the city's pace, at once hectic and painfully slow. People rushed cars with an empty seat or trucks with space in the bed even as traffic stopped for minutes at a time. Vehicles crammed the street as far as I could see, the distance obscured in the smoke of burning roadside trash.

The only clear geographic marker for Kinshasa is a widening of the Congo River called the Pool Malebo, formerly Stanley Pool. On the map, it nearly resembled a bull's-eye, an immense lake partially filled in with an island of sediment, around which the river flows. It separates the world's two closest capitals, that of the DRC from Brazzavilla in the Republic of the Congo, a former French colony.

Kinshasa, founded in 1881 by the American explorer Henry Morton Stanley and named Léopoldville after the Belgian King, served as a trading post where the river's navigable stretch ends. One of the challenges of colonization was that the river, though providing a route into the continent, began its descent to the ocean, just beyond the Pool Malebo, by rocketing down dozens of narrow cataracts. To link Léopoldville to the port, a railroad had to be built across Bas-Congo Province, a panhandle that attaches the country's massive inland territory to its scant twenty-five-mile stretch of Atlantic coast.

During the colonial era, Kinshasa's nickname was *Kin la Belle,* "the beautiful." Now it's referred to as *Kin la Poubelle,* "the trashcan." Heightening the sense of disorder is the construction underway in many parts of the city, fueled by the postwar rush for minerals. During the recent wars, the borders the DRC shares with nine other countries were often less boundaries than sieves through which its wealth escaped. Now, with the growth of industry in India, China, Brazil, and Russia causing an increased demand for raw materials, the minerals are often still sold illegally through the DRC's neighbors, notably Rwanda. The Chinese are renovating the capital and building highways into the Congo's interior in exchange for mining contracts, and the country's elite are profiting. Signs of commerce are everywhere, with new buildings going up helter-skelter even as those next door are collapsing.

The effect of all this was overwhelmingly claustrophobic, with a seventh of the country's seventy million here, many from the provinces for work or in refuge from ethnic conflict. One in five adults is HIV positive, and, unable to afford health care, the vast majority resort to faith healing and magic. In *Planet of Slums,* Mike Davis suggests that among the world's megacities, only the poverty of Dhaka, Bangladesh, compares to that of Kinshasa, where less than 5 percent of the population earn salaries, and the average yearly income is less than one hundred dollars. All along the street, young men in torn, colorless clothes sold goods or looked for work. They crowded into the road, trying to find rides. Six or seven at a time stood on a single rear bumper. They held onto tailgates or the back doors of vans, fingers hooked at the edges; at stops, they lowered a hand and shook it out, repeatedly extending it back to a familiar shape.

Group taxis crammed passengers in, many of them hugging baskets or synthetic gunnysacks. On my second day, I traveled without Evelyn, and it took me longer to get a ride. The Congolese barely had to gesture; they just leaned forward, revealing what they wanted with their gazes and postures. As I'd been taught, I lifted my arm and pointed my thumb or index finger to indicate the direction I would take at the next fork in the road.

Though I'd been told that the Kinois, the residents of Kinshasa, would work me over for every penny, on my first two rides, the drivers wouldn't let me pay. One steered a rumbling Mercedes, its windshield split, its sunbaked paint cracked like pottery glaze. Passing a crowd, he swerved to the roadside and handed me a brick of dirty Congolese francs nearly the size of a cinder block, asking me to give it to a stooped old man in a brown button-down shirt who hurried over to meet us. Maybe the driver didn't need money, I considered when he dropped me off, refusing my cash, telling me that he enjoyed the conversation.

Each time I visited the offices, Sally and Michael were finishing grant applications and ironing out plans for our trip. The staff rushed about, coming and going, making lists and compiling reports, their cell phones chiming and ringing, Skype beeping in the background.

As I spoke to Michael, he paused to rub his eyes and catch his breath, and I realized that what I'd been taking for exuberance may have also been the jitteriness of exhaustion.

"We've gone from being a small NGO to something a lot bigger overnight," he told me. "We've hired new office staff in the US, and we had to delay our arrival here so we could train them. And we've expanded our staff here as well. We have grants for work in the field, but not enough of that goes to operating costs, so we're struggling to maintain our offices."

That evening, some of the BCI Kinshasa staff left quickly, careful not to go home too late, when gangs armed with machetes came out. Known as *kulunas,* a word from Angola, from the Portuguese *coluna,* "column" (used for soldiers on patrol), the thugs prowled outlying neighborhoods, their faces at times painted like skulls. There were so many daily challenges for the staff and so many varied discussions in the offices—of landing strips in the rainforest, grant proposals for new vehicles, rural clinics running out of medicine, celebrities contacting BCI in hopes of seeing bonobos in the wild.

Sally joined the discussion, coming in from the next room to tell me that BCI was experiencing a sea change, a make-it-or-break-it moment. She worried about money, and in my short time there, I'd noticed that everyone in the Congo seemed to be asking for it, calling the offices and demanding it. Each time this happened, she explained deliberately to the caller what BCI could and couldn't do, when certain funding would arrive, that she and Michael were working on new budgets, more grants, and to be patient. She told me that BCI was barely managing to fund the people on the reserves, that she and Michael almost never paid themselves, and when they did, they ended up putting the money to an emergency somewhere in the field.

Over the next week, the BCI team decided to push back our flight to Mbandaka once, then again. Normally, they ran their trips separately, one staying in Kinshasa or DC while the other was in the field, living in mud huts for months at a time to support their Congolese partners as they established or oversaw programs. But they hadn't been to Kokolopori in over six months and had a lot to do. They chartered a bush plane from Mbandaka into the rain-forest with Aviation sans Frontières and sent the boats loaded with supplies to meet us at the reserve. Two of the Kinshasa staff, Bienvenu and Pitchen, were on board, as well as BCI's boatmen who were based in Mbandaka. After a month in Kokolopori, we would all return together to Mbandaka by boat.

Two days before we were to leave, and three after the boats' departure, Sally got a phone call: two outboard engines had died and the boatmen couldn't find parts in Basankusu, a town on the Lulonga River at the conflu-ence of the Maringa and Lopori, a day or two from the Congo. Eric, who had just arrived at the offices freshly shaved, a blue oxford shirt tucked into his jeans, set out to find replacement parts and put them on an upcoming flight to Basankusu. All day the Kinshasa staff bustled about, Dieudonné getting our photography permits since it is illegal to take photographs in the DRC without governmental permission.

We delayed once more, Sally and Michael repeatedly working until after midnight. Then, a week and a half after my arrival, we were ready. We loaded the bed of a white pickup with large yellow duffel bags printed with the letters BCI and drove back toward the airport as I stared out the truck window, tak-ing in the city's turmoil. Women paused between four lanes of rushing traffic, plastic tubs the size of laundry baskets on their heads. Shirtless men broke old concrete with sledges, piling chunks on the median, each muscle in their torsos knife-thin and close to the skin. Further on, boys played soccer in an empty lot among the scorched hulks of old trucks and heaps of smoldering trash. There were merchants in sooty storefronts, peddlers by loaded handcarts, students waiting for buses, office workers, men and women in pressed suits and skirts, climbing into taxis with mismatched panels, holes drilled along their edges, wires knitting them together.

Équateur

As we were about to climb the steps to the CAA jet that would take us to Mbandaka, a police officer and Dr. Nicolas Mwanza Ndunda, BCI's scientific director, ran from the N'Djili Airport terminal to give a package and contracts to Sally. Mwanza is a tall, jovial-looking man in his sixties, with a paunch and a small mustache. Sweat beaded on his forehead, and the sun had us squinting, the heat off the tarmac so palpable I could feel it in my muscles.

The other passengers hurried past us to claim seats as Sally read the papers, a subcontract for a grant that would employ staff from the Congolese Ministry of Scientific Research. She signed and handed them to Mwanza, and the officer began to lift his hand in an imploring gesture. She gave him the equivalent of five dollars in Congolese francs for letting Mwanza meet us.

After we took our places, not a seat remained in the narrow Fokker jet, the last six rows of which were loaded with bags and cardboard boxes heavily sealed with brown tape. It was hot inside, the passengers sweating, though we cooled down once we were in motion.

We left Kinshasa, crossing inland away from the Pool Malebo, heading east over Bandundu Province. Below us, forested rivers scored savannah plateaus, giving the landscape the look of interlocking puzzle pieces. Équateur was just above, bordering Congo-Brazzaville to the west, the Central African Republic to the north, and Orientale Province to the east.

Équateur is known for being the most heavily forested province in the DRC, and forty minutes into our trip, as we neared Mbandaka, I stared out the jet's window at the rainforest curving against the horizon. A distant plume of smoke rose from the endless rippled green, calling to mind a war photograph I saw years ago: a burning ship far away on the uniform ocean.

Before this trip, I'd studied the DRC on a map. Its lopsided bulk, in its place at the center of Africa, looked—just as the hackneyed metaphor says—like a heart. But maps don't do the Congo justice. The Mercator projection—which transposes the globe onto a cylinder or flat surface—misrepresents the area closer to the poles, expanding it. Relative to North

America and Europe, the Congo is far larger than it appears: at 905,355 square miles, it is 3.37 times the size of Texas, the eleventh-largest country on earth and the second largest in Africa, after Algeria. As of 2005, nearly 60 percent of it was forestland.

Though little of it was logged under Mobutu because of lack of transportation infrastructure, by the 1990s, 37 percent of the country's forests that could be exploited commercially were officially designated as timber concessions. With the war now over, much of the region has become more reliably accessible for systematic exploitation, so deforestation, which has been occurring at a rate of about 1 percent a decade, is likely to speed up.

When trees are cut down and decay, and especially when they are burned, they release CO_2 into the atmosphere. This carbon then absorbs solar radiation, warming the planet. Already, global deforestation emits more carbon dioxide than all of the transportation on earth—automobiles, airplanes, trains, and boats—combined, and nearly as much as transportation and industry together. Furthermore, each tree cut down has a double negative impact, not only releasing carbon but no longer assimilating it from the atmosphere. Through photosynthesis, trees create carbohydrates from CO_2 and water, synthesizing the carbon molecules with water and releasing oxygen as a waste product. In the process, the world's remaining tropical forests sequester 20 percent of global carbon emissions from fossil fuels, a number that decreases with logging and the clearing of land even as manmade carbon emissions rise steadily.

So dramatically have humans transformed the earth that in the early 1980s the American scientist Eugene F. Stoermer proposed the name *Anthropocene* for our current geologic epoch. Zoologists Guy Cowlishaw and Robin Dunbar write: "Not since the demise of the dinosaurs 65 million years ago has this planet witnessed changes to the structure and dynamics of its biological communities as dramatic as those that have occurred over recent millennia, and especially in the past four hundred years." Humans have devastated millions of square miles of habitat, and since 1600, eighty-nine of the planet's approximately five thousand mammal species have gone extinct, with 169 others critically endangered. More recently, agricultural and industrial revolutions have reshaped the world, changing the composition of the soil, water, and air, and the estimated current rate of extinction in rainforests alone, for all organisms—insects, plants, bacteria, and fungi—is 27,000 a year. Despite the severity of our impact, the entire 250,000 years of human history hardly compares to the damage we have done in the last fifty years, and given our current rate of expansion, hundreds, if not thousands, more animal species are expected to die off within the century.

In a way, the asteroid strike that most likely ended the dinosaurs' rule 65.5 million years ago and our current age are bookends, containing a long, largely continuous span of evolution and diversification of life that created humans, bonobos, and the rainforests as we currently know them. After the asteroid's collision, dust and ash filled the atmosphere, blocking sunlight and disrupting the food chain by killing off photosynthesizing organisms. When herbivorous dinosaurs could no longer graze, the carnivores that preyed on them also died, eliminating all top predators. The only creatures that endured were those that could subsist on insects and worms, which themselves bred in the carrion and detritus. One of the traits that has made us so destructive to our environment allowed our small, rodentlike ancestors to survive: they could eat just about anything.

After that cataclysm, the earth was a relatively quiet place, but over the next ten million years, it heated up significantly, and mammals thrived, spreading across the globe, speciating to fill ecological niches left vacant by the dinosaurs. That the subsequent transformation of the rainforest likely shaped modern humans reveals how changes in the environment can shift our path, transforming us from one kind of creature to another, with radically different behavior.

The planet's hot phase could have had a number of causes, from changing ocean currents to volcanic venting that released massive quantities of atmospheric carbon. Trees covered the earth nearly pole to pole, the Canadian Arctic and Greenland host to lush, closed-canopy forests, to alligators, tapirs, flying lemurs, hippolike mammals, and giant tortoises. Palm trees grew in Wyoming, where primates left some of their earliest fossil evidence. Though resembling squirrels in both size and appearance, they had the nails characteristic of primates rather than claws. With the planet so densely forested, they easily spread across Europe, Asia, and Africa.

By forty-eight million years ago, plant life had sequestered a great deal of atmospheric carbon in oil and coal deposits, and the planet cooled as a result of the continents' drift away from the equator. Until then, the earth had been in a warm phase, without significant polar ice, alpine glaciers, or continental ice sheets for 250 million years. The clustering of landmasses in the single massive continent of Pangea had allowed the warm and cold ocean currents to mix, maintaining relatively stable temperatures. But as the continents separated, they isolated the oceans, causing greater concentrations of cold water and the buildup of sea ice, so that sometime between thirty and fifty million years ago, average ocean surface temperatures dropped by a staggering eighty-six degrees Fahrenheit.

Cool periods tend to be arid, the planet's humidity trapped in ice, and the earth began to take on an appearance we would recognize. The interiors of continents dried out, and grass, which first appeared fifty-five to sixty million years ago, limited to the shores of lakes and rivers, evolved into hardier species. It eventually covered savannahs, which, though usually described as plains, are grassland with scattered, open-canopy woodlands. This dry habitat came to predominate in Africa and offered fewer sources of nutrients to primates, increasing competition and requiring more dynamic foraging. And as rainforests shrank to a band around the equator, primates, which had evolved into creatures that we might recognize as similar to monkeys, survived only in Africa.

Several theories exist for the monkey-ape split, 24.5 to 29 million years ago. It may have resulted from feeding patterns that evolved in part due to competition between primate groups in contracting ecosystems. One strong theory holds that when some monkey species evolved from eating only ripe fruits to being able to digest even those that are unripe—thereby increasing their own numbers and limiting the food supply for all other tree-dwellers—a few competing primates adapted to survive. The earliest ape—our first ancestor after the split—most likely resembled the gibbons, the so-called lesser apes, of which sixteen species survive in Southeast Asia. They are the most monkeylike ape and the fastest, most agile arboreal primate. With an average body weight of fifteen pounds, they swing hand over hand and leap through the trees rather than climb with all fours like monkeys. Such abilities no doubt allowed their ancestors to snatch hard-to-get food on small, peripheral branches, and thus to outcompete monkeys. Those among the first apes who had the longest reach would have been most successful, which would explain the remarkably long arms that gibbons sport today. Furthermore, brachiation (swinging from branches with the hands) would have favored the upright posture and the head shape and position that remain distinguishing traits of modern apes. Gibbons also lack tails, an appendage that helped monkeys balance on all fours in trees, but that might have been ill suited to brachiation and—in the case of the great apes—terrestrial foraging and travel.

Evolution, however, is unlikely to be so picture-perfect. Numerous factors are often at play, from the isolation of a few animals from a larger group to random DNA mutations that occasionally provide adaptive traits. When individuals colonize a new environment or live through a gradual climatic shift, those among them most capable of surviving these changes—and having the chance to produce surviving offspring—pass on their traits. In every group of individuals of any given species, there is variation. A high school classroom will have students with different heights, proportions, personalities, metabolic rates, immune systems, athletic abilities, and colors of skin, hair, and eyes. A hypothetical group of early apes is no different, and those with traits most suited to new circumstances will outbreed the others. When their successful offspring pair up, each new generation gets a double dose of survivor genes. If the change in the environment is particularly harsh and rapid owing to geological activity or new weather patterns, or if the competition with other animals is fierce, a bottleneck may occur: most of the individuals of the species die off, and the few who are left are likely to have adaptive traits. Even within a few generations, these adaptive qualities become more prominent and survivors begin to look different from their ancestors, whereas elsewhere, in other parts of Africa, where the environment is more stable, the species can remain relatively unchanged.

About twenty million years ago, not long after the arrival of apes on the primate scene, the next step in their evolution took place. From DNA studies, we know that the apes separated into two groups, the lesser apes and the great apes. A number of factors could have been at play. With diversifying monkey species dominating the canopy's diminishing food sources, it is likely that the larger and less agile of the gibbonlike early apes began foraging in the ground cover. Even today, unlike monkeys, great apes have the ability to digest a number of fibrous plants.

Environmental changes and the contraction of forests also could have influenced great ape evolution, and the simplest way to imagine the transition to a more terrestrial existence would be to picture a single group of early apes. They live in Africa, in the trees, but in a landscape particularly vulnerable to climatic drying. Though they are somewhat versatile, descending to forage for further sustenance, they never wander far. As savannah begins replacing forest, they compete for limited fruit resources with monkeys and with other apes, and have to venture farther on land. Those who survive gradually begin to resemble the earliest common ancestor of today's orangutans, gorillas, chimpanzees, bonobos, and humans.

Today, the least terrestrial great ape is the orangutan, which lives exclusively in Southeast Asia. Of the surviving great apes, its lineage was the first to split from the common ancestor of the African apes, fifteen to nineteen million years ago, and the only one to spread outside of Africa and survive. Of the great apes, they swing most easily—though far from displaying the agility of gibbons—and on the ground, they employ fist-walking, a likely precursor to knuckle-walking, the signature technique of chimpanzees, gorillas, and bonobos, who, being far more terrestrial, evolved to have friction pads on their middle phalanges. As for the surviving African great apes—gorillas, humans, chimpanzees, and bonobos—the splits in their lineages occurred relatively close together. Nine to eleven million years ago, the gorilla ancestor separated from the common ancestor of chimpanzees, bonobos, and humans. Five to eight million years ago, the human ancestor bade the bonobo-chimpanzee line farewell. And 1.5 to 3 million years ago, bonobos and chimpanzees went their own ways.

However, all great apes—humans included—continue to share behavioral traits, and one that is essential for all of them is nest building. Whereas monkeys and gibbons rest in trees for short periods, with little protection, great apes weave branches together to create bowls that can accommodate an adult. The practice may have led to deeper sleep that promoted greater brain regeneration and neuron growth. This behavior would perhaps have provided them the advantage of waking rested and clear-minded, and could have catalyzed the evolution of ever larger-brained apes, who reaped the benefits so long as they remained as committed to nests as we are to our huts and townhouses.

With so many factors influencing evolution, the genealogy is far from resolved, and new discoveries in genetics and fossils frequently call various aspects of it into question. Though the anatomy of chimps, gorillas, and bonobos suggests that their ancestors, unlike those of orangutans, continued to adapt to ground conditions, they also retained the ability to climb, allowing them to get food and take refuge from predators. One theory proposes that gorillas, chimpanzees, and bonobos are so terrestrial because their ancestors adapted to the savannah for millennia before finding their way to the remaining food-rich rainforests. And some genetic studies suggest that the human-chimpanzee split wasn't clean, their ancestors having romped on occasion. As for DNA, we share between 98.6 percent and 98.7 percent of ours with bonobos and chimps, 98.25 percent with gorillas, and 96.6 percent with orangutans. There is a dearth of fossil evidence from between nine and fourteen million years ago, and much of what we know about the earliest days of our evolution comes from studies of living great apes and their DNA. In many ways, we build evolutionary history back from surviving species.

Given that the chimpanzee-bonobo ancestor and the human ancestor evolved from the same stock—the same common ancestor who was neither chimpanzee-bonobo nor human—it's not surprising that there are some resemblances in social structures among the species. In fact, studies of chimpanzees and bonobos have shed light on the evolution of human behavior. Only a few decades ago, and especially after the World Wars, we humans strongly associated ourselves with the belligerence of chimpanzees, unable to deny our brutality. But over the last four decades, as we have become aware of bonobos, we've recognized a number of our other social traits in them, such as our proclivity for nonreproductive sex, our ability to construct largely nonviolent communities, and our practice of building peaceful coalitions.

But the greater mystery is how bonobos and chimpanzees, being so similar and having such a recent common ancestor, could have developed such divergent behaviors over a relatively short evolutionary period. Scientists have theorized that the Congo River formed at that time, between 1.5 and 3 million years ago, separating the common ancestor of bonobos and chimpanzees into two groups. While to the north the chimpanzees competed with gorillas for food, the bonobos lived in a lush enclave south of the river's curve, where certain aggressive traits were less essential for their survival. This theory, however, doesn't explain why there were no gorillas to the south of the river, and another argument exists for the evolutionary path of chimpanzees and bonobos, given that the Congo River may have formed millions of years earlier than once believed.

The bonobo-chimpanzee split roughly coincides with the beginning of our current glacial cycle 2.6 million years ago, which, relative to geologic time, rapidly transformed the planet and the great ape habitat. Though the earth had already been cooling for over forty-eight million years, the accumulation of polar ice sped up 5.3 million years ago, when the Isthmus of Panama joined North and South America, cutting off warm equatorial currents and cooling the Atlantic. Spreading ice reflected solar radiation into the atmosphere, preventing its absorption and starting a feedback loop that resulted in more rapid planetary cooling, and thus more ice. The term *ice age* is generally misused. Technically, it indicates a period during which substantial continental ice sheets exist in both the Northern and Southern Hemispheres. We have been in an ice age for nearly 2.6 million years, a time marked by interglacials, like our current warm period, and glacials, which most people erroneously refer to as ice ages. The glacials come in cycles of twenty thousand, forty thousand, and one hundred thousand years, mirroring shifts in the earth's tilt and orbit around the sun.

With this forty-eight-million-year sketch of earth's history since the planet began to cool during the Eocene, we can imagine a time-lapse film from space and see the movement of primates and forests to their current positions. First, we have a planet whose continents have nearly reached their present positions, though they are almost entirely green, forests fringing the poles. This coloring then melts away, the interiors of continents yellowing, flecked with green and outlined with it at the coasts, though a solid belt of forest still girds the planet's middle. With the exception of Africa, the continents that host primates become inhospitable to them.

The most remarkable change in forest distribution occurs 2.6 million years ago, with the ice age. Ocean levels drop and continental shelves appear as the planet's humidity gathers in ice more than two miles thick over much of the northern temperate zones. In places, glaciers stand nearly half the height of Everest, pressing the earth's crust so deeply into the mantle that today parts of Northern Europe and Canada are still lifting back into place. If we continue our time-lapse film, the ice age would show white spreading from the poles, the green-yellow savannahs desiccating, and the planet's rainforest belt withering to a few specks.

In *Demonic Males: Apes and the Origins of Human Violence,* Harvard zoologist Richard Wrangham and science writer Dale Peterson lay out one explanation for the divergence of bonobos and chimpanzees. They argue that even though tropical forests had been gradually retreating for millennia, the Congo basin rainforest, before the ice age, likely would have been much larger than now, allowing the common ancestor of chimpanzees and bonobos to circumvent the entire river system and cross over to the other side. But during the glacial maximum, the forest shrank, and survived only in the wettest pockets. Gorillas, who are vegetarians and sustain themselves on protein-rich shoots and buds, would have seen their food sources become scarce and their habitat dramatically reduced. They likely would have withdrawn to wet climates near mountains or died off, especially to the south of the river, where there was no mountainous terrain. The versatile chimpanzee-bonobo ancestor would have occupied more space and might, in certain areas, have lived largely in savannahs.

During the following interglacial, as ice caps melted and humidity returned to the equator, abundant rain carved new tributaries and enlarged existing rivers. Wrangham and Peterson explain that though the food sources optimal for gorillas would have reappeared in abundance throughout the basin, the gorillas would have struggled to return to all areas. Rivers would have hampered their travel, and despite the humid interglacial, the forests might not have returned to their previous size, no longer offering a clear path around the Congo's elaborate river system.

Judging by the gorillas' present habitat, it appears that they expanded only into the sections of the Congo rainforest currently inhabited by chimpanzees. The chimp-bonobo ancestors who lived in the same areas as gorillas faced limited resources and might have benefited by becoming

Empty Hands, Open Arms

significantly more competitive with one another for food, evolving toward chimpanzees. However, the chimp-bonobo ancestor across the river to the south, living without gorillas, had an easier time, benefiting from the diets of both chimpanzees and gorillas, as bonobos do today. With so many resources, it might have evolved to have increasingly less competition between individuals. Even now, chimps, just to the north of the river, rely much more on hunting. Of course, owing to the lack of fossil evidence, we can't easily judge whether the chimp-bonobo ancestor more closely resembled chimpanzees or bonobos, or had a unique disposition from which its descendents dramatically diverged.

Is a lesson in 65.5 million years of global history necessary to understand the planet's few remaining rainforests and the ways that apes now occupy them? If humans are the bookend, the driving force in a new mass extinction, it is clearly important to understand exactly what may be ending, and all that would be lost. The long, largely continuous evolution and expansion of species since the demise of dinosaurs appears, at least from our limited perspective, to be at a crucial juncture, with habitats being rapidly destroyed by humans. Given the exponential increase of human populations and industry, we must act quickly if we are to preserve remaining ecosystems at a time when few of us even understand their significance.

The story of this evolution changes how I see the forest—not as a natural resource or a feature of the landscape, but as a central factor in the story of our evolution. As it vanished, apes evolved and our ancestor separated from theirs. The only surviving members of their group took refuge in the equatorial forests that have existed in some form for millions of years, and they teach us more about the past and ourselves than fossils ever could. Sally Jewell Coxe often describes bonobos and chimpanzees as exemplifying the yin and yang of human nature, and their models shed light not only on how we can interact with each other, but on the ways an environment can cause us to change.

The plane banked and began to lose altitude, and I wondered how I would feel standing in virgin rainforest and seeing bonobos. As the last great ape that Westerners became aware of, they made us realize all that we didn't know about ourselves and the forest itself. Increasingly, though, as BCI's logo of a bonobo standing in a circle suggested, they represented the importance of coalitions to save that very forest. Today, Africa's rainforests are barely absorbing the carbon emissions of its cities, and the lesson in planetary history also serves to remind us of how carbon dioxide can transform the earth, and how the forests that we're cutting down are essential for sequestering it.

For years, studies of ice cores from glaciers have revealed that the current level of carbon dioxide is the highest the planet has known in the last eight hundred thousand years. New research, however, suggests that the last time the atmosphere held this much carbon dioxide was fifteen million years ago, when, according to the scientist Aradhna Tripati, a professor at the University of California, Los Angeles, "global temperatures were 5 to 10 degrees Fahrenheit higher than they are today, the sea level was approximately 75 to 120 feet higher than today, there was no permanent sea ice cap in the Arctic and very little ice on Antarctica and Greenland." Historically, global temperatures largely correlate to atmospheric carbon levels, and though temperatures are at their highest level in four thousand years, they are expected to rise at an unusually rapid rate over the next century, one too fast to allow most creatures to adapt. Some scientists have suggested that we are crossing into unknown territory, over a tipping point, where carbon emissions will create a domino effect, transforming the planet at an exponential rate. And yet our impact is increasing, a day in Kinshasa enough to make me understand the urgency of human need and hunger. The DRC's population—already the fourth largest in Africa after those of Nigeria, Egypt, and Ethiopia—is set to double to 140 million within twenty years. A glance from the airplane window sufficed to remind me of how isolated and unknown our few remaining rainforests are, how they can disappear without our knowing, and how much of a challenge it will be for humanity to work together to save them.

Mbandaka to Djolu

Ten minutes before landing, we crossed over the wide river again. Dozens of long forested islands split it into as many as five channels, yellow and brown sandbars visible beneath the water, carved by the current into shapes reminiscent of dunes. The jet coasted low, dropped its landing gear as my ears popped, and a minute later it banged down on the runway, all of us clutching armrests and gritting teeth.

We were let out into a sunny afternoon and crossed the tarmac to the yellow terminal, the main chamber of which contained two rows of wooden benches that looked like church pews. When I heard people say Mbandaka, I listened closely. The stress was on the first syllable, the *m* largely silent to my ear, at most a slight holding of the lips together before the plosive *b* sound.

Aimée Nsongo, a short, sturdy woman who was BCI's Mbandaka office manager, stood waiting for us. She commanded a group of young men who gathered the dozen large duffel bags, each weighing sixty or seventy pounds. We followed them outside the airport to where six Chinese motorcycles were parked. A single white pickup, rented by BCI, was in the gravel lot. The young men loaded the bags into the back while Aimée went inside to speak with agents of the Direction Générale de Migration (DGM) regarding the legal formalities of our travel in Équateur Province.

At least a dozen people sat in blue plastic chairs, drinking large bottles of Primus beer. We joined them as shoeshine boys gathered, along with vendors selling pineapples and bowls of large squirming *mpose* grubs, the larvae that rhinoceros beetles lay in rotting wood.

"Mmm—*mpose!*" Michael said as a young man held out a metal tub of what looked like thumb-size writhing maggots with pincers on their heads. He explained that both Congolese and bonobos eat them, and I would later read that they contain more protein than chicken and beef. He paid a cook to fry them in garlic, and they were delicious, with a texture and flavor like buttered lobster, the heads crunching lightly. We would spend the following weeks asking if anyone had *mpose*. They were our first meal in Mbandaka and would be our last one, a month later, again at the airport, before we returned to Kinshasa.

When Aimée finished with the DGM, we drove into the city along a paved road that, aside from a few humps, potholes, and fissures, was sound. Dozens of men passed the other way on bicycles, working the pedals with the laborious swaying of their bodies. Asphalt gave way to the wide red avenues of the city, multicolored umbrellas stuck in the roadside, vendors squatting beneath. Everything seemed tinged with the russet dust, concrete walls and buildings, people's clothes and skin.

Founded in 1883, Mbandaka was formerly called Équateur. It appeared on Henry Morton Stanley's maps at both the equator and the Congo River, like the joint in a cross. But he was mistaken; the city was in fact a few miles north of that imaginary line. Under Belgian colonial rule, the province became Équateur and the city Coquilhatville, a convoluted formulation commemorating Camille-Aimé Coquilhat, the Belgian governor-general of the Congo Free State. But within a year of taking over in November 1965, Mobutu gave the provincial capital its current name in honor of a local leader, soon therafter changing the Congo to Zaire and Léopoldville to Kinshasa.

During the Second Congo War, from 1998 to 2003, when Kinshasa was at times without electricity and water, crowds filling buckets at the river and carrying them home, Mbandaka and the surrounding regions suffered far worse. Opposing armies occupied people's land and homes, eating their food and robbing them. Hundreds of thousands, most of them civilians, died not only of violence but of starvation and disease.

Now, Mbandaka, a city of 350,000, had yet to recover from its years of penury. Its streets were filled with bicycles, but there were only a few motorcycles and the occasional car. For less than twenty cents per trip, a constant stream of bicycle taxis carried people across town, passengers seated on the padded racks behind the driver. The bikes reminded me of souped-up lowriders in the United States: reflectors and stickers; sparkles, colorful paint, and tassels; fancy rearview mirrors on long stems; pump horns and thumb-rung bells on the wide handlebars; passenger seats of red shag rug, couch cushions, or padded chair armrests bolted side by side.

The retro persisted at the hotel whose name we couldn't manage to identify, though we asked everyone. Four large concrete buildings stood in a fenced courtyard, each painted a different pastel. Our apartment had a living room, a stripped-down kitchen, and two bedrooms, one for me and the other for

Sally and Michael. The security guard told us it was the hotel of the governor, though we couldn't figure out if this was its name, if the governor stayed here, or if he owned it. The electricity came on briefly after sundown. As at Evelyn's house, the bathroom had buckets of cold water for bathing and flushing.

Two men from the bank came in the door, with gym bags loaded with 15,000 US dollars in Congolese francs, at least three dozen large bricks held together with rubber bands. The exchange rate was 900 francs to the dollar, and BCI would need small bills of 100 or 200 francs. Whereas inflation had made Kinshasa expensive, a fifteen-minute ride in a taxi or a street meal easily costing ten or twenty dollars, the economy in Équateur's rainforest was largely barter with almost no outside stimulus, and 100-franc bills—a little more than ten cents—gave the people living on the Kokolopori Bonobo Reserve currency for local products.

When Sally and Michael and the two bankers had finished counting money to pay trackers and reserve staff, as well as for the costs of the trip, there were five backpacks full of cash that they locked inside three large plastic duffels. It was already dark. We ate a meal of cassava, rice, chicken, fried bananas, and amaranth greens, cooked and carried over by Aimée's younger sister. Afterward, Sally continued making calls and meeting with people, and I was not surprised when I walked by her door and saw her asleep in her clothes.

Michael suggested that we take a walk and maybe grab a drink with researchers from CREF, the government's Centre de Recherche en Écologie et Foresterie whose staff had worked closely in the field with BCI for over a decade. Since our arrival in Mbandaka, a few of them had stopped by to say hello. As part of its goal to support Congolese agency, BCI had supported CREF, funding them to do wildlife surveys for each of the future conservation areas. Michael explained to me that given the distances they traveled, the researchers were the best source of knowledge about everything happening in the province, and he wanted to speak with them more. We locked the door, then descended the stairs and went outside.

Night in the city was nearly absolute, a wide swath of equatorial stars largely unfamiliar to my eyes, a few bright flares out across the city. It took us a moment to find the security guard, sitting near the gate in a folding chair, an AK-47 across his lap.

"Who stays in this hotel?" Michael asked in French. It was BCI's first time using it, and he wanted to make sure that Sally would be safe in the room.

"Only NGOs and government," the guard told him. "No one else comes in. It's very secure here."

We hesitated a moment, but the hotel's compound did look well contained, and Michael had spent considerable time in Mbandaka. He and Sally had never had problems in their decade of carrying cash and supplies in and out.

"Many people here watch out for us," he said, explaining that BCI was well known in Mbandaka. Then, as we walked out along the road, he told me the story of a young man the locals called Miracle Bonobo.

Since my arrival, I'd learned that many people involved with BCI have bonobo nicknames. For example, the Congolese often called Sally and Michael Mama Bonobo and Papa Bonobo. *Mama* and *papa* are terms of respect in the DRC, but it had taken me a while to get used to being called *papa* by people in the street, by Evelyn's maids, and by the staff at airports and supermarkets. BCI's oldest member, Dr. Mwanza, who was born in Bas-Congo in 1949 and earned his PhD in biology in the USSR, focusing on species reintroduction, is called Mpaka Bonobo, *mpaka* meaning "old" or "grandfather."

The story of Miracle Bonobo dated back six or seven years, to when BCI was still building credibility among the Congolese in the hard period after the civil war. The rebel- and government-held provinces had just reunited under a fragmented central administration when BCI assembled its team of boatmen. The captain was Malu Ebonga Charles, a green-eyed Congolese in his late forties whose grandfather had been German, hence his nickname— Le Blanc, "the white." The team often plied the long trip from Mbandaka to Kokolopori. Among them was Médard, a young Congolese man who became friends with Michael's eighteen-year-old nephew, Joey.

"My sister trusted me with Joey," Michael said. "It was summer vacation, and she asked if I could bring him back alive. I almost didn't, actually. He was all over the boat, hanging out with boatmen, and he and Médard became friends. Being on the pirogues—the dugout canoes—is BCI's vacation. It's the only time we get to unwind and relax. It can be challenging, of course. There are storms on the river, and accidents. But we love it.

"Joey was lying in the sun, hanging out with the boatmen, and we were stopping to swim often, but then he got malaria. He was so feverish that we had to stop to put him in the water to cool him down. We were giving him medicine, but it was taking him a long time to recover. Everyone on the boat really liked Joey, and after he went back to the US, Médard gave me a letter to send to him. In it was fifty dollars."

Michael paused in the dark. He was breathing a little hard and stopped, putting his hand to his mouth as if to cough or clear his throat.

"He told me," he said in a thick voice, "that Joey had talked about saving money for college. Médard wanted to send the money, but fifty dollars was half his monthly salary. It was barely enough to live on here. I couldn't believe he wanted to give away that money, and I insisted that he keep it. I told him Joey didn't need it.

"A few months later, in Kinshasa, Sally and I got a call. Médard and his friend had been hit by a motorcycle. They were walking here, in Mbandaka, at night, and the motorcycle driver lost control or swerved suddenly to avoid a hole. We never got the story straight. Maybe he was drunk. But he was going really fast. You see how dark it is. It killed Médard's friend instantly and left Médard unconscious and in critical condition. The hospital said that he'd suffered a massive head injury and would probably die."

We'd stopped walking and stood on the dark road, no sense of the city around us at all, just the vast, depthless night.

"Our team sent us photos of him. His entire face was swollen. His eyelids were as big as fists. He was bleeding from his ears and eyes and nose. The Mbandaka hospital had no one who could operate on head injuries, so we called a top surgeon in Kinshasa, and he said it would cost a few thousand dollars. He asked if the injured person was essential to our operations, if we really needed to have him airlifted there and were ready to pay this kind of money. We contacted everyone we knew to help with funds, and when I called my sister, she told me she'd just received a letter from Médard, another one that he'd sent himself, with fifty dollars in it. She immediately wired me two thousand dollars for the operation."

Again we were silent, Michael taking the time to calm his voice.

"We built BCI with an idea of family and community. We were a family. It didn't matter if you were American or Congolese, a scientist or a boatman. That was our vision. We would have done what we did for Médard for the others, too. What we didn't realize was how much taking care of Médard would make people trust us here. They want to take care of us, too. They know that we're doing this for them."

"And what happened to Médard?"

"The surgeon didn't expect him to survive. He was in a coma when we flew him to Kinshasa, but as soon as Mwanza came into the room, Médard woke up and recognized him. I don't know if the accident caused permanent injury, but now he seems fine. He's still with us. You'll meet him on the boat when we go back. People here remember the story. Everyone in the Congo is connected. The families are huge, so in a lot of areas more people are related than not. People called him Miracle Bonobo. It's made us realize, even now, when BCI is getting bigger, that we need to stay close to the people. A few months ago, the captain of the boat, Le Blanc, had a stroke, and we helped him get care. He's still not well, and this will be our first trip without him."

Michael and I arrived at the bar where CREF researchers often met up when in town. A dozen plastic chairs were arranged around crooked wooden tables set in gravel, and there was a raised dance floor with tall mirrors against one wall. But the CREF researchers had already gone home, which Michael said was unusual. He said that they called themselves *les beaux-frères de Jésus,* "the brothers-in-law of Jesus," and I admitted that I didn't get it.

"It's because Catholic nuns are called the wives of Jesus. They've nicknamed the local bar the Church of the Brothers-in-Law of Jesus. When they're in Mbandaka, they meet here for what they call *prier sans cesse,* 'ceaseless prayer.' These are the words a priest would use, though in this case they just refer to drinking."

Michael called to the waitress and began his own divine communion as a lively song blared on the sound system and people got up from a number of tables.

The Congolese are known for their love of dance. They value form in the way they greet, men ceremonially shaking hands and touching their foreheads side to side three times, women warmly kissing cheeks like the French, but adding one last kiss. When they dance, they are synchronized, the bar patrons—men and women—singing and moving together, watching their reflections in the large mirror on the wall. Kinshasa clubs have the mirrors, too, and people use them to learn new dances from each other, performing elaborate choreographies.

Later that night, I lay in bed, the room so dark it felt like a cave. Wind gusted outside, and I dozed and woke to doors slamming, curtains billowing. A storm front was pushing in, the one thing that could prevent our flight into the rainforest the next morning. I found my headlamp and went to close the windows.

As wind whistled over the city, I struggled to get back to sleep, thinking about Michael's story of Miracle Bonobo and what Sally told me about modeling BCI on bonobo society—the emphasis on taking care of each individual, regardless of his or her role. Outside, there was the occasional, distant clattering of wind-blown trash, the shaking of windows in their frames, and soon the steady drumming of rain against the dry earth.

After a few more hours of restless sleep, I reluctantly got up and packed my bag. The rain was letting up, and outside, the wet, red streets were empty but for the occasional bicycle. Since my arrival in the DRC, people had frequently complained about the lack of rain; Kinshasa was unseasonably hot and dusty. Unlike the Amazon, whose waters lower significantly during the dry season, the Congo remains level. The river begins south of the equator, flows north of it, and curves back across in a wide sweep over a thousand miles long, so it benefits from the rainy and dry seasons that alternate on opposite sides of the equator. But that year, Congolese said, there had been little rain. They'd never seen the river so low.

As Aimée directed the loading of the truck, Sally got through to the satellite phone of Marcel Falay, BCI's regional director in Kokolopori, to ask if the landing strip, nothing more than a field cut from the forest, was firm enough for the plane to land. He told her the rain had stopped there. The runway was fine.

At the Mbandaka airport, we drove onto the tarmac, where a single-propeller Cessna waited for us, AVIATION SANS FRONTIÈRES printed on its side. Started by former Air France pilots during Nigeria's war with Biafra in the late sixties, ASF, a nonprofit bush plane operation, had been expanding its routes through the Congo in recent years, as the country gained stability.

The two French pilots weighed our duffels on what looked like an aluminum bathroom scale, recording the numbers. On our previous flight, with CAA, Sally paid $5 for each kilo that exceeded our personal limit of twenty kilos, or about forty-four pounds. ASF charged $2.50 after a limit of fifteen kilos.

"This is what people don't get," she told me. "If you want to take anything into the field, you have to calculate not just the price but the cost of getting it from the US to Kinshasa, then from Kinshasa to Mbandaka, and Mbandaka to Djolu. That's why everything in this country costs a fortune. Transportation is a feat."

Already I'd noticed that bottled water and orange Fanta had gone from 1,000 francs in Kinshasa to 1,500 here. In Djolu, the few times that it was available, it would cost 2,500, even 3,000. The markup held true for diesel and gas as well, which was why BCI transported most supplies by canoe.

We were about to climb into the plane, the French pilots checking our pockets and passing metal detectors over us, when two DGM agents hurried from inside the airport and told us we'd skipped proper departure procedures.

Instantly, everyone was arguing, Sally and Michael fighting to be heard over the agents and Aimée Nsongo, who insisted that our baggage had already been searched twice upon our arrival in Mbandaka the day before, and that this was a private flight. Only when the two men heard Sally speak in

Lingala—a clear sign that she knew the customs of the region and wasn't a clueless foreigner—did they smile and relent.

"But you still have to pay airport taxes," they told us, "and we need to record your passports."

These weren't the made-up taxes I'd so often read about but simply the Go Pass tickets that airports sold. Though extortion apparently still existed in the airports and at the borders, the DRC's government had cracked down. Formerly, every official and soldier whom travelers met would harass them, accusing them of carrying banned materials or demanding passports, which only bribes would buy back. This practice of condoned corruption became institutionalized under Mobutu, whose government rarely paid its military. When the economy tanked, the people's survival depended on their ability to make money any way they could. Now, as the DRC struggled to rebuild after Mobutu's downfall and two wars, the soldiers, police, and administration remained neglected, unable to feed and house themselves, let alone their families, on their salaries.

"When people try to get money from us, we look at the situation," Sally told me. "We can negotiate or just walk away if it's something ridiculous. But sometimes we pay a little because that's how things work here. That's how people survive, and it creates goodwill and only costs us five dollars or less—usually a few francs. We wouldn't be able to do our work if we tried to fight every official we met. It wouldn't make sense."

When we were in Kinshasa, I had seen a book on Sally's desk: *The Empress and Mrs. Conger: The Uncommon Friendship of Two Women and Two Worlds.* The cover showed an old photograph of two women, one an elaborately garbed Chinese, and the other white, in equally elaborate turn-of-the-century Western dress. When I asked Sally about it, she explained that the white woman was her great-great-grandmother, Sarah Pike Conger, whose husband, a congressman from Iowa, was appointed ambassador to Brazil. The expats generally kept themselves separate from the local people there, but when Conger's husband received his next posting, as ambassador to China, she realized how little she knew about the Brazilians and how much her aloofness had cost her. She determined that she would learn about the Chinese and even forged a friendship with Cixi, the last empress dowager of China. The photo used for the book's cover is the only one in which the empress touches a Westerner, and Sally told me that as a girl, visiting her grandmother, she'd read the diaries of her great-great-grandmother as well as a book she wrote, *Letters from China.* She described how Sarah Conger wanted to set up her kitchen the way she liked and felt that the procurement of coal would be more efficient if she did it herself. But when she tried to streamline her staff, they became unhappy and ceased to work well. She realized that they had a system of exchanges that allowed for everyone involved to make a small profit and guarantee a livelihood. Though she wanted to run her house in a businesslike fashion, she saw that the Chinese system provided for more people and worked efficiently within their culture. To remind herself of such lessons and because of the affinity Sally felt with her great-great-grandmother, she kept a copy of *The Empress and Mrs. Conger*.

Having dealt with the agents, we climbed into the plane. As the pilots taxied on the runway, Sally took her phone out for one last call to Kinshasa. There would be no cell coverage in Djolu, no infrastructure at all, except for BCI's satellite phone that cost $1.60 per minute. But it was too late. The single propeller had gone to full speed, and we were racing forward, lifting from the runway. The forests of Équateur spread beneath us, green horizons in all directions, faintly rippled by the contours of the land.

In Kinshasa, when I'd told Evelyn's brothers that I would be flying to Djolu, the younger one had said, "I hope you have faith in something."

"What would you recommend I have faith in?" I'd asked. "In the pilot, the mechanic, or God?"

He considered the question.

"I wouldn't trust any of those three in the Congo."

The Congo is known for airline disasters and not meeting international security standards. Before coming, I'd run across an article about an accident in which a passenger brought an unconscious crocodile in a duffel bag onto the flight. As the plane was about to land, the crocodile woke and fought its way free. The terrified passengers ran to the front of the plane, throwing it off balance as it neared the strip. It crashed, killing the pilot and all the passengers except one. The crocodile survived, only to be dispatched with a machete on the ground.

We glided above the wide, split waters of the Congo River, then cut inland. For the next two hours, we traveled three hundred miles, the evenly textured forest passing beneath us. There were occasional variations: a few massive trees reaching above the canopy; some bright red foliage, in flower or leaves to be shed; then the skeletal fingers of a dead tree. Banks of mist gathered along thin depressions. The pools of a narrow river refracted glare through the hazy clouds. Moments later, there was just forest again, more regular than the sky.

As we neared Djolu, spaces cut from the forest came into sight, scorched circles of new fields from recent slash-and-burn farming. The landing strip appeared, a thin gash in the trees, a yellow line scored along its center. A dirt road ran beyond it, past a few mud and thatch homes, into the distance. The plane banked, then descended fast, the trees rising on either side.

The landing was so smooth I hardly felt the wheels touch. We slowed and stopped as dozens of children in torn and faded clothes ran from the edge of the forest and circled the plane. We got out, standing in a crowd of at least fifty of them, a dozen men and women greeting Sally and Michael, shaking their hands, the women kissing their cheeks, the men touching Michael's forehead with their own.

Each time I lifted my camera, the children flowed together in front of it. They called to see the screen after the shot, pushing in, trying to get a glimpse of themselves, screaming when they did, clutching my wrist and staring.

"Donnez-moi de l'argent!" they shouted. *"Bic! Bic!"* they said and lifted their hands, wanting pens. One of the pilots told me that at least twice a week he had to argue to keep his shirt, men coming from the crowd and insisting that they needed it more than he did. And seeing them, I didn't find this entirely unreasonable. With the exception of those who worked for BCI, almost everyone wore threadbare clothes—T-shirts disintegrated at the shoulders, hanging from their seams, and pants tattered beneath the knees.

Again, the Congolese took charge, villagers helping under the direction of Marcel Falay. Tall and broadly built, with a perpetually jovial expression, he was BCI's regional director and agronomist. He'd worked with BCI years before on a project. Afterward, when he was with another employer, he broke his foot in a motorcycle accident, and BCI had paid for his treatment. Later, when his contract finished, he returned to work for them, staying on even during the periods when they lacked funding.

As men and women who had been involved with BCI over the years shook my hand and introduced themselves, others loaded our bags into a Toyota Land Cruiser more battered than *les esprits des morts* in Kinshasa. BCI bought it from a dealer in Dubai in 2006, secondhand but in perfect condition, and had it shipped to Kinshasa, then upriver. As part of BCI's resource-sharing agreement with the people of the reserve, it had served for many community-development projects as well as tree planting. But a driver flipped it over an incline, and that, as well as constant use hauling people and goods, had left it dilapidated, the bumpers collapsing, the panels loose. BCI's other vehicle was stranded in Kokolopori, a Land Rover with a broken axle.

Michael climbed into the passenger seat with BCI's new photographic equipment. He would be documenting their work for the purpose of fund-raising. Sally and I each got on the backs of the two motorcycles driven by BCI staff.

The road through the forest was as narrow as a footpath, so sandy that my driver briefly lost control and had to slide to a stop. I expected the land to be largely flat, but it rose and fell, and following the path was like going through the hallways of an old mansion, one moment closed in and the next entering a large room. This was how I felt when the forest opened suddenly into a village, a dozen houses of mud daubed on woven branches, children in underwear running out to wave. Then the forest closed in again, the path winding between hillocks and declines, before we entered another room: this time a clearing around a stream.

The bridge consisted of seven narrow fifteen-foot logs laid side by side, the gaps between them wide enough to break a leg. Sally and I dismounted, and our drivers picked the flattest, straightest log and drove across. Then the Land Cruiser arrived. Everyone got out but the driver.

A young man walked across the bridge and turned. He lifted his arms, his index fingers raised, and with tiny movements of his fingers, he directed the driver. The Land Cruiser inched forward, front wheels on two of the logs. He kept motioning, a little to the left, but halfway across, it began to go too far, only an inch of its right front wheel still on the log, the rest over the water. The young man urged it back. The driver corrected, and as soon as the front tires touched the dirt, he fired the engine and raced onto the path, the wheels crushing the grass alongside it.

Ten minutes later, we came to a similar bridge and went through the same process, but the third one was longer, at least thirty feet, with planks laid across its logs. The Land Cruiser inched forward, the wood groaning beneath it. The young man directed with his fingers as the bridge swayed and creaked. Nearby, a fisherman sat in a narrow boat carved from a small tree trunk. Beneath high reeds that were reflected around him, he floated, watching without expression.

After climbing a rise from which the rainforest spread out, immense treetops rolling on to the horizon, we arrived in Djolu. To my eye, the only thing that distinguished it as a town was the absence of dense forest. With a population of ten thousand, it was without running water, electricity, or phones. At first glance, it resembled an agglomeration of small farms, the mud houses set far apart, separated by trees and gardens, colorful clothing and blankets drying on thatch roofs. Ducks, chickens, goats, and pigs wandered about. The occasional concrete building with a corrugated roof and crumbling, water-stained walls stood out, each belonging to a different regional leader and likely dating back fifty years or more to Belgian colonial rule. Wending everywhere, between trees and hedges, behind houses, were numerous sandy paths like arroyos. The beaten dirt roads were often sunk well below the surface of the land, the clay sculpted by running water. When the rainy season came, the town must have as many waterways as Venice.

We drove in front of the *stade*, the stadium, a raised stone foundation the size of a hut, with eight brick pillars, a metal roof, and some benches and concrete steps, all crowded with boys and girls. On the athletic field on the other side of the road, a ragtag bunch of boys were kicking a soccer ball. The children forgot about the game and pointed at us instead, screaming, "*Mundele, mundele, mundele!*"

This word, meaning "white person" or "foreigner," would be the mantra in Équateur. The children stared, wide-eyed, shouting it as if calling our names, and it took me a moment to realize that they were screaming it to draw other Congolese. They were announcing a rarity, many of them seeing their first white person in months, and farther out, in the villages, possibly their first ever.

Just past the stadium, we came to a six-room mud-brick house, the Djolu headquarters of Vie Sauvage, literally "Wildlife," the local NGO that BCI had spent years developing as their primary partner in the region. A fifteen-foot-high termite hill hid the building from the road, and children scaled its sides, gathering at the top to get a view of our activities, or reaching down to catch the hands of their friends and help them up. In the yard of beaten dirt was a *paillote*, a word that literally means "straw hut," though in the Congo it indicates a communal open-sided building with a thatch roof.

After some discussion with the Congolese staff, Sally and Michael decided to sleep in Djolu, at the Vie Sauvage headquarters. The forty-five-mile drive to Kokolopori took four hours if all went well, since the road was rutted, often with trees fallen across it and drop-offs on the sides. If we got a flat tire or broke down, we'd have to finish in the dark, holding flashlights out the window since the Land Cruiser's headlamps didn't work. Sally also didn't know the condition of the camp; she hadn't been there in over six months, and termites and insects were quick to devour rafters and the roofs of buildings.

We ate a dinner of cassava, rice, avocado, fried banana, and spicy stewed chicken in a red broth that was delicious poured over everything else. I dabbed a little of the *pili-pili* sauce on my food, the crushed hot pepper making me

Empty Hands, Open Arms

break into a sweat. We finished the meal with rainforest honey brought down from the trees, dark and liquid, poured into glasses to sip, or to be mixed with *lotoko,* a type of moonshine made from corn, cassava, or plantain.

Everyone appeared to know Sally and Michael, and stopped to speak. They discussed projects, people's families, and the reserve, then, inevitably, the diminished funding and financial difficulties. All seemed to be involved with BCI in some way, doing odd jobs for Vie Sauvage or working at the Institut Supérieur de Développement Rural (ISDR), the technical college that Vie Sauvage and BCI had founded.

Josephine Mpanga, a petite woman in her late thirties, stopped by, and I learned that she ran the biggest NGO in the territory after Vie Sauvage. Several years back BCI had jump-started her work with a microcredit loan and a few sewing machines, and she had since expanded a sewing cooperative into a program to employ women on a number of development and conservation projects.

With a straight spine, her posture authoritative if somewhat fatigued, she sat across from Sally and described how she hoped to spread her work to nearby villages. Sally listened, nodding or asking questions. Later, she told me that she wished BCI could support Josephine more, that Josephine was among the most determined leaders in Djolu.

Marcel came inside to tell us that we had to visit Djolu's newly appointed government administrator, and we followed him out. The sun had already gone down, the sky a deep blue that suggested the density of the darkness to come even as it silhouetted the palms along the road. Djolu is built on higher ground, and as we walked we had a view over the forest, the dark, misted curves of immense treetops set against the distance like mountains.

"Part of building social capital," Sally told me, "is maintaining good relationships with chiefs and officials, and showing them that we respect their authority. If they understand our projects and goals, then the community is more likely to understand and support us."

"It must get tiring," I said. At that point, after the day's activities and the constant human interactions, I was ready for bed.

She laughed, her voice a little hoarse. "Sometimes it gets to be a little intense, but I enjoy talking to people. And it makes things happen here. It's what's got us this far."

We stayed with the administrator for an hour, introducing ourselves and discussing regional projects, from those on the reserve to initiatives in Djolu and at the technical college. Even hours later, after we'd returned to the Vie

Sauvage headquarters and the generator had roared to life, people came to the door, pausing at the edge of the light, looking in, letting their eyes adjust as their smiles took shape and they called out Sally and Michael's names.

Several of them ran their own conservation areas that they had modeled on Kokolopori, getting trackers and eco-guards to volunteer with the promise of eventual employment once there was funding. Whenever possible, BCI had supported them with modest amounts.

Michael showed them photos he had downloaded of eco-lodges around the world, explaining possibilities for bringing tourism to the area. Local conservationists and villagers gathered around the table, staring at the computer screen. He told me that many people here believe a drab, American ranch house with tiny windows would appeal to vacationing foreigners, and he wanted to dispel this. He brought up images of open-air bamboo buildings, elevated bungalows with wooden floors and palm-thatch roofs. It might take another decade, but if the communities protected their forests and bonobos, ecotourism could fund them far better than agriculture or logging. As the men hunched around Michael's laptop, two teenage boys lingered in the door, listening and watching.

The headquarters doubled as a guesthouse for BCI and reserve visitors, and I went to my room, hardly bigger than its cot. Eight large cockroaches clung to the wall, as well as two gray spiders as big as my palm, with eyes that glinted like a single diamond when I shone my headlamp on them. I asked the building's keeper about getting a mosquito net, and he told me there were no mosquitoes at the moment, but I insisted, not worried about mosquitoes either.

I crawled inside the net, tucked its edges under the thin foam mattress, and lay down. I was exhausted, but the day's images kept coming back: the battered Land Cruiser, the fragile, makeshift bridges, the dire poverty. I wondered how much worse it must have been after the war, and how much effort must have been required to work in a place where the human need felt this suffocating. Many of us imagine carrying out dramatic changes in impoverished places, but few have the patience for the small, time-consuming, and seemingly endless details that make it possible.

I forced myself to stop thinking and drifted in and out of sleep for hours while Michael and Sally stayed with the others, their talk and laughter resonating late into the night.

A Sense of Place

Roosters woke me. They began at dawn, echoing each other's cries from across the town. My sleeping mind seemed to unravel, pulled little by little back into the world. Occasionally there were lulls and I dozed off, but then the crowing started up again.

It took me a moment to remember where I was. When I'd first moved to a city in my early twenties, to downtown Montréal, I lived in an apartment whose windows faced an inner courtyard. I sometimes awoke at night, disoriented, and had to go out to the street, to stand on the sidewalk in my socks, just to find my bearings, to see which direction was north. I wasn't sure what startled me awake those nights, at two or three o'clock—if I was used to freedom and big spaces, to sensing my place on the earth.

I often had a similar experience during my travels, a desire to look at a map and see how the landscape made sense, where the rivers originated, whether the mountains I was seeing were the beginning of a higher, more dramatic range, or just ragged, stony outcroppings stripped of earth by millennia of wind. The rises and curves on the map, and the winding human paths that conformed to them, remind me of something I once read, that the ancient Greeks perceived knowledge as a means of expanding the self, of feeling connected to existence. I couldn't name the African trees, the ferns and flowers and reeds, or say how they interacted, which roles they played within the ecosystem, but I was sure that if I could, my world would have seemed larger and more open.

Now, as roosters crowed and I woke up in a room the length of my too-short bed, I tried to connect this landscape with all I'd learned about it, to make sense of this spot on the map—Djolu, mud huts and dusty footpaths, a town harder to reach than the vast majority of places on earth. It lay at the heart of the Congo River basin, an immense territory covering more than 1.4 million square miles, its tributaries draining from Gabon, Angola, Rwanda, Burundi, Cameroon, Equatorial Guinea, Central African Republic, Congo-Kinshasa, and Congo-Brazzaville. Half of the basin's territory is rainforest, nourished by the tributaries on their way to the Congo, the fifth-longest river on earth carrying the third-largest volume of water. Djolu lies to the south of the Congo's arc, just north of the equator, near the Maringa River, in the middle of a landscape that has been forested almost continuously for millions of years.

Long before my first trips to Africa, from numerous photographs, I'd sensed something different about the continent, so visually unlike anywhere else: its high, rolling plains, its undulating landscapes and gradual, expansive basins, all unmistakable.

It hasn't been shaped in the same way as the other continents. Though it separated from South America about 126 million years ago, Africa remained largely unchanged for 100 million years, with virtually no rifting or volcanism. By 65 million years ago, erosion and the lack of volcanic activity had turned it, as geologist Kevin Burke writes, into "a low-lying continent with widespread deep weathering." I liked this image and found it easy to picture the endless, worn-out ranges of ochre dust, the landscape wind-scarped and cut with rivers.

This erosion continued until thirty million years ago, when Africa collided with Europe. The African plate ceased to drift, pinned possibly by its collision in the Mediterranean, or by the giant volcanic plumes that rose through the earth's mantle to create the Cape Verde and Afar archipelagoes. Only once Africa became static did the continent we know begin to take its shape. This large, flat expanse of deeply weathered land rested above a hot area, a convection circulation in the underlying mantle. Like a sheet of metal slowly warping above a flame, the continent changed its shape over millions of years. Plumes of less dense material rose from the hot mantle, pressing against the crust, at once thinning it by partial melting and pushing it up, warping its surface, initiating volcanic activity, and reactivating ancient faults.

The old Africa of low, eroded plains lifted into the landscape that geographers and historians have remarked on since Herodotus's time, a continent of long swells and basins. Whereas most continents have areas of extremely high elevation and others almost at sea level, very little of Africa is extremely high or low. The continent bulges from ocean to ocean, rising and falling in successive sweeps 125 to 1,250 miles in length. On the resulting tablelands are peaks, ridges, and escarpments created by millions of years of wind and water erosion. The elevation drops to both the north and west, marking the paths of the Nile and the Congo, the continent's two largest, though dramatically different, rivers.

The Congo is unlike other rivers in Africa. The gradual slope of the landscape usually results in slow drainage and immense deltas, as with the Nile, Niger, Zambezi, and Limpopo, all of which carried large quantities of sediment down from areas of the continent that were lifted. But Africa's basins and swells also cause internal drainage. As the continent was re-shaped, water that was unable to reach the ocean formed immense lakes, then spilled out into a new river, to another set of lakes, slowly working closer to the coast.

At first glance, the Congo basin fits this description, draining internally. For millions of years, it most likely formed a massive inland lake as the result of a geologic swell along the coast that blocked access to the ocean. But at some point in the last thirty million years, the Congo River cut through the highlands beyond the Pool Malebo and created an outlet, a 220-mile descent of narrow, violent rapids that possess, Adam Hoschchild writes, "as much hydroelectric potential as all the lakes and rivers of the United States combined." Over millions of years, the water rushing out from the land created the world's largest submarine river canyon, 497 miles long and 3,900 feet deep on the floor of the Atlantic, as well as an abyssal fan, a river delta composed of millennia of sediment, hidden beneath the ocean.

But the landscape where I found myself listening to roosters crow across Djolu's clustered homesteads is more ancient than much of the rest of Africa. The Congo basin is a craton, an ancient continental core dating back 2 to 3.6 billion years. Whereas much of the earth's crust is composed of relatively new material from plumes and rifting, cratons are typically thicker and deeply rooted, resistant to volcanism, which will occur at their edges but not their centers. While the lands of Africa swelled and broke open around it, the Congo craton held its place. East Africa lifted, drying out and losing its forests as it gained altitude, but the Congo remained lush. The waters drained from the newly raised lands, pouring into the low, immovable basin and making it one of the wettest places in Africa. Today, most of the DRC lies within what Alden Almquist, in *Zaire,* describes as a "vast hollow . . . the shape of an amphitheater, open to the north and northwest and closed in the south and east by high plateaus and mountains."

When the glacial cycle started in the Northern Hemisphere, a brief 2.6 million years ago, trapping vast quantities of the planet's moisture in polar ice, many African rivers, the Nile among them, ceased to reach the ocean, and the tropics withered. The Congo basin was one of the few areas to retain some of its rainforest. Though great apes likely died off elsewhere on the continent, small groups of them could have survived here.

As early as six million years ago, in the long cooling period leading up to our current ice age, our earliest ancestors became increasingly bipedal, spending more time on the ground. However, the severe changes caused by glaciation coincided with a rapid spurt in evolution that may have given rise to modern humans. The situation could have been similar to that of the earlier apes, only more extreme: the drying eliminated trees and created a hostile environment with few resources. Paleontologist and anatomist Kevin Hunt argues that as trees became much smaller and branches thinner, early hominids found that foraging by climbing was increasingly difficult; instead, they often stood on the ground and reached up for the fruit. Supporting this theory is the observation that today, among chimpanzees, tool use, carrying food, confrontational display, and looking over obstacles account for only 1 to 2 percent of bipedal behavior, whereas feeding, most often from the low branches of small trees, accounts for 85 percent of it. Again, if the environmental conditions were harsh, a bottleneck might have occurred, many of the early hominids dying off, leaving only those who were adapted to the new circumstances and capable of using bipedalism to their advantage, not only for foraging but also for hunting. Those human ancestors who could walk upright also used less energy during travel and freed up their hands to carry food, thereby nourishing themselves even when they couldn't forage successfully. They could also move between distant patches of forest more readily, and, as a result, provision more offspring.

In *Catching Fire,* Richard Wrangham offers an analogy to evoke the close bond that humans share with these early hominids. He gives the example of an australopithecine, an ancestor of modern humans that lived three million years ago, approximately halfway along the evolutionary path from our last common ancestor with chimpanzees and bonobos:

> Imagine going to a sporting event with sixty thousand seats around the stadium. You arrive early with your grandmother, and the two of you take the first seats. Next to your grandmother sits her grandmother, your great-great-grandmother. Next to her is your great-great-great-great-grandmother. The stadium fills with the ghosts of preceding grandmothers. An hour later the seat next to you is occupied by the last to sit down, the ancestor of you all. She nudges your elbow, and you turn to find a strange nonhuman face.

As for all of the grandmothers going back to the last common ancestor of humans, chimpanzees, and bonobos, it is conceivable that they could be housed in the United States's largest stadium, that of the University of Michigan, which hosted a record 114,804 attendees in 2011. In Richard Dawkins's essay, "Gaps in the Mind," he describes a similar thought experiment and writes that, in the lineage leading back to the last common ancestor, "you would nowhere find any sharp discontinuity. Daughters would resemble mothers just as much (or as little) as they always do."

Recent research suggests that there were numerous species of early humans, often overlapping or being rendered extinct as they spread out. *Homo sapiens*—modern humans—originated in Africa sometime before two hundred thousand years ago, then moved into Europe, killing off or absorbing the Neanderthals, adept dwellers of cold climates whose cranial cavity, despite our image of them as brutes, was in fact larger than our own. The Neanderthals left a significant trace of their DNA in humans living outside Africa (about 2.6 percent in mine, according to a genetic test), but *Homo sapiens* endemic to the Congo have no trace of *Homo neanderthalensis* in their genes. Nor do they, the Europeans, or Asians, have the genes of Denisovans, hominids living in Siberia forty to sixty thousand years ago, though the Melanesian and Australian aborigines share about 3 percent of their DNA with them. Numerous tribes of early human species likely dotted the earth, interbreeding and gradually forming our own species as we now know it.

Unlike in other parts of Africa, where volcanic activity has preserved traces of ancient peoples, the Congo rainforest leaves few fossils. Though migrations have crisscrossed the region, the soil of the forest is high in acidity, dissolving bones. What we know of human history here is limited. Before the arrival of the current racial majority, the Bantu, the likely inhabitants were pygmies, people thought to have evolved smaller because of forest conditions. Modern-day pygmies use non-Bantu words for many aspects of the forest and its plants, but speak languages derived from their contact with the Bantu, who spread from Cameroon and eastern Nigeria three thousand years ago. Empowered by Iron Age technology, the Bantu moved out in successive waves over centuries, in one of the largest expansions in human history.

Today, there are over seven billion humans, and no other mammal species can claim our rate of successful adaption. As Dale Peterson writes in *Eating Apes*, a book that describes some of the failures of major conservation NGOs and the degree to which logging and the commercial bushmeat trade are decimating great ape populations, "we are growing rapidly enough to displace, body for body, the entire world population of chimpanzees every day; rapidly enough to displace, body for body, the entire world population of gorillas every twelve hours; and rapidly enough to displace, body for body, the entire world population of bonobos every six hours at least." The destruction of other creatures' habitats has allowed this, though increasingly we are looking for other ways of living, our self-awareness being the trait that can most help us as our climate again changes and we question the future of our resources. In the process of trying to understand ourselves, we have become fascinated with our origins. But if we want to reconstruct the path of human evolution, the best way for us to understand what is lost or left only as rare, incomplete fossils is to consider the great apes, our closest cousins who are hunted to the verge of extinction. Though the reduction of great ape habitats likely began thousands of years ago as a result of human expansion, farming, and hunting, various factors have caused it to speed up exponentially. Booming human populations fuel the demand for timber and bushmeat, and modern weapons and motorized transportation facilitate their extraction. Even though laws forbid great ape hunting throughout Africa, they are rarely enforced, and few people know about them. Furthermore, as a result of both the local and global demand for palm oil, which is found in many Western household products, plantations are being created across Africa, resulting in massive habitat destruction. Lastly, the international race for mineral resources has funded the recent wars here, displacing communities, destroying the infrastructure, and forcing millions of people to rely on bushmeat to survive.

I was only beginning to grasp how the rainforest had shaped these people. It was a world of close horizons, walls of trees blocking my sight, the earth itself suddenly rising or falling, so that paths had to wind constantly around obstacles. Ever since I was a child, I'd thought in landscapes. I loved photographs of mountains, deserts, or plains, rolling hills or savannah, and only after staring at them for some time did I feel that I was ready to learn about their inhabitants, that I might understand them. But this terrain was unlike any I had known, and since our landing the day before, it seemed to me that the rainforest had absorbed the past, dissolved it like ancestral bones, and it would take time for me to begin to comprehend the culture here in deeper ways.

More and more cocks crowed, and when I opened my eyes, the light was stronger, brightly outlining the wooden window shutter and the bedroom door's uneven planks. There was the swishing sound of someone sweeping the dirt around the building. I got up and opened the uneven square of wood that fit into the empty window.

Willy, the keeper of the Vie Sauvage headquarters, a tall young man with high cheekbones, swept, moving the broom in controlled, rapid motions as sunlight spilled across the town, lighting up earthen buildings and palm thatch in incandescent shades of orange and yellow. He held one arm behind his back as he worked, bent at the waist, taking short steps, sweeping the dirt of the yard into a pattern of symmetric brushstrokes like those in a Japanese stone garden.

In the main room of the headquarters, I found Sally already deep in conversation with local leaders. She had told me about the delicate and time-consuming way in which social relationships were built. All morning, as I prepared my bags and the cooks readied breakfast, people constantly arrived to speak with her. They said they'd come to thank her and Michael for all that they'd done, before sitting down and explaining their needs: the lack of funds to educate their children, the suffering of a sick relative, the cost of medicine. Then they stayed, so that every task and discussion was slowed by the presence of people sitting in the plastic chairs, on the wooden benches, squatting in the shade of the overhang, leaning against the Land Cruiser's fenders.

Willy and Marie-Claire, head cook, hospital nurse, and the wife of Cosmas Bofangi Batuafe, a local conservationist also supported by BCI, tried to convince Sally to stay another night. They became visibly downcast when she explained that BCI had work in Kokolopori.

"If we stay another night," Sally told me, "then they get paid for cooking and taking care of the guesthouse. But we need to get to the reserve."

Behind her, the hood of the Land Cruiser was up, held in place by a stick polished yellow from use, five men looking closely at the engine. One wheel was off, and a young man was cutting squares from old rubber tubing with a handsaw to patch leaks in the tire's inner tube. Marie-Claire, whose round face had quickly regained its smile, began reciting prices, speaking Lingala though the numbers were in French, as was the word *franc*.

"No, no, no, no," Sally said, then answered in Lingala. From Marie-Claire's expression and bits of French, I could tell that Sally was saying the prices were too high. Briefly, Sally looked angry, but then she laughed and Marie-Claire did the same. I listened to Sally's new list of numbers, punctuated by *franc*. Marie-Claire agreed, and afterward Sally explained the interaction to me.

"Because the election held us back, people haven't been paid in a long time. We're only around for a month, so they know that this is their chance to make money, and the women in the kitchen want to work. There's virtually no cash economy in the area. People barter, but conservation brings in money that they can spend at the market."

It was almost noon when we finally crowded into the Land Cruiser, Michael and I sharing the front seat next to Jean-Pierre, the driver who, like many of those who worked with BCI and Vie Sauvage, lived in the reserve. Sally climbed onto the back of a motorcycle. Michael explained that Congo time required the addition of two or three hours to any plan, that if you didn't calculate the extra time you'd get caught in the dark on a road, or spend your visit to the rainforest in a state of constant disappointment.

Young men gathered to push-start the Land Cruiser, Jean-Pierre at the wheel, Michael and I crammed thigh-to-thigh next to him. A man in a red T-shirt hurried over and told Sally that we couldn't leave until we'd seen the local DGM official, that today was Sunday, so he wasn't working, and we'd have to spend the night. There was strict control on all aspects of travel in the country; before leaving Kinshasa, we had to get permits not only to take photos but to stay in Équateur.

All of the Congolese paused to watch, eyes static, curious but not too hopeful. I got the sense that the entire town was bent on keeping us there, but I also understood that we would probably leave.

Sally told the man that she'd already worked out an agreement to have the official driven by motorcycle to Kokolopori on Monday, but he shook his head. He said that the official must check our papers and passports to make sure that we even had permission to go to the reserve. She pointed out that BCI and Vie Sauvage had created the reserve, so why wouldn't it be legal?

Willy, Marie-Claire, the women who helped in the kitchen, and all of the lingerers watched, standing where they were about to wave good-bye. The men remained at the rear of the Land Cruiser, hands on the metal, ready to push-start it. In its cargo area, with heaped bags and jerry cans of gas, two young men—along to help with engine problems and repair flats—stared out the side windows without glass, and other villagers, unknown to us, crammed in like stowaways, until now keeping their heads low, looked out.

"Couldn't the official just come now?" I asked Michael.

"That'd be against the rules. The people here love their rules," he said and paused. "And they also love breaking them when it suits them."

In a place this impoverished, I realized, everything was currency, even laws and formalities.

Sally stared at the man a moment longer, as if evaluating how serious all this was. But as I was soon to learn, when the rules were ignored, no one was quite sure what to do.

"Oh come on," she said, speaking English now, and shouted to us, "Let's go!"

The men pushed the Land Cruiser. Jean-Pierre popped the clutch, and the tires grabbed at the earth as the engine sputtered and fired. Children scrabbled up the termite hill to get a vantage on our departure, then decided they'd rather be with the children running behind us. Two more young men jumped on our back bumper, clutching the edges of the glassless back window, and our convoy was off, racing along the rutted dirt road as people leaped aside and screamed "*Mundele!*" and pointed.

The path we were traveling was listed as a national highway, R401, one of the few bright yellow lines on the map of Équateur. There were four working vehicles in this entire area of seven thousand square miles, with a population of at least 250,000 in tiny, scattered villages, and the road was used primarily for walkers and the occasional bicycle or motorcycle. During the rainy season, it was impassible, too soft and slick, treacherous on the inclines.

As he drove, Jean-Pierre told me that his father was Belgian, that for some reason his siblings had been born almost white whereas he was black, though other Congolese saw him as white. He averaged about eighteen miles per hour, slowing for rain-gouged trenches and sandy hollows. Sometimes we rode in ruts where the ground was soft, crossed by gullies so deep that he almost stopped, letting one tire drop in at a time, the Land Cruiser shaking and rattling. Or we skirted drop-offs where the road narrowed, two tires over the edge, the vehicle wildly tilted as the earth scraped the undercarriage. On a few occasions, the hollows were on both sides, and the edges of all four tires hung as he steered, leaning forward, the rest of us staring down the wet inclines into the shadow of the forest.

From time to time, the path opened into a sundrenched village, a dusty yellow clearing smoothed from decades of feet. Jean-Pierre stomped the accelerator so that we soared past flapping chickens, ducks, goats, dogs, and pigs, past dozens of children who ran out shouting, in underwear or torn shirts. Everyone waved, families in doorways, men seated in the shade of their eaves, beneath the open-sided village *paillotes,* or beneath the patch of roof protecting the talking drum, a five- or six-foot section of thick, hollowed log with slits cut into it, which people strike rhythmically to send messages across long distances. Then we plunged back onto the forest path, branches lashing the Land Cruiser, the young men on the rear bumper ducking.

Two hours into our journey, we passed the fork in the road to Kisangani, the nearest major city and a regional crossroads where the Lingala- and Swahili-speaking parts of the DRC meet—only a ten- or twelve-day walk from here, Jean-Pierre told me. Michael explained to me that I should know the expression *kaka awa*, "just here," how the Bongandu, the people of the local Congolese ethnic group, answer all questions regarding time and distance. They delivered the words with the same assurance with which a parent driving a car says "almost there" to a child. To demonstrate this, he switched to French and asked Jean-Pierre how much farther we had to go, to which Jean-Pierre responded without hesitation, "*Kaka awa.*"

Three hours and two *kaka awa* later, he finally announced that we had crossed the boundary into the reserve. The forest was denser, its trees huge, crowding the path, which was even narrower and more degraded. The rainwater gullies were so large that Jean-Pierre opted to take us through them instead of on the remaining road, a narrow ledge several feet higher.

When we pulled into Yetee, the village where BCI kept one of its main camps in the Kokolopori Reserve, children and adults surrounded the vehicle. The camp was near the village, against the forest. Men were striking sticks together, singing as we got out. Michael began dancing with them, and they hooted in appreciation.

Someone took my arm and told me in French that it was impolite not to dance, so I joined the mass of people. They all had their knees bent, their butts stuck out, bobbing and swaying, shuffling side to side as they sang. Sally and Michael's names were distinct among the words.

The two motorcycles arrived with the rest of the BCI and Vie Sauvage personnel. The singing grew stronger as people began shouting, "Mama Sally!" They swarmed her, and she danced with them as our supplies were unloaded by dozens of hands and swept into a mud hut.

I didn't manage to retain all the names, as the reserve's staff were introduced in rapid succession, alongside those I had already met: local conservationists and BCI employees. After the singing had gone on for half an hour, we retreated inside to inspect our mud hut, which was built on a slope, tables and chairs tilted. There were four bedrooms, two on each end, and a center dining room with wooden chairs. The temperature inside was distinctly cooler, the earthen walls moist. Beyond the windows, the sunlight appeared white, erasing everything but the steady chanting.

We began unpacking as men with machetes gathered outside and cut up bamboo and tree branches, crossing the pieces and tying the edges with vine to make shelves and tables for us. By the time the sun's disk neared the forest, they had furnished the house. BCI and Vie Sauvage had several camps in different villages throughout the reserve and tried to alternate where they worked, so as not to create jealousy or rivalry. The simple presence of conservationists meant that scores of local people were hired to repair camp houses, as the mud crumbled a little with each wet season. Already points of light had appeared in the relatively new palm thatch, insects rustling inside the leaves, lizards hunting them, occasionally bringing down showers of dust.

As in Djolu, people came to ask what supplies we'd brought. Jean-Pierre arrived with his four-year-old daughter, a pretty girl who kept glancing up at us curiously. He told us that she had a fever and asked if we'd brought medicine. None of us were doctors, but the fever was low, and she had only a slight cough. We shared what we could find in our supplies, Advil and vitamin powder. One of the reserve's trackers came next, a tall, rawboned man, moving woodenly, ducking his head shyly when he looked at us. The previous night, he'd stepped barefoot on the cut stump of a sapling and gashed his heel. Sally washed it with peroxide and bandaged it.

Sick or injured people would come by often in our first days, telling us that there was no more medicine at the reserve clinic. Sally assured them that it was in the boat with the rest of BCI's field staff, and in the meantime, we shared what we had on hand.

Even the DGM official from Djolu, an aging man with hooded eyes and a small black beard, who arrived the next day by motorcycle, showed up with an injury that needed treatment. He had come to collect the fees that BCI paid to operate legally in the region. He unfolded a plastic grocery bag and produced all the forms relating to BCI's previous visits. One was so old and worn that he handled it like tissue paper, evoking the love of ceremony here. Gently, he opened it and laid it on the wooden table in the *paillote* as if it were a relic, the document's remaining ink pale blue, the folds in the paper worn through.

Sally paid a year's fee of one hundred dollars to operate in the region, and Michael called for *lotoko*, the local moonshine used in ceremonies or to show respect. One of the eco-guards brought a beer bottle with a folded palm leaf for a plug. As soon as Michael removed the leaf, a smell like rubbing alcohol permeated the air. He poured three fingers' worth into a plastic cup, and the official took a drink.

"Other NGOs, they come in here and they do their projects," the official said, "but they do them for themselves. They do their projects, and when they finish, they leave, and that's it." He waved his hand dismissively. "But BCI has given us a lot. You have made people's lives better. You are a part of us."

I was surprised to hear the official speak so dismissively about other NGOs. Even Michael and Sally appeared shocked. That was when the official told us about his injury, that on his way here, his son had lost control of the motorcycle on a sandy stretch and they'd fallen. He showed us the long burn on his ankle from the muffler, the skin darkened and papery.

As he drank, Michael and Sally went inside to get the medical kit.

The official looked at me and, still speaking French, said, "Is it true they do not even have children?"

"No, they don't," I said.

He shook his head, eyes still and serious, as if he couldn't imagine anything worse.

"They just work, helping people," he asked, softly, "instead of having children?"

I turned my palms up, not sure how to answer.

He nodded once, solemnly, and stared off, appearing sad for them. Nearly every man I'd met in the rural DRC had at least five children.

Sally and Michael returned with the medical kit and hydrogen peroxide. Together, they bandaged the official's ankle as he studied them, maybe trying to make sense of why they would do what they do.

But already, on our first day in Kokolopori, before his arrival, when Sally and Michael were still unpacking and the people kept coming and asking for medicine, I began to feel—to sense in my body in a way that had nothing to do with thinking—why they had chosen this life. There was no puzzle in the poignancy of human need, the way men and women showed their injuries and asked for help, requiring disinfectant or antibiotic ointment or a large Band-Aid, medical supplies that most North Americans had in their homes. It was not easy to see through the illusion that many of us harbor about helping others: that we must wait for scientists or doctors or governments. Aspiring to an ideal—to a grand vision of change—is often the enemy in such cases. We forget simple needs and how much each of us can do even with our limited resources.

The last person to ask for help was a young man named Mbangi Lofoso, a team leader for the bonobo trackers. He said that his daughter was sick, her arms and legs straight and rigid, her hands clenched, unable to open. She hadn't eaten in days now. Michael told him that he should take her to the reserve's clinic immediately, just seven miles away, in the next village over within Kokolopori, but Mbangi explained that he just wanted purified water for her, that he was already working with a traditional healer. Even later, when Sally and Michael offered to drive him and his daughter there, he refused. He looked hardly more than twenty, the skin of his face smooth, a hollow scar at the side of his throat, just to the right of his Adam's apple.

Afterward, Michael showed me the small river near the camp. We descended a steep path through the trees. A log bridged the water, and two children squatted on it, fishing for minnows. Hundreds of white and violet butterflies covered the smooth wood, pulsing their wings. Dozens more of them pressed together, fluttering in place. I had never seen butterflies like these: a few with white tails, others turquoise or tiger-striped. One had brown wings when they were closed, but the insides were baby blue, visible only when it flew.

As we walked onto the log, they fluttered up from in front of our feet, clouding around us, landing again as soon as we had passed.

The Bonobos of Kokolopori

If bonobo research and conservation have taken a firm hold in this part of Équateur, it is because of the Bongandu, one of several tribes that inhabit Équateur Province. Japanese primatologist Takayoshi Kano explored the region in 1973 by boat, truck, and raft, and by crossing hundreds of miles on bicycle, all the while asking villagers where the bonobos lived. He found that few remained in the west of their habitat, where they were hunted. But when he crossed east of the Luo River, where Kokolopori is located, he entered the territory of the Bongandu, and learned that there were numerous groups of bonobos lived in the forests.

Bongandu literally means people of the Ngandu culture ("bo" signifying "people," and "mo," as in Mongandu, referring to a single individual of the ethnic group). The Bongandu believed that bonobos walked on four legs only when watched, but otherwise went about like humans. Unlike the Congolese in neighboring areas, they saw bonobos as distant ancestors and had a taboo against hunting them. Consequently, there were large numbers of bonobos, and they were relatively unafraid of people. Kano established his first research camp in an area that, nearly two decades later, would become the Luo Scientific Reserve, not far from where the Kokolopori Bonobo Reserve has since been established.

The work done at Kano's research camp from the 1970s on set the foundation for our current understanding of bonobos, how they bond socially and sexually. Essential to their nonviolence, the Japanese researchers realized, is the stability of their groups. Since chimpanzees have to forage over great distances and expend significant energy to find limited food supplies that are patchily distributed, they travel in small groups to prevent competition among their own members. However, the bonobos have more varied diets and can remain in larger, more stable social groups that allow females to bond. Such coalitions, which tend not to exist in the chimpanzee world, permit female bonobos to limit the aggression of males and even prevent some from mating. Recent studies theorize that bonobos may have essentially domesticated themselves, females selecting those males best for group cohesion and thus gradually eliminating aggressive traits from the gene pool. Not only are the statuses of males determined by those of their mothers, but they will always side with their mothers during conflicts. And, even if the highest-ranking bonobo male attacks a female, all of the females will gang up on him and defeat him.

One of the mysteries of these coalitions, however, is why females forge such strong bonds when, as adolescents, they leave their family groups and travel to new ones to prevent inbreeding. How can unrelated females not find themselves competing for resources and male attention? The research of Takayoshi Kano and Gen'ichi Idani offers an explanation. When adolescent females come upon a new community, they each select an adult female in that group. Each one lingers nearby, observing the older female, attentive to her needs, and if the older female is welcoming, the adolescent approaches to groom, sit close together, or have sex. Though scientists have labeled the latter genito-genital rubbing, or GG-rubbing, Dale Peterson and Richard Wrangham write that this term "hardly captures the abandonment and excitement exhibited by two females practicing it." They suggest using the Bongandu's expression for it: *hoka-hoka*. The older female reclines and opens her legs, and the adolescent climbs on top. Wrangham and Peterson describe the act as resembling humans in the missionary position.

> Their hip movements are fast and side to side, and they bring their most sensitive sexual organs—their clitorises—together. Bonobo clitorises appear large (compared to those of humans or any of the other apes) and are shifted ventrally compared to chimpanzees. Kano believes their location and shape have evolved to allow pleasurable *hoka-hoka*— which typically ends with mutual screams, clutching limbs, muscular contractions, and a tense, still moment. It looks like orgasm.

Though sex among the females establishes a bond that likely strengthens the overall female coalition of the group, there are other factors that prevent male aggression. For instance, chimpanzee females emit an odor when ovulating, causing males to go into a frenzy and compete to breed with them, whereas female bonobos neither show clear signs of ovulation nor limit sexual behavior to their fertile period. The result is that males have no notion of individual paternity, and all males are caring and nurturing with infants. This strengthens the bond between males and females, and reduces the competition among males, supporting a social order that, compared with that of

Empty Hands, Open Arms

chimpanzees, is highly stable, based as it is around dominant females who maintain power until their deaths.

On our first trip to see the bonobos, we got up at 4:00 a.m., ate and dressed rapidly, then went out into the dark, to BCI's Land Rover this time. Michael had brought a new axle for it, but the reserve's mechanic had mistakenly asked for a rear one. Michael and Jean-Pierre had returned in the Land Cruiser to Djolu and had the broken axle welded. They'd also picked up Alan Root, who'd arrived by bush plane. One of the most influential figures in the history of nature documentaries, Alan had moved from England to Kenya shortly after his birth and spent his life there. His work had been syndicated worldwide for over thirty years, in the course of which he had been bitten by numerous animals, among them a python, a hippopotamus, and a puff adder. When a leopard bit him twice in the buttock, the Serengeti's chief park warden jokingly told him, "You know you're not allowed to feed animals in a national park." A mountain gorilla also bit him while he was filming in the Virungas for the Dian Fossey biopic *Gorillas in the Mist*. In her book by the same name, Fossey describes how Alan drove her from Kenya to her first research camp site in the Virungas and helped her get set up. Sally had coordinated his arrival so that he could evaluate how well habituated and accessible the bonobos here were for the ecotourism company Abercrombie & Kent. At seventy-five, he was tall and strong-looking, with gray-white hair, a goatee, and glasses.

The trackers as well as Sally, Michael, Alan, and I crowded into the Land Rover together, and it took us through the forest, going slow because of Alan's back, which had titanium rods in it from two helicopter crashes during his years of filming. The headlamps weren't working well on this vehicle either, so one of the trackers held a flashlight out the window. After fifteen minutes of grinding our way uphill and rolling through deep ruts, we stopped in front of a village and got out. There was a faint smell of woodsmoke as we walked past the dark mud huts, embers glowing beyond a doorway.

When we came to the edge of the forest, the head tracker took the lead. In his forties, Léonard Nkanga Lolima was a slight man, with a round, faintly feline face. Though he was not imposing, his gaze was unwavering, and he directed the trackers with reserved, almost imperceptible gestures, his quiet authority reassuring. He moved silently as we followed him into the smothering dark of the forest, along a narrow path. When I first met him a few days before and sat down to interview him about his work as a tracker, I was nervous. Having read Paul Raffaele's account of visiting Kokolopori in *Among the Great Apes,* I knew that Léonard believed Raffaele to be a sorcerer and feared him. The book offered no indication as to what Raffaele might have done to appear that way, but whatever it was, I didn't want to do the same. I must have come across as excessively polite and cautious, since Léonard later made efforts to speak to me on a number of occasions, as if to reassure me. Finally, I couldn't resist asking about Paul Raffaele, and when I did, a cautious, angry look came into Léonard's eyes. He and the others explained that Raffaele showed them a photo of himself holding a large snake. I knew the image; it was his book's author photo, in which an anaconda is wrapped around him. But for the Bongandu, nothing could be worse, as snake venom kills people, especially children, every year. They could conceive of no reason for a man to toy with snakes in this way, or—worse—to reveal his power to them, as if threatening them. The explanation surprised me and made me realize how easy it is to overlook a foreign culture, to project one's own values on another and speak before getting a sense of the person spoken to. Raffaele is an experienced traveler, and it's a mistake anyone could make.

The foliage on either side of the trail was nearly impenetrable, and I kept my headlamp aimed just before my feet so as not to trip on roots or branches. It had rained all night, the first rain since our arrival in Djolu. A nimbus of mist hung about tree trunks, and after half an hour, the sky began to pearl, dawn infusing low clouds.

Only when we passed small slash-and-burn tracts along the path could I see the outline of treetops. Often, where the dense forest had been cut away, oil palms, native to West and Central Africa, grew in the openings. One nearly blocked the trail, its wet fronds brushing my shoulders. Then we were back in the dense forest, mushrooms along a rotting log like a line of white disks in the dark, vines as thick as my arms dangling from trees.

For a while, the footpath was deep and narrow, cut by years of rain, no wider than my boot, and I had to place my feet carefully, one in front of the other, to keep from tripping. The weeds were shoulder-high, pushing in from either side, soaking my sleeves. I had yet to put my poncho on, the drizzle too faint to be bothersome and the heat of my body drying me.

Suddenly, a large white moth was flying just above my right shoulder, keeping pace, following my headlamp's gauzy beam through the humid air. It fluttered off, vanished. The ground before me dropped, descending steeply toward a stream, and when I glanced up from my feet, I had a vista of the exposed, rising forest on the opposite slope. The trees reared up, immense, pale pillars lifting the dark canopy high against a faintly silver sky.

When Léonard motioned us to stop, we had been walking for over an hour. We sat along a log. Gray light filtered down. We put on our ponchos as the drizzle intensified, seeping through the canopy and gathering on the bottoms of branches in large drops that plummeted the distance to strike loudly against the dead leaves of the forest floor.

Léonard told us that the bonobos had made their nests in the top of a tree bigger and higher than the others, a dense weave of vines hanging from it, like the tangled rigging of a ship. A hundred feet up, the trunk forked and then, higher, forked again, each branch as big as the trunks of nearby trees.

Bonobos' nests serve an important role in the rainforest ecosystem. As a group travels each day, sometimes as many as seven miles, they consume large quantities of leaves and fruit. Almost every evening, they make new nests, pulling branches together, snapping or just bending and weaving them, exposing the forest floor to the sun. In the night and morning, they defecate, and their droppings fall to the earth, carrying seeds that have passed through their guts largely intact. The seeds are mixed with fertile roughage and their hulls have been abraded by the digestive tract, making them more ready to sprout. In the patches of sunlight where the nests broke the canopy, the seeds grow more easily, taking root in the rainforest's thick loam. Because the bonobos travel so widely within their territory, they spread seeds, contributing to biodiversity. Without the bonobos—as well as the numerous other rainforest animals, from elephants, to buffalos, to birds—certain tree species might even go extinct.

With dawn, the forest began to reveal its contents, the stony phallic mounds of termites, some mushroom shaped, others veritable lingams, a foot to three feet tall. Mushrooms grew from rotting sticks, some white and pin-shaped, others vivid orange saucers. A few gray caterpillars with red and black markings crawled on my poncho, others on leaves. Called *mbindjo,* they, like *mpose,* provide protein for both the locals and the bonobos.

The clouds glowed, sunlight struggling through, and as we stared at the dense canopy, the sky was a million specks of mercury, the leaves like lacework around larger openings.

Branches began to shake, drops of water falling. A bonobo's arm weaved out briefly. A figure walked along a branch with a humanlike swaying of its shoulders. An adult bonobo gave its high-pitched hoot, and then a baby wailed, very much like a human baby, but just two or three times before it fell silent.

The canopy again ceased to move. Léonard told us that the bonobos would wait in the highest branches for the sunlight to warm them. Like us, they are slow to rise on rainy mornings. I pictured them seated on the immense branches, at the summit of this tree rising above the rest of the forest. They stared out over the green ocean, slowly blinking their black and luminous eyes. It was hard not to wonder at that primeval experience, of a creature so similar to ourselves living in such absolute elements, gathered with its family, sitting in peace at the line of forest and sky.

Staring up, I got vertigo and needed to look down for a moment before I could take a step. Above me, the dark interlacing canopy seemed liquid, the sky shining through like a reflection of light cast on the deep, shadowed water of a well. Each of the bonobos' movements caused the leaves to shimmer as if a pebble had been dropped in.

We waited for over an hour. Alan identified the calls of birds for us, the chiming of the emerald cuckoo and the low mournful fluting of the chocolate-backed kingfisher. Léonard explained that this particular community of bonobos had twenty-five members, three adult males, twelve females, six adolescents (three of each sex), and four babies.

Eventually, the branches began to shake in earnest. A large piece of deadwood fell and thudded against the loam. The bonobos all seemed to be awake, but waiting. The dark circles of their nests were barely visible.

They might have been feeding on *mbindjo* in the trees, Léonard told us. Along a high branch, a female walked on all fours, the pink bulge of her vaginal swelling clear even at this distance, a child following behind. Normally, bonobo infants cling to their mothers until they are four or five years old, but this one was larger, more independent.

Sally opened a bag and began passing around power bars and trail mix. This was a tradition she had begun, that visitors and trackers ate together, and she told me that it never failed to intrigue the bonobos. Food sharing is central to their culture, and often, when they come upon plentiful amounts, they have sex in excitement before sharing it. Sally preferred eating together rather than simply following bonobos with binoculars and cameras, which to her felt aggressive, as if we had come there just to take something.

"It's better to draw them to us," she said. "I've noticed that the demeanor of the people who are in the forest changes how close the bonobos come, and how long they stay with us. They love seeing humans share the way they do."

There was faint hooting in the canopy, flurries of movement as the bonobos moved closer to find out what we were eating and how we were passing the food around.

A bonobo stood on two legs and, holding a branch above it for balance, turned its broad head to stare down, its posture evoking that of a tightrope walker paused, contemplating the world below. Then it reached higher into the foliage, stretching the sinews of its long body before it lifted itself out of sight.

After we finished eating, we watched the silhouettes move off along the canopy, leaping at times. One used its body weight to make the branch it was on sway closer to a branch of the next tree, before it grabbed hold and crossed over. Léonard told us that the bonobos most often traveled on the forest floor; crossing from tree to tree required too much effort.

He again directed his trackers quickly, with slight gestures. Even as we spread out, he led us through the undergrowth, off the path now, pausing to break branches and place leaves so that, in case one of us wandered off with a tracker to take photos, the tracker could read the signs and we could all meet up again.

I'd bought my poncho online, assuming its soft waterproof material made from recycled plastic would be ideal for use in the rainforest. But I immediately saw its flaw. Unlike the smooth plastic ponchos that the others wore, mine caught every thorn in its weave. As I peeled briars away, wire-thin vines snared my boots and torso, and occasionally I had to stop and untangle myself as if from a net.

Alan pointed out a caterpillar with long white whiskers and a black head, a four-tuft Mohawk of black and white bristles on its back, and I wondered which of the more exotic butterflies this one became. It was the most spectacular caterpillar I'd ever seen.

Léonard warned me that it probably stung, that the prettier they were the more likely they were to be dangerous. He motioned us farther through the forest, the occasional rotten log compressing like a sponge beneath my boot.

Though slow to reveal themselves, the bonobos began to make more appearances, peeking down through the foliage with curious eyes, red lips vivid in their black faces. They had the taut, muscular arms of athletes, and their bodies were particularly graceful. As they studied us, they curled their long fingers around branches and tree trunks. We crept through the foliage, trying to see them more closely.

The large infant I'd noticed earlier hung for a while in an opening in the branches, eyes laughing, clearly entertained. He was suspended with his potbelly protruding as he examined us: strange creatures, our faces lifted. He glanced around with fascination, then disappeared into the foliage, and moments later an adult male swung to a nearby tree, one hand holding the trunk. He watched with the same curious and pleased air as the infant, lowering his eyebrows and pushing his lips forward, then faintly, sweetly simpering, as if unable to decide what face to show us. The black hair on his chest and the insides of his arms was thinner than that on his head and back, and his large pale testicles and thin pink penis showed between his thighs.

He studied us for a long time, occasionally glancing off, presenting his profile. He was an adult, but there was something particularly youthful about him, lighthearted, as if he hadn't taken on responsibility for his group yet, or simply knew that we were no threat.

The light through the clouds brightened, glittering against the moisture in his hair and fur, giving him a silver nimbus. He seemed so pleased looking at us that if he'd broken into laughter, I wouldn't have been surprised. He shook his head and reached up, his body not much smaller than a human's but more pliable and dynamic, and then he climbed out of sight.

These bonobos had been habituated by trackers who monitored them daily, but they were far from tame. I had observed chimpanzees at the Ngamba Island sanctuary in Uganda, and their muscular presence and aggressive gazes gave me little inclination to go near them. Signs warned that if one of them escaped the enclosure all visitors should stand in the lake, since chimpanzees are afraid of going into water. Alan had told me that chimps made him feel as if he were passing a street gang and had to avoid eye contact. This aggressive, dominant attitude appeared absent in bonobos, only the older females somewhat authoritative. They showed little interest in us even as the adolescent males watched us with wide eyes.

Following the Ekalakala group, named for a nearby stream, we wandered through the forest, taking pictures. Léonard knew their patterns. Each time he took me aside and told me to wait somewhere, I didn't know what to expect. I sat and watched the forest. Nothing moved. The others had wandered off, and I became convinced that Léonard was mistaken, that he was telling me to sit there for no good reason. Then, sometimes fifteen or twenty minutes later, a bonobo appeared almost directly before me.

At one point, Léonard suggested that Alan and I wait near a fallen tree, which had created an opening in the undergrowth where the sun shone into the forest. We crouched for at least twenty minutes before two bonobos came through the canopy. One swung himself down to the log and scampered across. But the other made a more dramatic entrance. He hugged the top of a thin tree and let it bend under his weight until he was upside down and his head was almost to the log. Then he flipped himself to his feet and released the tree, letting it snap back up. He sat, assuming pose after pose, looking at the sky, the ground, over his shoulder and back, then just stared off as we clicked photos.

He appeared deep in contemplation, though I had the sense that he knew exactly what we were doing, and wanted to be seen in his best light.

Yetee

The next morning, I was in one of the smaller huts in Yetee, sitting across from a village elder, a lean man whose muscled jaw and broad, veined forehead seemed tempered by years of authority. He'd taken off a straw hat and held it in his hands, and with each question I asked, he hunched a little, his French good though he searched for words. I wanted to know how his community felt about the work being done here for conservation.

"It's not enough," he said. "We need corrugated metal roofs for the schools. We need more schools. More clinics. More trucks and motorcycles and better markets."

"So you aren't satisfied with what the conservationists are doing?"

"It's not enough," he repeated, a comment that I imagined everyone in nearly every country would voice, often reasonably, for many situations in their lives.

"And if the conservationists left tomorrow and stopped their work forever, would there be something else that would allow the people to get money and medicine?"

He sat a long time, staring at me, chewing slightly, his jaw lopsided.

"No," he said, shaking his head faintly. "No, there's nothing else."

Yetee lay just within the reserve, a dusty expanse with a few dozen huts clustered off the road. Below, a small river curved around the slope skirting the village, and narrow paths descended to the various bathing and water-gathering points.

Though many people here wore newer clothes than the inhabitants in the villages along the road to Djolu, most had only one outfit. Shortly after Sally began paying salaries, a merchant arrived on foot, a bundle on his back. He put down a tarp just outside the camp and began selling Chinese-made soap, underwear, safety pins, hand mirrors, and batteries. Young men came through, leading goats tied at the neck with vines, or herding ducks. For dozens of miles in every direction, the reserve offered the only source of cash.

Guy Cowlishaw and Robin Dunbar define conservation biology as "a scientific discipline that aims to provide the sound knowledge and guidance necessary to implement the effective conservation action that will be necessary to maintain in perpetuity the natural diversity of living organisms." However, there are a number of views as to how this goal is best achieved, from setting aside parklands to establishing reserves like Kokolopori. National parks usually displace human populations, creating situations in which the former inhabitants lack a stable means of livelihood. With an estimated fourteen million conservation refugees in Africa alone as of 2005, some indigenous delegates have listed major conservation groups as more destructive to their ways of life than industrial corporations. "The battle for conservation by exclusion" has been lost, Cowlishaw and Dunbar write, and developing nations have been unable "to set aside huge tracts of land for conservation unless they were prepared to risk civil unrest."

As conservationists have turned away from national parks as a model reminiscent of the colonial period, they have begun to see local communities as their allies. Community-based reserves attempt to create distinct areas for wildlife and others that can be used by local people for farming or, at times, limited hunting and trapping. This approach also allows people to sell their goods to conservationists and ecotourists, and to work as trackers and ecoguards. Benefiting from the conservation economy is essential for local communities, given that otherwise "the external and internal pressures for the exploitation of natural resources will simply overwhelm the good intentions." By fostering a conservation-based economy and a new sense of stewardship, conservationists move toward the eventual goal of the local people fully managing the reserve. Critics of this approach point out the danger of local management in such unstable, impoverished nations, with so many external pressures, and they generally favor a degree of outside support, not unlike BCI's role in developing Vie Sauvage and advocating for them internationally.

In the Kokolopori Bonobo Reserve, the conservation accords that BCI and Vie Sauvage have created with the people allocate certain areas of forest for protection and other areas for agriculture. Slash-and-burn farming techniques are usually done a short walk into the secondary forest that surrounds the villages. Trees are cut down and burned, and the land is farmed. People use the patch for two to three years, until the soil is depleted, and then they leave it fallow for at least ten years. They rotate their fields within a certain area, and so long as the population density remains low, the cycle leads to little deforestation. Some hunting is allowed within the reserve as well, of duiker, buffalo, and small animals, though wire snares are prohibited.

In my conversations with Sally, I had learned how contentious the use of the forest can be. The people here see it as their birthright, as the source of their livelihood and nourishment, and they are reluctant to put it under the custodianship of outsiders. Conservation has to work carefully, aware of the ancient human relationship with the land, spiritual traditions, and tribal boundaries. It must also recognize how local people have for centuries endured exploitation by foreigners. The conservationists' vision for the forest must coincide with that of the Bongandu if they expect to attain their objectives. In the name of economic development, the West devastated much of its own forests, and conservationists must remind themselves of this when the temptation arises to take the moral high ground. The daily struggle for sustenance overshadows all talk of protecting wildlife. In working with the Congolese to preserve their forests, conservationists must know exactly what they are asking in each instance, in each distinct place and community, always being conscious of the economic stakes for local people, and they must forge common goals with them if conservation is to succeed.

Over the past few years, spending time in countries with catastrophic situations, I'd become skeptical of NGOs. Whether in Japan or Afghanistan, I'd seen how little aid and development money made it to the ground, how much of it got lost in bureaucracy and enriched people who least needed help. It was hard not to ask whether conservation NGOs were making concrete and lasting change, or simply providing careers for their founders and for staff and scientists. The conservationist Richard Leakey, in speaking of wildlife management programs, has emphasized the need not on "theories and experts," but for "the guys on the ground."

In the afterword to Dale Peterson's *Eating Apes,* Karl Ammann, a nature photographer and conservationist, defines "experts" as "highly paid . . . outside theorists and professional biologists." He asserts that conservation efforts need to focus more on supporting the people "who are already there, on the ground, supporting people who like people and who consider the studying of wildlife and habitat as a secondary priority." Being a scientist might be no more important to conservation than the involvement of those with the ability to understand people and work well within their culture. By partnering with local leaders and training communities in conservation methods, conservationists can address the immediate needs of people who are deeply invested in the well-being of their land.

Even on a small scale, I could easily see how generalized approaches and prefabricated solutions might not work in a place like Kokolopori. For instance, in many parts of Africa, microcredit programs are easy to implement, given that people can grow produce or make goods that they can quickly sell. In Uganda, Tanzania, and Kenya, lorries carry goods from market to market on paved and dirt roads, and battered cars serve as taxis for passengers and their produce. But in Kokolopori, if someone has grown rice or coffee, or has harvested and pounded cassava, and wants to sell it, the only option is to load it into a large, conical basket of woven vines and carry it, with a strap across the forehead, ten to thirteen days on the rutted path to Kisangani, where there are large markets. Or the would-be seller could choose the three-day walk to Befori, a small town on the river, where weeks may pass before a sluggish barge or riverboat arrives to carry passengers to Mbandaka, a trip that could take up to a month. Only a few people are fortunate enough to have rusty bikes with which they can bring supplies more rapidly to Kisangani or between villages. And after the costs of their own food, or of riding in a boat, they earn a pittance, if anything at all. Most prefer to stay where they are, eating what they grow, bartering when they can.

Arriving with BCI in the village, it all seemed fairly simple to me. But I was seeing a system they had spent a decade building: of camps with a clinic, generators and solar panels, and communication via radio; of trackers and local conservationists BCI had educated, funded, and supplied. On each of their visits, they left most of what they brought: tools, tarps, generators, and electrical cords, as well as boots and ponchos, bags of batteries and flashlights. And though the mud huts of Yetee struck me as impoverished, ten years before the village had been destitute, with no livestock, its cassava fields gone. The Congo had just emerged from a war that killed the majority of its five and a half million victims through starvation and disease; it was a place where, if you happened on a village, a man might come out to greet you, wrapped in a tattered cloth, then go back inside and give the cloth to his naked wife so that she could present herself. People resurrected techniques rarely used since the early twentieth century, of making clothes out of vines and raffia, the leaf fibers of a palm tree. Diseases were rampant, tropical ulcers hard to cure. Now they are fairly rare, and antibiotics are available. Here in the reserve, a doctor is on staff and there are few obvious signs of malnutrition among the children.

As for the bonobos, they are notoriously difficult to habituate to people, moving rapidly through the forest and wary of humans from having been hunted by soldiers during the wars. As Benoît Mathe Kisuki, the former administrative technical director of the Institut Congolais pour la Conservation de la Nature (ICCN), the Congo government's national park service, explained to me in Kinshasa, habituation can be dangerous for bonobos, because it makes them extremely easy to hunt. In Kokolopori, eco-guards had to be put in place first, and the villagers had to sign accords to protect the bonobos not only from local hunters but from outside poachers who might enter the reserve.

Once this was done, the bonobos were tracked regularly for years, until they became used to human presence. Vie Sauvage did this while continuously building support for the creation of an official reserve, explaining that it would be locally controlled and so overcoming the people's fear of losing the resources in their forests or of being forced out if Kokolopori were made into a national park. The most complicated part of the work wasn't the bonobos, despite the challenges of habituation, but how to satisfy a starving, traumatized people who had learned from a century of brutalization that outsiders would take what they owned and leave them with nothing.

After our first day following the bonobos, when Léonard led Sally, Michael, Alan, and me out of the forest into a small village, fifty children surrounded us, wanting their photos taken. A young man in shorts ran from a hut to the talking drum, and gave it only a few resonant strikes. Ten minutes later, the motorcycles began arriving from the camp in Yetee to pick us up, faster than I would have expected, as if the drum imparted urgency or authority, or the people held an ancient memory of respect.

But it was the children who stayed in my mind. While we waited, they swarmed about us, posing for the camera, others lifting their hands in front of the lens, trying to be included in some way, all of them then racing around to see the images on the LCD screen. Some of the boys did headstands and handstands, waving their feet in the air as others gathered around them to be included in the shot.

The crowds of children were suggestive of the extent to which the DRC's population is exploding. Even with livestock and cassava programs, the local people can barely feed themselves. They are in the greatest need of—and simultaneously pose the greatest risk to—the resources found in the rainforests, and they know that their relationship to the forests needs to change. Villagers said that even a decade earlier hunters had to walk three or four days from villages before seeing wildlife, and they understood that their traditional ways of surviving were failing. They asked me why more foreigners didn't visit and said that I should tell everyone I knew about the forests and the bonobos so that people would come.

Since my arrival in Djolu, and especially since I'd been in Kokolopori, whenever the villagers discussed projects on the reserve, the name that came up most frequently was that of Albert Lotana Lokasola. Even on our first day in Yetee, his name occurred often in the people's songs. They praised him for having founded Vie Sauvage. Sally had explained to me that this was BCI's first trip to Kokolopori without him. He had been the local leader BCI most supported, working closely with him on conservation efforts. Under his guidance, Vie Sauvage regularly provided BCI with reports on projects and wildlife monitoring. BCI used this material to apply for funding and worked with Albert to develop and manage further projects. The previous year, at the same time as the contested presidential elections, he had run for parliament and won, and was now in Kinshasa. He planned on dividing his time between Kokolopori and the capital, when parliament was in session, but listening to people talk in the evenings, I noticed that they were concerned he wouldn't return, that he would be too busy as a parliamentarian to do conservation.

The Congo's Bantu cultures revere great men, imploring them to save their people, to be a source of abundance. What I heard about Albert Lotana Lokasola evoked this traditional reverence, but it was also true that decades of government abuse had made the Congolese wary. Now they expected great men to serve their own needs and not fulfill their duties. Villagers said that Albert was always smarter than the rest of them, more talented in school, destined for success, and they considered his campaign promises, speculating as to whether he would become a corrupt politician or bring greater benefits to the region. The reserve was their livelihood, and they thought about the future and worried the way workers in rural America would at rumors of a factory closing or a lag in the economy that might hurt them. I couldn't help but wonder as well if he would have the determination and the resources to help them, and what the full scope of his ambition really was. But clearly, from the way the people spoke, even those who were concerned about his intentions respected him for all he'd done to build the reserve.

During my time in Kinshasa, I conducted interviews with Albert Lotana Lokasola and BCI's other partners. With Albert, I spoke briefly about his decision to run for parliament, and he admitted that it was controversial, that people feared it would distance him from Kokolopori and its communities. "But these last years," he added, "have been truly difficult. I realized that I must have influence on a higher level than just the reserve, that I can help conservation better if I am more involved in the government and have more resources."

He described how hard he'd worked to build the reserve, how in the beginning the big conservation NGOs wouldn't take him seriously. Only BCI did, and he partnered with them to achieve his goals. His work as a conservationist gave him a degree of power that threatened some leaders in Équateur, who, as he described them, used any change as a means to polarize the people in their favor. He wanted to free himself up to do larger projects, he told me, and not have to negotiate constantly with self-interested local politicians.

Hearing him speak, I recalled another statement by conservationist Karl Ammann, that the future of grassroots conservation is doubtful "until we can create political pressure from the top down." This had been perhaps the most challenging goal for BCI. BCI built their projects from the ground up so that they would be, as BCI advisor John Scherlis explained to me, "in touch with and rooted in local reality, organically growing in a way that is adapted to the local environment, and, only then, potentially stable and sustainable over the long term." Furthermore, having local leadership within the reserve communities ensured that the reserves would continue running in the event of a war or a change of government. But BCI had put significant effort into their relationships with the president, the ministers, and ambassadors, as well as the church leaders of the DRC. The ascent of Albert, and of people similarly educated in conservation, also had the potential to create top-down change. In Albert's case, that potential was reinforced and magnified by his success as a grassroots community leader.

In our conversation, Albert confirmed that conservation has to be integrated with the culture and needs of the people where it is being done, and that the Congolese know their forests but need training, leadership, and funding. The picture he painted was one of both collective effort and individual leadership. As he described the vision he shared with BCI—of saving bonobos by giving the people a livelihood through sustainable agriculture and livestock, education in conservation, and development of markets for local goods—I sensed that he was a man who rarely paused, who liked to set goals for himself.

Over the course of my conversation with him, and with other local leaders, I learned the protean nature of many Congolese conservationists. They had been soldiers, teachers, merchants, scientists, administrators, and politicians while remaining conservationists. The chaos of the country, the way relationship building depended not only on charisma but on a deep respect for the defiant character of the people and their pride in their forests and customs, meant that to work here successfully, conservationists had to let go of preconceptions, of what had worked elsewhere—of Western hierarchy and Western definitions of efficiency—and learn this country's history and traditions, acculturating themselves to the Congo.

Part II
Grass Roots

Albert Lotana Lokasola

In the days before leaving for the rainforest, I met with Albert at BCI's offices. He arrived in the company of his eldest son, a doctoral student in political science. Though not tall, Albert had an easy, authoritative carriage, the light movements of a man used to spending time on his feet and in the forest. The shape of his cheekbones suggested that he smiled often, and his eyes were expressive, at once enthusiastic and watchful, appraising those around him almost imperceptibly. He wore leather shoes and a black suit, and as we began the interview, he sat leaning forward, elbows on his knees, as if we might negotiate a project or he was ready to leave, to hurry out and set to work.

As the head of Vie Sauvage for a decade, Albert had partnered with BCI to build the Kokolopori Reserve, but I wanted to know about the years before he met them, before he became a conservationist. I wanted to understand how the Bongandu had perceived the roots of conservation in Kokolopori, how they had integrated it into their lives and explained it through their own culture. I asked, in essence, for him to tell the story of his life.

He considered my request, adjusting his posture, sitting straight as if calming his mind. When he spoke, the tone of his voice and the rhythm of his sentences sounded almost ceremonial.

"I was born the twenty-fourth of August, 1962. I was born in Kisangani, in the Kisangani Hospital. I was born in the middle of the war."

The conflict of which he spoke started shortly after the Congo's independence from Belgium on June 30, 1960, and its impact on Albert's life made sense in light of his father's social position—that of an *évolué,* Albert told me, a word that literally means "evolved." The *évolués* were an intermediary class of blacks established under the Belgians, largely as go-betweens. They were high-school educated—the highest level of education available in the Belgian Congo—though there was no test, no certificate to become one. A Belgian served as a godfather, introducing the *évolué* into white social circles, and the *évolué* would begin receiving invitations to places that weren't open to other blacks.

"One became an *évolué* after occupying a high position or after having been close to the whites. The whites would identify you as an intermediary, *un nègre* who wasn't entirely *nègre* and wasn't white either, but who was between white and black and served as a relay. They would accord this quality as if to flatter you, but in reality to use you better.

"You are called *Monsieur*," he explained. "You wear a suit and tie, and speak like a Belgian. You have just one wife, and your children attend good schools. You eat and laugh like a white person, and you measure your words carefully. But it isn't for your benefit. It was to better control you and the population. For a black Congolese, there wasn't a higher status than *évolué*."

Though Albert's grandfather had been a cook for a white family, a man not considered an *évolué*, he'd earned sufficient salary to send his only son, André, to school. His other child, a daughter, had died of a seizure during early adolescence, and his wife hadn't been able to conceive again.

In contrast to the many Congolese children with numerous siblings, Albert's father, André Lokasola, received his parents' full resources. He excelled at l'École des Frères Maristes, a technical college with both African and Belgian students, and while others dropped out, he went on to graduate, one of four Congolese students to receive a diploma. At the ceremony, whites arrived to recruit the graduates, and Albert's father became a *contre-maître*, the foreman of a woodworking atelier for a Monsieur Béleau, in Kisangani.

But independence was an insecure time for the *évolués*, who had conformed so closely to Belgian culture, and they would see their positions threatened in the years of violence that followed. The politics and conflicts of that era would transform the life of André Lokasola and shape the world into which Albert was born.

As for the Belgian government, it was reluctant to let go of such a lucrative colony. But as nearby African countries achieved statehood, the Congo demanded the same. Only with riots in Léopoldville (Kinshasa) and new political parties challenging the power structure did Belgium concede. Patrice Lumumba, a fiery thirty-four-year-old, was elected prime minister, and the older, far more conservative Joseph Kasavubu president. On June 30, 1960, King Baudouin I of Belgium, who had traveled to the Congo to be present at the independence ceremonies, spoke of the Congo's progress under colonialism and how his own country would guide it in the years to come, as if independence were but nominal.

President Kasavubu gave his own innocuous speech, and then Lumumba took the stage. He spoke of the Congo and Belgium as equals and announced that "no Congolese worthy of the name" would forget that independence had been won only through a fight—"a day-to-day fight," he declared:

> an ardent and idealistic fight, a fight in which we were spared neither privation nor suffering, and for which we gave our strength and our blood. We are proud of this struggle, of tears, of fire, and of blood, to the depths of our being, for it was a noble and just struggle, and indispensable to put an end to the humiliating slavery which was imposed upon us by force.

The speech burned itself into the consciousness of the Congolese, who'd never heard one of their own speak to Belgians like this. Though it made Lumumba a national hero overnight, his tenure was short-lived. Only a few days later, he raised the pay of all government employees except the military, a blunder that catalyzed the six-year period of conflict known as the Congo Crisis. The discontent exploded on July 5, less than a week after independence, when the Belgian lieutenant general Émile Janssens of la Force Publique, the Congolese army, convened a meeting of soldiers who expected the military to be Africanized. Janssens, refusing to allow black soldiers to serve as officers, wrote on a blackboard, "After independence = before independence," intending to remind them of their duty and that nothing would change. The outraged soldiers began to plunder the commissary, and rioting spread throughout the country.

Lumumba grasped at solutions, changing the name of La Force Publique, which dated to the beginning of colonization in 1885, to l'Armée Nationale Congolaise (ANC). Then, as Belgian military officers fled, he promoted largely untrained soldiers to replace them. But the chaos intensified, and Katanga, the country's wealthiest province, declared independence under Moïse Tshombe, who had the support of Belgian settlers and industries wanting to keep control of copper and cobalt mines. Not long after, South Kasai, the diamond-rich region, followed suit. These were the areas that had given the Belgian Congo its reputation as a "model colony," their roads, schools, and hospitals paid for by the state's share of the mining industry.

In the Belgian Congo, Albert explained to me, everything had been done to justify something else. To extract the country's wealth, the Belgians had claimed to be civilizing the Congolese. By providing basic services to the people, they could claim that the mining benefited the Congolese, even though it was enriching Belgium.

Within weeks of independence, the Belgian military had re-entered the Congo from Europe without permission, allegedly to protect Belgian citizens from rioting soldiers. The Congolese saw this as an act of aggression and possible reoccupation. Lumumba was infuriated by the colonial gesture, but only with the assistance of the UN was he able to make them leave. However, when Lumumba demanded that the UN use military force to help the Congo reclaim Katanga and South Kasai, the UN refused. He then requested the support of the USSR, and a thousand Soviet advisors soon arrived in Kinshasa. President Eisenhower had adopted a hard line against communism, and the United States viewed the Congo as a strategic reserve of cobalt, copper, uranium, and industrial diamonds. By threatening US interests, Lumumba set in motion the events that would lead to his death.

When the army began rioting, Lumumba turned to his personal aide, a twenty-nine-year-old journalist and former soldier named Joseph-Desiré Mobutu, and appointed him chief of staff of the army, commanding him to restore order. Those with memories of Mobutu from this time were impressed not only by his intelligence and physical presence—he stood over six feet tall—but by his courage. Larry Devlin, a CIA officer then stationed in the Congo, described Mobutu facing soldiers: "They were hollering and screaming and pointing guns at him and telling him not to come any closer or they'd shoot. He just started talking quietly and calmly until they quietened down, then he walked along taking their guns from them, one by one. Believe me, it was hellish impressive."

Though Devlin knew Mobutu well, and even saved him from an assassination attempt, he didn't foresee the dictator he would become. It was only later that the chaos made Mobutu decide he was more suited to leading the country.

The first coup d'état that Mobutu orchestrated was shortly after the arrival of the Soviet advisors. President Kasavubu denounced Prime Minister Lumumba's affiliation with the USSR and dismissed him from his position, and Lumumba responded by doing the same, ordering the president deposed. Both then commanded Mobutu to arrest the other, but Mobutu, after securing the support of the CIA, took control, arresting Lumumba and keeping the pro-Western Kasavubu in power. The Soviets left, and though Lumumba tried to flee to Stanleyville (Kisangani), he was caught four days later, on December 1, 1960. A month and a half afterward, he was murdered, his head most likely dissolved in sulphuric acid, his body buried in an unmarked grave.

But Lumumba's incendiary independence speech remained in the minds of the Congolese, and in Kisangani, Antoine Gizenga, the vice prime minister of the rival government formerly headed by Lumumba, continued his mission, receiving support from the USSR and China. He managed to hold out against the UN and Mobutu's government until January 1962. During that same year, while Katanga continued to resist and was finally defeated, Albert Lotana Lokasola was born in Kisangani.

Belgians were fleeing, threatened by the rampaging military and dissatisfied citizens, but as an *évolué,* Albert's father, André, had been close to the former colonial rulers and was also suspect to his fellow Congolese. He'd decided to continue his studies in Belgium, but just before his departure, his father died. The Belgians his father had cooked for had left, and shortly after he'd found a new job as a logger, he was crushed by a falling tree.

At the funeral, André's uncle, his father's brother, asked him to return to their traditional home in Kokolopori. He said that because André was an only child, it was his duty to come back; otherwise, he would be lost. The family, his uncle insisted, needed him in Kokolopori.

Under the Belgians, the national territory was divided into provinces, provinces into districts, districts into territories, territories into sectors, sectors into *groupements.* Each sector had a chief, or *échevin,* and each territory had a *bourgmestre.* When the Belgians left, the posts were filled with Congolese.

Albert's father was twenty-eight when he returned to his tribal village, Yalokole, situated in the middle of some of the densest, most biologically diverse forests in Équateur. No one in the Kokolopori region had his level of education, so the *bourgmestre* of the territory asked him to become an *échevin.* Though André had intended to study in Belgium, he was swayed not only by the splendor of his reception—women dancing, men bringing him gifts of wild meat each evening—but also by the political changes.

In 1964, a four-part rebellion began in which the revolutionary who would become the DRC's president thirty years later, Laurent-Désiré Kabila, participated. Among its soldiers were the Simbas of the Armée Populaire de Libération. Tribesmen whose sorcerers told them that in battle they would become lions, or *simbas,* anointed themselves with water blessed by witchdoctors and chanted *Simba Lumumba mai,* "lion, Lumumba, water," to make themselves impervious to bullets. The rebels captured nearly half the country, and when they took Kisangani, they declared it the capital of the People's Republic of the Congo.

Kasavubu was still president, and he appointed Moïse Tshombe, the former leader of the breakaway Katangan state, as interim prime minister to unify the country. In Kisangani, the Simbas held thousands of Western hostages and *évolués,* and to free them, Tshombe requested the support of the

Belgian and American militaries. He also hired hundreds of foreign mercenaries, who, along with the Congolese army, began taking the country back.

Believing that colonization was again being carried out in the Congo, with Tshombe as a puppet leader, six African countries—Algeria, Egypt, Ghana, Guinea, Mali, and Tanzania—moved to recognize the Kisangani government. As the mercenaries and ANC neared Kisangani, the Simbas forced the hostages into the street, making them stand in rows so as to dissuade an attack, but as soon as US airplanes dropped Belgian paratroopers, the Simbas began executing the hostages. Though more than 150 were killed, the paratroopers rescued nearly 3,000, and shortly afterward the mercenaries and government army took back the city. In the process of reuniting the Congo, the West was securing the resources it viewed as strategically essential to winning the Cold War: cobalt for fighter jets and industrial-grade diamonds used in the machining of engine parts. Tshombe forever lost popularity among the Congolese for having invited their former colonizer back, and Tshombe's decline paved the way for Mobutu's rise to prominence, despite his own role in coordinating the intervention.

During this time, in Kokolopori, many of the communities fled into the forest to avoid capture but left a few people, largely children and the elderly, to make the Simbas believe that the villages were still inhabited and to keep them from searching further. The Simbas had become known for taking all of the pretty women with them and lining the men up, inspecting them, and then executing those who didn't have callused hands and feet.

Albert paused, sitting, his elbows still against his knees. He thought a moment before he explained that his father was wanted by the Simbas not only because he was an *évolué* and held a position of leadership, but also because he was a member of the PNP, one of more than fifty political parties created after independence and perhaps the closest to Kasavubu's government at that time. When he tried to recall what the PNP stood for, he remembered only the epithets.

"They were called la Partie des Nègres Payés—the Party of Paid Negroes— or Pene Pene Na Mundele. *Pene* meant close, and *mundele* was a white person or a foreigner. It meant very close to the whites. The real name was probably Partie Nationale du Peuple or something like that."

Albert and his older sister, Gertrude, were staying in Yetee, his maternal village, when one afternoon five barefoot Simbas arrived along the path, carrying machetes and clubs. Albert was only three, but he remembered the moment and all that followed clearly.

The Simbas wore elaborate headpieces of small branches woven together

Empty Hands, Open Arms

as camouflage, and their silhouettes were terrifying against the sun. They had come to find out where the rest of the villagers were hiding in the forest, and they called to Albert and his sister, "Where is your *barrière?*"

An older man, Fabien Lokonga, whom Albert referred to as an uncle— nearly all villagers being related—had taught them that if Simbas asked about their *barrière,* "barricade," they were asking the location of the secret camp. He'd taught them how to respond, and the children told the Simbas, "Our *barrière* is at Bekongo."

But the Simbas knew that the camp had to be closer. They began pushing and slapping Gertrude, threatening both children with severe beatings if they didn't reveal its whereabouts.

Across the village, Fabien came out and called—Albert acknowledges the great courage required to do this—"You shouldn't mistreat those children. What is the problem? If you want to mistreat them, then you should come and mistreat me."

As the Simbas grabbed Fabien and began tying his hands, an old woman motioned to Albert and his sister from behind a hut. The two children quickly followed her past the buildings, beyond the sandy yellow earth of the village, into the undergrowth around the slash-and-burn areas, what he calls *les champs,* "the fields," though they were heavily grown up, ten-foot cassava plants mixed with trees and surrounded by forest. In the village, Fabien was beaten and told to confess the location of the village. He would refuse, and eventually be released, but not until Albert and his sister were far away.

Albert would forever recall hurrying from the cassava fields into the full rainforest, which seemed, suddenly, like a different climate, comforting against his skin. Though he'd been in the rainforest before, he'd never seen it like this. Everything had its own color, every color alive, his heart beating fast, the trees perfectly still, the air moist. Maybe it was because of the adrenaline and fear, or simply the contrast to the village, its exposed ground and buildings where all things appeared washed out in the sunlight, the same shade of dusty earth. He was seeing hues he hadn't known existed, a memory so vivid that it would seem to him, recalling this years later, that the eyes of children perceive more, have yet to be dulled to experience.

He followed his sister and the old woman through the towering trees, not pausing at narrow forks in the path, repeatedly ducking beneath undergrowth. The distance to the camp was less than two miles, his sister at times carrying him on her back when he fell behind, though he walked most of it, accustomed to traveling on foot, as most Congolese children were at his age.

For the next year, Albert lived with his family in the rainforest, in small huts hidden beneath branches. They learned to avoid or flee elephants, and the adults did everything possible so that children wouldn't cry, in case Simbas came looking. The people hunted only with traps made of twined vines, and ate caterpillars during *mbindjo* season, or mushrooms. They distilled salt from palm flowers and made soap from the ashes of vegetation.

One night, Albert woke to the sound of loud squeaking. *Tié tié tié.* There was an elephant shrew in one of his father's traps, a reddish-black mammal somewhat resembling a shrew but with long legs and the elongated snout from which it derives its name. Albert had never had a toy, and he wanted the small animal. Again, it was the colors that riveted him, the creature's fur shining in the firelight.

His father attached it to a cord and gave it to him, but it died within a few days because Albert couldn't figure out how to feed it. Even years later, at university, he would catch and try to raise elephant shrews to see what they would eat.

But several months after that first magical encounter with the forest, armed men came into the camp and took Albert's father away. The family learned that the Simbas had captured the nearby villages. They had lined up the men and said that unless they led them to André Lokasola, they would be executed.

The Simba in command told Albert's father that he would be taken to the new chief of the territory to be executed. But after days of walking, when André Lokasola arrived in Djolu, he recognized the head of the rebellion there; the man had been among those to watch him graduate in Kisangani. The new chief stared at Lokasola a long time, conflicted, no doubt seeing an individual of great value. It is difficult to know what might have been said between them, if André Lokasola was as gifted with words as his son would turn out to be, or if he was simply fortunate. Shortly after his arrival, he was no longer a prisoner but the secretary of the rebels' political office in Djolu.

Though his children and wife, Marie-Josée Bopoko, still lived in the forest, Lokasola worked for the rebellion while the government, with the help of Belgian and American forces and foreign mercenaries, took the country back village by village. When they captured Djolu soon after, André Lokasola was imprisoned and again sentenced to be executed.

This was the height of the Congo Crisis, a period of chaos throughout the country that saw the deaths of at least one hundred thousand people. Though he'd ended the conflict, Prime Minister Moïse Tshombe, the Katanga former-secessionist leader, had lost the people's support and was in constant conflict with President Kasavubu. Mobutu decided that the country needed the stability of a decisive leader whom the people trusted. In essence, having let Tshombe pacify the country and destroy his own reputation, Mobutu reaped the benefits. He launched his second and final coup d'état, which would begin his thirty-two-year dictatorship, though he claimed at the time that he would rule for only five, the same length of time as the Congo Crisis—as many years being needed to repair the country, he declared, as had been spent destroying it.

As Albert spoke, I traced the details of the country's history in how his father moved between worlds, leaving the white man's as an *évolué* and returning to that of his origins. As waves of ideology and war washed over the Congo, the people struggled to establish an identity muted by more than half a century of colonialism. Between independence and Mobutu's final coup, they changed roles and alliances often. If anything unified them, it was the knowledge that the real enemies were outsiders, white men with colonial interests and the desire to profit from the Congo's vast mineral wealth. Mobutu rose to power so prominently only because he succeeded in distancing himself, at least in the eyes of his people, from the very Western powers who were supporting him.

Earlier, when Albert had spoken to me of the challenges of conservation, I hadn't fully understood. The difficulty is more than a question of poverty or isolation, or problems with logistics and funding. The people have seen their resources stripped time and again, and as a result, their mistrust runs deep.

As for Albert's father, the entire Congo had only about a dozen university graduates and few high-school graduates. For any regime to execute an educated Congolese who was clearly amenable to changing sides would be folly. Again, André Lokasola's life was spared. People defended him, saying that he'd been forced to join the Simba rebellion against his will, and that he'd been a skilled *contre-maître*. As a result, he made his final political migration, becoming the chief of public works in the territory even as many of his rebel cohort fled or were slaughtered; he would ally himself increasingly with the values of his people, taking more wives and becoming a tribal chief, though remaining a government administrator for the rest of his life.

From Slave State to Failed State

One night, after the others went to bed, I left our mud and wattle house, my headlamp shining a pale swath in the dark beneath the abundant silver of equatorial stars. It reflected off the eyes of spiders on the path as I crossed the camp to the forest. The chirring of insects deepened with each step down to the stream. At the bottom of the hill, I paused, then walked out onto a log.

The night cries were resonant, the air almost palpable with the sound of frogs. As I listened, one group lifted their singing to a pitch, then dropped off as another, their voices entirely different, picked up. Some kept more or less steady, but when I turned off my headlamp, they remarked the change and the night got quieter. They slowly resumed their orchestra, and I distinguished at least four different kinds of frogs and grew accustomed to their intervals, their crescendos and pauses. A splash just to my side, at the reeds, startled me. The music again lulled. Above me, beyond the trees on either side of the stream, hung the ragged line of the starlit sky.

As I stood, listening, staring up, the night so dark I felt disembodied, it occured to me that I couldn't evaluate such a place. Have any of us ever known undisturbed nature? The stream seemed thriving, pristine, but hunters had passed through here thousands of times. Daily, villagers bathed, suds making rainbows, butterflies swarming bars of soap, alighting upon them and pulsing their wings.

The age of extinction in which we live is our creation, corresponding to the rapid growth of our population, and our industrial innovations. Environmental degradation has a long past here. Over a thousand years ago, the Bantu established trade routes for salt, copper, and iron, founding empires across Africa. In what was now the DRC, beginning in the late fourteenth century and lasting until the mid-seventeenth, the Kongo Kingdom ruled on the coast, and farther inland, the Kingdoms of Luba (1585–1889) and Lunda (1665–1887) thrived. From 1483, Portugal traded with the Kongo, converting its people to Catholicism and then, more and more, buying slaves, until, in 1665, it conquered the kingdom and created a puppet state. The

Portuguese shipped millions of Africans to the Americas, and during four centuries of slave trade, "America," as Thomas Turner writes in *Congo Wars: Conflict, Myth, and Reality*, "entered into the collective imagination of the Kongo community as the place where people went after they died."

The roots of exploitation ran so deep here that it was hard to fathom the impact. The recent wars were but the latest consequences of what was possibly Europe's most damaging colonial scheme. Africa's dark heart was not something the West found, but rather brought and continued to bring, selling weapons, propping up dictators, allowing material exploitation to run its course in any form. If the area became known for diseases, it was in part because the social structure had been destroyed, the people sickly, seeking refuge from slavery in the forest. Illness and parasites that had less impact on healthy populations thrived.

In 1884, with the Conference of Berlin, an event that formalized the European colonization of Africa, King Leopold II of Belgium took control of the Congo. The exploitation of everything living—people, animals, and forests—rose to a level previously unimaginable. From 1885 to 1908, he made the Congo his personal fiefdom, organizing it so as to extract as much profit as possible from rubber and ivory. Shipping weapons to the Congo and bringing raw materials back to Belgium, Leopold enslaved the population rather than pay workers, and the pressure to meet rubber quotas depopulated riverbank settlements and made the Force Publique push deeper into the interior in search of free labor.

The stories of atrocities in the Congo reached Europe first in anecdotal form and were quickly dismissed. Leopold's Force Publique, composed of African troops and Belgian officers, lived by a rule whose consequences would become the emblem of his reign: soldiers were not to waste bullets and had to account for each one fired by bringing back a human right hand. If they went hunting or missed their mark shooting at a fleeing slave and had to fire again, they compensated by harvesting hands from the local population, a practice that they developed solely to meet the stringent military requirements. This was one of the first times that the nascent art of photojournalism demonstrated its power to galvanize an international movement. Pictures that missionaries took of "mutilated Africans or their cut-off hands" were shown in protest meetings and published in papers, providing, as Adam Hochschild writes in his seminal book, *King Leopold's Ghost*, "evidence that no propaganda could refute."

Despite the lack of clear records, Hochschild and other scholars have estimated the death toll under Leopold to be ten million, approximately half of the region's population, this as much the result of starvation, exhaustion, and disease as of murder itself. Entire villages were enslaved to gather rubber and ivory, and as elephants and latex-bearing plants became scarce, men from various areas traveled farther, crossing into each other's territory and competing to fill nearly impossible quotas. Those who failed were severely whipped or killed as examples. Groups that rebelled were slaughtered, and once the rubber and slaves in a region had been used up, la Force Publique moved on to new areas. The strategy made Leopold one of Europe's wealthiest men, allowing him to initiate extravagant building projects, though he never set foot in the Congo, where he caused the disintegration of the social fabric.

The Congo gradually became the cause célèbre of the period, a little like Darfur today, with much outcry but little success. Roger Casement and Arthur Conan Doyle penned books on the subject, and Mark Twain ridiculed Leopold's claim to be on a humanitarian mission, issuing his now famous statement: "This work of 'civilization' is an enormous and continual butchery."

Speaking to the Congolese, I often wondered what they knew of that history, what might have been passed down through stories or taught in school. But when I asked, they said they knew nothing, even many of those with education. The average life span in the Congo is short, with many generations between now and 1908, when Leopold ceded the country to the Belgian government, and the Congolese have lived through many conflicts since then. More than unknowing, I saw a refusal in the gaze of the people I asked. There had been too many wars, too much to struggle against. The system had always been predatory in some way, whether during the Congo Crisis and the fight for independence, or during the colonial period, when, despite improved conditions and less brutality, the Belgians still implemented forced labor for mining, roadwork, and cash crops, punishing dissenters with the *chicotte,* a hippopotamus-hide whip.

At first, when I asked about that time, I saw people thinking, trying to remember which atrocity I was talking about, but then the refusal flashed in their eyes, as if at some point they had rejected the past, having realized that with it they couldn't move forward. Writers have speculated as to whether colonialism and its abuses made the people more vulnerable and ultimately accepting of Mobutu's corrupt and exploitative rule—whether, as journalist Michela Wrong writes, "a frighteningly efficient kleptocratic system effectively softened up a community for a repeat performance."

Thomas Turner, a professor of political science at the National University of Rwanda, refers to "the myth of the yoke," the Congolese's belief that their problems are the result of outsiders. Whenever Albert, Sally, or Michael speak of working with the people of Kokolopori and of protecting forests, the question of distrust comes up often. The people are keenly aware of the value of their land. I often heard numerous variations on the line, "The forest is our supermarket and pharmacy." It gives them cassava fields, vines to make ropes, wood and thatch to build houses; it provides elements for every aspect of their lives, keeping fires burning when the long rains come. It also provides bushmeat, their primary means of sustenance for thousands of years, an item to exchange and one used on many occasions, the social structure itself being traditionally built around the hunt.

An understanding of all this is essential if conservationists intend to work well with the Congolese. They have to see the reactions and fears of the people through the lens of their history. In this context, Albert was suited to formulate and achieve goals for both conservation and the community. The Congo's history is not abstract, but an urgent, often devastating force, obliging the people to find any possible way to survive. Every aspect of their environment has been crucial, and they have had little reason to believe that outsiders would understand this and have their best interests in mind. Only Albert could win their trust. They knew that he was a child of both the village and the forest, and sensitive to their fear of exploitation.

The nation that Albert grew up in was fractured, uncertain of its identity and of how it would function cohesively with self-rule. In May 1967, Mobutu announced the Manifesto of N'Sele, which marked the beginning of *le retour à l'authenticité*, "the return to authenticity." All Congolese were to give up European ways. Men would replace their suits and ties with long, high-collared jackets called *abacosts*, from *à bas le costume*, "down with the suit." Women were to give up miniskirts and dresses in favor of the *pagne* or wrap. Everyone was supposed to replace Christian names with African ones, and priests were threatened with a five-year prison sentence if they broke the new law when baptizing children.

In 1971, Mobutu changed the name of the country to the Republic of Zaire, from the Portuguese rendering of the Kikongo word *nzere* or *nzadi,* said to mean "the river that swallows all rivers." He even renamed himself Mobutu Sese Seko Kuku Ngbendu wa za Banga, which meant something along the lines of "the all-powerful warrior who, because of his endurance and inflexible will to live, will go from conquest to conquest leaving fire in his wake," though the quick-witted Congolese translated it as "the cock who leaves no hen intact." With more mercy than his name suggested, he went by Mobutu Sese Seko for short. This was also the time when Mobutism became the national ideology, public discourse glorifying his acts and referring to him as "Founder-President," "Guide of the Revolution," "Helmsman," and "Messiah."

Perhaps the only positive legacy of this period and its hardships was a shared sense of a Zairian identity that, for the first time, unified a country artificially mapped out under colonial rule. The Congo is composed of approximately 250 ethnic and linguistic groups divided among Catholics (50 percent), Protestants (20 percent), the indigenous Kimbanguist Church (10 percent), Muslims (10 percent), and indigenous belief systems (10 percent), though estimates for these groups vary and the practice of traditional forms of African religion at times overlap with the aforementioned faiths.

Increasingly, however, Mobutu's vanity showed. He became ostentatious, carrying a trademark cane and wearing a cap made from the skin of a leopard, a Parisian furrier supplying him with numerous duplicates. He went on frequent shopping trips to Europe in his private jet, and he paid for all of this by claiming large shares in the country's industries.

Mobutu's popularity faded, and even as he spoke out against corruption— *le mal zaïrois,* "the Zaïrian sickness"—his own excesses reached new heights. He survived assassination attempts, becoming paranoid and creating an inner circle that agreed with everything he did. He imprisoned or exiled even those who tried to warn him against his own mistakes. In Équateur, 710 miles northeast of Kinshasa, he built Gbadolite, an immense compound of palaces that came to be known in diplomatic circles as "Versailles in the jungle." Later in his rule, he had daily flights bring in flowers and shellfish. "They chartered Boeings like most people use supermarket trolleys," Pierre Janssen, Mobutu's son-in-law and a member of his court, recalled.

Under Mobutu, reinvestment in industrial assets stopped, and mines and factories fell into disrepair. What he didn't squander he hid away in Swiss bank accounts. The symbol of Mobutu that writers often evoke is his Villa del Mare, just down the coast from where King Leopold of Belgium had his own estate.

Mobutu presided over his country's economic decline even as its Mercedes-Benz imports hit a record high. The Congo's distribution networks broke down, access to goods became difficult, and prices shot up throughout the country. As wealthy Zairians became wealthier, the rest of the people ate their meals *à la morte subite,* "like sudden death," given that they never knew where food would come from, and when they found it, they devoured it on the spot. To have one meal a day was fortunate, and many families alternated between parents and children, eating every other day.

In light of a century of Congolese history, from King Leopold's slave state to Mobutu's eventual anarchy, it is no wonder that the people I encountered were so wary. In the villages, I walked past mud-daubed houses, observing crowds of children roaming about in tattered clothes, the adults masking their scrutiny with mastered nonchalance. The people had seen foreigners come and go, returning to their homes and safety during troubled times. Relationships here had been based on survival. There was no buffer zone between failure and starvation. If officials asked for a little extra money, they did so politely. The request had taken on a formal air. It would pay for their families' education, for their relatives' hospital visits. No one, especially not an official who had the power to ask, was exempt from being worked over for money.

Such opportunism wasn't recent, and the story Albert Lokasola told me of his father wasn't surprising. As a young man, André had lived through constant upheaval, uncertainty, and shifting values. After the Congo Crisis, Mobutu, who at that time seemed the leader the Congolese had hoped for, founded the Mouvement Populaire de la Revolution (MPR), which remained the only legal political party until 1990. Rather than be executed, André Lokasola had gone through three parties in as many years—the PNP, MNC (Mouvement National Congolais), and MPR (even becoming its administrative secretary in Djolu)—a skill of transformation-by-necessity that many would master during the decades of the new regime.

As Mobutu's politics dominated the Congo, Albert's father also became the chief of the sector of Luo, a collection of *groupements* in the forests of Kokolopori. It was here that Albert came of age, his father receiving gifts from the locals and impressing upon his son not only his ability to survive but their family's bond to the land, to its people and forests.

"Among my children," André Lokasola often told the villagers, "it is Albert who will be here with you. Albert will never leave you."

His father was well aware not only of his son's acumen but also of his ability to speak to others. As Albert grew up and went to increasingly distant schools, his father arranged for him to come back and renew his contact with the village, even when he was far away.

But education and then his career became the driving forces in Albert's life. He excelled in the village's primary school, said his former classmate and fellow conservationist, Pastor Jean Gaston Ndombasi, who remembered

Albert with these words regarding their schoolwork: "If he had eighty, we had sixty or seventy. If he had a hundred, we were relieved because we'd at least have eighty."

Albert attended a secondary boarding school in Mbandaka and university in Lubumbashi, where he did a degree in chemistry. Afterward, he moved to Kinshasa and took a placement test with Unilever. He was hired for management training and spent six years with them. Unilever wanted to prepare a class of Congolese who could replace the European expatriate staff, and sent Albert to work in the Ivory Coast for a year, then to Spalding, a town in Lincolnshire, England, for technical training. When he came back to the Congo, he replaced an expatriate as *formateur technique de l'usine,* the factory's technical trainer. But a year later, in 1991, the factory was slated to be sold to an Indian-Lebanese company, and he left it.

Listening to Albert, I could already see that he was not prone to dramatizing a struggle or likely to tell me how hard life in the country had become. He'd looked for new work, each time trying to get a foothold, to make a place even as Mobutu's regime was crumbling. But after an attempt at starting a career in Kisangani, he moved back to Kinshasa in 1994. He began what he called his *passage à vide,* "a passage in emptiness," a way of saying a period without work or clear direction. It proved to be difficult and formative, giving him the time to conceive a new vision of his future. But it was also humiliating for a man who had been so driven and successful to have to struggle without an income, to have to move with his wife and children to her family's home.

With the Cold War over, Mobutu had little support from the West, and the massacres that his security forces committed began receiving greater international scrutiny. He paid the military a pittance, forcing them to survive on bribes and extortion. They rented out their barracks for cash and lived with family, and planted cassava on their training grounds. Bureaucrats took similar measures, and Mobutu even once said on the air, "Go ahead and steal, as long as you don't take too much." His rule fostered a culture of abuse, of theft and skimming, that the Congolese still refer to as *tracasserie*—literally, the act of bothering or harassing someone.

But this abuse had deeper effects. The culture of corruption pitted the military and bureaucracy against the people. It was Mobutu's way of dividing and conquering, of using instability to prevent opposition to his weakening rule. He let the country's infrastructure fall apart, further isolating communities. The last foreign investors fled, leaving the Congolese virtually helpless against a predatory military and security apparatus. Organized crime thrived, stores and warehouses were plundered, and counterfeiting schemes devalued the national currency even as Mobutu was rapidly printing more money. Officials sold everything they could seize, and the Zairian ambassador to Japan even sold the embassy.

The 1990s were by far the worst years. Mobutu was absent, suffering from prostate cancer. The country was deeply indebted, the mines that had financed it antiquated and in ruins. The unpaid military rioted in 1991, looting Kinshasa. In 1993, when Mobutu printed 500,000-zaire notes, with an approximate value of one US dollar, no shopkeepers would accept the currency and the population dubbed the bills "the 'prostate' in honour of his afflicted organ." The soldiers who received them as pay rioted again, ransacking the country's businesses. Foreign entrepreneurs who underpinned what remained of the economy finally left. In rural areas, the disintegration of roads and infrastructure as well as the disappearance of schools and medical services caused people to flee to the cities, intensifying the chaos.

This was what Albert's *passage à vide* evoked, the search not only for opportunities amid overwhelming exploitation but for a new way of doing things. The name Lokasola, he told me, sitting across from me in the BCI office for well over two hours now, "means trailblazer. And Lotana is someone who is found in his place, someone who doesn't move. Things come to him. He does not go looking." And yet, during that time, he had never felt so bereft of his gifts. Until then his life, like his father's, had seemed charmed.

He told himself that he couldn't miss any opportunities, that he had to be vigilant. In Kinshasa, he spoke to everyone, trying to imagine new ways of surviving. He and his family were living with his brother-in-law in the Bon Marché neighborhood when he heard about Floribert Botamba, a man from Bosenge, a village not far from Kokolopori. He'd been working at Georgia State University with bonobos, and had only just returned to Kinshasa for a conference. Though Sally Jewell Coxe didn't know Albert yet, she'd been involved with primatologist Sue Savage-Rumbaugh's programs, which were then being done at Georgia State, and had even driven Botamba to the Atlanta airport, paying his extra baggage fees so he could bring more home to his family.

At the conference in Kinshasa, Botamba gave a presentation about language studies with bonobos. Albert was in the audience when Botamba showed a video about Savage-Rumbaugh's work. Seeing it, he felt possibilities begin to open up, the sense that he might create a project that offered him not only autonomy but creative and intellectual stimulation. He'd grown up in forests where bonobos lived, and in 1974, his uncle had introduced the Japanese primatologist Takayoshi Kano to the village of Wamba. Albert

Empty Hands, Open Arms

knew that bonobos were a charismatic species, and watching the video, he found himself riveted. The folklore of Kokolopori said that men and bonobos once lived together, but he had never realized the extent of their intelligence. He felt his mind working, everything fitting together. He might once again be close to his family and community, to the nature he had loved as a child, and help Kokolopori.

He informed himself about conservation projects in Zaire, about the Central Africa Regional Program for the Environment (CARPE), an initiative launched by the United States Agency for International Development (USAID). He inquired about getting grants to work with bonobos, but his fellow Congolese at CARPE just talked endlessly. He even wrote a project proposal to work with aphasic children in Kinshasa using Savage-Rumbaugh's approach to language teaching, and sent it to her.

He and Savage-Rumbaugh began to correspond. He wrote to her that he was returning to Kokolopori and intended to observe bonobos in the forests. She'd initially accepted his aphasia project but decided that she would rather fund him to look for areas in Kokolopori where there were bonobos so that she could someday study them in the wild. She gave him $500 to do so.

As Albert returned to Kokolopori, first by riverboat on the Congo River and its tributaries, then making his way over the dirt trail through the forest on the back of a motorcycle, he recalled his father's words: that Albert would be the one to stay with his people. It was the first time he understood the statement as prophetic.

Albert explained the value of the forests for conservation to his family and friends in Kokolopori, the possibility of attracting international funding to protect wildlife. But they couldn't see how the forest could be of interest to those so far away. Équateur Province, especially this part of it, had always been among the most isolated areas in the country. Even compared to Djolu, Kokolopori was poor. Its villagers referred to themselves in Longando, the local language, as *bato ba mbusa bokele,* "the people at the back of the house."

For two years, Albert observed where bonobos lived in the forest. To survive, he planted cassava fields. The country was creeping up on the cataclysmic end to Mobutu's reign, and after Albert's first year, he couldn't find transportation to Befori, the town on the Maringa River, halfway to Mbandaka, where he could sell his produce. The next year he was able to get only nine bags of cassava to Befori's market. But as a result of his time in the forest, and of visiting the Japanese research camp in nearby Wamba, he better understood how the bonobos were studied, and he could sense his ideas coming together.

He returned to Kinshasa, bringing back information about bonobos for

Savage-Rumbaugh, as well as field reports from Wamba to send to Dr. Takeshi Furuichi, a Japanese bonobo researcher. Albert stayed with one of his older brothers who was in the military and who worked with Mobutu's son, Kongolo, a man whose ruthless tactics to keep power had earned him the nickname Saddam Hussein.

Kongolo Mobutu had been a longtime defender of his father's regime, all the while extorting money, spying on political opponents, siphoning off the country's wealth. His new company, la Société Zaïroise d'Importation et Exportation (SOZADIE), had a simple concept. Being Mobutu's son and a powerful military figure, he was exempt from paying taxes on anything entering or leaving the country, and he set up the business so that people could pay him to bypass both the usual laws and the bribes necessary to move merchandise.

Albert felt that he had no choice. Despite planting fields he'd earned virtually no money. Everyone was making concessions, working for corrupt officials, selling themselves in some way to survive in a country where theft was a way of life. Though Albert became the secretary general of SOZADIE, he also found a position at the Ministry of Energy, and began working in the Water Department just after the first of the two Congo Wars had begun.

When you learn about a family or a person's life in the Congo, you sense the politics and wars like the features of a landscape, distant mountains beyond which it is almost impossible to see who people once were. Even the army lootings in 1991 and 1993—euphemistically dubbed *les évènements,* "the events"—are often used by people to pin down a date, to recall when they last saw a relative. Overnight, in 1997, with the end of the First Congo War and more than twenty years after Mobutu changed the country's name, people would suddenly no longer be *Zaïrois* but *Congolais* again.

But though Mobutu's downfall came suddenly as a result of Rwanda's military intervention, the people of Kinshasa saw their neighboring country's claim to have removed Mobutu as ridiculous. The Kinois had been resisting him for years, and to address domestic unrest, he had begun to democratize. For an invasion to topple him when he was politically weak and dying of prostate cancer made no sense to them.

And yet the Congo Wars were among the most complicated in modern history, ethnic tensions in the eastern DRC mirroring those in Rwanda, where conflict between the Tutsis and Hutus hadn't stopped since the end of the colonial period. Though ethnic division between the two classes had been institutionalized under German colonization, it became even more rigid after Belgium took over Rwanda in 1916. The discourse around eugenics was at its height in the West, and the colonial occupants saw a superior race in the Tutsis, who were taller, with larger skulls and paler skin. The Belgians issued racial identification cards, effectively ending all social movement between groups.

Though Germany and Belgium had supported the Tutsi monarchy, in 1959 the Hutus took over, killing between 20,000 and 100,000 Tutsis and exiling 150,000 more into neighboring countries, among them the Congo. But the core group of Tutsis who in 1994 would conquer Rwanda fled, after the 1959 Hutu takeover, to Uganda. Unable to attain full rights as Ugandan citizens, many of the young men entered the army as soon as they came of age. In the process of helping Tanzania overthrow Ugandan dictator Idi Amin so that Uganda's current president, Yoweri Museveni, could take power in 1986, the Ugandan Tutsis honed their military skills.

In late 1990, the Rwandan Patriotic Army (RPA), the military branch of the Rwandan Patriotic Front (RPF), invaded Rwanda, running an insurgency campaign that the Hutus resisted with the help of Zaire and France. The struggle lasted until 1993, when a ceasefire and power-sharing government were put in place. But on April 6, 1994, the plane of the Rwandan president, Juvénal Habyarimana, a Hutu, was shot down, killing him. Within hours, the Hutus went on a rampage, beginning a genocide that claimed the lives of eight hundred thousand Tutsis and moderate Hutus. The RPA again made an offensive, using the chaos in Rwanda to its advantage. By July 4, they entered Kigali, Rwanda's capital, discovering a city that had been largely destroyed and that reeked of death.

Unable to retaliate or maintain order, the Hutu government fled to Zaire, taking the nation's wealth and military. Over two million citizens escaped across the borders of Rwanda. Between thirty and forty thousand soldiers and 850,000 refugees arrived in North Kivu, around Goma, 650,000 in South Kivu, 270,000 in Burundi, and 570,000 in Tanzania. The Congolese in Goma later recalled feeling that an entire country had implanted itself in their midst. North and South Kivu, the Congolese provinces bordering Rwanda and Burundi, already suffered from ethnic divides, and the arriving Hutus murdered local Tutsis to solidify their positions.

Since the end of the Cold War, Mobutu had become largely irrelevant to the West, but he saw in the refugees an opportunity and supported the Hutu leaders, selling them weapons. As the Hutu military trained and the UN struggled to feed refugee camps, the RPF repeatedly insisted that the *génocidaires*—those who had committed the genocide—be brought to justice, and that the Hutus be disarmed. They understood well how an exiled group could develop its military prowess and spend decades preparing for an invasion, just as they had.

If the international community failed to take clear action, it was because the

United States and France had conflicting interests. Whereas the United States finally wanted to support democracy in Zaire and remove Mobutu, France hoped to maintain its influence in the region. At the time Zaire was the world's largest producer of cobalt, the second or third of industrial diamonds, and the fifth of copper.

The RPA went on the offensive by pushing into Zaire, sweeping hundreds of thousands of refugees back into Rwanda even as others fled west into the jungles. In planning their invasion, the RPF enlisted rebel Congolese leaders. Rising quickly to prominence among them was Laurent-Désiré Kabila, who, during the Congo Crisis, had attempted to lead a communist revolution in the eastern Congo. Che Guevara, who had traveled to the Congo in 1965 to assist with the revolution, later wrote of Kabila's undisciplined ways and his lack of "revolutionary seriousness." Kabila had spent the last three decades in Tanzania, smuggling gold and timber while running a bar and brothel. He'd received international attention only when his rebel forces kidnapped four Western researchers from Jane Goodall's chimpanzee research camp in Tanzania, then ransomed them after subjecting them to deprivation and communist reeducation.

Kabila brought little more than his name to the invasion, which, backed by Rwanda and Uganda, swept across the country. Many Congolese were eager to join, and numerous soldiers defected to the new cause. The primary casualties were Hutu refugees, many of them women and children, their numbers unknown though thought to be in the tens of thousands. Kabila's forces were backed not only by Rwanda and Uganda but, to a much lesser degree, by Burundi, Zambia, Zimbabwe, Eritrea, Ethiopia, Angola, and the South Sudanese rebel army. Only the National Union for the Total Independence of Angola (UNITA), an Angolan rebel group, and Sudan offered Mobutu some aid. His army was in shambles, the soldiers and officers preferring to sell the very weapons with which they would soon be defeated.

Within little more than six months, the largely Rwandan-led rebel forces had captured Kinshasa. At the airport, Zaire's elite tried to pack luxury items into jets, leaving Mercedes and BMWs, as well as heaps of designer clothes and stereo systems, just off the runway. Others fled in boats across the river to Brazzaville.

As for Albert Lokasola, what little work he'd found was gone within months. Many of the ministers left. Kongolo Mobutu's import-export company was short-lived, and his last days in the country were spent racing through Kinshasa with a military unit. Having drawn up a list of five hundred of his father's opponents, Kongolo tried to hunt them down and kill them before he fled. Having escaped to Morocco, his father died a few months later, on the same day Kabila claimed the presidency. Kongolo died two years afterward in Monaco, possibly of AIDS.

Albert was not extravagant in his description of this time. He spoke of it quickly, and I had to repeat my questions often. Whereas he recounted with ease the stories of his childhood, of the elephant shrew and his excursion into the forest, he spoke fleetingly of Zaire's last days. Given few words and left mostly to silence, his *passage à vide* became all the more poignant, the empty pages of his life written with his nation's history.

Only when Kabila took power did the Congolese have a sense of hope, that the country might again resemble the productive state of Mobutu's early days. Like all the others searching for a stable livelihood, Albert applied for every job, contacted every NGO arriving in Kinshasa until his search for employment bore fruit, and he was hired as the secretary-general of the Red Cross in the DRC.

Perhaps unsurprisingly, Kabila proved to be much like his predecessor, and soon he began to alienate the countries that had brought him to power. It didn't take long for the newly renamed Congolese people to realize that their country would soon be torn apart again, this time by a war funded by the mineral wealth that had been both the Congo's blessing and its curse.

The vast exploitation that ensued made the projects that Albert would undertake with Sally Jewell Coxe all the more urgent. The civil war would displace entire populations, so that villages that had honored certain hunting taboos *depuis la creation*—"since creation," as the Congolese like to say— would suddenly see their new neighbors skinning and cooking bonobos after a hunt. The economy and infrastructure declined exponentially, and the forests were unable to sustain the great numbers of people taking refuge there, many of whom hunted *nyama*—"animals" and "meat" being the same word in Lingala—without regard for their impact. This set the stage for the difficult work BCI and their partners would face a few years later, a Congo where people were starving and wildlife was on the verge of eradication.

Sally Jewell Coxe

After nightfall, Sally and I sat outside in reclining chairs cut from sections of bamboo and lashed together with vines. The evening mist had almost lifted, the stars coming slowly into focus. Nearly two decades had passed since Sally's first visit to Équateur, and though she had done so much work with the Congolese that it was hard to keep track of, she emphasized BCI's network as its greatest achievement. The organization had built relationships across the country with Congolese of all walks of life. It was precisely this social web that had allowed BCI to do so much on a relatively small budget, and Sally illustrated this point by describing a boat wreck in August of 2010.

"That was already a difficult trip. We'd brought a film crew from Australian Broadcasting Corporation TV as well as Michael Werner, an American filmmaker. We had the usual logistical challenges. On a visit to Lingomo, we discovered that the sixty-foot bridge before the conservation site had seriously deteriorated. The logs were so shaky that we couldn't take the truck across. Our team set out looking for motorcycles in the nearby communities and returned after nightfall."

By the time they crossed the bridge, cobbled together from stacked and crossed logs covered with roughhewn planks, they were exhausted, stepping carefully and avoiding the gaps with the lights of the headlamps. A thunderstorm began as they tied their equipment to the motorcycles with strips of rubber cut from inner tubes. Each motorcycle held a driver and passenger, both wearing backpacks, and in the pouring rain, they slipped repeatedly on the slick red earth.

After the film crew left on a bush plane, BCI departed on the pirogues for Mbandaka, accompanied by Michael Werner. Both he and Sally had a tight schedule. He was getting married as soon as he returned to the United States, and Sally had a conference in Aspen, Colorado. During their time in the field, Sally had told him how relaxing the river trip would be, just as she said to me—how it was the vacation after the hard work in the reserve.

Pirogues are dugout canoes, in this case forty-five feet long and nearly four feet wide. Though each had its own outboard motor, they were attached side to side so that they traveled as a single unit. Every year, Sally told me, the boatmen had improved the way they rigged up the bamboo beds and the roof over them, and that year was no exception.

They set off on the Luo River, the water high, the current fast, and the boatmen watching for trees that had been swept into it. Malu Ebonga Charles—Le Blanc—commanded the boatmen. He'd grown up on the Congo and had been running pirogues along its vast network of tributaries for three decades. Normally, the group didn't travel at night. They would tie up at fishing camps to sleep, though this doubled the duration of the journey. This time, with the water so high and little risk of hitting sandbars, Le Blanc kept the boats traveling all night, he and the young men taking turns resting.

"Before I went to sleep," Sally told me, "I was lying in my bed, under my mosquito net, and I remember writing, 'Le Blanc has the eyes of a cat.' They were green, and he claimed he had good night vision. The night was so dark. You couldn't see the moon or stars, and the jungle came right down to the river. There was no shore to speak of, just dense undergrowth and vines.

"I woke up after midnight to a loud thud and the boatmen yelling, 'Mama Sally, Mama Sally! *Mai ezali kozinda bwato!*' I put my hand down and felt the rushing water."

The boat's outboard had caught on the branch of a sunken tree, its stern pulled under. As the men tried to break it free, the pirogue filled. The eleven passengers moved quickly, throwing everything of value into the good pirogue, and all that was heavy and unnecessary into the water: cassava and an extra outboard. The boatmen cut away the cords attaching the tarpaulin roof to the good pirogue, and threw it into the one that was sinking. Sally focused on the sat phone, her computer, and the Broadband Global Area Network (BGAN), a portable satellite Internet terminal the size of a briefcase. Michael Werner took his film equipment and the footage he'd collected. Among the passengers were two students on their way to Mbandaka for school. One, a young man, clutched an empty jerry can, and a boatman was trying to take it so he could tie it to the baggage, but the boatmen had forgotten to pack life preservers, and the student shouted that he couldn't swim and refused to give it up.

As soon as Sally climbed into the safe boat, she realized that the bag with the money was in the other one, and she went back. For a flotation device, she took her Therm-a-rest air mattress. The pirogue was almost underwater, pulling the good one with it. They were caught in the middle of the river, where the water was deepest, far from the shore. As the current dragged the pirogue under, the boatmen told everyone to grab on to something, that they were going to cut the ropes.

It's difficult to fathom the mass of a pirogue, each one carved from a towering tree and weighing well over a thousand pounds: solid, thick wood that won't splinter if it hits sunken logs or sandbars. The boatmen were afraid that once they cut the pirogue free, the good one, already tilted sharply toward the water, would flip. They brought their machetes down, the ropes popped, and the pirogue lurched up, flinging Sally, the student with the jerry can, and a boatman overboard. Michael Werner caught Sally's ankle, and the boatman swam back and got in, but the student was swept into the current and lost in the darkness.

The edge of the overloaded pirogue was barely above the surface. Slowly, Le Blanc turned it as they called out to the student. They steered in the direction of his voice, and Dieudonné, a boatman whose name means "God-given," jumped in and brought him back. Sally studied the shores, moving her headlamp's beam over the jungle, knowing that if they sank, they would have to swim to that virtual barricade that likely harbored snakes and crocodiles.

After another hour inching along the river, they found a fishing camp and pulled ashore. They built a fire to dry themselves, but all of the fuel barrels and jerry cans had fallen into the water, and Le Blanc, who'd never in all his years on the river had a boat sink, worried that if they didn't set out now, they wouldn't find any of the fuel. He told Sally and the other passengers to stay, then left on the pirogue with the boatmen. Sally had run out of sat phone credit, so she hooked the computer to the BGAN and sent a message to Michael and the BCI team in Washington, describing what had happened and asking them to contact the sat phone company and buy credit. One of the CREF scientists, Yangozeni Kumugo, was with her, and he gave her their GPS coordinates. In her email, she told Michael when she would turn on the sat phone, not wanting to use up its battery. Later, as she dried herself at the fire, she learned that just before the accident, Le Blanc had taken an hour to rest, his cat's eyes closed, and that one of the boatmen had dropped the spotlight into the river, so they were navigating with the weaker beams of flashlights.

Le Blanc and the boatmen returned around 4:00 a.m., not having found any of the fuel. They waited until dawn and set out again, this time to the sunken pirogue. They dislodged the outboard motor and tied the pirogues back together, then started asking fishermen if anyone had found fuel. Though a barrel turned up, it had filled with water. A villager told the boatmen that a man had salvaged a jerry can of gas, but when they located him, the man demanded fifty dollars, which they eventually paid.

They now had enough fuel to get them to Mompono, part of the Bonobo Peace Forest where BCI worked with another partner, the Congolese conservation group Protection de l'Écosystème et des Espèces Rares du Sud-Est de l'Équateur (PERSE). Michael had called BCI's Kinshasa offices from DC, and the Kinshasa team had contacted PERSE via the HF radio system that BCI had given them. One of PERSE's staff, Anatole, began riding his motorcycle on a path along the river, carrying a jerry can of gasoline and hoping to connect with them.

From DC, Michael was raising several thousand dollars in emergency funds. He knew how expensive fuel was in the Congo's hinterlands, but his primary concern was a group of armed tribesmen, the Enyele, who had fought the Congolese army a few months earlier, then seized Mbandaka Airport before being driven east into the forest. They were the remnants of an insurgent group whose fighting in 2009, near the border of Congo-Brazzaville, had resulted in over 160,000 displaced people. No one was sure how many Enyele were still in the forests, or where they were, but they could have been near the BCI team. Normally, the pirogues would pass unnoticed through the area, but news of stranded Westerners would spread quickly. One of Michael's friends kept telling him that they needed to get an evac team with military contractors.

"This was one of those times," Sally told me, "that illustrated the strength of our network. Our team had contacts and connections throughout Équateur, from Kokolopori to Kinshasa, and as soon as word went out, there were friends and partners ready to help us at every stop. We bought fuel in Mompono, just enough to get to Basankusu, the first major port on the way to Mbandaka. We had money wired and bought enough there to finish our trip. But to make it in time for Michael Werner's wedding, we had to go all night again. We had a car waiting in Mbandaka, right at the river's edge, and someone at the airport letting the airline know that we would arrive. We got there literally five minutes before we were supposed to catch our flight."

Listening to Sally speak, as we sat in chairs on a grassy section of the camp, I couldn't help but try to make sense of her from what she'd told me about her youth, her childhood passion for exploring the forest and climbing trees, or when, as a teenager, she read *Silent Spring*, Rachel Carson's account of the impact of pesticides not only on animals but also on humans. Books had given me my first desire to travel and understand other cultures, and I could picture her as a girl, reading her great-great-grandmother's diaries, seeing life in fin de siècle China. The fact that she had helped create an organization whose strength was its broad network and its inclusivity made me want to understand what in her was so drawn to people in this way. Her desire to know everyone came across in her openness. She would spend hours in conversation and could tell me about almost every person who visited the camp.

From her stories, I learned that her father, Joseph Wentworth Coxe III, a psychiatrist, shared her openness. She described him as charismatic, funny, and compassionate, a voracious reader whose agitated mind kept him up at night. He taught her the principle of service, that people should give their lives to something. He'd studied medicine at the University of Virginia and later read the complete works of Sigmund Freud when he was a navy surgeon in the Pacific during World War II. He'd lost his mother as a child and been physically abused by the housekeeper who raised him, and reading Freud, he began to comprehend the depth of his trauma. After the war, he became a psychiatrist and married Jane Jewell, a Boston native and Wellesley graduate handpicked by the National Security Agency straight out of college to work as a cryptanalyst. Sally's older sister was born in 1955, Sally in 1960.

Sally grew up in western North Carolina, her father having found work at Asheville's famed Highland Hospital, where Zelda Fitzgerald died in a fire in 1948. He'd taken the job because it was one of the few places that didn't rely on electroshock to treat schizophrenics. He preferred to speak with patients and understand what had disturbed their minds. Sally noticed the way he looked at people, as if really seeing them, understanding them without judging, and she wanted to have this patience to learn how others lived. He showed the same care with her and her sister, helping them with homework, discussing literature and philosophy. He also treated poor people in the community, and since Asheville was in the Jim Crow South, he kept a home office that was open to everyone.

But his own health, both mental and physical, declined when he was relatively young. A chain smoker, he developed emphysema, and in Sally's telling, I got the sense of a man who found release from perfectionism through his addictions. She described him as a Jekyll-and-Hyde alcoholic: intent on being the best person possible, though each time he broke down and drank, he became violent, unable to remember his actions the next day. When Sally was twelve, he died in an accident, having driven his car into a bridge abutment on the Interstate. He was sober at the time, and no one knew if he'd fallen asleep at the wheel or crashed on purpose.

In the years that followed, she decided that she would study psychology, that it would help her figure out her father and herself. But after she enrolled at Williams College, she became disillusioned with Western psychology and interested in religion, anthropology, poetry, and art. She loved reading Nietzsche, Freud, Jung, Derrida, and Mircea Eliade, as well as the spiritual texts of the Sufis and Hindus.

In 1982, when she graduated and returned to Asheville, she craved a clear direction. Unemployment was high, and the country's culture of materialism reflected nothing she valued. She saw a career counselor who told her that she was suited for advertising because of the combination of psychology, writing, and art in her background. She joined a small ad office in DC and, after three years, went freelance, working mostly with nonprofits. Though freelancing gave her time to travel the American Southwest, California, Mexico, and Central America, she wasn't satisfied.

In 1990, she received a freelance contract to work for the National Geographic Society. The shelves in her family's summer home in Maine had been filled with the magazine, and growing up she had spent days reading issues dating back to the early 1900s. She loved the idea of working with the natural world, and later, when the National Geographic Society announced an opening for a full-time copywriter, she applied in hopes of transitioning to the magazine and writing articles.

One of her assignments was to promote the book *The Great Apes: Between Two Worlds,* which contained Michael "Nick" Nichols's photos of chimpanzees, orangutans, and gorillas in both the wild and captivity, as well as Frans Lanting's images of bonobos. Captivated, Sally read book after book about great apes. She met with Jane Goodall and George Schaller, a field biologist who'd studied gorillas, but she found Dian Fossey's story most compelling: how she'd befriended a gorilla named Digit, and how he'd been killed—his head, hands, and feet cut off by poachers to sell to tourists in Nairobi. Fossey then gave up her ambitions for scientific research and devoted herself to gorilla conservation. She didn't relent, protecting them until she was killed with a machete, likely by poachers, though her murderers were never caught and theories abound.

But when Sally learned about bonobos—creatures so much like us, with so many qualities that might teach us about ourselves—she became obsessed. Everything she'd read until then associated human behavior with that of chimpanzees, focusing on territoriality, belligerence, and aggressive sexuality. Bonobos were gentler and more cooperative in their use of resources, and they lacked the sense of paternity that obsessed other great apes, humans included. For Sally, they exemplified the qualities that humans should emulate if we were to ensure our own survival.

All her life she'd been looking for something to which she could give herself. Bonobos resonated with her on all levels. She read about the Japanese primatologist Takayoshi Kano, who habituated them in the wild, and Sue Savage-Rumbaugh, who was working with them in captivity. But while she could read endlessly about the other great apes, very little had been written about bonobos.

She ended up telling Nick Nichols, the photographer whose images appeared in *The Great Apes: Between Two Worlds*, how bonobos fascinated her. She'd met him at the National Geographic Society offices, and he'd invited her to interview him at his home in Charlottesville, Virginia, and to see his collection of mountain gorilla photographs. The images inspired her, as did his conviction that the world needed to know how these animals lived in the wild, and how humans treated them. He'd done investigative projects, going into laboratories to photograph chimpanzees locked in tiny cages, operated on and injected with diseases, hooked to electrodes. His work conveyed to Sally the intelligence and compassion of apes, and how they suffered. His photographs of medical research disturbed her, as did the images of great apes abused and eaten in Africa, and his stories of the problems surrounding conservation. She worked with him for several months before she told him about her desire to quit her job and write about bonobos, to help them by telling their story, and he encouraged her.

Over the weeks in Kokolopori, Sally told me these stories in snippets, during breaks in work or delays, and when she and I spoke, it was rarely without interruption. People asked her questions, or a new face arrived in the camp so that, midsentence, she lifted a hand to wave and hurried to greet the person. Even two years before, during Skype interviews, the demands of the BCI office and calls from the Congo had interfered. She would be describing how she first learned of the great apes' critical situation, and how she knew that—given the Congo's population boom, its political instability and poverty—bonobos would be next in line for extermination; then she would pause, derailed by the thought of how much she had to do, and switch the conversation to the to-do list in her head. This happened often on our trip as well.

"I learned more about my own nature reading about great apes," she said, "than in years of psychology courses. In bonobos, I saw a creature so much like us, one that has learned to cooperate—the closest thing to us on the planet, mirroring a side of ourselves that we often ignore."

She explained how important bonobos' sexual fluidity is to their closeness and happiness, though scientists often reduce it to a means of resolving conflicts or defusing tension—largely, she believes, because of Western discomfort with sexuality. She told me that it has been easy for humans to align ourselves with chimpanzees, as if we are pardoning male violence, saying it is natural, especially after a century with so many wars. She found the fact that coalitions of female bonobos prevent male aggression not only inspiring but important for people to understand. After all, what we can conceive of is often what we create. In focusing on attributes that we identify as masculine, we blind ourselves not only to how else we might live, but to other aspects of our nature: that a human from almost any part of the planet can travel to another culture and integrate. We have given little study to the wonder of our cooperative nature, of our ability to accept strangers or to be included, to adapt and, despite the risks, live among people with different histories and values.

Sally began thinking about how she could work with bonobos. At National Geographic, she knew Mary Smith, the photo editor who'd been the society's liaison with Louis Leakey's "ape ladies": Jane Goodall, Dian Fossey, and Birutė Galdikas. Leakey, whose work in paleontology and fossil discoveries in Tanzania changed the theory of human evolution, had started all three women in their field studies, believing women to be better suited to working with great apes since they were less likely to incite aggression. Along with Mary Ann Harrell, the National Geographic Society book editor, Mary Smith encouraged Sally. But Nick Nichols's words and experience resonated most, the idea that a young man from Alabama could creatively inspire people to see nature and great apes in a different light.

"All of my interests coalesced. I had a complete redirection of my life. I was very fortunate to be able to talk with people like Mary Smith, the end of the old guard. I was so lucky to be at National Geographic at the time that I was, with the veterans who had been there since the early days of wild great ape studies."

But it was Nichols who suggested that Sally work with Sue Savage-Rumbaugh. Though Sally loved National Geographic, after speaking with him, she decided to leave.

All that summer, Sally worked with the bonobos at Georgia State. Savage-Rumbaugh allowed her more access to the bonobos than was usual, noticing that she understood them, clearly adapting to their culture and even moving like them.

Sally spent many days in the university's forest. She played with Kanzi and Panbanisha, and they communicated with her using the plastic keyboards with lexigrams, though she saw that they understood more English than they had lexigrams to produce. They were also attuned to nonverbal cues—body language, the movement of her eyes. Bonobos use eye-contact more than do chimps and gorillas, with whom eye-contact is impolitic and often dangerous.

Empty Hands, Open Arms

Sally was fascinated by the bonobos' awareness and how, after the rare conflict, they would make peace. Though they'd briefly scream to voice their rage, they would then make up by having sex or rubbing genitals. Despite their strength—at least five times that of a grown man—they showed restraint. Their perceptiveness also impressed her, how they watched not only each other but humans, sensing moods and responding to them, trying to soothe or placate or be joyous.

Increasingly, she understood why Savage-Rumbaugh had worked to push the line between what was considered apelike and what was considered human. Jane Goodall had started this redefinition, showing that humans, who until then had been defined by tool use, shared this behavior with chimpanzees. She revealed similarities between human and chimpanzee societies: the experience of grief and love, the forging of strong interpersonal bonds. Savage-Rumbaugh pushed the question to one of language, of communication through symbols not only of concrete needs, but of emotions and ideas.

In the process of playing and speaking with them, Sally learned that the bonobos had dramatically different personalities. Panbanisha, Kanzi's half sister, was deep, observant, with a sense of still waters in her eyes. Kanzi was more affable, more of a showman, but he also cared for his siblings, especially the control subjects who didn't receive the training he did. He would take their hands to show them how to use the keyboard.

Panbanisha was five or six then, and she and Sally explored the forest, Panbanisha riding piggyback. Researchers left food stashes in various locations, and Panbanisha knew each one, first pointing to strawberries on her sheet of lexigrams, or cantaloupe, then directing Sally to that cache. They also played hide-and-seek, and when a researcher called, "Panbanisha, where are you?" Sally and the little bonobo sat, looking at each other, eyes wide. Sally felt like a child again, she and her best friend playing in the forest, speaking as much with words as with gazes.

Often, Panbanisha groomed Sally. She broke a twig, made it sharp, and traced it under each of Sally's fingernails. Then she bit off the ends of the nails. She inspected every bug bite and scratch, and Sally had to tell her each one was okay before Panbanisha moved on to the next.

Kanzi also groomed Sally, though he once peeked down her shirt, first looking up into her eyes to ask permission, in what seemed a gentlemanly manner. The difference between their species didn't appear to bother him, and when he was older, he would occasionally pleasure himself while looking at ordinary women's magazines, particularly turned on by the models in fur coats. But flirting was rare. For bonobos, females dominate, and Kanzi knew the hierarchy. His adoptive mother, the wild-born Matata, couldn't communicate well with humans, but he obeyed her. His abilities—from language, to building fires and cooking, to chipping knives like those from the Stone Age—didn't change that.

The bonobos were joyful by nature, and Sally had sensed that they loved to be happy and play. She felt sorry for Kanzi, that a creature with uninhibited lovemaking in his genes had no female companion. Like humans, bonobos have a strict incest taboo. But because his father had been used for breeding and his genes were overrepresented among zoo bonobos, Kanzi was given a vasectomy by those in charge of captive breeding. Over the years, however, the vasectomy failed. At the Great Ape Trust in Iowa, he fathered his first child, the baby Teco, whom Savage-Rumbaugh has been raising, further exploring the lines between human and bonobo culture.

But all that miraculous summer, Sally was planning to do an article—and eventually a book—about her experiences, believing she could help bonobos by writing about them.

"I was doing it as a participant observer," she told me, "thinking that I was going to bring the story back to *National Geographic*. It didn't work out that way, but I did get to bring *National Geographic* to Kokolopori twenty years later."

Though BCI would take the *National Geographic* team into the field in 2011, the work that would lead to this was just starting. After that summer with the bonobos, Sally joined the Bonobo Protection Fund. Founded by Sue Savage-Rumbaugh and Takayoshi Kano, it was the only existing organization focused on bonobo protection in the wild, though under the statutes of Georgia State, it was limited to research and education. Working with the BPF, Sally started the Pro-Bonobo Newsletter and raised more than $100,000 for the organization.

"That summer, Sue and I talked about visiting Zaire. Having spent so much of her life with bonobos, she'd dreamed of seeing them in the wild. It was my dream, too, and we decided to visit the research site at Wamba, where Dr. Kano had first habituated wild bonobos in the mid-seventies. We arranged to go with a group of Japanese researchers led by Dr. Takeshi Furuichi, one of Dr. Kano's protégés, and a film crew from NHK TV in Japan."

Sally earned money for the trip by doing freelance copywriting and began to study Lingala with Alden Almquist, who would eventually join BCI's board. An anthropologist who'd grown up in the Congo, he'd worked at the Library of Congress as a sub-Saharan Africa research analyst and literary examiner for over two decades. By the time she left for the DRC, she had a good base in the language, but a few months before her departure, the Rwandan genocide began. During the hundred days beginning on April 6, 1994, eight hundred thousand Tutsis and moderate Hutus would be massacred—most of them killed with machetes. The trip to the Congo suddenly seemed far more dangerous.

Sally had a college friend whose father had served in Vietnam alongside Brigadier General William E. Stevens, one of the first African-American generals in the air force. Stevens had a master's in national security affairs and African studies, worked at the Pentagon, and later, after leaving the military, would join the Africa-America Institute, an organization that fostered education in Africa. He'd been stationed in Africa on and off for decades, and he counseled Sally. He advised her to take three hundred American one-dollar bills, which back then were still accepted in the Congo, and keep them hidden for emergencies. If she was in trouble, she could show only small bills to buy help.

Well into the night before she left, she wrote copy to earn a little extra as her friends packed her bags and weighed them on a fish scale. Her bonobo habit had already been expensive, and this trip would cost her an additional $10,000. But once on the plane, she went back to studying Lingala and continued to do so after reaching Nairobi and flying into Bunia, a city in Zaire near the Ugandan border. Though the First and Second Congo Wars have since devastated Bunia, leaving it in a state of militia infighting over control of its gold mines, in the early 1990s it was quiet. The only place to stay, there as well as at Sally's next stop, in Nyankunde, was with Protestant missionaries.

These were the final years of Mobutu's regime, the country's economy in free fall, its remaining infrastructure disintegrating. Sally had traveled in rural Costa Rica and Mexico, but the poorest places she'd encountered there were far more developed than what she saw now. Even Bunia and Nyankunde were more developed than Wamba, where Takayoshi Kano had started his work twenty years earlier, deep in Équateur and less than sixty miles from Kokolopori.

Daily, Sally gave classes on the importance of the rainforest and had the children of Wamba teach her Lingala. She befriended two half sisters, Maki and Francine, who explained much about the Bongandu's culture. She accompanied them to church, to the river to wash clothes, or to their homes, learning to prepare local dishes and *fufu*—a staple food made by boiling cassava, then pounding it into balls the size of bread rolls that are eaten with sauces.

Each morning, at four o'clock, she went into the forest with Furuichi and the trackers. She spent her days with the villagers, making friends, perfecting her Lingala, and recording the folktales about bonobos that formed the basis of the Bongandu's hunting taboo. In one, a man climbs a tree to get honey but drops his rope and has no way down. When a bonobo comes along, the man is afraid, thinking the bonobo will throw him to the earth. But the bonobo turns and motions for the man to climb on his back, then carries him down. Months later, in the village, when the crops are ready to be harvested, the bonobos come out of the forest to eat sugarcane. The angry villagers throw a net over them, planning to kill them, but the man whom the bonobo saved picks up the edge and lets them escape. He tells his people how he was saved and makes them promise never to harm a bonobo again. This was one of many such tales, others describing bonobos and men living side by side, lost children who were led back to their villages by bonobos, or a man who left his wife alone and a bonobo who took his place as the head of the family.

Ever since Sally had fallen in love with bonobos, she'd followed her instinct and passion, knowing that once she'd learned enough, she would understand how she could help. Now, the pieces were coming together. She loved the rainforest and its people. It recalled her childhood, summers spent climbing trees, swimming in ponds. She wanted to test her limits and see what she could create and give back to the world.

She knew that she had to learn as much as possible, to speak Lingala fluently and understand the culture. The Bongandu were proud, and they spoke of the forests with a sense of authority. The forest was the source of their livelihood; their entire cosmology derived from it, spirits and mystery and sustenance, the forces of nature against which they balanced their lives. Conservation would require a delicate approach here—an understanding of the people, and the ability to listen.

On Sally's last day in Wamba, she went into the forest with the head tracker, Nkoy Batalumbo. She'd arranged with the village women to prepare a meal that she could share with him, and once there, they ate together. Seeing this, the bonobos came the closest that they had during the entire trip.

When Sally arrived back in the United States, she was already thinking about her return to Zaire. She continued with the Bonobo Protection Fund, but its meetings were contentious. She was learning that the human side of the bonobo world was rife with conflict. When it comes to chimpanzees, Jane Goodall will be forever in the minds of people, as is true of Dian Fossey with gorillas, or Birutė Galdikas with orangutans. But who would be the Jane Goodall of bonobos? Whose name would be attached to them, as their emissary in the human world? When resources are newly discovered, there is often a race to exploit them, and the same holds true in the field of science. With bonobos, there was room to do new studies and make a name.

"It was never my goal to be the next Jane Goodall," Sally told me. "I've often talked about the Jane Goodall syndrome as being at the root of much of the conflict between the female scientists. People thought that was what I was trying to be, but I wanted to unify people, to make a cooperative, unified force for bonobos."

In 1996, she planned her second trip to Zaire, selling most of her furniture for additional funding. She hadn't fleshed out her idea. Her vision of her work there was open-ended. She would meet people and learn how the country worked. But as she was preparing to leave, the First Congo War broke out. She waited, hoping it would be brief, that she could go soon, but nearly five years passed before she was able to depart. By then, millions of people had died, and thousands of bonobos had been slaughtered for bushmeat.

Africa's Great War

The wars that frustrated the efforts of both Sally and Albert received little of the world's attention and were later overshadowed by the September 11, 2001, attacks, the invasion of Afghanistan, and the buildup to the Iraq War. With Rwanda's support, Laurent-Désiré Kabila captured Kinshasa in May 1997, but while the country hungered for democracy and change, their new leader would prove to be a relic of an old world order.

Not surprisingly, Kabila quickly suspended the activities of political parties, announcing that he would rule by decree until the adoption of a new constitution. He declared that the transitional period would last only two years, but most saw him as reenacting Mobutu's role: appointing his cronies to draft a new constitution; arresting political opponents, journalists, NGO leaders, and human rights advocates; and having many of them beaten and whipped.

In *Dancing in the Glory of Monsters: The Collapse of the Congo and the Great War of Africa,* UN peacekeeper Jason Stearns questions Kabila's heavy-handed approach, asking, "Why did he squander the initial goodwill with such squabbles?" He explains that though Kabila was viewed as a liberator, his weak position caused him to lash out—that, having come to power in a rebellion coordinated and funded by Rwanda and Uganda, he "felt like the majordomo in a house owned and lived in by others."

Despite their relief at being freed from Mobutu, many Congolese quickly began to see the Rwandans as occupiers, Kinshasa's population chafing at the sight of foreign soldiers in its streets. Kabila feared being perceived as a puppet, and to remain president, he turned against his allies. On July 14, 1998, he replaced his Rwandan chief of staff, James Kabarebe, with a Congolese, and soon thereafter ordered all foreign military to leave the country, immediately flying out his remaining Rwandan military advisors.

Again, ethnic tensions in the Kivu Provinces flared. The very Congolese Tutsis who had fought so hard to remove Mobutu now feared for their safety. When Kabila, needing a loyal army, began funding the same Hutu military that had carried out the Rwandan genocide, the counterattack came quickly. The Rassemblement Congolais pour la Démocratie (RCD) formed and took the Kivus with the support of Rwanda, Uganda, and Burundi. James Kabarebe hijacked three planes and flew them full of shock troops to the DRC's Kitona Air Base, on the Atlantic coast. He cut off electricity to Kinshasa and would have taken the capital had Kabila not convinced Zimbabwe, Namibia, Angola, Chad, Libya, and the Sudan to help him.

The conflict that ensued involved a large part of the continent. South Africa brokered peace talks that failed, and the war quickly became about the Congo's mineral wealth, particularly as the global market for coltan was booming in lockstep with the popularity of handheld electronics. Rwanda and Uganda sold the Congo's coltan to US and Chinese companies, and diamond, gold, and copper smuggling were rampant. When Rwandan and Ugandan forces turned against each other in Kisangani in June 2000, their crossfire killing 760 civilians, injuring nearly 1,700, as well as damaging and destroying schools, businesses, and thousands of homes, their Congolese allies realized that the struggle no longer had anything to do with removing Kabila from power.

The Second Congo War was one of the greatest acts of looting in modern history, and while the World Bank labeled it a civil war, the UN acknowledged the detrimental role of foreign powers. The Congolese political scientist Georges Nzongola-Ntalaja calls it the war of "partition and plunder," and the evidence supports this description. As Dena Montague writes in "Stolen Goods: Coltan and Conflict in the Democratic Republic of the Congo," "Between late 1999 and late 2000 the Rwandan army alone reaped revenues of at least $20 million a month" from the sale of coltan, even though the mineral was not present in their own territory.

In many ways, the Second Congo War was the culmination of the country's long history of exploitation. It's hard to imagine a grimmer scenario: a military that has been poorly paid for decades fighting alongside halfhearted foreign soldiers with no personal stake in the Congo's future. Their only motivation was the wealth they could extract. The common soldier stole all that he could carry, but at higher levels, militia leaders enslaved villages, setting them to work digging coltan and selling it to foreign commanders. Agricultural produce, livestock, automobiles, appliances, and equipment stolen from the Congo poured into Rwanda, Uganda, Angola, and Zimbabwe, among other countries. In 2000, as Jason Stearns writes, the price of coltan soared "with heightened demand for cell phones and the Christmas release of a Sony PlayStation console." The price of tantalum—refined coltan—rose from approximately $10 to $380 per kilo. Copper prices increased sharply in 2001 because of the needs of the industrializing East. Even as Kabila was making desperate international deals selling minerals and diamonds to fund his military, the Rwandans and Ugandans were flying cargo jets out of the Congo full of the same.

Coupled with this pillage on the scale of King Leopold's was massive degradation of the Congo's natural heritage. Militias and soldiers cut down forests to make and sell charcoal, and destroyed habitat to extract minerals. They hunted for food and ran bushmeat markets. The Congolese were the victims of all soldiers; a military force's allegiance was irrelevant. Soldiers ate the people's food, stole their belongings, and raped women in many places where they were stationed. To survive, the Congolese had no choice but to hunt. Bushmeat became the staple, villagers moving deeper into forests, setting up traps, selling what they could. Areas known for their abundance of wildlife became empty overnight, with only the rare bird or small mammal surviving in the forests.

In January 2001, one of Laurent-Désiré Kabila's child-soldier bodyguards shot and killed him. There were many possible reasons, among them Kabila's decision to execute a commander to whom the child soldiers had been faithful, though a number of theories hinged on international conspiracies as well as Kabila's duplicity and refusal to introduce a democratic constitution.

A committee of military leaders nominated his son, Joseph Kabila, to take his place, believing they could control him. But once he assumed office, the younger Kabila set about consolidating his power and ending the war. He met with President Paul Kagame of Rwanda, and within the DRC, he laid the groundwork for a power-sharing government. He removed from authority men he saw as a threat to his government and the peace process. The West supported him, calling him one of a new generation of African politicians. In recent years, however, and especially since the heavily contested 2011 election, many fear that he will never become the leader they expected and hoped for.

The war officially ended in December 2002, but while a transitional government was formed on July 18, 2003, conflicts continued in the Kivus as well as in the Ituri region, in the northeast of the DRC, where it borders Uganda. The damage was long lasting, and the casualties from 1998 to 2007, mostly as a result of disease and starvation, were as high as 5.4 million. Approximately forty-five thousand are still dying from the effects of the war each month.

In Djolu territory, villagers described how soldiers removed wires from the few buildings that had them, taking light bulbs, sockets, and switches, stripping people of clothing, and raping girls of ten or eleven. Though the government remained in power here, the people, as elsewhere, fled into the forests, sustaining themselves with mushrooms, grubs, caterpillars, and bushmeat. Their cassava fields, harvested by soldiers, weren't replanted, so that after the war, there was no regular food source.

In DC, Sally concentrated her efforts on the Bonobo Protection Fund. She traveled within the US for its board meetings, writing copy to cover her expenses and visiting Sue Savage-Rumbaugh, Kanzi, and Panbanisha often, first in Georgia and later in Iowa. As Sally tried to understand how she could bring together what she'd learned in the Congo—about the needs of the people and their relationship to bonobos and the forest—with BPF's activities, she realized that BPF's mandate was too limiting. It didn't allow for the sustainable livelihood projects and community building necessary to promote conservation. Thinking back to the people she had met in Wamba, she understood that humans had to see themselves as part of the ecosystem. There had to be an explicit exchange, one based not on exploitation of the forest but on the people's protection of it in return for jobs and new sources of livelihood.

In 1997, on a night when the book tour for Frans de Waal's *Bonobo: The Forgotten Ape* came to the National Zoo in Washington, DC, and Sally was handing out literature for the BPF, she met several people who would become founding members of BCI, among them Alison Mize, the manager of the zoo's bookstore. Mize contacted her afterward, and they agreed that the Bonobo Protection Fund was too limiting. In 1998, they created the Bonobo Conservation Initiative. Its mission was to work in the spirit of bonobo cooperation to provide a network of collaborative action to protect the bonobos and their habitat, while empowering the Congolese to take the lead in doing conservation work and community organizing for protected areas.

Sally hosted meetings, inviting anthropologists, economists, and ecologists to look at how to save both an individual species and the Congo rainforest as a whole. They discussed engaging with the cultural values of local people and building an economy that would depend on bonobos. It soon became clear that unless they could harness the will of the Congolese, the bonobos would vanish. Sally considered how to expand on cultural taboos against bonobo hunting and teach the people that hunting and selling bonobos was illegal. If conservation could bring cash flow, the people would see the value of protecting wildlife, and if they were given the means to pursue an education in conservation, they would gain prestige and their local expertise would benefit the conservation effort.

In 1999, Sally traveled to Europe and Japan to continue her education and invite the few bonobo researchers to participate in BCI's efforts. She wanted to involve as many people as possible and thereby increase the available knowledge about bonobos and conservation. The most important connection she made was with Takayoshi Kano. She stayed with him in Japan, and he became the honorary chair of BCI's advisory council. Sally was still torn between writing about bonobos and trying to make the story she wanted to write happen. Together she and Kano went over his collection of folktales and signed an agreement to co-author a book about Congolese bonobo folklore. She copied his notebooks of folktales told by the people of Wamba since the mid-1970s, as well as cassette recordings of their stories.

Back in DC, Sally met everyone she could from the Congo, getting to know members of the Congolese diplomatic and expat community. She was excited about her work and wanted to learn from them as well as to share the importance of her project—of bonobos and their habitat.

BCI advisor John Scherlis told me that BCI's staff and partners had raised awareness of bonobos in the DRC, in its national, provincial, and local governments, in its ministries, and in its private sector. He pointed out that Sally had done the same in DC, "among the Congolese diaspora, with whom BCI has a very close relationship—unlike any other conservation NGO." A USAID white paper corroborates John's observation, explaining how conservation organizations can increase their effectiveness by networking and partnering with African diaspora communities. The report cites BCI for its "tremendous success" in doing just this and suggests that BCI's work alone could be the subject of a case study.

Sally's vision was to have BCI build grassroots support for conservation while also doing the "top down" work that Karl Ammann described as essential for conservation's long-term survival. She was educating the Congolese political elite who circulated in and out of the United States, many of whom knew little or nothing about bonobos, and though it might appear that she was far from creating political pressure, she was building relationships and social capital. Contrary to the view of politics that sees leverage and even threats as necessary to force negotiations, Sally's focus was on mutual respect, which has by and large facilitated her work in the DRC.

As the war raged on, BCI raised money to support Claudine André, a Belgian conservationist who had grown up in the Congo and founded Lola ya Bonobo, the world's only bonobo sanctuary, which took in orphaned infants confiscated from traders who were selling them as pets. BCI also produced radio shows that would be aired in the DRC. Reports described massive quantities of bushmeat feeding the various military forces, and to counter this, BCI prepared broadcasts. Using the folktales that she and Takayoshi Kano had gathered, Sally worked with Congolese in DC to make recordings asking people not to hunt bonobos. She was able to get the thirty-minute shows, which consisted of a mix of music interspersed with legends, broadcast on both the Congo's eastern and western fronts.

She began planning the trip to Kinshasa that had been delayed by the outbreak of the Second Congo War. No matter how she explained her passion to her friends and family—telling them that it was spiritual, that she felt the need to do something more meaningful, to take risks and make sacrifices—they were afraid for her. Millions were dying in the Congo, the little news that made its way out describing mass rape, the rampant spread of HIV, and the enslavement of the people to exploit and smuggle minerals. In the eyes of the West, the entire Congo seemed a hopeless bloodbath.

Sally received a grant from the National Geographic Society's Expeditions Council to return with the Japanese to Wamba and see how many bonobos had survived the wars. The grant was designed to set the stage for the visit of a *National Geographic* team who would write a story, and the project for which Sally received her grant was conceived in three parts, with three separate expeditions culminating in Dr. Kano's return to Wamba.

BCI also received a grant to do a pre-feasibility study for protected areas for bonobos. The donor was the Global Conservation Fund, endowed by Gordon Moore to create new protected areas around the world, and administered by Conservation International (CI). Russell Mittermeier, CI's president, exhorted the BCI team to think big, to assess the prospects and plan for the largest reserve possible. Sally woke up one morning with the idea of a Bonobo peace park. The Congo then appeared as if it might break into three countries—the Uganda-aligned north, the Rwanda-aligned central east, and the government held south and west—and the best way to keep the bonobo habitat intact would be a peace park, a protected area sited to include contiguous parts of more than one country. That bonobos might serve as a symbol of peace in a war-torn region also rang true. The return to Wamba would be just the first step in gathering information for the future Bonobo Peace Forest. But with war continuing and the national infrastructure in shambles, a year of planning and networking in both the Congo and the United States would be essential to get the team there safely.

Since 1994, Sally had remained in contact with Brigadier General William Stevens, and in 1999, he'd become chairman of BCI's board. He introduced her to the DRC's ambassador to the United States and offered to assist with security for the National Geographic expedition and accompany her to

Empty Hands, Open Arms

Kinshasa. Through BCI's board member Zihindula Mulegwa, known as Z, she arranged a meeting for herself and General Stevens with President Joseph Kabila. She'd met Z, a part-time pastor and journalist with a degree in conflict resolution, at the Congolese Pentecostal church in Arlington, Virginia, and he'd told her that he and Joseph Kabila were friends. When Kabila took power, he requested that Z return to the DRC and become the presidential spokesperson. By then, Z had been on BCI's board for over two years.

Sally and General Stevens arranged to fly to Kinshasa to meet with Kabila, but the day she was supposed to leave, in June 2001, one of her close friends was killed in a motorcycle accident. Sally missed her flight and arrived late in Kinshasa. Stevens and Z had met with Kabila and received an enthusiastic reception. Months later, when Sally returned to Washington, the Congolese ambassador would request her aid in preparing the first public reception for Kabila in the United States.

In the DRC, Sally began setting up the National Geographic expedition, hiring BCI's first employee, Jean-Marie Benishay, a young man who'd written his university thesis on bonobo social structure. Her primary Congolese partner for the trip was Dr. Mwanza Ndunda, then director general of the Congolese government's ecological research institute, CREF. Unlike other protected areas, which were administered by the ICCN (the government's park service) and the Ministry of the Environment, Wamba was a scientific reserve, under the jurisdiction of the Ministry of Scientific Research and legally administered by CREF as part of the Luo Scientific Reserve.

Mwanza had devoted his life to conservation, but the chaos and corruption of the Mobutu years and the ensuing wars had frustrated his ambitions. He studied biology and conservation at the University of Kisangani before receiving a scholarship to do a PhD in the USSR. He recalls arriving in Moscow in December and almost getting back on the plane to go home, but he stayed, doing his research in Moldova, learning Russian, and writing his dissertation—in Russian—on species reintroduction after he successfully reacclimatized Japanese deer. This was in the late sixties and early seventies, and to support himself, he would travel to West Germany and buy blue jeans, then sell them in Chisinau; a few pairs allowed him to study for months.

After his return to the Congo, he translated his dissertation into French and was hired to work with Japanese researchers studying gorillas in the Kivus. He went to Japan twice for training and colloquia before becoming the general director of CREF and being stationed in Équateur, where he worked with both Kano and Furuichi, returning on several occasions to Japan. But under

Mobutu, CREF's funding never arrived. He and his researchers were barely able to live off their salaries, and the moneys allotted to science were taken by corrupt bureaucrats. The situation became much worse during the wars, years that he spent fishing and planting cassava so that he could feed his family. With the country reunited, his goal was to build CREF into the scientific institution it was meant to be, and given BCI's mandate to develop local leadership and resources, Sally saw CREF not only as essential for the 2002 National Geographic trip but as the future backbone of operations in the Congo. They had the personnel to do what was most needed: survey the forests and determine where the bonobos were.

Those who met Sally on her first trip back to Kinshasa were struck by her tenacity, the way she spoke with everyone, explaining the importance of bonobos and the rainforests, a topic that seemed surreal with the country on the verge of collapse. Sally and the BCI team worked to get the government's approval for the National Geographic expedition and met with WorldSpace Satellite Radio to discuss the potential of Radio Bonobo, a multidisciplinary program she hoped to launch.

BCI had determined that the best approach in the DRC would be to use established networks to educate people. The two strongest influences there are music and the Catholic Church. Sally managed to set up a bonobo commission within the church and educated priests about conservation, resulting in the DRC's Congress of Catholic Bishops's decision to formally back BCI. Popular musicians exerted a comparable influence on the culture. The Congolese respected them, and Sally worked toward producing a radio program in which musicians would sing of the natural heritage of Équateur, using folklore to remind people of their ancestral commitment to protecting bonobos. The broadcasts also discussed health issues, from the dangers of eating apes and disease transmission, to sanitation, malaria, and HIV prevention.

The cost of working within the DRC, of making connections and hiring people to go into the field, and getting materials into Équateur, was exorbitant. The Japanese research camp in Wamba was occupied by DRC government soldiers who hunted in the nearby forests and harassed the villagers, and Sally had to find a way to remove them. And yet she was going broke. She knew that she had to engage fully with the challenge that she was taking on with BCI, and she sold off the last of her stock portfolio even as she applied for grants.

"I don't think I've ever doubted the project," she told me. "It kept me going. It didn't feel as if it was just me. There were so many connections. One of my favorite lines is from W. S. Merwin's 'Provision': 'I will take with me the emptiness of my hands / What you do not have you find everywhere.' That has been my experience. Things and people just kept showing up. Every time I thought that there was no way to go on, something happened."

This was during the first phase of the Central African Regional Program for the Environment (CARPE) under USAID, and the focal point for CARPE in Kinshasa was Evelyn Samu, the Congolese woman whose home I stayed at during my time in Kinshasa. She had organized a conference on protecting biodiversity in times of war, and as a result, Sally heard about her.

"It's important to point out," Evelyn told me when we spoke in her Kinshasa home, "that at that time people didn't know much about bonobos. We talked about chimpanzees. We talked about mountain gorillas. But the person who came, aside from Claudine André, who was taking in orphaned baby bonobos—yes, she talked about them—but the person who really talked about bonobos in their natural habitat was Sally."

Sally and Evelyn became friends, and Evelyn gave Sally a space in her office. Later, when Sally ran out of money, Evelyn let her stay in her house.

"But the man I was seeing at the time," she recalled, "he was convinced that Sally worked for the CIA. 'See,' he would tell me, 'look at her. She's carrying all of that camera gear. Do you really think she's here for apes? Who's she working for? What's this organization—BCI? It doesn't even exist. There's nobody involved with it. She has to be CIA. You need to be careful with her. Get her out of your house. Get rid of her.'"

Evelyn hesitated, her features chiseled and aristocratic, her gaze direct.

"At first I didn't believe him, but then I thought about it. There were almost no Americans left in Kinshasa, and Sally had appeared out of nowhere. She even spoke Lingala. I'd believed she was there to work with bonobos, but how could I know? And her story about being broke. Maybe she wasn't really broke. Americans weren't known for going broke in Kinshasa. So maybe she'd used that as an excuse to get close to me. I couldn't imagine what the CIA might want with me, but those were strange times, and during the war, anything seemed possible."

Records suggest how strange life in Kinshasa must have been. Mobutu's regime had collapsed, the elite fleeing with luxury items amassed over decades, and Laurent-Désiré Kabila had arrived, a rebel and smuggler who knew nothing about running a country. As for the CIA, it had long had a presence in the Congo. The country's natural resources had always received the attention that its people did not, and the Congolese knew that most foreigners were there for the diamonds and gold.

Even in Kokolopori, people were often wary, asking if I was really there to see bonobos. At one point, a teenage boy stepped from the shadow of the *paillote* near our hut and held out a copper ingot. I took it, the chunk of metal easily weighing ten pounds. He told me that he found it while digging in his garden and asked if I wanted to buy it. The men who usually lingered in the *paillote* all watched, eyes narrowed, waiting for my response, and I called to Marcel, who tromped out of the hut in his rubber boots. He towered over the boy and asked a string of questions in Lingala, then turned, snatched the copper, and went back to the hut.

"What was that about?" I asked him a few minutes later.

"*Ce garçon?*" he said, "that boy? He doesn't own the copper. I'll give it to the chief later. The boy brought it just to see if maybe you're not really here for the bonobos. Everyone is suspicious. They still have the old way of thinking. When a new person comes from outside, they want to see if he's really here to dig up the land and steal the copper and gold, because those are the stories the Congolese tell about foreigners."

In light of this—that even in 2012, the Congolese were worried about being exploited, having their land dug up or their forests cut down—I had no difficulty imagining the reception Sally must have had, arriving in wartime Kinshasa on a shoestring budget and trying to advocate for a virtually unknown species of great ape when most people were still concerned about the RCD rebels and Rwandan military renewing its push west and taking the capital.

Eventually, though, Evelyn Samu relinquished her doubts, realizing that Sally was untiring and clearly working for the sake of bonobos. But Evelyn's story wasn't unusual. The Mobutu years had left the Congolese with an ingrained skepticism and the knowledge that anything was possible. If their leader could build Versailles in the middle of the jungle, fly in flowers and shellfish daily on Air France flights chartered for each particular item while the population starved, why wouldn't a lone American woman who spoke Lingala have been trained by the CIA? Even Z had his doubts at first, confessing that he also wondered if Sally was CIA. Still, he helped her, waiting for the moment when she might ask more of him, or question him on other issues.

Given the suspicion in the country and the degree to which the people had been exploited, only Sally's decision to focus on building relationships allowed her to win their trust. The relationship that she would cultivate with Mwanza would create support for BCI in the Congolese scientific community. Even more important was the alliance she would establish with Albert, whom she first met when Furuichi recommended him to help clear

Empty Hands, Open Arms

the landing strip in Djolu, a job that required taking the necessary supplies in boats up the river.

By then Albert was living in Kinshasa, though he had been forced to move frequently during the early years of the Second Congo War. He had helped the Japanese researchers, making sure their trackers were paid and bringing their reports back to Kinshasa. And he'd founded the Fondation pour la Protection de la Vie Sauvage et de l'Environment, an organization that existed largely in name and through which he envisioned carrying out his future conservation projects once he had funding. His most recent return to Kinshasa, shortly after the second war began, had been on two dugout canoes lashed together, both with motors.

He had brought his mother with him, thinking that she would be safer in the capital. But several days into the trip, the boat passed the port of a village where two armed soldiers stood on the shore. The men shouted for the pirogues to stop, and when the captain ignored them, they hurled grenades into the river. Everyone on board ducked as jets of water detonated from the surface. The captain turned the boats to the land, and the soldiers made the passengers get out and pushed the men into a line.

Albert stood in the sun alongside the others as more soldiers came from the village a little less than a mile away. They were members of Jean-Pierre Bemba's rebel force, the Mouvement de Libération du Congo (MLC). The officer in charge commanded the men to take off their shirts and inspected their shoulders to see if they had marks from wearing weapon belts or any other telltale signs of soldiery. Seeing that Albert was heftier, he asked if he was a colonel, shouting in his face.

The officer decided that the passengers and crew would have to stay in the village until the war was over. They spent a month there, the boats remaining in port. One night, some of the passengers escaped, but Albert, having his mother to take care of, couldn't.

Though the rebel soldiers became more vigilant, Albert and the crew decided to corrupt several of them, since they didn't appear to enjoy their jobs. Their officer had gone on a day trip to another camp and left the village guarded by six soldiers. Albert and the others gave them what money they had and promised them further rewards in return for help escaping.

The soldiers refused, saying that they would be executed, but Albert had a gift with words that would serve him in the years to follow, when he worked to consolidate Kokolopori into a reserve, and again later, when he ran for parliament. He explained that it was wrong to hold innocent people, that the soldiers should come with them and escape as well, that they would be happier not living under the heel of their officer.

One by one, the men and conspiring soldiers walked the mile between the village and the boats so as not to draw attention. The officer was supposed to return by dark. There were two boats, but only one of the engines fired. As they tried to get the other to start, they saw figures running from the village and realized that the officer and his men had returned earlier than expected.

Lashed together to travel in tandem, the boats pulled out unevenly with just one engine. The soldiers began firing from a distance, and Albert and his mother hid with the other men in the livestock hold.

The second motor finally started. Just beyond the port was the confluence of a smaller watercourse and a little farther past it, the main body of the river turned. As the soldiers fired and ran, the boats passed the embouchure and rounded the curve. Unable to cross the water, their pursuers were soon out of sight.

When Albert arrived at Baringa, a government-controlled town in Équateur, troops from the FAC, the Forces Armées Congolaises, gathered on the shore. He and the others tore a white shirt into strips that they wrapped around their foreheads. They shook tatters of white. They held up the soldiers' guns by the barrels, extending the stocks in a show of surrender.

As soon as they landed, Albert and the others were separated from the six rebels.

"What happened to them?" I asked, and he explained that they were sent on to Boende, the capital of one of Équateur's districts, then on to Kinshasa.

"Were they executed?"

"No," he said, but then he explained how terrified the FAC soldiers were of the rebel army. All night, they shot constantly into the air. Albert and the others huddled together, expecting counterattacks, but nothing came. Eventually, they realized that the enemy wasn't there. The soldiers were simply trying to scare off the rebels or comfort themselves. Albert grasped the absurdity of the war, the front hardly moving, soldiers not wanting to fight, possibly not even knowing why they should, just wasting ammunition against the night sky, as if the sooner it was used up, the sooner the war would end.

Albert and his mother traveled 125 miles to Boende and took a boat to Kinshasa, where he continued to look for work. He went to conservation meetings with CARPE and USAID and explained potential projects in Kokolopori until he realized that everyone he met was interested in talk, but that no one was going to give a Congolese funding. He applied for grants and continued going to conferences, but he told himself that the people he met seemed to have confused conservation with conversation—an easy mistake, just two letters misplaced, but a world of difference. One night, having cocktails on the roof of the US embassy and discussing all that needed to be done, he decided that he'd had enough.

By then he was working at the Red Cross, and it was at his office there that he first met Sally. She explained the need to have the landing strip cleared and found him easy to speak with, enjoying his sense of humor. He told her his ideas for conservation, about the Fondation pour la Protection de la Vie Sauvage et de l'Environment, whose name he'd shortened to Vie Sauvage after he'd been hired at the Red Cross. He'd realized that the unwieldy names and long acronyms so popular in the DRC weren't necessary. The Red Cross had a simple elegance, so why not Vie Sauvage?

Sally realized that he was familiar with a significant area in the bonobo habitat and open to working with outside organizations on conservation— that he was exactly the sort of person BCI should support. Though she was just getting started, Albert agreed to help with the National Geographic trip, wanting to work with her in whatever capacity. When I pressed him on why he would be so quick to help Sally, who was struggling to fund herself, he answered simply: "I immediately saw that she was interested in the Congolese in a way that others weren't."

When they were together, Sally tried to learn everything she could: words in Lingala; who worked in what area and what they hoped to achieve; what the people in Équateur knew, how they perceived the bonobos, the wildlife, and forests, and how they would respond to her ideas. No other Westerner had spoken to Albert this way. He believed that if he helped her accomplish her goals, she would do the same for him.

Like Albert, Mwanza saw in Sally an opportunity to expand conservation. He and his researchers had their headquarters near Lac Tumba, a lake in the Congo basin on whose shores stood an old research station built in the 1940s by King Léopold III of Belgium. The building had a lab with marble-topped counters and a library with books from the 1940s, and yet, despite foreign conservation funding being allocated to the DRC, Mwanza's researchers worked barefoot and had no funds to go deep into the forest, much less materials for proper tracking. They didn't even have money for pens and paper.

During their years in the region, the CREF scientific staff had seen bonobos in the forests near Lac Tumba. In hopes of getting his researchers working properly again and doing a scientific bonobo survey to the west of Lac Tumba, Mwanza put together a proposal for a $2,500 grant, an insignificant amount by the standards of conservation NGO expenditures. But everyone he met turned down his requests, one person even admitting that she'd been told to do so by Furuichi, who, since Kano's retirement, had been Mwanza's primary partner.

"Furuichi told her," Mwanza recalled, "that he would give me the money himself. He wanted to keep the monopoly on CREF's researchers. He said that he would give me eighty dollars and a few rain ponchos, so that I could go into the forest. I said no. I want a program. I have to send researchers. The area is vast."

Instead, Mwanza gave Sally the proposal. She had told Furuichi that she wanted to find additional funding for Wamba, since there was very little money for the community's needs, only for trackers and the expedition. But as she explained to me, Furuichi had replied that he didn't want her to raise more money, and though she didn't understand his reasoning, she respected that he was a scientist with an established site and might not want to spread himself thin. She also realized that working with Albert and Mwanza fit better with BCI's philosophy, to support local leaders and communities, and to use local knowledge to protect large areas for the future Bonobo Peace Forest.

Though I contacted Furuichi by email to get his take on what happened at that time, he declined the interview. According to Mwanza and Sally, however, when Furuichi found out that they would be working together, he told Sally not to and said the same to Mwanza.

"I got angry," Mwanza explained to me. "I told Furuichi, 'I run a government organization, and I am free to collaborate with whomever wants to work with us. If I can work with Sally in Lac Tumba and with you in Wamba, I don't see a problem.' But Furuichi wanted to be CREF's only partner for the bonobos. He kept suggesting that I stop working with Sally, but I told him no, that I saw nothing wrong with Sally that I should stop working with her."

When Sally returned to DC, she set about trying to find funding for Mwanza and Albert.

On a day at the end of August 2001, she received a phone call from a man in New York City. He told her that his name was Arnold Bob and that he was a traveling street performer. Each year, when he went through San Diego, he stopped at the zoo and did puppet shows for the bonobos, who watched eagerly. He told Sally that he'd been involved in a legal case and received a windfall compensation of $2,500. He said he wasn't a man of means, but he wanted to do the best thing possible for bonobos, so he'd contacted BCI. She told him that she had a proposal for exactly $2,500.

Around the same time, when President Joseph Kabila announced his intention to visit Washington, the DRC ambassador, Dr. Faida Mitifu, contacted Sally to help plan his reception, then scheduled for mid-September. On September 11, BCI's executive director at that time, Angus Gemmell, who went on to found BCI Australia, came running into Sally's office, shouting, "The fucking Pentagon, man! The fucking Pentagon!"

From her office window, they could see the smoke rising from where the hijacked airliner had struck the Pentagon.

Later that afternoon, the phone rang. It was Arnold Bob again. He was in New York City. He wanted to send the money that very day and was determined to find a means.

"I need to do something good for the world today," he said, "however small."

Michael Hurley

Kokolopori is a little more than sixty miles north of the equator. The weather wasn't too hot, the days peaking in the high eighties, the nights in the low seventies or high sixties, cool enough to sleep. The dry season lasted until April, and I hadn't seen a single mosquito, not in the village or the forest, not even after sunset.

Evenings, the staff of Vie Sauvage and BCI gathered with Sally and Michael in the hut, where they sat around the table to discuss work. But this night was quieter than usual, and Michael and I went out to the *paillote* to talk. I put my headlamp on low and set it on the floor, the light warm against the yellow dirt, the darkness beyond the thatch eaves as solid as a wall.

Michael had been telling me about Engindanginda, the sacred forest, an area in Kokolopori where the locals traditionally do not go. According to them, there was a battle many generations ago, and the spirits of the dead remain. But as with other taboos, this one was breaking down, hunters skirting the area's edges, going a little closer to the lake glimpsed at its center, though no one, according to the stories, had gone all the way in. In 2005, Albert and Michael discussed doing a quick survey there to see what species inhabited the area while it was still relatively untouched.

"When Albert and I decided to go in with some trackers," he told me, "the chiefs, notables, and spiritual leaders from the villages came to do a ceremony for us. They dug a hole in the ground and went up to it one by one. They started yelling and making threatening motions, then took a swig of *lotoko* and sprayed it from their mouths into the hole. Some of them had headdresses and spears, and they shook the spear at the hole, then passed the bottle to the next person. At the end, the spiritual leader said some words. Then the men came over and gave us a pat. They touched us and said it was over, that we would be protected from the demons.

"I thought they did this for everyone, but Albert told me it was special. He said no one had ever gone all the way into the sacred forest and returned alive, and that since I was the first *mundele* entering it and they considered me family, they wanted to make sure I was safe."

Throughout Équateur, there are areas known as sacred forests, places where hunters aren't allowed. Later, when I wrote to Albert about the name of the one in Kokolopori, he would tell me that the real meaning of the name Engindanginda had been lost over the generations, but that it may stem from *yoko y'engunda,* meaning "lake of those beetles in charge of burying feces." In the legend, however, the beetles play an important role in the war between Kokolopori and nearby Nsema, possibly consuming the flesh of the dead whose blood formed the lake in the sacred forest. In the name Engindanginda, the repetition conveys magnitude, as in very large beetles. But there were two other explanations that he offered: *linginda* means a special war dress, with *bongindanginda* meaning a very big war dress; and *lingunda* means deep, with *bongundangunda* meaning a very deep lake. He wrote: "Therefore, Engindanginda would be that mysterious deep lake stemming from the war between the Kokolopori and Nsema people, where Coleoptera buried corpses or bodies, and blood turned into a lake."

The battle happened before the time of the Belgians, and over the generations the people of Kokolopori heard strange sounds from the sacred forest, coming, they believed, from the lake at its center. Likewise, the hunters who went to the lake never returned.

"I really remember what one of the trackers said," Michael added. "He told me it was important to figure out what was going on in the forest, to find out what was killing people. He said that it could be methane gas rising from the lake, so that people would die and sink into the swamp. Or it could be demons in the forest, the spirits of the place. I found it remarkable that he considered both possibilities equally likely, the scientific and the traditional explanation. Other people claimed there was a huge snake that lived there. Someone had seen it. Still others said there was an immense crocodile and that they had heard noises like those of elephants, though they hadn't seen any."

Michael was convinced that danger from crocodiles, leopards, poisonous snakes, even swamp gas, could be avoided with precautions.

"I had spent about a month exploring different parts of Kokolopori, trekking about fifteen kilometers a day. There was a different feel each day depending on the forest type, sometimes swamp forest that required wading through water up to our chests, other days secondary forest that was almost impenetrable, where we had to slash our way through the undergrowth, and sometimes primary forests that seemed like walking in a green cathedral, where the canopies didn't allow sunlight to hit the forest floor, so shrubs and ferns and other lower-level plants didn't exist.

"To enter Engindanginda, we started before dawn. I was looking for the differences between this forest and the others. I was especially attuned to the sounds, as the trackers had talked about the strange noises there. I can't say I heard anything different, but I was more aware of every bird, every creaking tree. Before arriving at the edge of the lake, we chopped through about half a kilometer of a plant with spear-shaped leaves larger than my chest. Then I heard Albert call ahead, and we entered into an area of sunlight, looking at what appeared to be a fortress of a species of palm growing up to twenty or thirty feet, entangled and covered with thorns. We paused to get our breath and soak in the place. . . . Once in a while there was the short song of a bird or an insect chirping, but the quiet was almost like a blanket that covered us. It seemed like we were in a place of worship, and we all agreed that it wouldn't be right to slash our way through the palms to enter the lake. Albert said that before doing something like that we should work it out carefully with the village elders, as it felt to us that we would be desecrating a shrine. We all seemed to relax after that decision, as it was sort of a rationalization for us not to go farther. We all were a little concerned that there could be some truth to the stories."

Watching Michael with the Congolese, I often had the sense that he, like Sally, wanted to know every detail of their lives, to understand their reasoning and ways of being in the world. But his words about the village leaders saying that they considered him family rang true, and a number of children in Kokolopori's villages had been named after him and Sally. Like Sally, he interacted with the people easily, enjoying their company, spending his downtime talking with them, listening to their points of view, debating with them, often deferring.

His attitude called to mind what he had told me in interviews about his childhood, how he grew up, with parents who believed in sacrificing personal goals for the sake of family and cohesion. In many ways, they were responding to their own experiences of solitude and isolation. His father's parents had substituted wealth for warmth, living off the inheritance of their paternal ancestor, a Michael Hurley who'd left Ireland for the United States in the 1840s, not poor but with businesses and investments and plantations in Cuba. This man's sons were playboys. They joked that their goal was to spend the family wealth before they passed on, and they did.

Michael's grandfather was the only one who married. His son, Joseph

Manuel Hurley Jr., was an only child, come late into his parents' life of wealth and status, overseas investments and art collections. He spent his first five years on the French Riviera, raised and fed by his maid, his mother enjoying breakfasts in bed, often away. The idea of a close, loving family became his dream, one he shared with Michael's mother, Jean Heyer, whose family had immigrated from Germany in the 1800s. Joseph Hurley graduated from Harvard College, then Harvard Business School, and became a stockbroker, limiting his ambitions so he could enjoy raising his children.

Michael was born in Beverly, Massachusetts, in 1952. When he was five, the family moved to Hamilton: a place of hunt clubs and fox chases, where the first streetlight in town was installed for a horse crossing near the polo fields. The area had stone walls and rivers, swamps, lakes, and forest, and wasn't far from Boston or the ocean.

Not long after moving there, he walked into his new backyard and climbed onto a tree stump. In the brush just below him lay a gleaming white-and-copper-banded necklace. But when he crouched and reached for it, it moved. He jerked his hand back and ran to find his father, who came and killed the snake with a shovel.

They brought the two-foot-long snake inside, and his father looked through the *Encyclopedia Britannica* until he found it—a milk snake, an uncommon serpent known to eat rats and mice, good to have around the house and not dangerous, though often mistaken for a copperhead. There was that moment, the father and children at the table, all realizing his mistake, and then, finally, after a silence, he cleared his throat and admitted his error.

After that experience, Michael set about learning the scientific names of all the reptiles and amphibians he could find, and spent his summers in the swamps or at the Audubon Nature Camp. At home, he developed a collection of live animals including chameleons, iguanas, pythons, boa constrictors, a young alligator, and a large snapping turtle that a nearby sanctuary was going to kill since it was eating the ducks. At the Audubon camp, he won a competition in which he identified leaves and feathers, and as a result was selected to attend Wildwood, an overnight camp. The experience catapulted him through other courses and trainings, through Phillips Exeter Academy and finally Harvard, where the classes, he recalled, were significantly easier.

Anthropology, however, and not science, inspired his next passion. The idea of different worldviews fascinated him, how within another's culture the world could be transformed—or how he might be, seeing it that way.

He gradually focused his studies on shamanism, looking at whether anthropologists should participate in a culture to understand it. Students and professors spoke about the importance of objectivity, but how could he understand a foreign worldview while rooted in a supposedly objective Western culture?

During this time, when Michael questioned the usefulness of his studies, his father, who had sacrificed satisfaction in his career and had the obligation of raising and educating five children, gave him a key piece of advice.

"Do anything," he told him, "but whatever you do, use this time to learn as much as you can. Don't worry about getting a job. If you learn as much as you can at college, that will stand you well. That will be good for you. Don't try to focus on one technical thing, and don't try to select something that will help you earn money. If you do that when your mind is forming, you will lose so much. And if you become a stockbroker, I will shoot you."

And so Michael focused increasingly on folklore and mythology, looking at different cultures and their cosmologies. Maybe, he told himself, he could figure out what to do later in life by understanding what made people think the way they did. But when he graduated in 1975, the United States was suffering from one of its all-time highest unemployment rates, and having a degree in folklore and mythology, with a minor in witchcraft and magic, wasn't a way to get a job at Merrill Lynch. The only other technical skill he had was from his student job, working as the chef's assistant at the Harvard Business School, so when he graduated, he became a cook. He also got married right out of university to a woman he'd been dating; it seemed the thing to do. Though he had a dream of moving to South America and living in the forest, they didn't have enough money, so they moved to Florida and he took a job on a private yacht with a glass bottom under the galley—which sounded like paradise until he realized he'd be in the company of wealthy alcoholics for months to come.

When he moved to Washington, DC, at twenty-three and found a job in finance, he wanted to understand how the system worked. He had no background in it but was taken on at Walker & Dunlop, an old mortgage banking firm, and as his impulsive marriage fell apart, he taught himself government-related finance, reading the code of federal regulations cover to cover and studying low-income housing. By 1982, he was appointed to the Grace Commission, tasked by the White House with investigating government waste and inefficiency.

After the commission and his divorce, he visited Ireland and, without intending to, began a walkabout, spending nine months there, overstaying his visa. He enjoyed feeling light and wanted to learn how to live with very little. He hitchhiked and was put up in old farms and cottages, met musicians and fellow travelers.

When he returned to Washington, he wanted to find his way back to his college passions. At that time, DC was a hub for industrial films, the second most important city for the film industry after LA. He served on the board of the Washington Film and Video Council, and he traveled to a variety of places, among them the Amazon and Pitcairn Island in the southern Pacific Ocean, to do research and produce documentaries. His trips to Haiti and Easter Island made the strongest impressions on him, both having suffered similar environmental disasters as a result of deforestation.

Increasingly, Michael's interests resembled those of his college years. He studied medicinal plants and set up conferences that brought the practitioners of mainstream medicine together with those of alternative medicine. At that time, scientists were spending millions collecting samples from around the world—leaf, blossom, fruit, bark, inner bark—screening each element for antifungal, antiviral, and antibacterial properties, among others, and he ran another conference on the business and science of medicinal plants. He became increasingly interested in the ethnobotanical approach, in which researchers learned about plants from shamans whose ancestors had been in the forests for thousands of years, passing down knowledge.

This all came to a stop when the woman he was living with at the time was diagnosed with Lou Gehrig's disease. For five years, he took care of her, using up his savings. Nothing had pushed him closer to questioning his existence, its value and purpose. After her death, he thought back to his time in Ireland, when he'd owned nothing.

From an acquaintance with whom he'd worked on the conferences, he learned about Sally and her work. They met at a gallery opening in the spring of 2002, and talked all night, discussing their travels, folklore, and different worldviews. In the weeks afterward, as they started seeing each other romantically, he began attending BCI meetings.

"I was so overwhelmed at the time," Sally told me. "There was this huge network—a matrix of people and connections I was maneuvering and weaving together. Most people got confused and lost in the situation, and Michael just got it."

In July, when she was about to return to the Congo for the National Geographic–funded expedition to Wamba, BCI was growing, its phone ringing frequently, and Michael offered to stay at her place and keep tabs on things while she was gone.

In the Congo, Dr. Mwanza and Albert had been organizing the details of the trip. Albert had already left the Red Cross when Sally received a grant from the US Fish and Wildlife Service to do surveys of bonobos at Kokolopori, the first step toward a possible protected area and all that it entailed. He had decided that he wanted to dedicate himself fully to Vie Sauvage.

But wartime challenges remained, and when Albert arrived in Djolu, he was carrying a GPS to help prepare for the bush plane flight that Sally and the expedition members would take to Wamba. He had papers giving him permission to travel, *un ordre de mission*—a longtime formality in the Congo, used by Mobutu to keep outsiders out of his more profitable or restive areas, and continued during the war, the military forces being deeply wary of spies. Albert carried *un ordre de mission* from the Red Cross as well as one from a military general, but he was worried that the GPS would attract attention. He met up with several of his brothers at Djolu and continued on toward Yalokole. Only when he arrived at a military roadblock and his brothers walked past, ignoring the soldiers, was the party stopped and interrogated. The soldiers examined the GPS and his travel documents, but they couldn't find fault in his explanation. Nonetheless, to show their power and demand respect, they had Albert's brothers strip and lie facedown on the road. They whipped them to show Albert not to be too confident of his power, he supposed, but they also spared him because he was protected. Then they returned the GPS and his papers, and he and his brothers continued on.

The state in which Albert found his people stunned him. Almost no one had clothes. The cassava fields had virtually vanished back into forest, having been dug up repeatedly by soldiers and not replanted. Sally would see the same thing upon her arrival with the expedition. The people appeared shrunken, many of them sick, having contracted AIDS from the occupying soldiers. The two closest friends Sally had made in 1994 were half sisters Francine and Maki, whose father, Papa Bandja, had helped Takayoshi Kano set up his camp in the seventies. Both sisters died of AIDS after being raped, and Papa Bandja, their father, had been shot and killed outside his home by soldiers, men with whom he had disagreed—over what, Sally didn't know.

She had planned to return with Dr. Furuichi and Dr. Mwanza to the moribund Japanese research camp in Wamba, which was now occupied by four soldiers who terrorized the people, threatening them if they weren't fed and taking their daughters as servants. That February, Sally had finally met with President Kabila, and though he'd agreed to give her ten minutes, they'd spoken for two hours, discussing the Bonobo Peace Forest and the conceptual link between conserving natural resources, stabilizing local communities, and helping maintain peace within the country. When she told him about the occupied research camp, he arranged for her to be accompanied by a high-ranking officer who would ensure the security of the expedition and ask the soldiers in Wamba to leave.

Upon the expedition's arrival in the camp, the officer greeted the soldiers, inviting them to drink *lotoko*. They sat together near the dilapidated buildings, the day muggy. He gradually befriended the men before explaining to them that the site was a government research center. By the order of the president, he said, they had to leave. After a tense moment, the soldiers agreed and gathered their possessions, bundles of objects they had stolen from the villagers.

Unlike on her first trip to Wamba years before, when Sally spent nearly three months in the camp, this time she stayed only a week. Furuichi refused to let her go into the forest. He reconvened the local trackers and sent them out to look for bonobos. The main goal of the expedition, besides confirming the status of the Wamba bonobos, had been to see the people, to rebuild relationships and reestablish the camp. Everything the Japanese had brought over the decades was gone. To fulfill her obligations as a recipient of the National Geographic Society Expeditions Council grant, Sally had to gather as much information as possible for the second and third stages of the expedition, when they would return with more people.

According to Sally, the tension between her and Furuichi lasted throughout the trip. He wanted her to curtail activities, to stay at the camp and not circulate among the people. She didn't see the bonobos and hardly renewed her contacts. She could have ignored Furuichi's constraints, but she chose not to, intending to avoid conflict with him. But from that point on, as she recalls, the walls went up between the two of them. She had no idea what she could write in the grant report. She felt that they had accomplished little, and yet she thought it would be impolitic to explain to National Geographic what had happened.

On the day she returned to Kinshasa, she came down with her first case of malaria. Sick and sweating, she could hardly leave her rented flat, and when she returned to DC, she finally called Furuichi and tried to discuss future plans for conservation. He said that he didn't want to get involved with her work, and not long afterward, he contacted the National Geographic Society directly and renegotiated the project she'd begun so that he could receive a scientific rather than an expeditions grant.

With Michael, she talked through BCI's vision, of an organization built on the knowledge and skills of the Congolese, and that made change from within rather than impose it. Through their discussions, their plan for BCI became clearer and reinforced their decision to focus on Congolese partners and community leaders. As Michael wrote to me in an email:

> Effective and sustainable conservation is a complex multi-sectoral program requiring holistic approaches and methods. Biological science is only one element in a sound conservation program. It must include anthropology, sociology, economics, politics, public relations, community development, healthcare, education and more. Yet historically at least 90% of conservation programs and projects and organizations are driven by and led by biologists.

He also offered the following explanation of what he has come to term "vertically integrated philanthropy," which would connect donors at the top directly with beneficiaries at the bottom—as opposed to the general trend by which "donors fund intermediaries to implement programs that have been developed in the US or Europe by 'experts' who often have little connection with people on the ground." He gave the example of a philanthropist who goes trout fishing in Montana. This person would hire a local guide to lead him to the best fishing spots, not a PhD ichthyologist from the University of Miami. He went on to say that though conservation—and its success—is immensely more complex than fishing, conservationists often neglect to consider or consult local knowledge.

> We often miss opportunities to gain valuable and even necessary information because we do not respect the knowledge and wisdom of local and indigenous people. The questioning of local hunters and villagers yields almost the same results as standard transects and recces implemented by scientists. In addition, the active involvement of locals in the process also leads to enhanced cooperation and buy-in to later-phase conservation programs. The same certainly holds true for community development programs. . . . Lack of resources in local communities should not be equated with lack of knowledge.

Working toward these ideas, Sally and Michael and the BCI team applied for more grants and continued supporting Vie Sauvage and CREF. At that time, there were a few field research sites for bonobos, some involving conservation on a small scale, and the Lola ya Bonobo sanctuary in Kinshasa, but no large-scale operations aimed at protecting extensive portions of the habitat, with the exception of Salonga National Park, which had been established by Mobutu in 1970. The Congolese wanted support for bonobo conservation, and Dr. Mwanza and Albert had demonstrated what they could achieve with minimal funding. When Sally's sister sold a family house in Maine, Sally spent her portion of the money to develop Kokolopori. Not long after, Michael's mother died, and he put his inheritance into BCI.

Sally decided that supporting Mwanza and bringing recognition and funding back to CREF had to be at the core of BCI's strategy if they were to encourage a Congolese movement for conservation. This would create teams of scientists who could do the work necessary to help community leaders establish reserves. But the process of transforming BCI into a full-fledged conservation NGO was grueling to say the least, and even as they received donations and began projects, they applied for additional grants to keep CREF and Albert working. Determined not to break the momentum of the Congolese conservationists developing protected areas, Sally and Michael ceased paying themselves. They financed Albert's trips up the river with supplies and found further training for CREF researchers so that they were well versed in the best techniques for surveys, among other conservation practices.

Eventually, though, more substantial grants began coming in, and establishing the Bonobo Peace Forest in one of the poorest, most remote regions on earth began to seem possible despite the odds.

Economics around the Campfire

Days, in the village, it seemed as if there was no other world. Sunlight flooded the open space, filling it like a bowl, the rainforest a wall all around. Even when I stepped into the forest's shadow, I could see that this part of it had been largely tamed, made an extension of the village, trails cut through the heavy undergrowth to the river. I didn't have to go far, though, to see how much higher the trees were, strung with vines, the ground cover impenetrable.

When I began this project, it was during a time when my life felt too small, my career mediated almost entirely through an LCD screen and the computer so integrated into my existence that my unrest seemed to flash, in my periphery, like an error light. I realized how little time I spent in nature whereas I'd been in it constantly as a child, first in British Columbia, exploring forests and streams, and then in Virginia, where the forests were denser, loaded with vines, poison ivy, and deciduous trees. Years later, pursuing ambitions, working or researching in various cities, I began to have the same dream, of a forest, its trunks dark and wide. Nothing happened in this dream, except that I breathed more easily.

I am not a forest dweller, and having moved often since early childhood, I struggled to imagine the Bongandu's familiarity with the land. How did it feel to grow up in a world where the social order was structured around the forest? My paternal grandfather spent his entire life on the coast where the Saint Lawrence River becomes the Gulf of Saint Lawrence, in rural Québec. He could foretell the next day's weather by studying the water and sky. He knew when each fish migration would begin and how to read the health of the sea from what he found in his nets. In eastern Canada, when foreign factory boats decimated the cod stocks, the social order nearly collapsed. People migrated to cities for work, complex fishing cultures became isolated communities surviving on welfare and alcoholism was rampant. It helped me to look at the forests similarly. In Kokolopori, the traditional communal hunts that brought the villages together had become rare due to the lack of wildlife, and a sense of confusion persisted. Women could earn more money raising livestock than men could hunting. What happened to a culture's hierarchy, its stories and codes, when what it was based on vanished? And what would it be like to think that the ocean itself could disappear, as the people here knew that the forest might someday?

Many of those who write about the bushmeat trade acknowledge traditional subsistence hunting, that it is normal for rainforest people to supply their families with protein in this way. The problems arise when logging companies cut highways through the rainforests, their workers needing steady rations and their trucks carrying this meat to urban markets where, due to the demand for it, people pay more than they do for farmed meat like beef. Traditional hunting practices and reverence for the forest once limited how many animals could be killed, but modern weapons in the hands of a growing population and the demands of cities and towns have made the bushmeat market one of the primary economies of the rainforest. River barges passing through the forest are heaped with bushmeat, and traveling merchants buy it from villagers in canoes so they can resell it in commercial centers. The hunters who enter by logging roads are efficient, cleaning out areas, leaving only the smallest creatures. The roads also open the forest to refugees, who build villages where none were before, compounding the effect of hunting.

While wars ravaged the DRC, just to the northwest, in the Republic of the Congo, or Congo-Brazzaville, European companies demonstrated the power of industrial logging techniques that could soon be replicated to the south. The proponents of logging claim that it brings wealth to impoverished countries, but as Dale Peterson writes, it is actually "giving the cash wealth to one group, the urban rich, and taking the biodiversity wealth from a different group, the rural poor." Logging diminishes the forests' capacity to sustain the people living there. The types of trees most often logged have always been crucial to the livelihood of rural people, not only for materials but for medicine and food. And they don't grow quickly. Some of the sapele trees (*Entandrophragma cylindricum*) that loggers cut are four hundred to nine hundred years old, making them "approximate contemporaries of Leonardo Da Vinci."

Logging proponents have argued that the removal of such old trees would have little impact on the rest of the forest, but the complexity of these ecosystems defies the imagination. Conservation biologist Lee White illustrates the relationships between forest species with the story of an elephant that defecates in AD 1000, its feces containing the seeds of *Baillonella toxisperma*, locally known as the moabi tree. Though many sprout, only one isn't consumed by the forest's animals and insects. The seedling takes root, but for twenty years it doesn't reach more than a yard in height, until a storm fells a massive tree and opens a hole in the canopy. As White writes, "This event initiated a race. . . . Forest species growing in the center of the opening were scorched by the sun and died. Other plants were broken by elephants feeding on the lush vegetation in the gap, or were bent into nests by families of gorillas." The moabi survives, lifting with it the vines that have grown around its trunk, carrying them to the sunlight. Only when the tree is one hundred years old does it bear fruit for the first time. White describes the many plant species and creatures living in its limbs, and how, when monkeys eat its immature seeds, none sprout and years pass before it flowers again. Three centuries later, the moabi produces fruit every three years, its large crops attracting numerous species, even Iron Age humans moving their village to be closer to it. Its branches become home to birds, primates, and plants, orchids covering its trunk. The story ends when the tree is one thousand years old, over two hundred feet tall, nearly ten feet in diameter, when loggers cut it down and a bulldozer drags it away. White's point is that we must not lose sight of geologic, or deep, time when working with the rainforest. Conservation is enriched when we understand not just how to preserve, as Cowlishaw and Dunbar write, "the biological processes that underpin living systems," but also "the ecological-evolutionary processes that gave rise to the communities as we now find them and that continue to drive them." It is important to understand how long it took for the rainforest to develop, that its biodiversity is a product not of decades or even centuries, but of millennia.

As for humans, it's impossible to conceive of the forest without them. The most isolated areas are affected by people hunting and harvesting fruit and insects that are also fed upon by animals. However, while humans have likely been in the Congo basin for the past one hundred thousand years, systematic logging of the oldest trees is very recent and has an extreme impact; the extermination of these trees radically disrupts the ancient ecological balance.

Logging also threatens traditional subsistence economies, which are deeply entwined with the ecosystem. Ancient trees provide material for multiple aspects of people's lives—for building, medicine, and food—and they are the ones that host the most caterpillars when other food sources become scarce. As Dale Peterson writes, "In the subsistence economy, biodiversity represents wealth as palpably as coins in the pocket represent wealth in the cash economy, and the empty forest is as serious a disaster as the failed bank."

With the disappearance of elephants, buffalo, and sitatunga, which were hunted for meat prior to the wars, many Congolese people have become desperate. And at the present rate of human encroachment into the forests, the bonobos have little time. If the much larger population of Africa's chimpanzees could be reduced to 5 percent of what it was a hundred years ago, the bonobos, who may number as few as five thousand and are spread over 139,000 square miles, need concerted human effort now in order to ensure their survival.

The plan that BCI hoped to implement would avoid two scenarios: national parks and isolated conservation "islands." For the first, local people would have to be displaced, creating conservation refugees. National parks frequently lack funding as well, and hunting often continues within them, exacerbated by the fact that they become a no-man's-land, administered by absentee landlords. During several meetings in Kinshasa, the Congolese in both the government and the ICCN told Sally that they didn't want more parks. These conversations helped transform her vision of a "Bonobo Peace Park" into the "Bonobo Peace Forest," in which communities would remain to manage and protect the land—their land.

In the second scenario, preserving isolated forest "islands," the animals living within them no longer breed with animals in other areas, resulting in genetic drift. Less movement of populations results in less genetic diversity and, therefore, less potential to adapt to environmental changes. And as a result of inbreeding, the impact of negative recessive genes becomes much more significant, including possible catastrophic outcomes from disease. Furthermore, as the habitat surrounding the protected island is destroyed, habitat compression may occur, with increasing numbers of displaced animals taking refuge in the remaining pristine area, leading to heightened levels of competition over diminished resources. BCI's goal, in contrast, was to establish a network of reserves linked by corridors, within which wild animals could move as they wish, with the opportunity to join and breed with other groups.

The challenge with avoiding the national park model lies in making conservation a viable and attractive option for local communities. To do this, one of the concepts on which BCI based their work was the conservation agreement. Dick Rice, BCI advisor and former chief economist at the nonprofit organization Conservation International, pioneered the use of this approach in developing countries. As Rice explained to me, "The lack of tangible economic value is one of the most serious threats facing the world's dwindling stock of biodiversity." Rice's solution to this dilemma was to make conservation itself a source of economic benefit through formal quid pro quo agreements. In Kokolopori, the clear agreements between local communities and BCI/Vie Sauvage stipulated protection of bonobos and their reserve's habitat in exchange for employment, health care, and other benefits.

"These agreements are some of the most cost-effective investments around," Rice said. "It's a way to connect the supply and demand for conservation. That is, the people on the ground who are willing to protect a particular place or species in exchange for the willingness and ability of those in developed nations to pay for that. The problem is that without a mechanism to put those two things together the funding often gets diverted into paying for meetings and travel rather than conservation. Formal agreements are a way to break out of that cycle and channel money into incentivizing concrete results."

To implement a lasting conservation agreement, Albert had to work carefully with the people of Kokolopori. He had more than the necessary familiarity with the local culture, understanding the subtle connections in the community and its relationship to the forest. But he didn't want to hand Kokolopori over to an outside organization or the national government. The people living in the reserve would never forgive this, and it was very unlikely that the reserve could succeed without their goodwill and support. He was one of them, and he wanted Vie Sauvage to grow from them. Similarly, BCI made clear that it didn't want to control the resources of Kokolopori or dispute the leadership of Vie Sauvage, but rather to strengthen its capacities. At one point, when BCI and Albert first began working together, he offered to serve as BCI's regional manager. But Sally told him that she felt it wouldn't serve him well in the long run, and that BCI's goal was to build the capacity of Vie Sauvage, empowering the community. Later that year, in 2002, Albert and Vie Sauvage signed a memorandum of understanding with BCI, stating their common goals. As BCI's partner, Albert would manage the region and be paid a monthly salary.

With BCI's support, Albert began laying the groundwork for a reserve in Kokolopori. In French, the process is called *sensibilisation*, meaning to help people become aware of a subject, to educate them. Before he could begin to think about community consensus, he had to explain why bonobos and the forests were important to other countries. Once villagers and local leaders were in agreement with his goals, he could set up preliminary accords, first to zone the forests in partnership with the villagers and their leaders, then to do a complete wildlife inventory to international standards and train a staff of trackers and eco-guards. He explained to them how the community development projects would be integral to the work, and how the local people would earn livelihoods managing the reserve.

Travel in the Congo is slow. Each time you stop in a village, you are expected to pay respect to the local leaders, to explain what you are doing. In this way, Albert repeatedly met with each village, where he had family, where people knew and trusted him. He told them about the growing international interest in bonobos, that Westerners wanted to protect them.

The natural place to begin explaining this was a fact I often heard the Congolese repeat with wonder, as if I might not have known: "There are no bonobos anywhere else in the world. They live only in the Congo."

Villagers often described the moment that they learned this, explaining that they had no idea bonobos and the Congo were so special. This knowledge, combined with reverence for their forest—their belief that it is one of the oldest places in existence, unchanged, as they liked to say, since God created the earth—inspired them.

Day after day, Albert traveled from village to village. He spoke solemnly to the people and their seated leaders in the shadow of the *paillote,* dozens of village men squatting around the elders who occupied the few chairs.

The talk turned from the wonder of bonobos and their forests—all they contained that might be of interest to Western scientists and even tourists—to more concrete economic matters: how the people of Kokolopori could get funding to protect their bonobos and other natural resources. Albert painted a vision of the future. There would be money for people working for the reserve, a clinic, and more schools, all funded by conservation.

The question the village elders asked in return was simple: "And what about our forests? We need them for hunting, for gathering food and planting fields. If we support your bonobo project, will we lose control of them?"

Albert responded carefully, reminding them that even ten years before, a hunter could walk into the forest and not too far in, he would begin to see all sorts of wildlife—monkeys and boar and antelope.

"But now," he said, "a man has to walk at least a day before he can find animals to hunt, and often two or three days, into the deepest forest, far away. Once those animals are gone, and once more of the forest has been turned into fields, what will happen?"

The clear truth of the argument spoke to the elders. Everyone knew how much had changed, especially since the wars. Albert explained that with conservation, the forests would renew themselves, the animals would return, and there would be funds just for making this happen. They would not be giving anything away, or selling everything they had. The villagers agreed to give Albert a chance to prove that he had good intentions, that the foreigners he was working with would support them and didn't have other motives.

At this early stage, the greatest danger was that of jealousy and power imbalances. Even the slightest action could be used to polarize people. Local chiefs or politicians might fear that Albert was gaining power and claim he was stealing the people's forests or conspiring with foreigners to do so. In order to prevent such views from taking root, he needed to win the villages over one by one.

He began with those where he had family, convincing them to supply volunteers. Then he picked trackers and eco-guards, no more than a single paid person from each village, so that each one's monthly income of twenty-five dollars would change that village's status. In Congolese families, as in many African families, relatives expect wealth to be shared, and men with some power are quickly seen as "big men," entitled to respect. In essence, Albert had to create a power structure in which the benefits would descend from Vie Sauvage and people would have an interest in defending the organization against other politicians and leaders—a need that would arise before too long.

With little funding, Albert did broad inventories of the forests and began habituating two bonobo groups to humans. The aftermath of the war made this difficult. Soldiers had hunted bonobos, and the great apes wouldn't be quick to forget how dangerous people could be. Most of them had seen members of their families killed. When the first trackers began habituation, the bonobos hurled branches and showered them with fecal matter. The largest male bonobos displayed by lifting their arms and hooting, but more often than not, the bonobos simply fled or hid within the dense forest. The trackers followed them every day, recording the GPS coordinates where the bonobos built their nests before sunset. The next dawn, trackers would go to that spot and resume following them. Many thought it could take at least six years for the bonobos to become comfortable with human observers, but with BCI's support in funding, Albert's community leadership, and the constant work of the trackers, they achieved partial habituation within two years. National Geographic Society–funded photographer Jeffry Oonk visited in 2004, and got close enough to take what Sally considered some of the best bonobo photographs ever.

Each time BCI struggled with funding, Albert was immediately in a vulnerable position. Whenever he came into contact with local chiefs, they asked for money—five dollars here or there—and some immediately got drunk on *lotoko* and made further demands: more schools and clinics; the corrugated iron roofs that were a sign of status. Worse, some people began to see Albert as the wealthiest of the new big men. His clothes were better than theirs, after all, and he rode a motorcycle, something virtually absent after the war.

If his project was to survive, he couldn't let them forget that he was one of them; that he, too, was struggling on their behalf. But many villagers in that region—as I experienced during our visit—are quick to demand everything, asking for the clothing I wore, the bags I carried, convinced that someone who could buy a camera and a computer must have endless riches back home, as would have been the case under Mobutu. The divide between rich and poor has been so wide and is so deeply ingrained in them that they struggle to understand that there are people who have the means to help them but who aren't rich, and conversely that there are people who don't have the money to save everyone and yet aren't poor.

As I spoke to Albert, he explained the three great challenges involved in building and maintaining a reserve.

"The first comes from the community where you want to create the reserve. The people like their forest. They live from it. They don't want people to put limits on their use of the forests. They are also afraid that foreigners will take their lands. On one side there are the young people and on the other the old. Those who lived through colonialism remember what it was like. The others didn't live through colonialism, but they are old enough to be an important part of the population. So you have to find an appropriate discourse. If you make a practice of lying, you will be caught in your lies, and you will fail. But if you tell too many truths, there will be too much light, it will be too blinding, and you will fail. You need a leader who is trusted because of his story. The Lokasolas are generally trusted because of my father. This is the first challenge. You must know how to talk to them.

"The second challenge is to find money. It is impossible to get money if you are Congolese and you are not partnered with a Western NGO. The third challenge is managing people in a very poor area. Some people are jealous of those receiving benefits, and others feel that they are not receiving enough. They feel that only some are getting privileges from everyone's forest. You have to know how to please everyone."

As Albert and I spoke in Kinshasa, Michael came to the door and asked how the interview was going. When I told him what we were discussing, he said that Albert was skilled at navigating the space between the Bongandu's changing society and their ancient culture, especially in places where there was incredible conflict and need. He recalled Albert presiding over meetings with hundreds of people desperately wanting something. A conflict arose around some promised change not yet made, or insufficient funds. People were shouting at Albert, shaking their fists. Then Albert became extremely calm and spoke in a singsong voice, his eyes riveted on their faces, moving from one to the next. After he finished, everyone sang his praises.

When I asked Albert how he did it, he replied, "I am part of them. I am from them. I have some element of their heart in myself, and I can perceive how things are in their head and heart. By feeling them during conversation, I can anticipate. . . . What you say depends on the audience, on people who are before you, and you can read the expressions on their faces while you are speaking. When you say something that hurts them, you sense it quickly, and correct yourself. When I say, for example, that we are going to go into the second strata of the forest, and I can see in their faces that this is too much, I quickly add that it's not necessary for us to go there now, but that we might go there someday."

Albert explained that he wasn't simply adapting his discourse to the people, but learning what was possible from them—where, when, and at what pace the work could be done. He was adapting to their thoughts and feelings so that conservation could move forward with their support and goodwill, and benefit from the strength of a unified community. As simple as this sounded, it was profoundly different from how outsiders—from Kinshasa or from the developed world—generally dealt with these communities.

Albert explained that to get the initial community accords to protect bonobos and set aside certain parts of the forest, he brought together all the traditional village chiefs.

"*Nous sommes arriérés,*" he told them, "We are behind. I, your brother, am, too. But we have this forest. I can't bring you anything that will help you for a long time. But we have a resource that can be found behind our house. It's this forest here. I have gone to university. I know the value of the forest. I know what the forest can bring to our lives. And I have friends who can help us manage this forest for our own good. I ask you to have confidence in me so that we can create a reserve here where we live."

This was Albert's approach from 2002 to 2004, when he and Sally established the first accords: agreements of intent outlining how the people of Kokolopori would try out this approach to conservation and see how the communities would benefit in exchange for limiting hunting and farming. But the accords weren't easy to get, and he opted for an approach that proceeded one step at a time. He knew not to push too hard, and that people would need to see benefits in exchange, as well as proof that he wasn't there to exploit their resources and goodwill. So he broke it down, doing one accord at a time, for each step in the process.

"The first thing to say was, 'Listen. We can manage this forest. The limits aren't our concerns at the moment. What we should do is accept that the resources are important to us, and that we should sign an accord based on this principle.' The discourse needs to be wed to the context. Once people accept the basic premise, you can move to the next step. 'We want to make this reserve, but it is true that we can't protect the entire forest because it will suffocate us. We need to find the animals that we need to protect. So I ask you to sign an accord to do an inventory of the animals. And because men and animals live together, the next step is to study and find what people need. Not to mock you, but to understand your needs.'"

Albert's words startled me—his notion of mocking people. Again I could see the importance of local leadership. It is easy to forget how people might feel about foreigners looking in on their needs and struggles. One NGO study in the area around Djolu determined that the vast majority of people possessed only one pair of pants. It hadn't occurred to me until then how easily such a project could humiliate the people. For decades, I had run across reproductions of Walker Evans's photographs of rural Alabama families in the Great Depression—evocative portraits of people living in squalor. But years after having seen them for the first time, I read that many of the children in them later refused to be associated with the images. The memory of that time was too painful. They had gone on to live normal American lives and were eager to leave behind those years of brutal hardship, when they were barefoot and clothed in rags, living in shacks.

This is a common oversight in humanitarian and development work, and with the creation of reserves in desperately poor areas. The people there are conscious of everything they own, every detail of their environment that keeps them alive, and they are extremely conscious of what they don't have, of feeling diminished by those who hope to help them. Albert knew how to walk this fine line, not judging or imposing rules, but eliciting involvement and support. He explained that the next step in the process, once the inventories were finished and there was a better sense of the forests, was to discuss what could be eaten. This, too, was delicate. You could not condescend to people or make them feel controlled, Albert told me. As an example, he gave the critically endangered salongo monkey (*Cercopithecus dryas*). With the people of Kokolopori, he discussed the possibility of protecting the salongos—only two hundred are thought to remain, and Kokolopori is the only place in the world where they are known to exist—and making them a resource for ecotourism. He wouldn't say that hunting the salongo was wrong. Rather, his discourse was indirect, presenting information so that the people could come to understand how they could save a vanishing species and make their own decisions.

"And there are animals that the state protects legally," he said. "So we need to make sure that the protected animals aren't eaten. We discuss where the animals can be protected—so, 'In this area they can't be protected, because that's where we go hunting.' You have to listen carefully. You can't push or question, or the agreement will fail. You have to listen and discuss which zones will be for conservation and which for hunting. Once you have established these laws, you can begin to study the free land. They discuss what they need in their schools, the need for a clinic—all the things people need and want. Once all of this is done, you call the ICCN. The ICCN puts together the documents to make the reserve and this gets shown to the minister, who then helps create the reserve."

But just as Albert had to work closely with the people of the thirty-five villages within the reserve, he had to be the liaison with BCI, accompanying them in the field, supporting their work, and providing them with the documents they needed in order to secure further funding.

Albert told me that from early on in his friendship with Sally, he guessed that she must have studied psychology. "You can't fight against someone who is not fighting with you. She never takes credit for her work or says that she is the one paying. She says it is Albert doing everything. And I tell people that Sally is a good person whom they should respect."

He described how she would often stay in Kokolopori two months at a time, meeting with people in the villages, getting to know their goals and struggles.

"She is a person who draws others to her. She achieves this because she's not conflictual. She's a *maman*. Michael will sometimes take one step too far. Michael's greatest strength is the quantity of work he can do. He can write four or five projects. I appreciate his capacity for work. Where he can be weak is in diplomacy. Each person has a weakness. She is very strong in diplomacy. I would make her the American secretary of state. You can argue with her now and three hours later we let it go. What is her weakness? She pardons people too easily. She forgives people their failures too quickly. She is led to understand the good side, though this is also an advantage. But if she were more cautious, she wouldn't draw as many people. Michael will push at times. Sometimes Michael and I, we are like . . ." he hesitated, "*deux elephants dans une casserole*"—two elephants in a saucepan.

"Is this a Congolese expression?" I asked.

"Yes," he said. "*Jo cu mi balene na jocu moko.*" Then he laughed for a long time.

When speaking of Albert's broad base of experience, his willingness to make sacrifices and live in the forest villages when he could be in Kinshasa, Michael confesses that he has at times become frustrated with Albert's tendency to take on too much. Albert was already overloaded with commitments—methodology trainings that BCI helped finance, a course on conservation in Costa Rica, and the Wild Foundation's World Wilderness Congress in Alaska—when he decided to do a second degree in science, this time in biology, in Kisangani, so that he could be better equipped as a conservationist. As a result, he struggled to be as available as BCI wanted. Conversely, Albert told me that one of Sally and Michael's flaws was that they often worked in states of emergency, and that he found this distracting when he was busy. Still, the three of them, along with the BCI and Vie Sauvage staff, have repeatedly worked through conflicts and accepted differences to achieve their goals.

What became clear to them over the next years was that in order to save a species, they had to build an economy. Because of Kokolopori's remoteness and lack of infrastructure, microcredit doesn't work easily there. But BCI facilitated a sewing project and a market for household goods, as well as small-scale palm oil production and the sale of salted fish. It also tried to run a riverboat that would bring goods to the market, and had plans to convert locally produced palm oil to bio-fuel.

During the war, cassava fields had been left untended, and the flies that carried the African mosaic virus had spread and were killing most of the crops in the region. BCI helped establish programs for disease-resistant cassava—a crop that the locals dubbed Lotana, after Albert. Furthermore, BCI's investments in the community enabled people and cooperatives to raise more livestock, weaning the people off hunting. In fact, livestock husbandry—*élevage*, as it is known in the DRC—is currently BCI's foremost community development project, along with sponsoring women's groups. The community's productivity allows BCI—whether alone or with researchers, photographers, and film crews—to buy local meat and crops, and bring money into an area that, while it had no real cash economy, had cash needs.

Despite the focus on economics and community development, BCI and Vie Sauvage didn't lose sight of the fact that their concern was not just for the people's welfare, but also for nature. When Albert spoke of conservation, he paused to describe animals he had seen, the experience of coming upon an elephant or a leopard in the forest. He told me of a time during habituation when the bonobos became so comfortable that they walked past a tree where he was sitting, so close that he could have reached out and touched one, and that briefly, he could imagine himself as one of them.

Even in the camp, in that dusty bowl of earth exposed to the sun, as Michael and Sally met with local leaders and Vie Sauvage's staff, they worried that there was so much work that they wouldn't get to spend time with the bonobos. The way they spoke of the forest echoed the words of World Wildlife Fund cofounder Sir Peter Scott, who described "wildlife and wilderness" as "natural treasures [that] must be preserved in perpetuity just as certainly as the great art treasures of the world."

Today, there are larger issues at stake than when Scott was writing in the early 1960s, and the "value of wildlife and wilderness to mankind" of which he wrote has increased immensely. The environmental crisis is changing the climate at a speed no one could have predicted fifty years ago. At one point in our discussion, Albert told me that he was amazed when he first visited Washington, DC. He hadn't expected to see any trees at all, much less squirrels running throughout the city's parks and backyards. He and the other Congolese thought that Americans had killed all of their animals and cut down every tree, that this was why they were trying to save them in Africa. The experience brought home to him that the work he was doing had greater stakes, that the rainforest where he'd grown up was crucial not just to the survival of his people or for the sake of its beauty and the bonobos, but for the health of the planet itself.

Human Cultures
and Cultured Animals

Our first week in Kokolopori, Sally and Michael worked at renewing connections, paying the staff and trackers, and evaluating the progress of a number of projects, from farming to the new buildings in the camp. The boats from Mbandaka had arrived at the port of Befori, a five-hour drive on a road much worse than the one we took from Djolu. Supplies were arriving daily, first the medicine for the clinic and the electrical equipment. Normally, the boats would follow a smaller river directly into the reserve, but the water level was too low, requiring arduous shipments in the vehicles.

After our first foray to see the bonobos near Yetee, we set out with Alan Root for Yalokole, the next major village in the reserve and Albert's hometown. We were in the Land Cruiser again, the Land Rover's axle having broken a few days after it was repaired. We would visit a landing strip under construction inside the reserve in order to provide Alan with a sense of ecotourism possibilities, then see the salongo monkeys. Afterward, we'd spend a few hours on the river in a dugout canoe.

The company that Alan Root was working for intended to sell tours of the three African great apes, all of which are found in the DRC. Gorilla tourism had been growing in the eastern Congo, a significantly more dangerous region because of rebel groups and ethnic conflicts, but there were not yet any developed programs for ecotourism in the much safer but more remote region where bonobos lived. In Rwanda and Uganda, ecotourism had become a multimillion-dollar business, focusing largely on mountain gorillas, whose global population numbers only 880 as of 2012. In Rwanda, a day's visit could cost $750 for a permit, $400 for a tracker, as well as transportation and housing. The booming ecotourism economy motivated both the people and the government to protect gorillas and their habitat, to make the gorillas part of their culture and a source of pride. They even held naming ceremonies for newborns the way they did for their own children. BCI's goal was to achieve something similar for bonobos, and they hoped to show Alan the potential for doing so in Kokolopori.

I had taken to riding on the Land Cruiser's back bumper, alongside the young Congolese men who tended to the engine, changed flats, and refueled. The bumper was preferable to being crammed inside with passengers on the metal floor, diesel sloshing in plastic jerry cans. But it also required alertness, as the ride was a two-hour rodeo of ruts and rain-eroded hills.

The young Congolese showed me how to hook my fingers against the metal ridges just inside the window. We dug our toes against the bumper, which was broken at the center and so loose that it wobbled and flexed with each pothole. Unlike the Congolese, I had shoes to protect my feet. The back doors closed only with the help of a bungee cord, opening slightly with each bump, and the greatest threats, aside from falling off, were getting a finger pinched or being hit in the face by a low-hanging branch. Each time the Land Cruiser plunged through foliage that churned against the roof and sides like the brushes of a carwash, the three Congolese called out, and we crouched low. My right hand clutched the side window, and after one such plunge through undergrowth, a dozen dark thorns decorated the skin of my forearm like pins in a map.

As usual, children charged from the huts that occasionally lined the road, screaming and waving. Parents and older siblings grabbed toddlers who didn't know better and ran forward, sensing that the vehicle was the source of excitement.

I only feared for my own safety once, when we rushed around a curve and came upon a handsome black duck sleeping in a tuft of grass. Jean-Pierre swerved, veering wildly against the forest, the two right tires falling into a deep rut hidden in the weeds. The bone-jarring drop would have been frightening enough: my knees slamming against the back door, the bumper sagging, the Land Cruiser pitching suddenly at an angle, the forest lashing us, its branches bent and released with a sound like a thumb moving over a deck of cards. But then the Land Cruiser bucked as we left the rut, and our feet rose briefly from the bumper as we hugged the metal. After a few fishtails, we settled back into the two shallower ruts of the dusty path.

I was grateful when we neared Yalokole and the villagers ran out, stopping us. They shouted and waved palm fronds, then loaded Sally and Alan into chairs and heaved them up, all the while singing, sweat streaming down their faces. The entire village ran, Michael and I taking photographs, jogging as the people—hands reaching from all directions to steady the wooden chairs—shuttled their guests into the village.

At least thirty girls, some as young as five or six, most in their teens, began singing and dancing in a large circle around boys who pounded the drums.

This went on for hours, the girls slightly crouched as they shuffled forward, behinds lifted, raffia tied at the base of their spines and swishing like tails to the rhythm of their hips.

To get out of the sun, we sat in the large village *paillote* as people carved up pineapple and brought forest fruit the size of small apples—red, with large pits and a thin layer of sweet pulp—and others that they told me the bonobos loved, resembling thick red string beans, their hard pods containing a peppery white mash around black seeds.

On the other side of the *paillote,* the mothers began dancing. Their song was much quieter, without the hoots and calls, the blown whistles of the younger women. Sally joined the mothers, raffia tied to her waist. The song was so hushed that when I went to record it, I could barely hear it over the lively cries on the other side of the *paillote*. Did this say something about motherhood here? The villages were crowded with children, and the mothers were fatigued, cooking, watching over their offspring, constantly working. Maybe the hushed dance of the mothers, with their sideways shuffle and hands softly, dryly clapping, told of the quiet work that went on behind society, underpining it. Whereas the young women danced in a circle, turning out as often as they turned in, the mothers faced inward, often silently taking a step, falling in toward each other with another faint hand clap, then drawing back again.

One of BCI's cornerstones is Information Exchange, developed by everyone involved with BCI, under the guidance of Sally and Alden Almquist, who brought a PhD in anthropology and long experience in the forests of the DRC to bear in introducing many of the activity's core principles. For Information Exchange, the BCI staff met with the local people and asked them questions about their culture and goals, then described their own vision so as to learn how the villagers perceived it. I once asked Michael what made it special— why the emphasis on it? Was it just to have knowledge of where the bonobos live and the people's attitudes toward them? He explained that too often in the past, outsiders who wanted to help the Congolese in fact hurt them and their traditions, making it harder to win their trust in the future.

"For instance," he said, "in 2006, BCI received a grant from UN GRASP's [Great Apes Survival Partnership] Conservation Center, Micro-Credit & Enterprise Project. Jean-Marie Benishay, who was then BCI's national director for the DRC, met with the women of Yalokole. While the grant was focused on training, women's sewing, soap making, et cetera, BCI was interested in integrating a village well into the program. Jean-Marie discussed this with the women doing the project, but they weren't very receptive. They didn't want to appear ungrateful or negative, so they didn't speak up immediately. It was only after going through the Information Exchange process with its structured feedback and sharing—after the women really understood that this would be their project and their decision—that they voiced their concerns. We had thought that the women stood to benefit the most, since they wouldn't have to carry water for miles every day, but they explained that going to the river was their only time away from the men. They go with their children and sometimes see their sisters and aunts from other villages. They talk and tell stories, and the children play together. If there was a well in each village, they wouldn't see each other so often, and they'd be under the heel of the men all day. They actually said, 'We wouldn't be able to be with each other away from the men and talk about them.'

"The point," Michael concluded, "is that in many cases, projects are decided upon and designed externally, and that's why they fail."

Briefly, across the *paillote,* in a far corner of the village's main clearing, the men struck up their own song. They were tapping sticks together, singing rhythmically, sweating and laughing. But not long afterward the girls took over again, hooting and crying out, and when I walked back to their side, they shouted and waved their arms, singing and dancing more furiously, swishing their raffia, putting on a show.

"Do you know what they're singing?" asked Claude Baombo Bakengola, Vie Sauvage's financial officer, who recently moved from Kisangani to the reserve. "They are singing that they are young, that they must push the old people away, because young people are made to be in love. They are made to do anything for love and can't worry about what the old people think."

But it wasn't until the next day, after we saw the salongo monkeys, that we arrived at a smaller village near the river and saw the truly furious dancing that the young Congolese are capable of. The girls and young women wore threadbare tank tops, some red and white, others brightly patterned, and had bundles of orange and yellow raffia tied at the small of their backs. The boys who drummed were no more than twelve or thirteen years old, and stood with postures of power, chests lifted, shoulders rolled back, caps pulled low over their eyes, one with his visor off to the side. It looked as if they were posing for the beginning of a rap video.

The girls began the dance on their knees, as if bowing to the boys, who then started to drum. Soon the girls were up, dancing in a tight circle around the drummers, but one caught everyone's attention. Her back curved from side to side as she lashed her hips with her yellow raffia. She was maybe fifteen or sixteen, beautiful, smiling, her teeth perfectly straight and white. Her face, like those of all the girls, had been rubbed with ochre, white lines painted irregularly on her cheeks and forehead, her throat and shoulders, and just above her breasts. The lines were short, in groups of four, like pale claw marks, and looked as if they'd been made with a fork.

Though the drumming boys appeared blasé, their eyes half-lidded, they pounded harder as she danced. Sweat soaked her red tank top, and the raffia accentuated the movement of her hips. She knew she had the crowd's attention. She sang loudly, calling out to the sky, shaking her arms in a way that left no doubt that the origins of American popular dance lay in this continent. One strap of her red tank top fell down her shoulder. She didn't touch it, danced harder, the boys keeping up, sweating now. The other strap began to slip. She smiled, her pretty face lifted to the sky, the sun flashing on the metal hoops in her ears, a single green plastic bead in each one. The other strap fell, and the rest of the girls kept glancing over.

I looked around. Everyone's eyes kept darting to the four white stripes above each of her breasts, which were now solely responsible for holding up her tank top. The Congolese are largely modest people and don't go barechested, and it was hard not to wonder what she was up to.

A bent, very old woman shuffled from the crowd. I hadn't seen her until now, her face wrinkled, mouth scrunched up, hair in a few large gray cornrows. She grabbed the girl's arm with one hand and pointed at her breasts with the other. The girl pulled her arm free and with a shrug flipped the straps back into place and kept dancing, chin lifted, eyes to the sky.

There's a saying, "The Congo makes Africa dance"—a reference to how often its songs are heard throughout neighboring countries. But in the Congo, music is the great communicator, on par with religion, the rock stars and preachers at the culture's helm. It appears to be the medium through which all people most easily find expression, whether of joy, sadness, or futility. Gérard Prunier's meticulous account, *Africa's World War: Congo, the Rwandan Genocide, and the Making of a Continental Catastrophe*, describes how, even when Kinshasa appeared as if it would fall in the Second Congo War, many night clubs picked up a new song called "Titanic": "In spite of the growing threat of AIDS casual love affairs flourished. There was a kind of defiant despair in the air, as if tomorrow would never happen. If people were going to go down, at least they would go down singing."

Even in Yetee, when the supplies were brought from the boats and BCI's Mbandaka staff joined us—efficiently setting up the camp and giving the trackers batteries and new equipment—one of them brought his laptop. Saved on it were hours of music videos from Kinshasa, and each evening, while the generator ran and we all charged our various batteries, a crowd formed outside the next hut over. Thirty, at times forty youths watched images of Congolese luxury, buxom women dancing in rhythm near new cars, shaking their breasts and bottoms, men dancing and laughing and eating. The rhythmic music reminded me of Caribbean dances or Jamaican rap with a slower cadence, the country music version of rap, as if sung to people who would be line dancing, as the Congolese often appeared to be doing in Kinshasa and Mbandaka clubs.

Singing is at the core of Congolese culture in a way it is not in the West. Though Westerners listen to music, few of us break into song while walking or fishing or doing work. The Congolese sing often, sometimes softly to themselves, at others in unison, or for the arrival of guests. Their relationship to song reminded me of how Westerners express good or bad news. If I call a friend to tell him about a success or failure, I often notice that I'm repeating myself long after I've conveyed the information. We tend to talk something out in the same way that a singer repeats a chorus. We share our good news five times with the same person, with a few variations in how we describe it, often because we're self-conscious, afraid to be repeating ourselves. And even if our conversation changes topics, we loop back, interjecting our contentment, the way a song constantly returns to its central theme, until we've exhausted the impulse to talk.

Early in BCI's development, when they used music to raise awareness about bonobos and reinforce existing cultural taboos against hunting, Jean-Marie Benishay approached Werrason, one of the Congo's greatest pop stars and the self-titled *Roi de la Forêt,* "King of the Forest." Werrason's influence can be compared only to that of Michael Jackson in the eighties. The Congolese memorize his songs and dance moves, and, along with other musicians, he sets cultural standards, inciting youths to dress in new, innovative ways. When he agreed to record a radio spot that explained the importance of bonobos, BCI became famous overnight in Mbandaka. The concrete result of the broadcast was that people watched for orphan bonobos for sale in the markets. Until then, the people and even the police hadn't known that it was against the law to hunt or sell bonobos. When BCI was starting, virtually no one in the government knew anything about bonobos—the ambassador, the minister of the interior, the president; even Mwanza, years before, as a young man working in a zoo in Kinshasa, couldn't distinguish them from chimpanzees. BCI began airing the Werrason broadcasts in 2005, and suddenly the people they met in Équateur Province would approach them enthusiastically, wanting to share information or discuss bonobos. The broadcasts also strengthened BCI's relationship with the provincial police.

To create change in Équateur, BCI engaged on a deep level with the local cultures, and the village songs echoed this, with references to Albert, Sally, and Michael, to bonobos and conservation. BCI's vision has always been to invest in the Congolese people, and the social capital that has fueled their projects has grown in many ways from their concern for their partners, as was apparent in the story Michael told me in Mbandaka, of Miracle Bonobo, the young boatman struck by a motorcycle and airlifted to Kinshasa, or of others they helped.

Such successes, however, are fragile. BCI's greatest struggle occurred after Kokolopori became an official reserve in 2009. The people believed that benefits would increase dramatically, but BCI received less funding that year. They struggled to maintain the programs that were in place, and to pay trackers and ecoguards. Conservation efforts springing up in other areas faced the same challenges. Cosmas Bofangi, a local conservationist, has successfully habituated bonobos in the Lingomo region, several hours from Djolu. He explained to me that his people first volunteered and now are paid six months of the year. He is able to keep morale up and is himself doing a degree in conservation at ISDR, the technical college that BCI and Vie Sauvage built in Djolu. But sporadic funding erodes trust. As conservation expands, it is difficult to keep pace with local expectation.

If BCI, Vie Sauvage, and others like Cosmas have survived this difficult period, it is because they've realized that small NGOs can compensate for limited funding with the loyalty and participation of the local people. The Congolese do not want to be eternal foot soldiers of conservationists who come from outside, whether from Kinshasa or foreign countries. BCI and Vie Sauvage have addressed this, first by sending promising employees to get diplomas in conservation at the Tayna Gorilla Reserve's school, the Tayna Center for Conservation Biology, in the eastern Congo, and then, more importantly, by creating ISDR. It is this college that the local people speak of with the most hope, mentioning its information technology courses, which are open to the community, as well as the longer programs in conservation and sustainable agriculture. They are also proud that it was conceived and implemented by Congolese to achieve a goal that the community shared. One of Albert's campaign promises was to expand it and get it national accreditation, which he has recently done. At a glance, its two buildings of rough brick seem only a little better than the rest in Djolu. Inside the main classroom, wooden chairs are scattered about and a single chalkboard lashed to two bamboo poles leans against the wall. But many young women and men in the area see it as the best way to establish themselves, to earn respect in their communities and gain opportunities, and it is a lesson in how a small amount of funding can create dramatic change. One of its first female graduates, Béatrice Mpako, became assistant administrator of the Boende district (including Djolu and other territories), showing the power of education to change a woman's status even in such a patriarchal society.

The theme, of course, is inclusion, that conservation will create the means for the Congolese to become their own conservationists, to have their own experts. The most successful conservation scenarios appear to be those in which the inclusivity works both ways—in which the Congolese are integral to the vision just as the foreign conservationists participate in the local culture.

Even in Kinshasa, during a dinner at Evelyn Samu's home, when BCI's employees and partners gathered, the feeling was strikingly familial. At one point they stood in a circle to welcome new members. Giving Bonobo names is a BCI tradition, both playful and serious, and is deemed an honor. Mwanza, Mpaka Bonobo (Grandfather Bonobo), must approve all names, being the elder. That night, Evelyn Samu became Mokambi Bonobo (Leader Bonobo), and Richard, the new accountant, was promised the title of Mbongo Bonobo (Money Bonobo) once he'd settled in. Michael explained to me that they did something similar in Kokolopori, creating a title of *chevalier de la forêt* "knight of the forest," and celebrating Léonard's skill as a tracker with feasts and dances and songs.

But to engage consciously with a foreign culture requires patience and care, and conservation projects are more likely to become self-replicating when their ideas connect with the values of the local people. The process is less like planting than grafting, connecting foreign conservation practices to the customs that are already in place, since the Bongandu have long recognized the importance of bonobos and acknowledged their human qualities. However, in order for conservation to succeed completely, it also requires support from the general public in the West, the people who donate to conservation causes and who vote for leaders who support them—people who understand that the bonobos are worth saving. But westerners are only beginning to recognize the emotional and mental complexity of great apes.

In 1871, the British anthropologist Sir Edward Burnett Tylor offered what would become the modern definition of culture: "that complex whole which includes knowledge, belief, art, morals, law, custom, and any other capabilities and habits acquired by man as a member of society." But culture remains a tricky concept, often considered exclusive to humans though studies have shown repeatedly that animals, especially great apes, have cultures as well. The question might remain academic were it not so crucial in determining our judgments regarding which creatures deserve protection and which ones can be eaten or have their habitats destroyed. If we feel that culture is a purely human construct, and that animals, as Descartes asserted over two centuries ago, are machines whose brain movements can be influenced through external training, we quickly come to conclusions resembling those of his student, Malebranche, who, when his neighbor asked why he was thrashing his dog, declared that animals are "inanimate machines"—"Do you protest if I beat a drum?" If we believe, even on a subconscious level, that we are dealing with machines, or simply with meat, then arguing for an animal's protection becomes difficult unless it provides benefits to us, material, scientific, scenic, or otherwise.

Increasingly, however, the research of primatologists points not only to highly developed ape cultures in the wild, but to the creation of cultures among captive apes as well as between apes and humans. Dale Peterson and Richard Wrangham write: "Apes are caught between two worlds, of human and nonhuman consciousness. Ape observers are caught between two parallel worlds, between being convinced of apes' mental complexities and finding them hard to prove." They are right that the scientific mind will want harder proof than variations of bonobo culture observed in captivity, such as the way the bonobos in the San Diego Zoo used hand-clapping to ask for things and then, as they were moved to other zoos, taught the gesture to the bonobos they encountered. When Sue Savage Rumbaugh speaks of the human-bonobo culture that she lives in, I understand what she means: her bonobos made very human gestures; they looked me in the eye, appearing aware of the combination of reactions their behavior might elicit from me. Their easy familiarity was unlike that of the wild bonobos who—some amused, some surly—accepted our presence, at times with curiosity, at times with wariness, going about their daily feeding with an eye cast back, just in case we turned out to be like those humans they ran across during the war, who hunted them with guns.

Though the increasingly large body of knowledge around ape behavior is providing an immense record of their mental complexity, we are capable of understanding a lot about apes from a few examples. For instance, in *Brutal Kinship,* a book of photographs and essays looking at the way humans subjugate chimps to their needs, Nick Nichols describes the unique culture of Tai Forest chimpanzees, one element of which is their use of stones as both anvils and hammers to open nuts. Like the cultures of humans, that of the chimps is passed from generation to generation. "Tai mothers teach their infants the skill of cracking the shells without crushing the kernels carefully and patiently—cleaning the anvil, putting the nut in just the right position, even molding the infants' fingers around the hammer, adjusting the lesson to the little one's level of skill." Similarly, Jane Goodall points out that various groups of chimps observed throughout Africa show different sets of tool-using cultures, which they meticulously pass down through the generations.

One of the most compelling presentations of ape culture is to be found in *The Great Ape Project: Equality Beyond Humanity,* a collection of writings by both ape experts and others who have had contact with apes, examining the possibility of a great ape personhood act that would offer apes the same legal protections as humans. The arguments are exhaustive, looking at biological, cultural, ethical, and legal issues. For example, Richard D. Ryder, a psychologist whose work defends animal welfare, states that great apes challenge the foundations of our conventional morality, which, he argues, is based around altruism. Humans, Ryder explains, show altruistic behavior "motivated either by a (learned) sense of duty or by a spontaneous feeling of empathy based upon the awareness of others' sentiency and, in particular, their capacity to feel pain or distress." However, though great apes show clear signs of sentiency, which Ryder evokes as "the greatest mystery of the universe," humans rarely recognize their conscious suffering.

A glance at a Nick Nichols photograph—at the eyes of a chimpanzee that has been imprisoned for years with little food and no sunlight, or experimented on with surgical operations—is enough to convey their pain and dissolve the boundaries between us and them. Their haunted gazes are undeniably human, damaged in ways we would recognize in another person. African hunters describe how, when cornered, chimpanzees beg for their lives in the same way humans would, bowing, stretching out their arms, their faces pleading. And Koko, a lowland gorilla who has learned sign language to communicate with humans, can discuss what happens when someone dies but shows clear signs of discomfort when the subject is her own death or that of a friend. Jane Goodall describes the range of emotions in chimps, how orphans can die of grief after losing their mother, or how youths "gambol around, somersault, pirouette, and sometimes break off to hug their mother in sheer exuberance. Chimps have a sense of humor, and they can also be embarrassed." Decades of Sue Savage-Rumbaugh's writing reveal parallels between the behaviors of bonobos and humans. A series of photographs in *Apes, Language, and the Human Mind* shows bonobo facial expressions that are immediately recognizable: mirth and curiosity; concern and hesitation; and, in a request for comfort, a plaintive pout so compelling that, seeing it, I feel inclined to reassure the bonobo myself.

Unless we think that only humans have a right to live or deserve a public outcry when killed, there can be no justification for not caring. Even the smallest amount of empathy gives us a window into our kinship with great apes, a sense of how much we share with them. And as for their altruism, we have only to recall Sally's stories of going into the forest with Panbanisha or Kanzi, the way they would worry about her health, groom her and examine every scratch and bug bite.

We can find similar stories in all species of great apes, and yet the sentiency of non-humans remains problematic for us, given that we lack the tools and opportunities to perceive it. In all fairness, the same has been true historically among human societies, who have demonized each other and been incapable of recognizing similarities across the boundaries of language and culture. But just as we increasingly understand foreign societies, our observations of gorillas, orangutans, chimpanzees, and bonobos have provided us with enough information that we can begin to understand their social and interior lives. They play with toys and make up imaginary scenarios; they also watch TV and become concerned about the lives of the apes they see there. They recognize themselves in the mirror, lie to hide misbehavior, learn sign language and teach it to their children, and use language that is self-descriptive, humorous, and metaphorical, as well as that which refers to events in the past and future. Even in the wild, Wrangham observed a two-year-old chimpanzee whose mother was soon to give birth playing with a piece of wood as if it were a baby. The young chimp was almost surely excited about having a sibling, and was treating the wood like a newborn, carrying it in all the same ways a mother would, even playing with it in his nest.

Writing about the use of chimpanzees for medical testing, Jane Goodall points out that if their brains, central nervous systems, immune systems, and blood compositions so closely resemble those of humans that they can serve as stand-ins for us in experiments, it should follow that the two species share intellectual and emotional qualities as well. It would seem that people choosing to use chimps for medical research are either oblivious to this contradiction or ignoring the evidence of our similarities. Philosopher James Rachels writes: "A fundamental moral principle, which was first formulated by Aristotle, is that like cases should be treated alike. I take this to mean that individuals are to be treated in the same way *unless there is a relevant difference between them.*" He points out that humans believed themselves to be set apart from the rest of creation until Darwin challenged this vision of humankind and offered a new one in which we share a common heritage with the rest of the animal kingdom.

Do humans, as several authors in *The Great Ape Project* suggest, perceive the animal kingdom as a hierarchy that culminates in human superiority and goodness, and has the way we self-servingly define superiority blinded us to our similarities with our great ape cousins? Some scientists even emphasize the violent traits of chimpanzees in order to distinguish them from humans, describing how chimps in lab cages throw fecal matter and scream. Rather than address the injustice that caused this pent-up fury, they use the anger as a justification. We don't put forth similar arguments for humans, concluding that because of prison violence, inmates can be used in laboratories.

Bonobos, on the other hand, challenge our sense of superiority, and some writers have subjected their putative goodness to scrutiny. In his *New Yorker* article, "Swingers," Ian Parker questions whether the bonobo, "equal parts dolphin, Dalai Lama, and Warren Beatty," has been too idealized. He goes on to enumerate every violent act a bonobo can commit, from hunting for meat to inflicting pain on one another. He tells of a group of females who chewed off the fingers and toes of a male in captivity, and reports another story of females severely beating a male in the wild.

Though it's true that bonobos will eat meat, their observed prey are few and small compared to those of chimpanzees, who have been witnessed killing dozens of monkeys each month. And while bonobo researchers spend years documenting a few isolated cases of violence, chimpanzees and humans frequently injure and slaughter other members of their species. Furthermore, as Frans de Waal points out in *The Bonobo and the Atheist: In Search of Humanism among the Primates,* bonobo aggression seen in captivity, with females attacking males, is almost always the result of zoo staff misunderstanding bonobo social structure. "For years," he writes, "zoos had been moving males around, thus causing disaster upon disaster, because male bonobos get hammered in the absence of their mom." Over the centuries, writers have repeatedly documented the rise of violence with the breakdown of human social structures, and it is no wonder that bonobos also respond poorly to forced displacement and the destruction of the family unit.

However, that female and male bonobos have varying ranks, and that both can initiate sexual interaction, resembles our conception of an enlightened society more closely than does the near dominance of every male over every female among chimpanzees. Male chimpanzees battle for the alpha position, and male bonobos do not, nor do they gang up on females. Wrangham and Peterson describe bonobos as "chimpanzees with a threefold path to peace. They have reduced the level of violence in relations between the sexes, in relations among males, and in relations between communities." Even recent brain studies of chimps and bonobos confirm that their respective cerebral structures correspond to their observed behavior: bonobos have higher levels of anxiety, are more risk-averse, and have increased restraint.

And yet can the motivation for their behavior be reduced to instinct and biology? Or is it possible that cultures and social relations vary among bonobo groups in ways more closely resembling humans? Takayoshi Kano writes that bonobos "are rich in individuality, and the personality of individuals probably exerts a strong influence on the character of social relationships between group members." He goes on to explain that field studies at Wamba reveal different group "personalities" that are likely to be rooted in the way various particular individual personalities compose them. It is of course the distinct character not just of bonobo groups but of all apes that makes them such rich subjects for research. For instance, apes communicate often with gestures whose meaning varies dramatically between groups within each species. The flexible nature of this symbolic communication gives us a glimpse into how language might have emerged.

The challenges facing great ape conservation lie not in their culture or behavior, but in ours—in our inability to empathize, our refusal to accord them sentiency. We often fail to see the subtle line of influence, the way animals and humans are constantly shaping each other's culture. We have a long history of integrating them into ours. We have domesticated them for food and work, and created complex societies around herding or horsemanship. If we killed lions and wolves and made them into symbols, it was because they were both our predators and competitors in the hunt, and human respect for them was adaptive, since those who lacked it often got killed and didn't reproduce. Likewise, humans are still adapting, creating symbols with flagship species to protect the natural resources necessary for our survival. In this way, conservation has promoted the growth of coalitions between Congolese and Americans, as well as between organizations and governments. President Joseph Kabila has learned about bonobos, and the Bongandu are increasingly interested in protecting other creatures, so that the flighty salongo monkeys we observed only after much effort—their black faces framed with a line of white, orange fur at their throats, the rest of their bodies brown and khaki— have come under their care.

But the way humans use symbols is not simple. We know the transformative power of an icon, how it can serve as a reminder of a quality that humans possess. By aligning ourselves with it, we find our behavior subtly changed, our consciousness shifting away from a categorical identification with chimpanzee behavior. We have found aspects of our society that we increasingly value represented in a non-human species—equality between the sexes, group cohesion, the lack of war. Like bonobos, we enjoy non-procreative sex, and we form social bonds more easily than do chimps, who wage war when intruders come into their territory. We can travel into distant rainforests and discuss the preservation of resources and species, and speak, as BCI does, of a family model for their organization. We do not have to be naive about bonobos to see them as a symbol, and to diminish the value of this symbol does not serve us well, either when we are using it to protect the few remaining rainforests or the creature itself.

During my stay in Kokolopori, I repeatedly saw that the symbol of the bonobo does draw people together. When villagers dance and praise the work done for bonobos, when schoolchildren learn the ancient folktales or when traditional singers, funded by Vie Sauvage and BCI, travel from village to village, performing songs about bonobos, the result is as palpable as that of Westerners hearing Biblical parables that encourage virtue.

In *Apes, Language, and the Human Mind,* Sue Savage-Rumbaugh and her co-authors, Stuart G. Shanker and Talbot J. Taylor, remind us of our illusions of superiority and its risks. They address language as the long-held bastion of humanity, and examine it in a way that the Congolese villagers who greet us repeatedly with song might understand well.

Language is a funny thing. It permits us to think that we know things that indeed we do not know. It permits us to talk about things rather than to do them and to think we have actually done something by talking rather than by acting. It permits us to think that by talking in unison, we can come to act in unison—forgetting that the more feeble the link between word and deed the less likely words are to alter deeds. Should we wish to act in unison, it is far better that we sing than that we speak.

Language is a funny thing. It permits us to think that other species are not able to communicate the purposes or intentions of their actions to one another, nor to coordinate their behaviors, nor to plan their actions. It permits us to think this because it permits us to avoid hearing the kind of talking that other species are doing.

Empty Hands, Open Arms

Territory and Power

While bonobos as symbols might sound quaint in the context of rainforest villages or community building, the importance of the coalitions they represent shouldn't be minimized. Traveling, I've often encountered disillusioned youths who have worked with NGOs, whether humanitarian or conservation, and who are heading home, finished with saving the world. Their stories are remarkably similar: infighting, power grabs, projects that have more to do with the people running them than with what or whom they are trying to protect.

If the stories told by those involved with BCI and Vie Sauvage are to be believed, the greatest challenge to the conservation work being done by BCI and its Congolese partners isn't government ministries, corrupt officials, or decayed infrastructure, but rather competing NGOs. As Sally explained, BCI's greatest challenges began with the arrival of the large conservation NGOs that came to the Congo under the auspices of USAID. With the end of the Second Congo War, USAID initially decided to allocate fifty-three million dollars to the Congo basin, funds that were to be matched by hundreds of millions more from donors and governments abroad. The resulting project, the Congo Basin Forest Partnership (CBFP), set about dividing the Congo basin into twelve "landscapes" and putting the big international NGOs—the BINGOs—in charge.

CBFP's mandate emphasized partnership and resource-sharing with those already working on the ground. However, there were some regions where none of the BINGOs had worked, and while BCI was one of the few organizations already operating in these regions, it was small, nothing compared to the larger, more established structures of the World Wildlife Fund and the African Wildlife Foundation. BCI's 2011 revenue reached $1 million in 2011, compared to $26 million for AWF and $238 million for WWF. BCI met with AWF, which had yet to work within the Maringa-Lopori-Wamba landscape (containing Kokolopori), providing it with information for its bid to become landscape administrator. And yet while AWF's proposal used information from one of BCI's studies of the region, it didn't credit BCI, and shortly after

AWF had been made landscape administrator, it distanced itself from BCI. As Alden Almquist recalls, the person he had worked with at AWF told BCI that the subcontracting was being organized in Kinshasa.

In the decade that followed, AWF would resist sharing funding with BCI, preferring to set up its own projects. When BCI petitioned to receive a portion of the funds directly, Sally recalled how USAID told her that BCI had to work through AWF. Between 2002 and 2011, the United States government invested $98 million in the twelve CBFP landscapes (at least $50 million of which was matched by foreign donors); of the millions that AWF received for the landscape that contained the Kokolopori Bonobo Reserve, only $3,650 went directly to BCI—in 2004, to support a survey. Even though the Kokolopori Bonobo Reserve was an integral and ecologically rich part of the landscape and made a nationally gazetted protected area in 2009, it was left off AWF's CARPE/CBFP map of the landscape for several years.

While in Djolu, I visited the AWF office, a handsome brick building on a rise overlooking the rainforest. It was one of the few places in the area with satellite Internet, but despite their better funding, AWF's operations here struggled, like BCI's. They had had a large solar panel installation outside for months, but no one who worked there knew how to hook it up to the batteries, so the only power came from the generator, which broke down often. Some of the employees were friendly and told us that they ran the generator and Internet two hours twice a day for the benefit of the community, but the man in charge of the generator told us, as soon as we arrived, that there was no fuel, and turned it off.

I spoke to Phila Kasa Levo, the young Congolese man in charge of the Iyondje conservation area, which consists of the two of Kokolopori's thirty-five villages that decided to work with AWF (the remainder currently working with BCI and Vie Sauvage). There, bonobo habituation was being done under the leadership of a Japanese researcher, and Phila explained the problems they faced: among them, a lack of boots, ponchos, flashlights, and batteries. When I asked him about the Kokolopori Bonobo Reserve, his response in no way suggested conflict between BCI and AWF. He spoke of it as a model site whose successes he hoped to emulate. I got the sense that there was no conflict between Congolese, only between the two NGOs' administrations.

"BCI's biggest problem," Albert told me, "was its war with AWF over the landscape. BCI started before AWF was in the landscape. AWF came and ignored the work done by BCI, but they took some of BCI's research. AWF and BCI were put in the same landscape, but AWF wanted to minimize the work done by BCI constantly to stop the competition. . . . The battle with AWF was destructive for BCI. The partners, the donors, put their confidence in AWF, and the financing of BCI in the landscape suffered."

Albert went on to explain that he and BCI created Djolu's technical college with no money from AWF. "If you want to have people involved with sound management of natural resources, what's first?" he asked. "They need an education. Even if we put this money into the region, no one is educated, not even the directors of the territory." The success of the college, he told me, was that other NGOs, even AWF, hired the graduates. This was exactly what Vie Sauvage and BCI intended; his only regret was that an alliance with AWF could have made the college larger, better equipped, and available to more people.

He explained that over the years the Bongandu had come to appreciate the community conservation economic model. By protecting forests and bonobos, they could receive outside support, generate new livelihoods, and increase the likelihood of foreigners visiting. Sites with habituated bonobos were rare, so researchers, conservationists, and cinematographers had come. Over the years, BCI brought in a BBC scouting crew for a documentary; a *Time* magazine reporter; photographer Christian Ziegler and science writer David Quammen for *National Geographic;* a film crew from ABC TV Australia; a Harvard graduate student in evolutionary anthropology who carried out months of field research on the bonobos; a scientist from the Max Planck Institute who trained field staff in biological survey techniques; filmmaker and journalist Michael Werner; Paul Raffaele, who wrote a *Smithsonian* magazine article about the bonobos that he later used for the bonobo section in his book *Among the Great Apes;* Arne Schiøtz, Danish herpetologist and former head of conservation for WWF-Europe; several members of Conservation International; and Russell Mittermeier, head of CI, chair of the IUCN Primate Specialist Group and one of the world's leading primate conservationists.

"This built confidence," Albert said. "It grew and grew and grew. It reached a certain level. But once it attained that level, it began going down again because of expectations. People thought that all of their problems would go away with the creation of the reserve. But it takes more than the creation of the reserve. The demand is too great, and the means are few and don't always arrive on time. We now have the bonobo clinic and the college. And maybe when we build the new landing strip close to the reserve, that will change things. But people are now asking if maybe the reserve, is something that will go nowhere. The immediate need is to be more creative so that the movement will gain energy."

The feeling that everyone deeply involved with BCI and Vie Sauvage has is that they missed a crucial opportunity, having been excluded from millions in CBFP funding when they were already established in the area. They had hoped to combine forces with AWF and reduce expenditures by not duplicating offices and field equipment.

Though BCI's growth was in many ways too fast for its capacities, passionate Congolese conservationists continued to come to them. Anthropologist and BCI board member Alden Almquist told me that Sally had a good eye for leaders, that she knew how to work with the church and find leaders who had a foot in both worlds, the modern and the traditional, who could lead the people but also run the organization. The seeds BCI had planted with the Congolese, the respect they had earned there, and their passion for bonobo conservation expanded their influence despite the missed funding opportunity. And as with many such expansions, this one brought further conflicts.

During my time in Kokolopori, I looked for evidence of discord with AWF. The Congolese I spoke to couldn't explain it, and the person who managed AWF in the region during that time answered my request for an interview by saying that he was too busy to talk. He agreed to take questions by email, but never answered why BCI hadn't received significant CBFP funding for Kokolopori.

Cosmas Bofangi, who runs his own conservation area, had done trainings with AWF and expressed considerable appreciation for them, but he also pointed out the difference between them and BCI. "BCI works with the community to get everyone involved. Their work is participatory. Instead of dictating, like the model of AWF, Sally wants to work with the people, above all with the people of the local population, and to get the entire community participating in conservation."

Later, I spoke with BCI advisor John Scherlis. He studied evolutionary biology and zoology at Harvard and Cambridge Universities and has worked in conservation for decades. Having supported BCI since its creation, he addressed the conservation world's preoccupation with credentials. He pointed out that Sally and Michael's lack of scientific background had hurt them. "The downside is that they did lack a certain amount of knowledge. But the biggest downside is probably that they don't have the credentials as something to flash, like the password at the door of the speakeasy. If they had PhD degrees from the sort of universities from which they have undergraduate degrees, or if their undergraduate degrees were in different disciplines, they probably would be viewed very differently. On the other hand, the fact that they arrived unburdened by the disciplinary and institutional cultures, and that they looked to the local people more for how to move ahead, rather than implicitly assuming that they themselves had the answers, was an advantage. I think the essential thing, certainly for Sally, is that she sees her work in terms of building relationships with people."

Scherlis explained that communication and openness to other perspectives had been BCI's foundation, but that Sally and Michael were too overworked to use their strengths to their full potential. He had spent years supporting BCI, and like almost everyone involved, he had worked for little or no pay. This was a comment I heard echoed when I asked others to give their criticisms of BCI's approach. There was always a long hesitation and then some references to it being disorganized or often in crisis-management mode. But each person I asked also pointed out that if BCI weren't struggling for funding, it wouldn't have these problems.

That said, in the course of my research, I also heard frequent criticism of big NGOs and their use of funding. Many cited their corporate structure as the problem, the costs of sustaining a large organization and promoting it, the expenditures on conferences and hotels, on flying Western scientists into the field. Is it possible, I found myself asking, that conservation has been shaped less by sustainable work models than by the desire to stay ahead of competitors among the conservation NGOs? And if BINGO employees are moving up through the ranks to better positions, should the same support and financial security not be offered to those who run the small NGOs?

For people familiar with development and conservation work, stories of NGO infighting have become a cliché. But in a country like the DRC, it's disheartening that NGO squabbles remain such an obstacle when the needs are so great and the stakes so high. Trust in places like Kokolopori is fragile, and the lack of coordination and support between NGOs erodes the people's faith in foreigners, further entrenching the culture of wariness. Though the people of Kokolopori and many other regions of Équateur have embraced change, they stand at crucial junctures, at once enthusiastic for the work to be done and dissatisfied with the slow development, fearing that they will be let down once again.

In light of how common such conflicts are in even the most idealistic of fields, it's hard not to wonder if we can make significant and lasting change without changing ourselves, and particularly our cultural values and our sensitivities to power. Without awareness of how it works, or of the expectations that other cultures have of those in power, conservationists will almost surely run up against conflicts.

In Kokolopori, as elsewhere in Central Africa, the people's expectations of those who hold power affect the way projects must be carried out. In *Political Legitimacy in Middle Africa: Father, Family, Food,* Michael G. Schatzberg warns that "middle Africans inhabit a political realm whose boundaries can differ substantially from those prevalent in parts of the West." The "big man" (*mokonzi* in Lingala) establishes a community of relatives, allies, and dependents whom he sees as a family of which he is the head. Mobutu ruled Zaire in exactly this way, as a personal fiefdom, portraying himself as the father of his citizens. But the true impact of this worldview is seen in how the father negotiates with others, and in the "unity and indivisibility" of his power. Schatzberg writes:

> Contrary to the historically recent Western experience, power in middle Africa cannot easily be divided or shared, a usually implicit understanding and assumption that is nicely captured in the Zaïrian/Congolese cultural axiom, "*Le pouvoir se mange entier* [Power is eaten whole]," which is dispersed throughout a wide range of current Zaïrian/Congolese discourse.

Though the notion of this indivisibility was established culturally in the pre-European Bantu civilizations, colonialism reinforced it, whether in the form of the Léopoldian colonial administrators known in Kikongo as *bula matari,* the crusher of rocks (a name first given to Henry Morton Stanley), or the Belgian Congo's paternalism, in which, as Thomas Turner and Sandra W. Meditz write, "coercion or the threat of coercion never was far from the surface." Unfortunately, in their dealings with local big men, Westerners often unwittingly slip into that role themselves. And our greatest failures often occur when we do not understand how we influence the broader cultural context. For instance, Ian Parker describes an interaction between the German bonobo researcher Gottfried Hohmann and local Congolese people.

> The men of Lompole had convened around him, their arms crossed and hands tucked into their armpits. Hohmann remained seated and silent as an angry debate began—as Hohmann described it, between villagers who were unhappy about the original deal that compensated the village for having to stop hunting around Lui Kotal (this had involved a bulk gift of corrugated iron, to be used for roofs) and those who worked directly for the project and saw the greater advantage in stability and employment. Hohmann had finally got up and delivered a forceful speech in Lingala, Congo's national language. He finished

with a moment of theatre: he loomed over his main antagonist, wagging his finger. "It's good to remind him now and then how short he is," Hohmann later said, smiling.

This is a disturbing scene. A researcher or conservationist who appears in the forest and negotiates the protection of bonobos in exchange for certain benefits for the people may think he's written up a one-time deal. But if he expects his work to continue and good relations to endure, he must see himself as those people do, as a big man with more resources than they could ever imagine, and with the responsibility to share the benefits. It may not be a social order that appeals to us, but if honored, it is one that maintains a certain balance, allowing the big man his prestige so long as his "children" do not go hungry.

Though maintaining power has likely always been demanding among the Bantu—leaders earning respect by demonstrating the ability to fulfill responsibilities as "fathers" of their families—the Mobutu years made this power structure even more complex and tenuous. While the big man once existed within the known world of the village and the forest, his resources and actions visible to the scrutiny of the people, power in those years shifted to a realm of the unseen, to foreign wealth and politics in the capital. In many ways, it took on grotesque proportions, as big men became capable of transforming a place overnight, the way Mobutu did with Gbadolite, building palaces in the jungles. The people saw that big men had the means to feed all of them, but that the traditional order of accountability had been lost, and that big men used the old rhetoric of indivisible power to take only for themselves.

In the center of Djolu is a tall metal radio tower, held in place with cables. The people recall that the Canadians came in the seventies for logging, but then, after many surveys and much talk, they left. On a number of occasions, villagers told me the story and pointed to the thin tower, the town's most noticeable feature. Though they had lived beneath it for over thirty years, they asked why the Canadians built it and left it, as if worried that this could happen again with new opportunities. The tower had come to represent both a missed opportunity and the inexplicable decisions of those in power. They wanted to understand the forces influencing their lives—not to trust that foreigners in distant NGO headquarters would take them into consideration, but to participate in decisions themselves.

Since Albert had been elected to parliament, the people of Kokolopori had begun to question his intentions. He won a battle against a local politician who accused him of stealing the forests, but when I spoke to the villagers, this accusation didn't appear to concern them. They seemed divided as to whether, after entering parliament, he would have the power and resources to make radical change in the region. He had promised to expand the college and develop the economy, to build schools and clinics, but this is the talk of all politicians, and the Congolese have heard their share. The other half of them feared that now he would be lost to them, just another politician accumulating wealth and living luxuriously in Kinshasa, his true motivations and resources beyond their sight. I asked him about this, and he said that for him the greatest challenge was people's impatience—that a politician has to run both a sprint and a marathon, developing a long-term vision while quickly achieving short-term goals to satisfy the needs of his constituency. He acknowledged just how difficult the situation had become.

But what makes it more complex is that even now, having examined the beliefs and distrust of the Congolese, we Westerners aren't necessarily well prepared for community building—for getting accords signed, reassuring the people, and creating reserves. We are too easily fooled by those aha moments when we think we've figured everything out and have a privileged perspective. In fact, the Western culture of power is equally complex. If the Congolese build coalitions under the auspices of big men, we individualists all want to be recognized as big men, and few of us are willing to concede our own goals or prestige to the larger vision.

In this sense, Ian Parker's assertion that "the challenges of bonobo research call for chimpanzee vigor" is an apt evocation of how competitive bonobo research and conservation have become. Parker's final paragraph suggests the degree to which professional ambition can overshadow the big picture.

"What makes humans and nonhuman primates different?" Hohmann said. "To nail this down, you have to know how these nonhuman primates behave. We have to measure what we can see today. We can use this as a reference for the time that has passed. There will be no other way to do this. And this is what puts urgency into it: because there is no doubt that, in a hundred years, there won't be great apes in the wild. It would be blind to look away from that. In a hundred years, the forest will be gone. We have to do it now. This forest is the very, very last stronghold. This is all we have."

Even if a serious evaluation of conservation is beyond the scope of Parker's article, his send-off reinforces a short-term vision of the forest. After all, if the forests are doomed by 2107, what is the point of conservation? The forest's value beyond research is passed over in this context, and Hohmann's dismissal (at least in Parker's portrayal) of the Congolese who live in the forest replays an age-old challenge: foreigners are using their land while offering little in return.

Increasingly, the Congolese want power to be honored within the terms of their culture, and conservationists to take their interests into consideration. NGOs and researchers may steamroll local leaders for the sake of their ambitions, but by supporting the Congolese and establishing shared goals, they might inspire them to take up conservation for themselves, a step that would likely improve the outcomes of research.

Albert also pointed out how rarely Westerners recognize Congolese conservation efforts and the ways foreign conservationists have used local people to achieve their goals while giving them little credit. The Congolese are often nameless, even invisible, in the writing about conservation. In a *National Geographic* article about great apes, published in 1992, a small add-on article mentions Wamba:

> A real drama occurred in 1987. During [Takayoshi] Kano's absence, soldiers appeared at Wamba to capture bonobos to give to foreign dignitaries. The trackers refused to lead the soldiers to the apes and were beaten. After the soldiers killed a cluster of bonobos to collect an infant, Kano's chief tracker put himself between soldiers and another group. He said they would have to kill him before they could kill any more bonobos, and the apes were saved.

"Kano's" chief tracker is Nkoy (which means "leopard"), and despite having been beaten and threatened with death, he remains nameless. Rather, he is described as an extension of Kano, an object on the scene. In the eyes of the Congolese who spent years in the field, tracking, keeping notes, and risking their lives while foreign researchers came in for relatively short visits and then received praise for their courage in going to the Congo, this kind of omission is not insignificant.

Albert experienced this dynamic himself when Conservation International's Senior Director for Central Africa, an American, traveled to Kokolopori in the company of a British reporter for *Time* magazine. After the creation of the immense Sankuru Nature Reserve in northeastern Kasai-Oriental Province in 2007, the reporter contacted BCI. He visited Kokolopori because it was more accessible, and when he penned his April 21, 2008, article, "Eden for the Peaceful Apes," he referred to the visiting CI director frequently, although the man had never been to Kokolopori before. The article doesn't mention

Albert, and a photograph's caption describes the visitor from CI as "persuading," "seated, being introduced during a conservation campaign in Yalokole." He sits at a table while Albert, unnamed even here, stands, speaking to the people he has worked with for years. And while the article mentions André Tusumba, who led the effort to create Sankuru, there is no photo of him. A reader might think that the reserves owe their existence to the visitor.

In many ways, prestige and the celebrity status of the Western "big man" seem to be greater impediments to effective conservation than the Congo's poverty and lack of infrastructure. A more inspiring send-off than any we've seen so far would be the end of *Demonic Males,* in which Wrangham and Peterson meditate on the violent potential of the human intellect and on what we can learn from bonobos.

> If we are cursed with a demonic male temperament and a Machiavellian capacity to express it, we are also blessed with an intelligence that can, through the acquisition of wisdom, draw us away from the 5-million-year stain of our ape past. . . .
>
> Temperament tells us what we care about. Intelligence helps generate options. And wisdom can bring us to consider outcomes distantly, for ourselves and our children and our children's children . . . and perhaps even for the minds in the forest.

If bonobos serve our culture well as a symbol of peace and coalitions, it's not because they are perfect; they are simply more skilled at maintaining harmony, aided by the fortunate fact that they have adequate resources. As Peterson and Wrangham make clear, changing human behavior is essential to the success of our species, and this requires a change in how we manage and share resources. The importance of transforming ourselves may also be why Sue Savage-Rumbaugh found herself among *Time*'s one hundred most influential people: she not only discovered how bonobos can communicate using human language, but also conveyed what that says about how both they and we can adapt.

The failure to use our symbols to their fullest potential lies entirely within human culture. The myths of Western culture are as great a challenge as any notion of power among the people of Équateur. We have our own deeply entrenched complexes of prestige and territoriality, to which we are often blind. If we want to succeed in conservation, the solution sounds trite, though it is in fact deeply challenging: we must make space for other organizations and approaches, and support each other, no matter the differences.

Empty Hands, Open Arms

Part III
Sankuru

André Tusumba

"*Je m'appelle* André Tusumba. I was born the twenty-sixth of January, 1962. My father was also Tusumba André. I am his homonym. He died a year ago, on the fourteenth of November, 2011."

So André Tusumba began his story, placing himself with names and numbers, his own and his father's, then his mother's, who died on April 10, 2001. He was one of fifteen, his father having had two wives. His mother had seven children, his *marâtre*—his father's second wife—eight.

We were in Kinshasa, before my departure with BCI to Mbandaka, in Evelyn Samu's dining room, at a table that seated a dozen. Her granddaughter and niece, both two, played outside. The maids watched over them, occasionally calling out. On Matadi Road, a vehicle with a broken muffler passed, the reverberations of its engine banging off the walls.

André was hard to read, his posture somewhat military, his eyes still and unrevealing as he spoke. I had run across his name in articles about the creation of the Sankuru Nature Reserve, and I had heard Sally and Michael describe his conviction and incessant work. He was dressed modestly, in jeans and a button-down shirt, a baseball cap in his hands. Occasionally, when he emphasized a word, the strength in his features came to the surface, his cheekbones broad and high.

"As a child, I had two loves," he told me, "soccer and goats. Each day after Catholic school, around three o'clock, I would take our goats to graze. We had 117 goats."

This was the first image he shared, a ten-year-old André climbing the hills of Kivu, not far from the border with Rwanda, a thousand miles east of where we sat.

As he spoke of the goats, he dropped his gaze, smiling faintly, the military aspect gone. I got the sense of a man whose heart is close to the surface, who gives himself entirely when he cares about something.

"I knew the goats," he said, "and they knew me. And so sometimes, in the evening, I let them be and went to play soccer." He described his friends arriving, making goalposts by jabbing sticks into the flat surface of a dirt road. They saw the dust cloud to the east before they heard the hammering of the big truck's engine, and they played until it was almost upon them. Then they grabbed the sticks, kicked the ball into the sloping pasture, and jumped off the road. The ball was made of bunched plastic bags that André had sewed together and wrapped with a piece cut from his mother's house-dress, an act for which his father beat him with a belt.

Sunset spread along the horizon, the mist golden over the dark blue curves of distant hills. André scored one last goal, grabbed the ball, and ran off. The other boys were used to seeing this. The goats knew their daily schedule and had returned home.

"Though I grew up in North Kivu," he told me, "my origins are in the province of Kasai-Oriental, in the district of Sankuru, the territory of Katako-Kombe, from the same village as Patrice Émery Lumumba. We are from the same *groupement* as Patrice Émery Lumumba. In our family we are all relatives with him. But we did not have the chance to get to know him because my father was a soldier. Around 1952, he did his military training in Kivu."

Under the Belgian colonial administration, André's father moved to North Kivu, a far more affluent province than Kasai-Oriental. He married there, and André was his second son, followed by a daughter. At home, his father made them speak the Tetela language of Kasai, even André's mother, whose native language was Mashi, the Shi language of Bukavu. Outside their home, with their friends, they spoke Kalanga or Swahili.

After independence, his father worked for the Service of Public Works and Land Management. For his job, they moved to Bukavu, then to Goma, on the Rwandan border. Later, they would move to Rutshuru, where his father started a coffee plantation and continued to raise cattle and goats.

André was proud that his father's uncle was Lumumba. He often asked his father why he'd never returned home, and his father said that his parents were deceased, that he'd built a life here that they never could have had in the much poorer Sankuru area. But André was conscious of his homeland because of the Tetela language that he used with his family.

Those years, his brothers didn't herd the goats that their father raised to sell for meat; only he did, and it was the only time he could play soccer. His mother refused to eat goat or sheep, and wouldn't even cook pork. André followed her example. If his father slaughtered one of his goats, he wouldn't touch the meat, eating cassava and *pondu*—stewed cassava leaves—instead.

As his love of animals grew, he became more curious about them in the wild. When he was in sixth grade, he went to Virunga National Park with his teachers.

Virunga dominated the region around the Zaire-Rwanda border, and boasted massive volcanoes, forests with leopards, elephants, gorillas, and hippopotami. He loved watching the animals, and with his friend Théophile, he began going often, climbing to the volcanoes to stare over the rolling hills.

"Are there also wild animals in Kasai, like those in Virunga?" André asked his father one night.

"Yes," his father said. "There are many, many wild animals in our province."

"Someday," André swore to him, "I will return to Kasai and go into the forests and see all the creatures that live there."

From his childhood, the strength of his conviction was clear, passions and loyalties dominating his personality. When he was ten, he confronted his father, who, after he took a second wife, began to ignore André's mother and to beat her when he drank. The priests at school had drilled into the students respect for their parents, and André never would have lifted a hand against his father, but he put himself between his parents and took the beating.

Over the years, André repeatedly told his siblings, "Anyone who drinks like our father will be unhappy in life." To this day, neither he nor his siblings use alcohol, and the only two drinks he has consumed have been glasses of champagne: one when the Sankuru Nature Reserve was officially established, the second when he and BCI were put in charge of Sankuru's carbon rights by the Ministry of the Environment.

He also told his siblings *Malheur à celui qui prend une seconde femme*, "Misery on whoever takes a second wife," and none of them are polygamous. As a child, he asked his mother to stop drinking, and she agreed. But his father never did.

The other conflict with his father concerned soccer. It was the pastime of the loiterers and louts in Goma, and though his father banned it, André skipped school to play. By the time he was fourteen, he was playing on the region's official team. His mother and siblings sneaked into the city to watch his games, but his father knew nothing about his son's growing fame. They lived a long walk from the city, and it was populous enough for André to lead a second life. It also seemed as if people, knowing about the conflict and admiring André's skill, conspired to keep him a secret. But gradually his father caught on, and when André was seventeen, a major first division game was scheduled and his father finally heard about his son's talents.

Shortly before the game, his father told André to spend the evening ironing clothes. As André did so, his siblings left and hurried to the city to watch the game. His father lingered, then, at the last minute, also went to the stadium, curious to see if his son was as good as people claimed. André stopped iron-ing and ran to the city along another path to meet his team. That day, the match was close, no scores made until the very end, when André drove the ball into the net with his head. But before the celebration could begin, even as his team was trying to hoist him up, he broke away and sprinted home, bathed quickly and returned to ironing clothes.

"That evening, over dinner, my father asked where I had been. I said, 'I was here—you gave me chores.' He asked my older brother where he'd been. He said, 'I went to see the game.' He asked my younger sister, and she said, 'I also went to see the game.' He looked at me and said, 'This time I'm going to beat you not for playing soccer, but for lying.' And so he beat me with his belt." André laughed and slapped the table. "But at least after that, he would tell me not to forget to go to soccer practice."

By the time André finished high school, Zaire's economy was in a slump, the country's infrastructure disintegrating, and his dreams began to seem impossible. His father couldn't pay for the education of so many children, but his mother, who had never gone to school, told André that if he didn't have a university degree, he would someday be the servant of his friends. She offered to help pay with what she earned from planting a field of beans, and he took a year off to work and put aside money. He did an employment test and was offered two jobs, one as a journalist for Radio National Zaïrois, the second managing human resources for an aviation company. He chose the latter, then went to university, where he was shocked to discover how poorly funded it was, how quickly everything was falling apart.

By then the Mobutu regime was growing weak. Services in the country were rapidly deteriorating, corruption everywhere. He hated the injustice, the police and military harassing people, taking their goods in the name of made-up taxes. For those who dissented, there was only prison, exile, or death.

He still played soccer, and this would prove to be his salvation; fanaticism for the sport made him a local celebrity, and even the police and military respected him. When he was attending university at the Institut Supérieur Pédagogique de Bukavu, he asked his mother to move in with him because he couldn't stand how his father treated her. He was doing a degree in his-tory, and as he read about nations and their wars, he saw the common theme, the rejection of oppression, the fight to create change and freedom, to rebel against old systems and corrupt regimes. Already in his first year, he be-came director of the Jeunesse du Mouvement Populaire de la Révolution, the student division of the MPR, Zaire's only party, in which membership was obligatory for all citizens.

Still, André longed for the fall of Mobutu, and one evening he cut a photograph of Lumumba from a copy of *Jeune Afrique* and put it on the bulletin board, where students gathered every morning to chant, "Mobutu, Mobutu, Mobutu." A crowd formed, and when people started asking who had put Lumumba's photo there, André called out that he had done it.

When the police arrived and asked him if he knew what doing this could cost him, he answered, "Do you know that Lumumba is the national hero and that he is the father of our independence?" He was taken to the Services de Securité Militaire. They wanted to know where he'd found the photo, and he told them about the magazine. Due to his youth and popularity, they warned him and let him go. But his action only increased his fame among the students.

Because the government had ceased paying university officials, they began selling classroom chairs and tables. Then they started asking the students and their parents to pay, and they established a quota system, taking only a certain number of students from each area.

André was in his third year when he organized a demonstration. In 1987, most of the European priests who ran the institutions had left, and the state had taken over the schools. But there was still a priest as rector, Père Milani, a tall Italian in his early seventies who loved soccer. By then, André was the student spokesman, popular not only for his politics but also for his skill on the soccer field.

André first tried to negotiate with the officials for affordable tuition. He and the students put together a memo and sent it to the school's directors. But when it was ignored, they decided to deliver it to the governor's offices. André organized a nonviolent march of over a thousand students to take it there, but the police shot tear gas canisters into the crowd, then beat the students with clubs.

"The next day, I was invited to the office of the institute's general director. As I arrived in the hall, I saw seven police officers waiting. I knew what could happen when you took action. I didn't want to be a martyr. I just wanted to fight the system I hated, and when I saw the police, I understood right away. I was ready for anything, even death, but I believed my popularity would protect me.

"The police wanted to know who was behind the protest. They had a list of students, but the other leaders had already escaped across the border to Rwanda, and were on their way to Europe. I said that I was just trying to protect student rights and that the demonstration was peaceful, but they put me in prison, alone in a cell for a month."

Days passed, and his friend Célestin Chishibangi brought him study notes for his classes. André learned that many students had run away. Relatives had to pay to bring prisoners the only food they would receive, and Célestin paid to bring him the notes, which André studied even though he had been expelled from the university.

A month later he was released, and when he walked into the institute, Père Milani was waiting. The lean Jesuit would leave a few months later, following the others back to Europe, but he helped reinstate André—not just because he'd been a good student, but because the soccer team hadn't been the same without him.

Since high school, André had been close friends with Guillaume, the younger brother of Pierre Kakule, the head conservationist of North Kivu's Tayna Gorilla Reserve, who would go on to win the 2005 Condé Nast Environmental Award. Visiting the reserve, André learned from Pierre of the similarities between himself and gorillas, as well as about bonobos. He could see how quickly the wildlife was disappearing in the areas he'd hiked as a boy, but after their conversations, André went on to read articles about the environment, about global warming and a hole in the ozone layer.

This was one of those moments when, as André spoke, I could see what might have come of his life if his energies hadn't been consumed by survival, with feeding himself and his family. But Zaire was disintegrating, and André focused on building a teaching career. He finished his degree in history and gave courses at the technical college in Goma. He was twenty-five, and soon married a twenty-two-year-old graduate in English from Bukavu. By 1992, he was the syndical delegate for the teachers of Goma. Salaries were rapidly diminishing, and they used SIDA, the French acronym for AIDS, to describe the situation: *salaires insuffisants difficilement acquis*—insufficient salaries acquired with difficulty.

When he was thirty, living in Zaire had become a daily struggle, and he left his family to teach in Rwanda, at the Collège Saint André, sending money home. He gave courses in history and geography, and continued playing soccer. It was 1993, and Kigali was heavily militarized. Hutu soldiers were everywhere, even civilians were carrying clubs, and every Tutsi was a suspect. When the *collège*'s Tutsi custodian was taken by the police, André spent a day at the station until he got him back.

Some mornings, there were bodies in the street. Again the servant disappeared, and this time André could find no trace of him. Then a friend with whom André played soccer, Janvier, was shot and killed in front of his house. Three days later, André gave up his courses, packed his bags, and

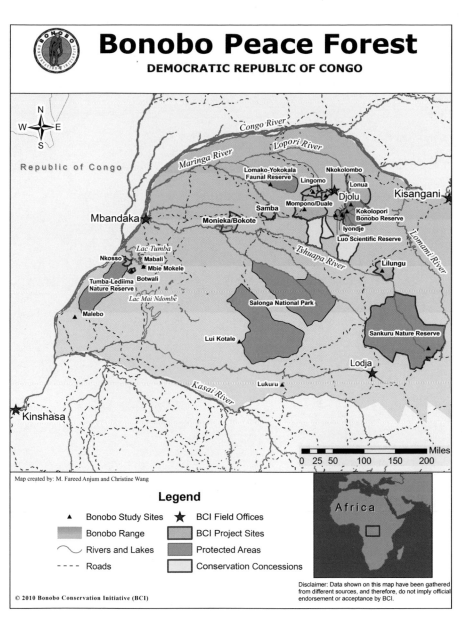

Bonobo Peace Forest
DEMOCRATIC REPUBLIC OF CONGO

Congo River

Lopori River

Maringa River

Republic of Congo

Lomako-Yokokala
Faunal Reserve
Lingomo

Nkokolombo

Lonua

Djolu

Kisangani

Mompono/Duale

Samba

Monieka/Bokote

Kokolopori
Bonobo Reserve

Iyondje

Luo Scientific Reserve

Mbandaka

Lac Tumba

Nkosso

Mabali

Mbie Mokele

Botwali

Tumba-Lediima
Nature Reserve

Lac Mai Ndombe

Malebo

Lui Kotale

Tshuapa River

Lomami River

Lilungu

Salonga National Park

Sankuru Nature Reserve

Lodja

Kasai River

Lukuru

Kinshasa

Miles
0 25 50   100   150   200

Map created by: M. Fareed Anjum and Christine Wang

Legend

▲ Bonobo Study Sites   ★ BCI Field Offices

　 Bonobo Range   　 BCI Project Sites

〜 Rivers and Lakes   　 Protected Areas

- - - - Roads   　 Conservation Concessions

Africa

© 2010 Bonobo Conservation Initiative (BCI)

Disclaimer: Data shown on this map have been gathered
from different sources, and therefore, do not imply official
endorsement or acceptance by BCI.

BCI Reserves Map.
© BCI, Created by M. Fareed Anjum and Christine Wang

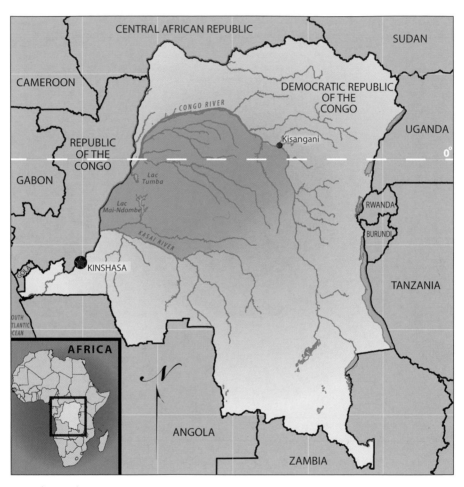

Bonobo Habitat Map.
Created by Chris Auger for the Bonobo Conservation Initiative

Democratic Republic of the Congo Map.
Washington, DC: Central Intelligence Agency, 1998. Credit: Library of Congress Geography & Map Division

Sally Jewell Coxe and Iboko, a bonobo that BCI saved from a trader in Mbandaka. 2005.
© BCI, Credit: Hurley

Bienvenu Mupenda, chief of operations, Nicolas Mwanza, scientific director, Eric Epheni, communications coordinator, and Papy "Pitchen" Kapuya, program assistant and logistician.
Credit: Béchard

Michael Hurley and Iboko. 2005. Mbandaka.
© *BCI, Credit: Coxe*

Evelyn Samu, national director, and Richard Demondana, finance manager.
Credit: Béchard

Arriving in Djolu by bush plane.
Credit: Béchard

Children push-starting a motorcycle.
Credit: Béchard

Directing the Land Cruiser across a bridge.
Credit: Béchard

Children playing with a ball made with the natural latex from a vine.
Credit: Béchard

Kanzi at the
Iowa Primate Learning
Sanctuary (formerly the
Great Ape Trust).
Credit: Liz Rubert-Pugh

Bonobo in Kokolopori.
© *Christian Ziegler, National Geographic*

Bonobo in Kokolopori.
© *Christian Ziegler, National Geographic*

Bonobo in Kokolopori.
Credit: Béchard

Albert Lokasola.
Credit: Béchard

Albert Lokasola performing the knight of the forest ceremony in honor of Léonard Nkanga Lolima, head tracker.
© *BCI*

Sally in the forest with trackers at Kokolopori.
Credit: Ingrid Schulze

Jean-Pierre (in white cap) and village men working on the Land Cruiser.
Credit: Béchard

Beginning of village dance within the Kokolopori Bonobo Reserve.
Credit: Béchard

Children in Kokolopori.
Credit: Béchard

André Tusumba.
Credit: Béchard

André speaking to community members in Sankuru.
© *BCI, Credit: Hurley*

André and Michael filming a bushmeat market in Lodja, the administrative
center of the Sankuru district. Standing next to Michael is Bantu Bungi, an
ICCN Technical Director and specialist in Zoonotic Disease transmission.
© *BCI, Credit: Eric Epheni*

Albert Lokasola, André Tusumba, and Dieudonné Mushagalusa, deputy
national director, with Sally Jewell Coxe.
© *BCI*

Children and woman in Likongo, Pastor Jean Gaston Ndombasi's community conservation area under development near Kokolopri.
Credit: Béchard

Fisherman on the Maringa River.
Credit: Béchard

Basankusu, a town on the Lulonga River at the confluence of the Maringa and Lopori.
Credit: Béchard

The boat arrives in Mbandaka, where Dick Rice, BCI advisor and former chief economist at the nonprofit organization Conservation International, joins us.
Credit: Béchard

returned to Goma in the night, realizing that he himself would be suspect for his friendships.

In Goma, one of André's friends was an advisor to the governor and offered to find André a job as an advisor to the vice-governor. But Joseph Kanamugiri, a Tutsi friend from Rwanda, visited and asked André if he wanted to sell veterinarian pharmaceutical products in Kivu. They traveled to Bunia and made more than they'd expected, since local suppliers had vanished with the breakdown of infrastructure. They then began selling throughout Zaire.

André was finally able to pay for his siblings to attend school, and he had them come to live with him in Goma. But according to him, his wife couldn't stand the invasion of her privacy, and she told him he had to choose between her and his family. He promised that his siblings wouldn't be there forever, and she and André already had a two-year-old boy. But she left anyway, taking their child, and returned to her family. He asked her to come back, but she refused and eventually married a member of Mobutu's family.

When the genocide started in Rwanda, André was no longer able to get veterinarian supplies. Joseph, his business partner, fled to Goma, taking refuge in André's house, and when the Rwandan Patriotic Army (RPA), largely composed of the descendants of exiled Tutsis in Uganda, invaded Rwanda, the entire Hutu government fled into Zaire.

"I believe that Zaire's hardship began with the genocide," he told me. "Goma was a city of five hundred thousand, but over a million Hutus came. They brought their government, their banks, their police, everything. An entire civilization implanted itself in ours. The Hutus demanded all of the food, and their military began killing Zairian Tutsis and taking their homes." He described that this was done with the tacit understanding of the Zairian military, who hated the local Tutsis.

"And Joseph?" I asked. "Was he killed?"

"No, he wasn't. The Hutu military had an understanding with the Congolese Army. I was well known in Goma for soccer, so I could do more or less what I wanted."

He described how the RPA fought all the way to the border, killing Hutu soldiers, how there were so many bodies in Lake Kivu that no one would use the water. People died from dehydration and diarrhea, and corpses lay in the streets, tractors coming through daily to pick them up.

One afternoon, André saw a refugee near his house. She leaned against his neighbor's wall, then just died, falling to the ground.

Another day, after a brief rain, he found a small girl tied to her dead mother in the street, the woman having succumbed during a cholera outbreak. He took her and raised her as his own, looking through the Bible that night to find her a name.

Since André could no longer get veterinarian supplies in Rwanda, he had to find them in Kampala, the capital of Uganda. He married again, had another child, and moved to Butembo, not far from Uganda, taking his youngest siblings with him. He struggled to provide for his family, and the Ugandans he knew wanted Zairian coffee, so he drove it across the border and brought veterinarian supplies back in the empty vehicle. His greatest challenge was negotiating with soldiers who tried to extort amounts that exceeded the value of his goods. His fame as a soccer player no longer protected him, and business became a constant struggle. When a friend in Uganda offered to introduce him to André Kisase, a fellow Tetela from Kasai and a known rebel Zairian leader, André accepted.

He met Kisase in his home near Kampala. Kisase was reserved but clearly happy to speak to someone who knew his tribal language. They discussed the situation in Zaire and their shared hatred of Mobutu. For André, who'd struggled for so long to feed his family while being robbed daily and seeing his society deteriorate into anarchy, Kisase's talk of war made sense. There was no other solution, he realized, and so, when Kisase proposed that André begin military training in Uganda, he agreed.

A few months later, in 1996, when the RPA invaded Goma to push the Hutu leaders out and repatriate the refugees, Kisase told André that this was the time to liberate their country. With the entire border destabilized, the Alliance des Forces Démocratiques pour la Libération du Congo–Zaire (AFDL), led by Uganda-backed Kisase and Rwanda-backed Laurent-Désiré Kabila, invaded. André was Kisase's aide-de-camp, but not long afterward, early in 1997, Kisase was killed.

"You were there when he died?" I asked.

He shook his head, looking down slightly. "That I cannot speak of."

History books do not offer a clear account of Kisase's death. He was the only rebel with a force of any size before the Rwandans began courting Zairian leaders. Their immediate reason for wanting Mobutu removed was his support of the Hutu *génocidaires*. Whereas Kabila followed the Rwandans' orders closely, earning himself the nickname *Ndiyo Bwana* ("yes sir" in Swahili), Kisase wanted a revolution for the Congolese, and frequently challenged the Rwandans. Some accounts state that as he departed his military camp in North Kivu, Kabila's bodyguards accompanied him and killed him on the road, but there has been no definitive report.

If André shifted his allegiance to the Rwandans, he told me, it was only because he wanted Mobutu removed. Zairians were flocking to the cause, Mobutu's soldiers fleeing west. The people's frustration had at last been harnessed, and they supported Kabila because they were hungry for change. But the decay of the Zairian state was far greater than anyone could have imagined, and the war went quickly to Kinshasa. André arrived there the day after the capital fell.

His joy was short-lived, however, as Kabila's nepotism began immediately. The country's new leader named relatives and friends from Katanga to positions of power. Nothing that André had fought for was happening.

"Everyone kept asking Kabila if they could have elections and a multiparty state, and he said no. We saw another dictator in the making. We wanted to eliminate Kabila before his dictatorship took root."

André was working for the Conseil National de Sécurité in Kinshasa, or National Security Council (CNS). The Rwandans had followed his activities during the war, and when Kabila expelled them and the new war started in 1998, they asked André to come back. They saw that he had the makings of a leader, speaking French, Lingala, Tetela, Swahili, and Mashi, as well as some Kinyarwanda and Luganda, the languages of Rwanda and Uganda. They gave him further military training in Rwanda and placed him as a technical consultant for Ernest Wamba dia Wamba, a soft-spoken professor who had spent years in academic institutions in the United States and now was the president of the Rally for Congolese Democracy (RCD), the rebel force opposing Kabila.

André admitted that the Rwandans made serious mistakes early on, and eventually began simply looting the country, but he defended their initial involvement. "When the Congolese write about Rwanda, it's always in the wrong way. If Rwanda was an occupying force, then Zimbabwe and Namibia would be occupying forces, because they were fighting in Kabila's stead, as was Angola. . . . But now that there are no more occupying forces, what are we going to do with the Congo? Let's stop accusing people. Yesterday we accused the Belgians. Now it's the Rwandans. But the Belgians aren't here anymore. The Rwandans aren't here. The Zimbabweans and Angolans aren't here. This is a Congolese problem. This country belongs to us. We have to accept that we have an obligation to our population and our country; otherwise, we'll find occupying forces everywhere."

André is referring to "the myth of the yoke," the view that many Congolese hold of, in the words of Thomas Turner, "a passive Congo, vastly rich, preyed on by outsiders." They believe that foreign governments have been stealing from them, manipulating their politics, and that the Rwandans and Ugandans came as "agents of the West." But while André acknowledged that the Rwandans and Ugandans ultimately did exactly what the Congolese expect outsiders to do, he rejected the idea that the effort to topple Kabila was misguided, and he believed that if Kabila had remained in power, he never would have allowed true democracy. André knew that the RCD would be hugely unpopular among many Congolese, but he didn't want to endure another decade of powerlessness and poverty.

Today, given the Congolese's hatred of the RCD, it is difficult to recall just how much Kabila's rule resembled that of Mobutu: suspending political parties and managing more than half of the nation's funds himself. His encouragement of racial hatred against Tutsis, the murders of Congolese ethnic Tutsis, and his use of the former Hutu army and *génocidaires* as his personal force tipped many of those in the east in favor of the Rwandans. Ernest Wamba dia Wamba stated that his mission was to establish democracy, and many like André supported him.

When the war broke out, Kabila funded the Mai Mai, the numerous rebel groups that arose to protect territory or for larger political and economic reasons. The RCD massacred civilians ostensibly in an attempt to stop the insurgency or as reprisals for their own losses, and its lack of manpower and funding transformed it into what Jason Stearns describes as "a predator that sucked resources out of the population and provided next to nothing in return." Telling his story, André admitted that the force he supported had done a great deal of harm.

At first, he was in charge of logistics, provisioning RCD troops and managing their movement. Then he began recruiting, wanting to explain to the people why this war was important. Eventually, he decided that he should lead the 3,700 Congolese men who'd chosen to join, and he put himself through military training alongside them. But the war only dragged on, and as it did, further divisions emerged among the rebels.

"All wars are won with a population," André told me. "If the population believes in a cause and takes it to heart, then they support the war. The first war was supported by everyone. The second war didn't have the support of everyone. The Congolese didn't understand why people rebelled against Kabila so quickly. The rebels had Rwanda and Uganda for support. The population didn't appreciate the second war. But the second war was very important because Kabila wanted to be a dictator even more than Mobutu had. The nepotism that people denounced under Mobutu was starting again. We were in a state of auto-proclamation, where there was no government. The politics of Kabila weren't adapted to the real world. He should have kept good relationships with allies, but relationships with neighboring countries were worsening."

In May 1999, the RCD took Lodja, the administrative center of the Sankuru region, and André found himself a seat on the first plane there. He had never been able to reach Sankuru before; he'd lacked the money and leisure, and the area had been cut off owing to the country's degraded infrastructure and the *tracasserie*—soldiers harassing travelers constantly. For the first time, he observed the forests broken with savannah, yellow clearings like puzzle pieces in the vast green covering that thinned to the south until it gave way to open land. He recalled his father's stories, how he'd said the region was full of wild animals like those in the Virunga National Park.

In Lodja, he spoke to the local people and explained the RCD's purpose, meeting with community leaders and assuring them that they would not be mistreated. He tried to dispel the belief that the RCD was a Rwandan invasion with no support from the Congolese. To the contrary, he told them, thousands of Congolese had joined the struggle precisely because they wanted a democratic state.

In 2001, when the RCD was putting a military governor in charge of Lodja, the people there requested that André be given this position because they felt he understood their needs. The RCD agreed to make him vice-governor, and he set about establishing better relations with the people and punishing military abuse.

Once, he learned that a Mai Mai group had captured a village 110 miles away. Though the governor recommended a counter-attack with one hundred soldiers, André insisted on taking fifty, since there were only seventeen enemies in the village with light weapons, and he didn't want more soldiers than he could watch over. When he set out, he rode his motorcycle in front of the truck that carried his troops. If they arrived before him, his soldiers might blame the villagers for allowing the Mai Mai to enter, and there might be reprisals.

Once there, he discovered that the Mai Mai had left after killing the head of police. André's soldiers wanted revenge, but he said that if they did anything, he would shoot them himself. From there, he went to the neighboring village, where his father's family was from. André was scouting the area with two bodyguards when seven Mai Mai approached, all of them local people who had formed a rebel group. His guards wanted to shoot, but he ordered them not to. He saw the old weapons the Mai Mai were carrying, and he doubted that they had ammunition for them. They got within twenty yards, staring at him, and he just stared back, commanding his men to do nothing. As André recalled, his two guards ran.

"I always focused on my goal," he told me, "and made up my mind to achieve it. One of my rules was to never allow myself to see anything negatively. I perceived all in a positive light so that I would succeed."

Staring at the advancing Mai Mai, he told himself that nothing bad could happen to him in his paternal village—that he must know these men and that they must be aware of his reputation for fairness. He put the power of his will into his gaze, commanding them not to attack. One of them called him by name.

He spoke with them for a long time, listening to their grievances. Over the course of the next week, he managed to get more than a thousand Mai Mai to come out of the forest. He explained that they had to rebuild their country, to work together. He met with the chieftains, establishing relationships that he would use again years later to create the reserve. The chiefs told him that they were angry at certain abusive commanders, police, and administrators, and André had them removed from the region.

"Fear," he told me, "makes you do bad things. Fear makes you do stupid things. My entire life I knew I could go to prison or die, and I made peace with it. You made up your mind to fight for the country, *la patrie*, and you elevated its value so that you could fight for it."

But André's greatest challenge in the RCD involved Sankuru and its wildlife. Though he'd dreamed of returning to his paternal homeland and seeing its animals, the only sign of them was in markets full of bushmeat. He recognized the smoked carcasses of monkeys and occasionally of what appeared to be a great ape, bodies dried whole, with faces intact and long human hands. He knew that there were no chimpanzees south of the Congo River, and he'd heard that bonobos lived only in Équateur, north of Sankuru; Pierre Kakule had described them. He wondered what these apes were.

As he observed the steady flow of bushmeat out of the forests to feed the soldiers, he realized the extent of the devastation, the degree to which his country was being pillaged. The Rwandans and Ugandans were extracting mineral resources even as the local people were forced to hunt wildlife to feed themselves. He spoke to other officials in the RCD, but they thought he was crazy. Lambert Mende Omalanga, a former vice prime minister under Mobutu, the elected deputy with the most votes in the Sankuru region, and the current presidential spokesman for Joseph Kabila, recalls believing that André had an ulterior motive, that he was trying to gain power, or that he'd simply lost his mind. When I met with Mende in his office in Kinshasa, he told me that at first he strongly opposed André.

"But André was doing very important work. Above all, he didn't give the impression that the interests of nature and people were in conflict, or that nature should be for the use of tourists who come from outside. The idea is that it's necessary to integrate the people into nature's protection, so they can make money doing it. And André put all that in language that was easy for everyone to understand, so they could see that it was in their interest. There was much opposition, but he convinced us, and we have become his partners."

All across the Congo, the war was decimating wildlife. In the Kivus, militias set up camp in the Virunga National Park, the oldest in Africa. They were exterminating thousands of hippopotami, running a bushmeat and charcoal business with the nearby towns. Park guards were equipped with high-powered weapons and fought low-grade wars on their territories, militias making reprisals by executing gorillas after the guards tried to block their activities.

But in Sankuru's forests, there was no enforcement of laws protecting endangered species. André learned that the great apes he'd seen in the markets were indeed bonobos, and as vice-governor, he put out a military order against the killing of bonobos, elephants, and okapis, the other flagship endemic species of the Congo, a relative of the giraffe with zebra-like markings.

The Kasai region had always been known for its diamond mines, which had contributed to Kabila's—and now the RCD's—funding. But as he argued with the local leadership, he told them, "The diamonds you have are nothing. This—the animals, the forests—is the real wealth."

Over time, André felt his interest in politics diminishing. Amid the chaos, the dislocation and exigencies of survival, he'd lost contact with what was most important to him. He wanted to be in the forest and work with the villagers. What would happen to them if the soldiers and townspeople ate the remaining wildlife?

His vision would focus increasingly on bonobos after a tribal chief gave him one as a present. She was little more than a year old, an orphan whose family had been slaughtered by hunters, and even as André received her, he again had to explain gracefully to the chiefs why they shouldn't do this.

He named the bonobo Henriette, after his sister. He and his wife washed and fed her, amazed at how affectionate the tiny creature was, clinging to them, looking in their eyes the way their own children did. He told his wife about the Lola ya Bonobo sanctuary in Kinshasa, which he knew about from Pierre Kakule, but with the war he couldn't take the bonobo there. They decided to raise her, feeding her, speaking to her, letting her be part of their family.

He was amazed how quickly she learned from them, following in their daily rituals. But she was a baby, and housebreaking her would take some time. One afternoon, when he was on duty, Henriette went into the sleeping quarters of the household's military guards. André had told them to keep their door shut since Henriette liked to explore. Inside, she defecated on the bed of Kokongo, a severe man who, when he saw what she had done, beat her to death with a stick.

André came home a few days later, and when his wife told him, he could hardly breathe. He learned that the guards had given Henriette to the neighbors, who had begged for the carcass and eaten it. André wanted to punish Kokongo, to punish all of them, but this would achieve nothing. He sat the men down, and, barely able to control his fury, he said, "You have just killed our national symbol."

The men struggled to understand, and André explained—the rarity of bonobos, that they lived only in the Congo, that they were intelligent and capable of emotions like humans. He repeated details that Pierre Kakule had told him, how bonobos gave birth only every five years, how they built their homes in trees and lived in complex social groups.

Afterward, André considered what else he could do to educate people. Henriette was the gentlest individual he had ever known. He'd seen so much war, so much death, and the idea of a creature who didn't kill made him wonder how humans could lose themselves so deeply in violence. Could people live similarly, resolving disputes without murder? Why shouldn't humans make peace like bonobos, he asked himself. Why shouldn't this be their credo?

He decided to found Action Communautaire pour la Protection des Primates de Kasai (ACOPRIK). He spoke to those who'd thought he was crazy, the governor and other powerful men in the region. He asked them to join and support his project, and they did, listening to him—a man whose conviction they had come to respect, if only because it could not be swayed—as he promised that conservation would be the future of Sankuru.

Defending the Vocation

After Laurent Kabila's assassination in 2001 and the transfer of power to his son, Joseph Kabila, André knew that the war would begin winding down.

"His son is better, far better," he told me. "We still have a long way to go, but he is much better."

By 2004, the country was in the process of reunification. His vice-governorship had been a military position, and with the war over, he resigned. He didn't see any reason not to. Joseph Kabila had accepted a multiparty state and free elections, and André was ready to devote himself to ACOPRIK and creating a reserve in Sankuru. Having seen so much waste of resources and human lives, he wanted to do something meaningful. From his readings in history, he understood the importance of decisive action, that it was necessary to stop the large-scale slaughter of wildlife and protect the forest.

"My training is as a historian," he said, "but conservation is my vocation." Heeding this calling, he focused on educating the people. As in the first war, his vision came together faster than he expected, as if he were again racing across the country, longing for change, though in this case as well, after an initial success—the creation of the Sankuru Nature Reserve in 2007—he would find himself mired in conflict.

Much as Albert had, he spoke to local leaders, explaining that their natural resources could either be exhausted or maintained and treated as renewable resources.

"In everything I do," he told me, "I think about what I can leave, how I can pass on the heritage of my work." He has hardly shifted his posture in over an hour. He sits perfectly straight, his hands on his thighs. He hesitates now, his expression different, slightly pained, as if he is searching in the story to find what he could have done to avoid the controversy that would cripple progress in the Sankuru Nature Reserve.

When he visited the villagers, he told me, he spoke not of what the people could dig up and sell—diamonds or gold—but of what they could maintain, of how tourism and conservation would increase the value of the forest. He asked how much they earned from killing elephants. It was a small sum compared to what they might earn as eco-guards. He asked the pressing questions. Was hunting as easy as before, or were the animals disappearing? What would they do when there were no animals left to sell? Exploitation had been the model for profit in the Congo for so long that it was hard for people to believe that an educated Congolese like André didn't want to manipulate them for his own interests, or that he cared about the well-being of their villages.

He bought a motorcycle because the roads of Sankuru were too bad for cars, and he drove wherever there were bonobos. He taught people about great apes and recorded where they were said to live. In many villages, he created small groups to support the protection of bonobos, to teach others about their importance and the possibilities for a sustainable future.

Months at a time, he made his way through the forest, over a thousand miles on winding paths. The Congo is a land of rivers and streams that swell with each downpour, and he often had to stop and strip his clothes, tie them in a bundle, and carry his motorcycle across rushing water. He rode 130 miles to Lomela, 75 to Djonga. In each village, he would talk to the people. He rarely progressed more than seven or eight miles an hour, coming upon a watercourse every three or four miles, again undressing and hefting the motorcycle across.

He saw that the communities' only source of sustenance was the forest; they relied on it for wood, water, game, mushrooms, black pepper, roots, edible leaves. The Sankuru region was the watershed for five of the Congo River's major tributaries, and he gradually explored its landscape. The population seemed to be growing, slash-and-burn agriculture expanding.

"I knew that deforestation would harm the watershed," he told me, "but how could I ask people to live differently? I often traveled a hundred kilometers without seeing a clinic, school, or pharmacy. The population lives in a state of deprivation that you can't imagine."

Like Albert, he had the skill of speaking to the people, of making them see his vision while asking them to do only what could be managed in the present. He focused on bonobos, describing the diseases that humans could contract from eating non-human primates. He explained the possibilities of conservation and tourism, of getting funds from the international community. In many villages, people had never seen a motorcycle. They had never heard talk like this.

Over the years, villagers began calling him the *osediketu,* "bonobo man," in the Tetela language. When children heard the engine of his motorcycle, they ran from the villages shouting *Mototuwaiketu*, "The motorcycle of the bonobos!" But only in 2004 and 2005, as the country's infrastructure recovered and military tensions eased, did it become possible for him to communicate with Kinshasa and travel there to look for support. He knew he couldn't start a conservation movement without linking to a larger network, but he recalled how people involved with WWF and AWF only wanted to talk and offered no concrete guidance.

During those years, André had been in touch with the gorilla conservationist Pierre Kakule in North Kivu. From a distance, Kakule mentored him, buying him a computer and a printer as well as fuel for the motorcycle when André began to go broke. Working with the Dian Fossey Gorilla Fund International, Kakule ran a school for conservation and landscape managers at Tayna, and BCI had sent several promising students there for training. This time, when André called him to discuss the difficulties of getting support given that Sankuru was a mining zone and outsiders didn't know about the presence of bonobos and okapis, Kakule suggested that he contact BCI, saying that their approach might be effective there.

"Up to this point," André explained, "most NGOs didn't go into Kasai. It was the diamond region, and under Mobutu, access had been strictly controlled. No one believed me when I told them about the bonobos and okapis. But Pierre told me what BCI had done, and that they were interested in working with Congolese conservationists."

In September 2005, at the GRASP (Great Apes Survival Partnership, of the United Nations Environment Programme) meeting in Kinshasa, André met with Sally. He recalled her warmth, feeling as if he'd known her for years. Sally and BCI's team sat down with him and placed a map on the table, asking him to explain where he'd traveled and what he'd seen. They asked for an activity report, and he wrote one up and gave it to them. Nothing was promised at that first meeting, but he was sure they would work together.

The GRASP conference was the first time he found himself in a room full of people who cared about what he did. When Sally introduced him and said he had come to tell them that there were bonobos in Sankuru as well as in Kokolopori, both the foreign and Congolese scientists in attendance were surprised. They didn't know where Sankuru was. They asked, and he explained that it was at the heart of the Congo, just below Équateur. He reminded his audience that there was no border for animals, that they didn't need visas or passports.

After the GRASP conference, BCI signed an accord with ACOPRIK and sent a preliminary scouting mission. Jean-Marie Benishay, then BCI's national director, traveled with André in Sankuru. The people who'd seen André so many times were surprised that he'd brought a well-dressed visitor from Kinshasa, someone who wanted to know about their territory. Maybe the *osediketu* hadn't been totally crazy, or maybe he'd just found someone equally crazy.

The rains came often in the forest, and the paths filled with mud and water. They didn't see the sun for days, only mist, and they couldn't dry anything. Even their bags with spare clothes were soaked. When they came to a village, they had to build a fire in a hut and dry their clothes, standing naked and asking the people not to come inside.

The journey was arduous, with both men on the light motorcycle in addition to nearly ninety pounds of gas in jerry cans and backpacks full of sardines, biscuits, clothes, and tools. Fallen trees often blocked their way, and André recalled one evening when they were driving in a hard rain to reach the next village where they would spend the night. They came to a large fallen tree. In the light of their headlamps, they looked for a place in the forest where they could take the motorcycle around it. Thunderheads blocked the moon, and as they carried the bike through the underbrush, Jean-Marie began to shout. At the same time, André felt prickles up and down his legs, in his groin and armpits, as red army ants swarmed up his body. They pulled their clothes off, running and thrashing through the bushes.

They traveled 745 miles altogether that week, and saw six dead bonobos in the markets, as well as okapi skins. As soon as Jean-Marie reported this to Sally and Michael, BCI set about looking for further funding from the United States Fish and Wildlife Service.

They launched a second expedition in April 2006, this one accompanied by CREF scientists. The Sankuru villagers were stunned to see the *osediketu* followed by five bonobo motorcycles. He had ten people with him, scientists who spent money on food, on lodging, and spoke enthusiastically to the local people, beginning the process of Information Exchange. André recalled the festivities, the dances, the liveliness of the people who suddenly felt valued. In one village, the chief brought out bottles of what he said was a special *lotoko* for the CREF researchers, members of the "brothers-in-law of Jesus" who often congregated with the Mbandaka team. After an hour the men were falling over. André, who didn't drink it himself, recalled never having seen men so drunk, and when he asked what was in the *lotoko,* the chief told him it had been brewed with marijuana.

The researchers recovered, and over the next few weeks, they worked their way deeper into the rainforest, finding communities so isolated they'd been untouched by the war. ACOPRIK, BCI, and CREF focused on the eastern part of what would become the Sankuru Nature Reserve, seeing live bonobos as well as okapis. The existing okapi reserves were in the far northeast corner of the DRC, and like bonobos, these animals hadn't been known by the scientific community to live this far southwest. The researchers also saw rare monkeys, the blue monkey and owl-faced monkey, and an unknown species. There were still elephants, which had been nearly exterminated elsewhere during the Mobutu era.

When Jean-Marie Benishay returned, he told Sally and Michael that the challenges in Sankuru would be much greater than those in Kokolopori. The poverty was devastating. And unlike people farther north who had ancestral traditions against bonobo hunting, some people in this region actually used bonobos for medicinal and ritual purposes. They ground the bones and rubbed the ash on women's bellies for fertility. Educating the people would be much more challenging than elsewhere, but BCI and ACOPRIK persisted. Gradually, with the aid of an Information Exchange team that BCI sent in, André helped establish an accord with twenty villages that agreed not to hunt bonobos.

One of the people who most supported André, eventually becoming the president of the administrative committee of ACOPRIK, was his cousin, Michel Kitoko. Michel was born in Sankuru in 1967, and shortly afterward his mother left his father, abandoning him. His father was a doctor, but he struggled to feed all his children from several wives, a task that became increasingly difficult as Zaire's infrastructure disintegrated and he had to travel to distant towns and villages to make money.

When Michel was eleven, his father acquired several hunting rifles from a German who was leaving the country, as many foreigners were at that time. Michel's father taught him to fire them and, impressed by his son's skill, sent him out each day after school to hunt. During school vacations, Michel left the house for weeks, living in the forest with the other men.

But as he got older, each time he saw his half siblings and friends with their mothers, he felt so much pain that he hardly knew what to do. He'd never seen his mother's face, not even in a photo. When he was seventeen, he asked his father's permission to find her. He knew only that she'd gone to live with her older brother in Kivu, and so he walked two hundred miles through the forest. After nearly a week on foot, he reached Kindu, a city where he'd heard his mother lived. The people there told him that she was in Bukavu, so he continued another two hundred miles, by foot and then by train to Lake Tanganyika, the longest lake in the world, where he took a boat, then another train, only to discover that she wasn't in Bukavu. People knew of her, though, and said she'd moved to Goma. He crossed Lake Kivu and searched in Goma, gathering clues from the people he encountered. Finally, in Rutshuru, he met his mother for the first time, finding what he'd hoped—that she was joyful to see him.

During that reunion, he also met his cousin André, and by the end of his three-month visit, he and André were close friends. His mother wanted Michel to stay, but he told her that he was in charge of the hunt and that he'd promised to return home. And so he did, again on foot.

But his journey began once more not long after. He was a good student, and his father sent him first to Kinshasa, then to Morocco to study. His older brother, who worked in Europe, paid for Michel's education in law and political science. Michel then moved to France, where he passed exams to qualify for his degree. He was still there during the wars, and it was André who called to tell him that his family was safe.

Michel didn't meet André again until 2005, in Kinshasa, at a small restaurant with plastic chairs on the Boulevard de 30 Juin, named for the date of the Congo's independence. They discussed the RCD, Michel telling André that the Congolese saw them as invaders, and André defending all that he'd done to fight dictatorship. It wasn't their talk about the RCD that most shocked Michel, however. Rather, he was stunned to learn of André's passion for conservation.

"He wants to protect the bonobo," Michel recalled saying to himself. "I told myself that he was crazy. He was protecting the animals I killed over there. That made me emotional. He's going to defend the animals that we kill and eat! I thought he needed something else to do. So I started trying to think up something that would help him find himself in life again."

But when Michel returned to France, he began researching what André had said, and he was startled to discover how right his cousin had been. Because he'd grown up in forests, he'd always thought that the world was full of nature. He also learned about bonobos, and since it was much easier to do research in Europe, he began sending André information. Michel admitted to himself that André was on the right path, and in the course of his research, he became so obsessed that he started attending ecological and conservation conferences in Paris.

"I was shocked that they didn't know why we were eating the animals. They say we shouldn't eat them. They had never eaten them. But they don't care to understand why we were eating them. . . . I would go to conferences to tell them to stop condemning us. You have to understand our reasons. For us, the forest is the supermarket. There's not even an agriculture or livestock program in place, so what are the people going to do?"

He'd gone to the conferences with the innocence of the uninitiated, thinking he wasn't qualified to be there, only to discover that he was the only one with actual experience of the rainforest. He told them he had been raised to hunt, and often did so to feed his family. "They had no idea of the human need. I tried to explain it: 'You have made these people into your enemies. How will you work with them to make change?'"

When Michel next saw André, he shared his expertise, both from his research and as a former hunter. He knew how the people from these areas thought, and that ACOPRIK had to improve their living conditions in order to succeed with conservation.

The next expedition BCI organized with ACOPRIK catapulted the project forward. They brought scientists from the Institut Congolais pour la Conservation de la Nature (ICCN) into the territory and proposed establishing one or two community-based reserves that would link to the projected Bonobo Peace Forest. But when the ICCN's people saw the rich biodiversity of Sankuru—not only okapis, bonobos, and rare monkeys, but hippopotami, Congo peacocks, and elephants—their response was dramatic. They called the bushmeat trade in Sankuru an ecocide, and they moved toward creating a reserve more quickly than they had with Kokolopori, which was already functioning like a reserve although it had yet to receive that legal status. When discussions about the boundaries of the projected Sankuru Reserve began, BCI recommended that it be a third of its current size, focusing on the territory from Lomela to Katako-Kombe, along the Lomami and Tshuapa Rivers. At the national level, the discussion became enthusiastic, officials seeing both the need to protect this core watershed of the Congo River and the possibility of using the forests to develop carbon credit programs that would allow for the sale of credits to companies that chose to decrease their carbon footprint. There was also the question of governance, and since Sankuru had comprised a single administrative region for decades, the ICCN decided to make a community-based reserve on a larger scale than had previously been attempted, so as to keep the political and administrative boundaries of Sankuru intact.

The term *ecocide* is hardly extreme in light of the conditions not only in Sankuru but throughout Central Africa. Though a healthy rainforest can sustain about one person per square kilometer, many parts of the Congo basin now have a density of five to twenty. These populations are expected to double every twenty-five years, and already by 2004, Central Africans were consuming an estimated five million metric tons of bushmeat a year, or, as Dale Peterson writes, "the equivalent of some 20 million cows and steers." In 2000, the bushmeat trade had an estimated profit of almost one billion USD.

Of the animals slaughtered, apes are severely affected because of their slow reproductive cycles and their high intelligence. Female bonobos begin to develop their pillowlike genital swellings when they are seven, and though they leave to look for a new group at eight and are sexually mature by nine, they don't bear offspring until they are between thirteen and fifteen, just before they reach their full adult size. Pregnancies produce only one child, and mothers nurse for five years. Their infants, like those of humans, require learned behavior to survive and remain dependent through their adolescent years. Parents must invest a great deal of time and energy into raising and educating them, and this in itself limits the number of offspring they can produce. Like humans, bonobos develop large brains, and this also means a slow growth rate, since brain tissue consumes more energy than almost any other body part. In the typical life span of a bonobo—fifty to fifty-five years—a mother can have only five or six children, one every 4.6 years.

André understood this. Though the forests of western Sankuru were degraded and overpopulated, he intended to prevent further encroachment as well as logging concessions. He knew the classic scenario: loggers cutting roads that quickly become rivers of meat; trained hunters accessing new areas that they "empty" systematically; and European-financed logging trucks carrying the smoked meat to larger markets or cities. Such roads bring migrant workers trained as loggers, as well as their families, into the unfamiliar forests, where the only source of protein is bushmeat. With western Sankuru, André planned to create a buffer, teaching people the value of the forest and eventually funding its protection through carbon credits, while in the eastern region, he would focus on active wildlife conservation, hiring eco-guards and—once the area was free of hunters—habituating bonobos.

He traveled throughout Sankuru, teaching people, and their confidence in him grew with each survey and training program, and with CREF's increased presence. ACOPRIK led an expedition to meet with community leaders, explaining the purpose of the reserve, the ways it could create a sustainable economy in the future. The villagers said they were ready to do this, and they signed an accord that André took to the ICCN.

On November 6, 2007, the Sankuru Nature Reserve was officially signed into existence, one of the largest in Africa at three million hectares. BCI put out a press release that newspapers around the world picked up. The *New York Times* and *Time* magazine published articles on Sankuru. Suddenly, there was an 11,802-square-mile nature reserve and a great deal of good press, but no funds to enforce laws against hunting and logging. Former Canadian prime minister Paul Martin called BCI's offices in DC, speaking to Sally and Michael, and asking how the reserve had been created with so little funding.

Almost immediately, before BCI and ACOPRIK could start their work in earnest, the controversy around Sankuru began, nearly bringing work in the reserve to a standstill and damaging relationships between ACOPRIK and the local people. John and Terese Hart, an American husband-and-wife team of scientists who had been at the GRASP conference where Sally and André told people about the presence of bonobos in Sankuru, had since received funding and initiated surveys in the Sankuru region, unbeknownst to BCI. Their findings confirmed those by ACOPRIK, CREF, and BCI, and in the scientific world, announcing the presence of bonobos, okapis, and an unknown monkey species in a new region represented a significant discovery.

Sally recalled, "When we found out they were conducting surveys in that area and the news about Sankuru came out, I wrote to them in the interest of collaboration. But when the announcement came out, they launched a major attack."

It began on Thanksgiving 2007 with a series of emails that Terese Hart addressed to Sally but that she copied to a dozen people directly or indirectly involved with bonobos, as well as donors. She wrote that the villagers in parts of Sankuru not only were unaware of the reserve, but that the Administrative General Director (ADG) of the ICCN wasn't aware of any international NGO participating in Sankuru, and that his goal was to create not a reserve, but a park. Unstated in this correspondence is that the Harts had wished to establish a national park that included the eastern section of the Sankuru reserve. In response, Sally explained that she had been working with the ADG, and that he was fully aware of BCI. Over the next few emails, Hart questioned ACOPRIK's role, and whether Sankuru's boundaries had been properly established.

In 2008, Terese Hart wrote a blog post, suggesting that villagers in Sankuru wanted to kill André for selling their forests. It begins: "We had been hearing rumors for almost 7 months that in a series of isolated villages, the Djonga villages, something had gone wrong for conservation. We had to find out what." What Terese Hart doesn't acknowledge in the blog is that she had email correspondence with BCI for months before the entry, and that she had been opposed to the creation of Sankuru for other reasons. Instead, she asks rhetorically if

ACOPRIK had stolen chickens and goats, or made off with a village woman, before saying that the villagers claimed that ACOPRIK had manipulated their signatures in order to "push through" the reserve.

Her reference to villagers believing that André had sold their forests—an accusation that she doesn't fully address or resolve—is odd. While community reserves allow people to stay and participate in conservation, her plan to create a national park would require inhabitants to leave. The Harts' current maps show their projected national park just to the east of Sankuru, hugging the boundary, with a surrounding "community conservation zone" that overlaps with the eastern section of the Sankuru Nature Reserve.

Hart presents one other argument for the conflict between ACOPRIK and the villagers, stating that it stems from a "murderous opposition" that developed between the Tetela of the Savanah and those of the forest. As proof, she cites a historical event from the 1960s, and though I tried to confirm such ethnic tensions, everyone I spoke to—from the presidential spokesman Lambert Mende Omalanga, who is from Sankuru, to Michel Kitoko, André Tusumba, and others in the region—said that they were aware of no such "murderous" tensions. They said that while there were occasional rivalries between politicians from different districts, this was standard across the Congo, if not across Africa and the world, and that no conflicts among the Tetela kept them from working together. André pointed out that if such murderous tensions did exist, Hart wouldn't have had to read about a fifty-year-old event to learn about them. He and those he worked with insisted that any conflicts in the area were the result of the Harts' polarizing local people against ACOPRIK, using money and influence to create divisions so they could justify creating a park. I tried to contact Terese and John Hart to get their side of the story, but John never responded, and Terese declined the interview.

In Kinshasa, when I spoke with Benoît Kisuki, he presented a stark view of the Harts. He had worked for more than twenty years in conservation, first on the Okapi Wildlife Reserve that the Harts themselves helped establish in the Ituri rainforest, then as the administrative technical director of the ICCN and now as the national director for Conservation International.

"The Harts," he told me, "were doing biological prospecting in the zone of Sankuru and toward Maniema and Orientale Province. They thought the biological prospecting would lead them to create a national park in the interior of the DRC, in that particular zone. They really wanted to be the first to establish that protected area. At the same time, when they hadn't yet achieved their objective, BCI was in the process of working on the politics of the Bonobo Peace Forest and with local organizations, Vie Sauvage in Kokolopori and ACOPRIK in Sankuru. . . .

"I remember when André Tusumba arrived in my office when I was administrative technical director and he showed me the documents with the vision he had. He talked about BCI, whom I already knew because they had worked on Kokolopori. Afterward, we met in my office with André and BCI to understand the reality on the ground. I thought the idea was excellent, and I proposed creating a reserve. They asked how we would go about doing so, and I took my two directors and sent them to the area to determine the limits. . . . They worked with André there. They had two objectives for this mission. The first was to assure that local communities and tribal chiefs were truly aware of the idea of creating a reserve, and the second was to find out whether ACOPRIK was known by local communities. . . . When I had the proof from my colleagues that ACOPRIK was known in the area, that they had a site, that the tribal chiefs and even the local administration supported the idea, and that there was support from BCI for the financial aspects, I set about putting together the document for the creation of the reserve. And suddenly we create the reserve, to the great surprise of the Harts. The reserve included the zone that the Harts would propose to include in their future protected area. This created a problem because we had done this before them. . . . They even tried to produce scientific evidence that showed that this was a reserve only on paper and had no biodiversity."

Benoît defended the reserve's value, which he saw as lying in its biodiversity, carbon credits, and location in the watershed of the Congo River. He explained that André was proposing a green economy rather than the exploitation of minerals that enrich only people from outside the region, and that even though the Harts claimed Sankuru to be lacking in biodiversity, part of the same protected area that they were proposing lay within the reserve. And yet the idea that the whole reserve was without bonobos took hold.

None of the people I interviewed denied that Sankuru's southwestern forests have lower levels of wildlife, nor did they dismiss the Harts' skill as conservation biologists, or the value of their planned protected area. Sally and André acknowledged that based on wildlife inventories alone, the ICCN might not have included the entire Sankuru area in the reserve. But given the amount of bushmeat in the markets around the Sankuru forests, the ICCN wanted to act quickly and decisively. As conservation biologist Michael Soulé writes, "In conservation, dithering and endangering are often linked," and "the risks of non-action may be greater than the risks of inap-propriate action." Furthermore, not all reserves or parks have consistently high levels of biodiversity; even the Wildlife Conservation Society (WCS) report that recommends funding the Salonga National Park over Sankura specifies that the park "contains *several areas* with high bonobo densities" (emphasis mine). *The World Atlas of Great Apes and Their Conservation* confirms this: "Bonobos seem to be absent or at low density in the central parts of the Salonga National Park." The authors go on to state that though the park has few bonobos compared to the region in which Wamba and Kokolopori are situated, there are significant populations in its northeast, where "government involvement and application of laws are poor . . . and hunting is a current threat."

Likewise, in Sankuru, the forests in the southwest have seen more hunting than those in the east and north. It seems clear in retrospect that the ICCN privileged the importance of the watershed. They wanted to expand wild-life habitat and protect the remaining animals as well as slow the encroach-ment of humans. If we were to look at the national parks on the East Coast of the United States when they were first established, we'd see nowhere near the biodiversity there is now. Much of the Appalachians were farmland, heavily hunted and logged. But one of the principles in creating a protected area is to rehabilitate the environment so that species can expand into it, to create natu-ral corridors that allow animals to breed with other groups. The East Coast of the United States has far more forest today than it did a hundred years ago, and in many places, locals report the reappearance of species not documented since the nineteenth century. The Sankuru Nature Reserve was made to protect not only the areas with high biodiversity, but also those around them, allowing animals more habitat and reducing human pressure. Lastly, the Ministry of the Environment intended to initiate carbon credit programs that could foster a local economy based on forest protection. This would create a buffer zone and a sense of investment for the people.

One other important factor heavily influenced the ICCN's decision to make all of Sankuru into a reserve. John Waugh, a consultant in conservation strategies and planning with more than twenty-five years of international experience, explained to me that there are patterns of land ownership and histories that go with land. "Land units," he said, "are social units. If, in creating a conservation area, you take a piece of land from one group and a piece of land from another group, and mash them together, you are actually forcing two different groups to work together. Even if you produce the best co-management arrangement possible, you interject a lot of complexity into the arrangement. The communities may represent different clans, or even speak different languages. There's a strong chance that they have a history of competing interests. If you reorganize these patterns without understanding the complex relationships between people and the land, you risk totally ignoring the social dimensions, and that's a real problem in terms of sustainability of the conservation enterprise."

The Harts' plan was to create a park on land composed of different administrative regions and even provinces, whereas the more feasible project would be for them to make a protected area that abuts Sankuru and supports its conservation efforts by creating an even larger buffer around its zones of high biodiversity. "If you look at the eastern portion of Sankuru," Michael Hurley told me, "east of the Tshuapa and west of the Lomami, the part where the Harts say the biodiversity is rich, you still have an area larger than possibly any other bonobo protected area in the DRC, aside from Salonga."

In a time when conservation efforts are struggling, it is difficult to understand why the Harts launched their attacks. Was it scientific jealousy, a question of competition for limited funding, or the fear that they were being scooped on a huge discovery, this being just another example of the conflicts in bonobo research that began with Coolidge and Schwarz over a tray of ape skulls? Or did they genuinely see no potential in any of the land within the Sankuru Nature Reserve? Michael believed they wanted to save face, given that they had received funding to work where they claimed no one else was doing research.

But André had a slightly different take: "The people saw the Harts as having a colonialist attitude. When they come, they impose on others—'You come here. We'll pay you this much'—rather than speak to people. They would take people from other provinces, from Orientale, to the Sankuru area, to work in those communities. They started marking areas off, making transects, without communicating with people. They didn't realize that the people living in Sankuru know these species. The idea of discovery is only for the foreigners. It is not for the local people."

Benoît confirmed this view, saying the Harts were "of that class of people who believe that they should come and teach conservation to the Congolese. They are still of that old class, and when there is a local organization that tries to work for conservation, and we have to help it to move forward, they don't believe in those politics."

Terese Hart's blog describes the landscape in language that could possibly be taken as colonial, referring to "the rather daunting task of leading the first mission into a truly unknown forest." Even the title of the Harts' 2007 grant proposal to the US Fish and Wildlife Service includes the line, "discovery and conservation of the Tshuapa-Lomami-Lualaba Landscape." John Scherlis explained to me that their descriptions suggested they didn't pursue working relationships with local people like Albert or André, who could "pull aside the curtain for them to make [the landscape] less daunting, less unknown."

With their growing desire for agency, the Congolese are increasingly sensitive to behaviors they perceive as colonial or autocratic. Even if Western conservationists see themselves as creating positive change, local people might view them no differently than other, more self-interested outsiders. And while models of partnership give less prestige to individuals, their inclusive structures promise larger, more coherent projects, with a sense of community investment that offers greater probabilities of success. In *Primate Conservation Biology*, Guy Cowlishaw and Robin Dunbar write that for community-based reserves, "one key factor contributing to their failure is that the goals of the local community are often not the same as those of the conservationists who support the project." In contrast, BCI's focus on communication and community integration may be precisely what has allowed them to produce such significant results despite the fact that their limited funding is spread over so many areas and projects.

The public nature of the Sankuru controversy had the opposite effect of building consensus, however, and BCI and ACOPRIK struggled to receive grants for the reserve. In 2008, the International Union for the Conservation of Nature (IUCN) Netherlands, part of a global alliance of scientific professionals dealing with nature conservation (not to be confused with the ICCN, which is a Congolese government institution), decided to grant BCI 84,995 Euros (about $132,000) to begin work in the Sankuru Nature Reserve. This was designated to kick-start development and sustainability projects and would pay for further surveys, more trackers, and eco-guards to protect bonobos and other species. The focus of the work funded by the grant would have been in the eastern part of the reserve, where the Harts had begun working. However, shortly after an IUCN conference in Barcelona that Michael and Sally didn't attend because of lack of funds—a meeting that Terese Hart did attend according to several sources—the moneys were rescinded.

The rescinding of the IUCN Netherlands grant was a turning point, the halt and digging of trenches. What could have been a success story, the creation of one of the largest reserves in Africa, became the opposite, dividing rather than unifying people. The infighting broke both the enthusiasm of the local people and eroded their trust. Local agency, the sense that people in a given area can make real change, is fragile after so many years of corruption and imposition by outsiders. Some village leaders sided with the Harts, possibly seeing their ability to get funding. And politicians jumped on the bandwagon, realizing the value of the reserve and how they could use it to influence public opinion to their benefit. ACOPRIK struggled to maintain the enthusiasm of the villagers, some of whom turned on them, resuming hunting. Others stayed loyal, bringing them orphan bonobos whom ACOPRIK then sent to the Lola ya Bonobo sanctuary, creating a strain on everyone involved, because the sanctuary had insufficient funds. In one year alone, ACOPRIK sent seven orphans. André saw others, who were too sick to be sent, die in his wife's hands as she was trying to nurse them and Sally looked for money to get them to Kinshasa.

Following the financial crisis of 2008–2009, funding became even more scarce. BCI paid trackers and ran projects not only in Kokolopori and Sankuru, but also six other areas under development. Sally and Michael often diverted their own salaries to needs in the field, and for André, the hardest moment came when he had only three dollars left in his house, which his wife planned to use to buy food for the family. He was supposed to email a report to BCI, and he would have to pay exactly three dollars for the Internet use at a nearby business.

She said, "You're telling me that you want to spend the money for Internet when we need food."

"*Oui, madame,*" he responded.

She went into the bedroom, came out, and threw the money at him. He took his flash drive and ran to send the documents. When he returned, he went to a small garden he'd planted near the house and began harvesting what he could find. But his wife refused to eat with him.

Not long after, BCI began paying him $500 a month even though they lacked funding for Sankuru. They bought him a new motorcycle when his ceased to work and supplied him with radios to communicate with people in the field. BCI also took over costs of ACOPRIK's students, who were being educated to work in the reserve.

Having been further marginalized in the conservation community, Sally and Michael looked to carbon credits to support the reserve. In Kokolopori, BCI had been working on proposals for Clean Development Mechanism (CDM), the first carbon credit program under the Kyoto Protocol, a 1997 international treaty that obliges signatories among industrialized nations to reduce greenhouse gas emissions. CDM worked through reforestation and preservation of forests that would allow the reserve to sell credits to industrialized nations or businesses. But international standards for carbon credits were still being formulated, and for Sankuru, BCI hoped to develop a contract with the government that would put BCI and ACOPRIK in charge of how they were managed.

In speaking of Sally and Michael, André recalled their determination.

"I saw how hard they tried. They weren't working miracles, but they were nourishing my hope with small solutions. They were giving me enough to sustain what I'd already built. I fully understood the depth of Sally's tenacity at the end of 2009, when we were negotiating with the government so that the reserve could manage carbon credits. On each of her trips to Kinshasa, she met with government officials and spoke with the minister of the environment. Once, just after she'd left, I had a conference with the minister, but he refused to sign and told me to forget the proposal. I called Sally and she said, 'André, you do not have the right to forget about that proposal. You have to go see him again. This isn't just for Sankuru, but for all people.'"

BCI's goal was to develop a protocol for Reducing Emissions from Deforestation and Forest Degradation (REDD), a carbon credit system that allowed reserves to work with several different international programs. But given that there was no precedent for REDD carbon financing in the DRC, the process took six months. BCI developed a contract with the help of the DLA Piper law firm, which had offered its services pro bono, supporting BCI from both its DC and Brussels branches. At the BCI Kinshasa offices, when the ICCN was holding a commission with BCI on REDD, the staff joked about the *troisième bureau,* the third office. The *deuxième bureau,* the second office, refers to where one goes to have an affair. The third one was the parking lot outside the Ministry of the Environment, where vendors sold Cokes and phone cards, and BCI's staff waited each time the commission was to be convened.

André recounted in his sparse manner how, at yet another meeting, the minister insisted that he needed to speak with Sally. André called her, she took the next flight to Kinshasa, and they signed the contracts—the first-ever government contract for REDD in the Congo.

Though he described 2010 as *une année en calvaire,* "a year of calvary," their project was accepted. Shortly after, Sankuru received a grant to develop carbon credits from Norway and the UK's Congo Basin Forest Fund (CBFF, not to be confused with CBFP) for REDD, which is now being implemented. This funding has been arriving slowly, administered by the African Development

Bank through a cumbersome financial and administrative process that wastes valuable time.

"The effect of the conflict over Sankuru," André stated simply one afternoon, as he and I stood in the sunlight outside BCI's offices, "was more bonobos dead, more elephants dead, more okapi dead. Nothing has been gained from it."

Though conflict in conservation and between scientists is far from unusual, it needs to be addressed precisely because of the impact it has on funding and managing reserves as well as on unifying local people, and because of the way competition skews even the scientific reporting that we take to be objective. The conflict with the Harts also highlights two different approaches: that which prioritizes the values and methodologies of a scientific field and that which respects local knowledge and social boundaries of people as well as their leadership. In *Science and Public Reason,* Harvard professor Sheila Jasanoff writes,

> There is a growing need . . . for what we may call the 'technologies of humility'. . . . They call for different expert capabilities and different forms of engagement between experts, decision-makers, and the public. . . . They require not only the formal mechanisms of participation but also an intellectual environment in which citizens are encouraged to bring their knowledge and skills to bear on the resolution of common problems.

Were they to frame their work according to the goals, knowledge, and social boundaries of the local people, the Harts might be significantly more successful. Their strengths clearly complement those of BCI, and had they chosen either to develop local capacity with BCI in eastern Sankuru or to establish their own protected area just to the east of it, both groups most likely would have been far more successful.

Despite this conflict, however, the importance of Sankuru was again recognized internationally. In December 2009, alongside Wangari Maathai, Jane Goodall, and Russ Mittermeier, BCI was honored at the fifteenth Conference of Parties to the UN Framework Convention on Climate Change in Copenhagen, for its efforts to save Sankuru's huge rainforest. In her capacity as founder of the What Is Missing? Foundation, Maya Lin granted BCI $12,500 to support their "Fair Trade" Community Carbon Initiative. She described Sankuru as "the largest REDD project in Africa and one of the largest on earth" and stated, "we feel it is especially appropriate to support and endorse this precedent-setting model carbon offset project. We congratulate BCI for the remarkable work it's doing to help find solutions to the biodiversity and climate change crises."

The Congolese also celebrated the achievement. Internationally known Congolese pop star Papa Wemba, who had grown up in Sankuru, joined the effort just as Werrason had for Équateur, composing and recording a song about bonobos and ACOPRIK.

Even as I write this, work continues in Sankuru. REDD projects cost millions to implement, and the zoning of forests is arduous. Sankuru clearly does need more resources directed at conservation, but the current funding will finally set projects in motion. ACOPRIK and BCI continue to educate local conservationists, more than a dozen having finished their studies in 2012. For development, André envisions one thousand agricultural starter kits going out, as well as fishing kits. Of the eighty-five people who already received a monthly salary, sixty trackers each get fifty dollars a month.

"Before," André told me, "even if they shot a buffalo, they couldn't get fifty dollars. The most they would be able to get is ten dollars. But they can't get them out and get the money. They couldn't even get that much from killing an elephant."

ACOPRIK still struggles with the consequences of the conflict between conservationists and has had to expend significant energy and resources on self-preservation rather than on getting work done. As a result, conservation funding isn't used as efficiently or as quickly as possible, at a time when environmental degradation is increasing exponentially. If anything, self-sacrifice in the largest sense of the expression is called for, to put aside personal ambitions and professional pride, to make coalitions that will be imperfect because humans are, in order to achieve concrete goals on the ground.

Viral Conservation

We'd been in Kokolopori for more than two weeks, the days mostly hot. Sally, Michael, and the BCI team worked with Vie Sauvage, frequently meeting in the *paillote* to go over reports, expenditures, and the details of projects involving reforestation and maintaining habituation.

Every few days, a different group of twenty or thirty women arrived in the camp from another village on the reserve. They entered singing, clapping, and stomping, and formed a circle in front of our hut, the words "Mama Sally" clear in their song. They'd known her for years, from her previous trips, and they came bearing gifts of chickens, eggs, and vegetables. One group even showed her a newborn girl named Sally.

Other conservationists visited as well, and Roger Afelende, a tall, thin, baby-faced man in his early thirties, turned up one afternoon on a motorcycle. Michael told me he'd created his own community-protected area where he lived in Nkokolombo, tracking a bonobo group in forests that could be reached after a motorcycle ride sixty minutes south of Djolu, followed by an eight-hour walk west. Roger told me that his trackers had seen an albino bonobo who spent more time on the ground than the others, and made her nests in small trees rather than in the canopy.

I'd often heard stories of the community-based conservation projects locals had launched after being inspired by Albert and BCI's work. Roger's was the most recent, and the albino made the idea of visiting the site appealing. I discussed it with Michael; he wanted to go but had too much work.

After a few days of planning, I was ready to head back to Djolu, but Roger told me I couldn't ride with him. He was hesitant to explain why, so Jean Gaston Ndombasi, another homegrown conservationist, explained that this excursion to Yetee had been Roger's first time using a motorcycle. Jean Gaston told me to climb on with him. He was small and thin, in his late forties, his light brown skin tight over the prominent bones of his skull, his eyes slightly jaundiced. He couldn't have weighed more than 140 pounds, and I was nearly 190. I told him this was a bad idea.

"*Ce n'est pas vrai*," he said. "It's not true. I can take you. It's not a problem."

I hesitated, but he waved for me to get on. As soon as I did, he cranked the accelerator and we weaved around a deep rainwater gully before careering down the hill toward the log bridge. He braked, aimed for one of the logs, and shot across, then up the road, gaining speed. I glanced back to where Roger was only just setting out, riding slowly. He soon disappeared from sight.

The sun dominated the sky, the shadow of a distant thunderhead on the horizon. It was two in the afternoon, and the yellow trail was at times a tunnel of shadow beneath the canopy, at others in sunlight so hot it felt like a hand pressing against my forehead. I wished for a helmet, or that we were going slow enough for me to wear a hat.

Before a flat stretch of clay, Jean Gaston accelerated, and the wind brought tears to my eyes. On either side were immense clumps of silvery-green bamboo that burst skyward. As he gained speed, the tires made a skittering sound on the leaves covering the baked earth. Ahead, the trail turned to golden sand, and he crouched like a jockey. Rather than slow as I expected, he sped up.

The tires plowed in and the motorcycle fishtailed, wobbling and swimming to the side of the path. Three women carrying woven baskets with straps across their foreheads jumped into the forest. Our tires bumped the shoulder, and we swerved to the other side. My heart pounded as I tried to let my weight sink, to stabilize the bike. Jean Gaston repeatedly pulled us out of a fishtail.

As soon as we were beyond the sand, he shouted back, "You're a good passenger. You don't make me fall." Then he cranked the accelerator again.

There had been many people in the camp at Yetee, and I didn't know Jean Gaston, only that he was the environmental inspector for Province Orientale and had been developing a conservation area in Likongo, a five-hour drive to the south of Kokolopori, whereas Djolu was to the west. But now, as we passed eight young men stumbling along the side of the path, he called over his shoulder that he was a pastor.

"You see," he told me, "these men, they have finished work, but they do not spend their money on food. Instead they buy *lotoko*. I do not drink or smoke. It is not the will of God. Some of us must set examples for the others if we hope for our country to survive."

I agreed, but my thoughts were on my survival as he cut wide S's, avoiding potholes, and splashed through sandpits as deep as those on a golf course. Each time he lost control, he crouched, hardly reacted, and when the bike drifted to the side, where there was now a ten-foot drop to dark, descending forest and massive tree trunks, he waited until the fishtail was almost at an end, then popped the bike onto the narrow crust of shoulder, inches from the edge, accelerating again.

He called something over his shoulder.

"*Pardon?*" I asked.

"*J'ai dit*—I said, if we believe in God, we will not have an accident."

I hoped that he had enough faith for the two of us, and it seemed he did as we repeatedly slalomed through sand. I'd often traveled by motorcycle, alone or with friends, or on motorcycle taxis in other countries, and I'd never seen anyone drive through sand this way. I would have preferred that he stay focused, but he called explanations over his shoulder, telling me that four young half-naked men with large woven baskets on their backs, singing, were walking the two-week trek to Kisangani's market. He said the same of young men herding pigs or goats. He raced past others, boys with bamboo over their shoulders, one with his rusted bicycle loaded with long wooden poles cut from the forest, tied to the central beam with vines.

Then Jean Gaston talked about his conservation area, and all the sacrifices he had made to educate locals and train trackers, to build a lodge for the visitors who had yet to come. He worked in Kisangani and used his money for conservation, inspired by Kokolopori. God made man the curator of the earth, he explained, and it can be Eden if we so choose. Otherwise we will destroy it all and our punishment will be that we'll have nothing for our survival.

The clouds I'd seen earlier had become a massive front, black along its bottom, blue striations of rain below. At the top, a darker, bruised blue reached high into the atmosphere, blurred all along the distance, like windswept strands of hair. The dry season hadn't ended here, and there had been just one night of rain, before we'd gone to see the bonobos. Since then it had been dry and hot, and everyone had been speculating as to when the rain would finally arrive.

We passed through a sodden village, the soaked sand firm, the palms dripping, and Jean Gaston paused from describing the vast forest through which his people tracked bonobos to tell me that God was protecting us from the rain. I pointed to the oncoming front. Wind blew hard, and he wiped his eyes, freeing them of grit. But he told me that God would not let the rain touch us.

In each tiny village—rows of wattle huts, the occasional house of mud bricks—the path widened into long, sunbaked commons with a few palm oil trees and a talking drum. We swerved past ducks, downy gray ducklings, chickens that screeched and flapped from beneath our wheels, piglets, goats, and puppies running in confusion.

Just beyond each village, the road became footpath again, ten inches wide, with rutted weeds on either side. It wound through the forest, and Jean Gaston leaned with the curves.

"The really difficult part," he told me, "is getting funding. Madame Sally and Monsieur Michael are doing everything they can, but these are not easy times."

"No, they're not," I agreed, craning my neck as we rounded a bend.

"I have been working on cassava production first. That allows people to eat and feel secure. The other projects take more time."

At a curve, we came face to face with three boys on a rickety bicycle, a large one pedaling, a small one on the handlebars, and a medium one squatting on the rack behind the seat. The bike swerved into the undergrowth and toppled, the boys flailing. Jean Gaston barely paused from explaining how the cassava was resistant to mosaic disease.

Passing thunderheads had left wet swaths, so that every ten minutes we plunged from rain-cooled landscapes back onto the glinting path. Jean Gaston was picking up speed again even as I could see the golden glow of copious sand far ahead.

"And I am starting pisciculture," he told me. "Do you know what pisciculture is?"

We plowed from the full shadow of the forest into deep sand and sunlight. The wheels felt as if on ice, the motorcycle swerving to the left as, thirty feet ahead, on the right, a boy rode his bike into the sand. I sensed the inevitability of our next swerve, our weight about to carry us to the right. The boy pedaled hard to stay upright in the sand, and just as we lost control and swerved, he did as well, his bike cutting to the other side, six inches between us as we passed.

A young, ink-black woman watched, just off the path. The irises of her almond eyes blended against her skin, giving her a beautiful, feline gaze. She had a woven basket on her back, its strap across her forehead, and her round breasts were naked, twin infants in her arms, each of them sucking at a nipple, rolling their eyes to the motorcycle.

"Pisciculture," Jean Gaston said, "is when you find a natural spring in the forest and dig a large hole and let it fill with water, then put fish in it. You can feed them so they get big fast, and you can sell them. It's a lot of work, but everything's a lot of work, and without these sorts of projects, there can be no conservation. You can't save bonobos if the people are starving."

When we rolled into the dirt streets of Djolu, completing the usual four-hour drive in two, the town was soaked, long mud puddles in the roads, children drying themselves in the sunlight.

"We have arrived," Jean Gaston called to me. "And look! God has protected us from rain and from danger."

At the Vie Sauvage headquarters, I took my previous room, with the ubiquitous roaches and spiders I had grown used to, but by nightfall Roger still hadn't arrived. We assumed he'd had a problem with his motorcycle, and I spent part of the evening speaking with Cosmas, who was also establishing a reserve. He'd habituated bonobos and won community support through development projects, and planned to have his area legally gazetted.

Roger arrived the next day, one of his tires having repeatedly gone flat so that he had to rent the front wheel of someone's motorcycle. Late that afternoon, only an hour before sunset, Roger and I rode to his house in Nkokolombo, our bags tied to the back of the motorcycle with strips cut from inner tubes. He drove poorly, braking in the sand unlike Jean Gaston, so that several times we nearly wiped out.

Our first stop was in a small village not far from the landing strip. We pulled up to the hut of the *chef du groupement,* a female chief, which was rare—her father having had no sons. She walked out in a skirt and white bra, trying to get her blouse on but putting it on inside out, then pulling it off before getting it right. Without a word, she grabbed the Nalgene water bottle from my hand, sniffed its edge, and, clearly disappointed, shoved it back into my hand.

She and Roger spoke quickly in Longando.

"What does she want?" I asked him in French.

"She was hoping that you had brought *lotoko* for her."

And then everyone just stood, the *chef du groupement* staring off, scowling, a tight gray headwrap on her skull. Her sons and the other village men approached, one after another, to shake my hand, smile, and nod. Then, as if having received a signal I'd missed, Roger got back on the motorcycle, and I joined him. The sand was so deep that the rear tire spun as we pushed forward with our feet, carving a long, winding line until we were back on the path.

"Do we have to stop at many more places like this?" I asked.

He hesitated before shaking his head slightly. *"Non."* A moment later, he called over his shoulder, "You want to go fast?"

"We've already lost a day, and we don't have much time."

I was concerned about formalities, that the novelty of my visit would oblige us to stop often. If the hike to his site was as arduous as everyone said, we'd have to hurry so we could get back in time to meet BCI on their next trip to Djolu.

Until now, in Kokolopori and Djolu, Roger had come across as subservient, nodding and currying favor with more established conservationists, always at the edge, quick to help with bags and hardly speaking. But I was soon to receive a lesson in local hierarchy.

The sun had set as we neared his village, the trees cut away on either side of the path, the air blue in the shadow of the broken forest. He blared his horn and kept his thumb on it until he reached his house, then rode twice in a circle in front of it and stopped. He dismounted as women, children, and a few men hurried out. They began singing and clapping their hands.

Roger, who until now had communicated in a near whisper, spoke in a booming baritone, and the people fell silent. His jaw suddenly appeared long, thrust forward. He motioned to the members of his family one by one, introducing his father, his brothers, his older sister. He took me to see the unfinished mud-brick lodge where ecotourists would sleep someday. The name of his future reserve, Nkokolombo, was painted on a metal sheet, and he commanded me to take photos, though the absolute equatorial night was almost upon us, and the camera's flash blotted out the details.

He asked me to sit in a small room in his house, on a chair, then left. In the light of a single lamp, the room filled up around me, neighbors arriving, and nearly two dozen boys crowded in, standing and crouching. Two doorways led outside, in the front and in the back, and the people filled them. They pushed open the wooden shutters and stared in the windows. Small children squeezed and peeked between legs. Adults stood on tiptoe to see past each other. At least forty sets of eyes studied me. I tried to start conversations with the young men, but they were too shy. They stared as I waited for the better part of an hour. I could only imagine how exotic I must be, strange enough that they could gaze evenly, studying my face and my hair.

And then Roger returned, having gone to get his wife, a pretty young woman who followed him in. He held up an infant boy by the armpits and told me that it was his son.

"I have five children," he said. "She finally gave me a son."

"Where are your daughters?" I asked.

"Somewhere else," he said.

That night I slept in a room with cockroaches and gray spiders. From an open-faced building just outside, where the women cooked, firelight flickered, shining through chinks in the mud bricks and the gap beneath the roof thatch. Boys laughed in the next room over. I'd hardly fallen asleep when Roger knocked. The gray dawn had replaced the glow of the fire.

Though we set out quickly, Roger stopped often to show me his projects, among them a nursery for seedlings that he and his volunteers used to replant old fields. Then we left the motorcycle with his in-laws because they lived closer to the conservation area, and he and I met up with three of his trackers. We walked into the forest, and for two hours, the trail often passed through slash-and-burn fields, some scorched and smelling of cinder, others with dozens of small freshly cut trees lying crisscrossed, the foliage still drying, and yet others with manioc shoots reaching high above my head.

We entered the gloomy older growth, into what the local community hoped would be the Nkokolombo Bonobo Reserve. The path carved through the loam of the forest floor. Red or black ants crossed it in narrow streams that flowed like liquid, or rivers dozens of feet wide. We'd run, stomping our feet, then crush the biting ants on our legs with our palms.

At a clearing several hours in, Roger told me that this was where his village had relocated during the war. One of his daughters was born there, and during those years, he learned much about tracking and wildlife. Later, when he'd heard about conservation efforts in Kokolopori, he was eager to apply his skills. For three years now, he and his trackers had been volunteering, following a bonobo group that repeatedly fled. Nkokolombo is closer to Djolu than is Kokolopori, and saw far more hunting during the war, much of it by soldiers from areas without taboos against eating bonobos. The surviving bonobos were extremely wary, and habituation had been slow. The trackers lost them for days at a time, and Roger told me that he needed outside expertise. Then he started a line of reasoning I had heard often, saying that I must return to the United States and tell everyone about the forest and the Congolese who were protecting it, and ask them to come see the forest, too.

At Roger's signal, we paused in a camp with a single wattle hut, where the trackers cut sugarcane and a bunch of bananas. Tiny sweat bees clouded around us, burrowing into my hair, covering my forearms. To my surprise, three women with babies tied to their backs arrived on the trail from which we'd come. The first was Roger's wife, and holding bags of food and cooking utensils, they glided effortlessly past us, chatting as they stepped one by one over a massive rotting log with a tree growing from it, roots veining the decomposing wood.

We set out again, with the women this time. Despite their loads, they hardly appeared fatigued, but we were soaked with sweat. Over the next several hours, we walked in streams as often as on land, the water cool on my feet, the bottoms sandy. The current was red with the tannins of disintegrating leaves. The one time I asked how much farther the camp was I got the answer I should have known to expect: *"Kaka awa."* Finally, after nearly eight hours, we passed beneath an immense fallen tree, between two branches as if through an arch, and came into a clearing with five small huts in an L formation. A row of palm trees grew along one side of it, and at a bench, in the shade of a small tree, a man pounded cassava in a hollow log, white powder dusting the ground around him. Though only trackers lived here, working in shifts that lasted a few days or several weeks before returning to their village, the camp was well tended. Gardens whose plants I didn't recognize added touches of green, and beyond the sandy earth, the trees were immense, pillaring the sky, their thick branches tufted with ferns, hung with vines.

I checked the GPS device that BCI had given to Roger:

N 00.30126
E 022.18418
Alt. 435 m

Over the next four days, we searched while the trackers' wives kept the camp. Each morning at four o'clock, the trackers rose from their bamboo beds in the huts, and I from my tent, which I'd pitched in a cassava field to distance myself from the crying of babies and the sand fleas. The trackers sang Christian songs with Roger, nine men chanting softly in Lingala, the only recognizable word being *Jésus*. They'd lost track of the bonobos a few days before my arrival, and we set out looking for them, finding their empty nests in a high tree, as well as the nest of the reported albino in a much smaller one, halfway up to the canopy. A few times I heard the raw, repeated screech of a great blue turaco, a bird whose broad wingspan appeared silhouetted against the sky.

One by one, when they were alone, I asked the trackers to point to something that was the color of the albino, and they each pointed to a different bright yellow object. Bonobos were known to be uniformly black, and I wondered if this one was not an albino but simply a very old bonobo, which might have explained why it slept lower in the forest. But if it was an albino, it might

Empty Hands, Open Arms

simply be sensitive to the direct sunlight of the high canopy. The trackers also insisted that a second bonobo in the group had two white stripes on its back, one on either side.

We continued, but we saw only bonobo prints in the mud. Finally, after four days in the forest, I had to meet up with Sally and Michael. They would already be in Djolu to meet an Australian crew from VisionQuest who had arranged with BCI to fly in to Djolu. They intended to shoot a segment of a 3-D film on great apes.

Before I left, I shared what extra supplies I had in my backpack. Roger's wife had an infected eye, and daily I had been putting antibiotic ointment on her eyelid. I gave her the remaining cream. Her eye had already improved dramatically. One morning, when the trackers saw me taking vitamins, they asked if I would share. Later, they told me that their ailments had vanished, that they no longer had chronic coughs or sore throats, that I had very strong medicine indeed.

My last evening in the camp, as thunder boomed in the distance and the horizon darkened, a hard wind setting up, I crouched with the men, my notebook open, and recorded the names of the gigantic trees around us. I jotted the following words:

Bokongu. Very tall and thick, next to it *Bokanga,* thin with a burst of branches at the top, very high.
Beele. Pale trunk. Gives sweet fruit.
Botuna. A little out of sight and hard to see.
Bokangu. Very hard wood. The men say it holds carbon gas inside, that it makes a hissing sound when you cut it, as all of the gas escapes.
Bokombe next to it. No leaves. I am having a hard time telling them apart.
Bokotombolo. Bosenge. Lifake.
Massive trees. Forest and storm linked. Hulking clouds, orange in the evening.

In the days to come, the downpours would be more frequent, the sound of thunder often reaching us from a distance.

We returned the next morning without photos of the strange bonobo, Roger downcast, asking if I would come back, telling me that he was working hard at habituating the group but that it took time.

We returned to his village to find a council of furious elders, and I discovered that Roger had bypassed getting their permission, wanting to spare me the trouble. In our absence, BCI had met with them and made peace, apologizing for the mistake and explaining my purpose there.

"Did you see the bonobos?" the elders asked.

"No."

They smirked. "You did not see the bonobos because we did not give our approval."

I glanced at Roger, and he hung his head.

"It's true," he said. "If the elders are angry, the bonobos will not come close to us. This was a mistake."

Later, in Djolu, Sally told me that BCI always got the elders' approval before going into the forest. A few elders, on trips to Djolu's market, to see friends, or to watch soccer games, stopped by and patted me on the shoulder, laughing. They sat with me and discussed the forest and the benefits of community-based reserves, and explained that Roger was young and impulsive, and needed to learn patience. I confessed with some reluctance that I probably shouldn't have hurried him so much. I hadn't had the sense that he was listening, but he'd rushed me to the camp as I'd requested. If anything, I was the one who hadn't respected the local leaders.

Months later, when I was in Washington, DC, I met with Alden Almquist. Having moved with his parents to Équateur Province a year and a half after his birth, and fluent in Lingala, French, and English, he was skilled at explaining Équateur's culture in terms that Westerners could understand. His father was a doctor, missionary, and preacher, whom the people protected during the uprisings after independence. Alden began his university studies in Kisangani early in the Congo Crisis and recalls being able to walk through the shot-out windows of the buildings as easily as through the doors. He continued the degree in the United States, finished a PhD in anthropology, returned to Zaire on a Fulbright to study rites of passage in a traditional hunting village, and later wrote a great deal on Congolese culture, including the section on "Society and Its Environment" in *Zaire: A Country Study* and "Horticulture and Hunting in the Congo Basin" in *African Rain Forest Ecology and Conservation*. When I told him about my trip with Roger, he explained to me that the Congolese have traditional notions of conservation, some of them based in "firstness," the idea that those who have been first on the land have power over it and deserve respect.

"Firstness," he told me, "is one of those cultural categories of explanation that doesn't have a good analogue for us because it involves nonmaterial entities and agents, which we don't honor. There are ties that the first settlers form with the land, and if new people come in, they are under obligation to ask for permission for hunting, farming, and fishing from the lords of the land—and they are called that, the lords of the land. One of the things BCI did when Sally and I went in 2003 and 2004 was to go around and form these little bonobo committees, and meet with the lords of the land. They are the people you go to if you're an immigrant, or if you are a relative who wants some land to farm. And in each place the extent of the rights varies. In some places, the chief pretty much has the clout over who gets what. But the lords of the land always have a spiritual authority, and people in the know go to them, because if they turn against you, or you act against them, they can do what they call 'closing the forest,' another category of analysis that Western conservation has scorned. . . . It means that if you go hunting, you won't kill animals. If you go to do surveys, your surveys will come to naught. Whatever your activity is in the zone, it's not been opened to you. . . .

"Firstness ties into that. Whoever is on the land first is understood to have certain powers over success in that land, in whatever form success takes. And that also includes fertility. If you try to enter an area and live there in contempt of whoever has authority over it, you shouldn't be surprised by stillbirths, fertility issues, illness."

Alden explained that the village where he was doing fieldwork wasn't of the same ethnic group as those in Kokolopori, but it was in the same cultural area, and had similar practices. While the Belgians had moved most villagers closer to the roads in order to use them for forced labor and offer them services, the people Alden worked with still lived deep in the forest. He also told me that the spirits of dead elders attended events and were referred to in the same terms of address and reverence as those the people used when speaking to living elders. The ancestors are there as long as someone has a living memory of them, and they influence both how power is wielded and how the balance of nature is maintained on the land.

Alden's words resonated with Michael Schatzberg's *Political Legitimacy in Middle Africa*. Schatzberg explains that though Westerners don't have to believe in the Congolese worldview, we have to recognize their model of causality if we hope to understand their decisions. Even at the national level, under Mobutu, politicians believed that his regime poured magical substances into the Congo River to control the people, and that he briefly banned foreign beer so as to force the population to consume domestically brewed, mind-controlling potions. Some have attested that payments to Mobutu's witchdoctors took up 3 percent of the government's budget, more than the Health Ministry. During the 1974 World Cup, Zaire sent a plane full of witchdoctors to cast spells, and in other situations, the power of the ancestors has been said to change the outcomes of national sporting events and whether the Congolese adhere to "symbols of national unity." Schatzberg writes that his own political analyses of Zairian politics were incomplete because his theoretical orientations "did not consider the possibility that sorcery was important to understanding politics at the national level. Sorcery, after all, was beyond the parameters of the political as they were implicitly understood in most Western social science."

With regard to conservation, Alden continued in this same vein: "There was a form of what we would call magic, *pomoli*, where if a hunter used it, he would kill more game than usual, but the whiplash would be that members of his lineage would sicken and die. That's how you knew that a hunter was working the dark side in increasing his kills in the forest. . . . But what I like about it is that there's a balance between human extraction from the forest—life in the village and life in the forest—and if you took too much, more than your share, from the forest, you were punished. . . . I was fascinated by the fact that they were basically practicing conservation measures. They only hunted during the rainy season. In the dry season, they were back in the village. . . . And when I would go out with them, they rotated trapping areas in each lineage's hunting areas. They actually had the forest demarcated."

He described the intricate trails, camps days away with crops planted around them, as well as log bridges just beneath the surface of the water, so that you appeared to be walking on the stream. When he'd asked whose trails they were on, the people told him they belonged to the village. He'd wanted to know why they had two sets of trails, since they required so much maintenance.

"They'd say, 'We have to let the animals rest. We've been hunting and trapping them. The guns frighten them.' Others would say, 'We have to let the animals give birth.' These were explicit, codified conservation statements by indigenous hunters. And those are about the only things that Westerners will listen to grudgingly in the context of conservation. With the other stuff I talked about—firstness, opening and closing the forests, the powers of the spiritual world over the outcomes of your activities in the forest, and your good relationships among people as a key—there's scorn: 'It's superstition. It's categories of explanation that we didn't author, and therefore do not honor.'"

Alden told me that he chose to support a vision of conservation that was African-based, with strong local leadership, and that used local traditions to reinforce conservation. Albert later corroborated Alden's view, explaining that in Équateur people view certain parts of the forest as sacred and have banned hunting there because animals go to these regions to give birth. He speculated as to whether myths about sacred forests like Engindanginda are in place only to keep hunters from disturbing the animals during this time, and whether stories of the sacred forest could be used to encourage conservation. Even BCI's scientific surveys began with local knowledge, the Congolese who knew the forests guiding the researchers, a tactic that scientific studies are increasingly showing to be as effective as transects. As a result of BCI's approach, every site surveyed, in more than twelve areas in Équateur, contained bonobos.

If there was one thing I understood from my conversations not only with BCI and Vie Sauvage's staff but also with the local Congolese, it was how specific conservation is. Generalized theories and strategies must be secondary to the reality of each place: the way the war has affected the people, their relationships with various governments and power structures, and their beliefs and traditions. Personal relationships and cultural understanding matter above all else.

"When Sally and I developed our approach to Information Exchange," Alden said, "we were looking for a way to use African ideas, delivered by African voices, for African audiences in conservation, instead of importing Tarzan with credentials. We've had a history of using the folktales, disseminating them. I know the way ideas spread in Africa. Even though ethnic groups were allegedly conflictual, healing cults would spread among them, and everyone knows that all of those New World crops spread like lightning through allegedly balkanized, tribalized Africa."

Though a lot had changed since those early depictions, I got the sense that knowledge was still studied and shared, that when an idea reached a village, everyone mulled it over, debated it, and passed it on. I saw evidence of this in Roger's work. He had learned about conservation through word of mouth, then attended Information Exchange training in Kokolopori with Alden Almquist in 2008. After participating in surveys and Information Exchange with BCI and CREF in Lingomo and Mompono, he used his salary to start his own NGO, transforming his community.

This is what I found most interesting about Kokolopori, that the local people's understanding of the work being done there makes the project, in essence, self-replicating. BCI's staff have built relationships with them, exchanging knowledge. Both groups are aware of each other's struggles, knowing that no one has the full support necessary to achieve their goals on their own. And because decisions are made nearby, the people assimilate the nature of the work and are learning to replicate it.

The result of all this is a conservation movement that might be characterized as viral. Regardless of their level of education, local people have numerous ways to participate, and whereas they might oppose a park that excludes them, they understand how community conservation improves their lives. They have seen members of their community who once struggled win respect and become conservationists. Albert was elected to parliament, and the conservation graduates from the ISDR technical college, both men and women, have found jobs with larger NGOs and received government positions. Most importantly, the people are interested in more than the immediate material benefits of conservation; they feel ownership of conservation's long-term vision, and they know that their forests are degrading and the wildlife is vanishing.

The Congo I was encountering could not be more different from the images that dominate the media: a country of such inhumanity that we find it incomprehensible. Blinded by the old trope of the dark heart of Africa, we fail to understand how our material and political interests have contributed to the suffering of the Congolese. Rather, we dismiss their hardship as an African phenomenon. We refuse to acknowledge even how our appetite for the newest technology has accelerated the environmental degradation. In *Dancing in the Glory of Monsters*, Jason Stearns writes: "If all we see is black men raping and killing in the most outlandish ways imaginable, we might find it hard to believe that there is any logic to this conflict." Among the results of such media portrayals is that we fail to recognize the culture that has evolved within the rainforest, a sort of living Rosetta Stone that can both open the complex ecosystem to science and offer a framework for conservation.

Over the previous month, I had noticed that Sally and Michael wore too many hats, writing grants and running offices in two countries while being leaders in the field, negotiating projects, and coordinating visits. They seemed disorganized and overwhelmed at times, but they did listen to the people, and when the villagers spoke to them of the forest, they abided by the cultural rules and found a way to work within them, knowing that this approach would have enduring results.

However, their relationship to cultural stories isn't naïve. Neither Albert Lokasola nor BCI believes that conservation should be left in the hands of starving people, practiced on the basis of folklore alone. War, migration, logging, and overpopulation have profoundly altered people's relationship to the natural world in many parts of the Congo. Still, the traditional beliefs of rainforest inhabitants endure in many places, and conservation is more likely to take hold when their cultures are respected and, where possible, used to complement the scientific view.

Cultural understanding is one factor among many in creating a successful reserve, from community accords that prevent hunting to legal protection at the national level, to international funding. These are all part of a complex web of relationships that link Washington, DC, London, Oslo, and other capitals to Kinshasa—to Kokolopori, Sankuru, and the numerous Bonobo Peace Forest sites under development. And yet if that web is to connect not just to educated Congolese like Albert and André but to all the people in the forest, understanding their history and values is crucial. When they see conservation as an organically integrated part of their livelihoods and personal ambitions, they are far more inclined to take up its cause and reproduce its projects independently.

Back in Kokolopori, after almost five days with Roger, I found the camp busy. The villagers came out to watch the 3-D film crew lugging their equipment about. With the help of trackers and eco-guards, the crew carried everything into the rainforest to shoot scenes of bonobos. One night, the cameraman projected his footage on a sheet in a hut, the villagers passing around the 3-D glasses, seeing their bonobos hanging in the air before them, just above the rough-hewn table with its bowls of pineapple chunks.

The film crew's advisor was Ian Redmond, the zoologist and conservationist who, when working with Dian Fossey, had discovered Digit's decapitated body. He went on to become a leader in the campaign to ban the trade in African elephant ivory, found UN-GRASP, found and still lead the Ape Alliance, and serve as the ambassador for the UN Year of the Gorilla in 2009, which focused on conservation issues, education, and advocacy for gorillas. He had participated in over fifty documentaries for the BBC, the National Geographic Society, and the Discovery Channel, among others. As he and I sat in bamboo chairs beneath a tree in the camp, I asked questions and he shared knowledge gathered from his thirty years working with great apes. Later I read one of his essays, in which he states that the rapid dwindling of the great ape habitat was "not the result of a concerted effort to eliminate them," but "a case of collective negligence." He goes on, "The hard reality is that the relatively small sums available for conservation are no match for the massive economic pressures to exploit or destroy ape habitats. And the 'haves' can hardly point the finger of blame at the 'have nots' . . . whilst ignoring their own role in the equation." His words echo the point that so many books on the Congo make, reminding outsiders of their role in the difficulties here.

A few days later, as soon as the film crew left, Sally, Michael, and I went into the forest for the last time on the trip. We found the bonobos quickly, a dozen of them feasting on the leaves of a tree. They sat just above us, their testicles and vaginal swellings hanging as they stuffed their mouths. The younger ones appeared fascinated by us, the older females largely indifferent, giving us only the occasional glance. We were with them for several hours, until finally, one by one, they went to the edge of a large limb and grabbed a branch on a nearby tree, pulled it closer, and jumped.

I followed a juvenile as he traveled low in the foliage. He seemed to find me entertaining and went ahead a short distance before stopping and watching me approach, his dark eyes gleaming. Then, when I got too close, about a dozen feet away, he moved deeper into the trees before stopping again and observing me work my way through vines and brambles, as if nothing could be more ridiculous than how humans get caught up in the foliage, tripping and crawling.

The next day, Sally and Michael went back to sending reports and grant applications through the BGAN, the portable Internet system that had failed us for most of the trip. Using the sat phone, Sally called the company to discover that the besieged Syrian government had blocked satellite Internet communications, since rebels there were using the same equipment to create off-the-grid Internet networks. Each time the company unjammed the Immarsat network, the Syrians blocked it again. Finally, after repeated calls on the sat phone, Sally was online. She and Michael had told me that they usually treasured their time in the field because they could get away from the computers, but on this trip they felt as if they'd hardly left the office.

Over the last week, storms had repeatedly blown through, but on our next-to-last afternoon, the inside of the hut darkened and a damp wind gusted in the spaces between the wattle and the thatch. A few loud drops struck the roof before the onslaught began, one of the heaviest downpours I'd ever seen. I leaned in the window, gazing from beneath the gushing eaves. Puddles gathered, rivulets saturating the earth until it could hold no more. A stream formed, rushing, six feet wide, finding every declivity as it crossed the camp. The current deepened, pouring toward the main road where dark water already rushed in the wheel ruts. The two streams joined within seconds, gouging the road, digging a trench that wound its entire length to the small river below the village.

Michael had looked burned out all day, working on reports, but now he stood in the door, his face radiant, as if he could finally breathe, as if there was nowhere else he'd rather be.

A day later, on a hot morning, the sun boiling moisture from the ground, we packed our bags in preparation for the five-hour drive to Befori. From there we would take the pirogues that, after six days and nights, would return us to Mbandaka. We would first follow the Maringa River to where it joined with the Lopori, and became the Lulonga, rivers in the DRC often changing names at each confluence. The Lulonga would then carry us to the Congo River, a little more than 40 miles upstream of Mbandaka.

When we were almost ready, a group of trackers gathered in the doorway. They usually didn't arrive in the camp until after dark, when they'd watched the bonobos go to sleep and recorded the GPS coordinates. Their faces were grim, and after speaking to them, Sally told us that the eight-year-old daughter of Mbangi Lofoso, the young tracker who'd come to us on the day of our arrival in the camp, had just died.

They were holding a wake, a *matanga,* down the road, and we walked with the trackers to pay our respects. Thunder again boomed in the distance. Scattered dark clouds moved above us, wind blowing through the dense foliage at our sides.

Michael told me that even though Sally paid to have Mbangi's daughter taken in the car to the clinic, the family delayed and continued with traditional healers. When they finally saw the doctor, it was too late. According to tradition, Michael explained, the mother's family would come to inspect the situation, to determine if the girl's death was the result of witchcraft.

We reached a small village of half a dozen buildings. A group of women stood in the weeds near the road. They had finished bathing the girl and were dressing her. One of the men there asked if we had a camera. Only I did, having carried it in my backpack with my notepad.

"Will you please take some pictures of her for us?" he said.

Michael held my bag as I carried the camera into the group.

She looked fragile, thin after over a month without eating. The women had powdered her face and put a new camouflage T-shirt on her, then wrapped her in patterned blue and gold cloth. The father, Mbangi, the young tracker with the scar on the side of his throat, stood close. Thunder resonated over the forest as my camera clicked.

The woman who picked up the girl wore a pink blouse. She crouched, supporting her on her knees, one hand on the back of her small head, the other holding her mouth closed. The woman's fingers were dark against the girl's skin. I didn't know what I was looking for, what type of image, how they would want to remember her. A few raindrops fell as the woman cradling her cried, and dark spots appeared in the white powder on the girl's face. Her hand kept drawing my attention. She hadn't been able to open it for a month, her fists cramped shut, though now the fingers were loosely curled in her lap, almost peaceful. The camera clicked, and Michael touched my arm.

"I think that's okay," he told me softly.

The woman wrapped the girl and hugged her to her chest, then stood and carried her into the family's house. We ducked through the low door. The inside was dark, filled with dozens of people singing and hammering on drums. The only word I recognized was *hallelujah*. The girl lay on a sheet of woven caning, on a bamboo pallet. We stood in the humid, suffocating dark until the song had finished and people had spoken. When we left, others were arriving. Two young women came running, screaming and weeping as they crossed the village, arms lifted, and almost threw themselves through the dark door of the pulsing house.

The River

The road to the river at Befori made the journey between Djolu and Kokolopori seem easy. We stopped often as the young Congolese who rode with me on the back bumper cut away fallen trees. There were a few old brick Belgian and missionary homes, this region known for coffee plantations before the national infrastructure degraded and the last of the expatriate community fled in the early nineties.

Small clouds passed all day, no rain but for a few scattered drops, and as the sun hit the horizon, golden against the forest canopy, we reached Befori. I'd imagined a port town with markets and rows of shanties, but there was just the grassy shore, a few small huts, and a woman cooking fish in a pot over a fire. The only boat was ours, a vessel composed of three forty-five-foot-long dugouts lashed together side by side, with a neat roof of blue tarpaulin over the center. The dugouts had been carved from massive trees and sat low in the water. One was reserved for fuel drums and two were for people, bamboo cots set head to foot inside, each with a thin foam mattress. In the rear of the boat, there was an open space with more fuel, where the boatmen steered the outboard engines.

The next morning, while the boat was being loaded, we visited Likongo, Jean Gaston's conservation site, motorcycles shuttling us through bamboo forest and across rotting log bridges, each trip taking more than an hour. BCI received its warmest welcome yet: ceremonies and talks and dancing. The local people held a symbolic wedding between their community and BCI, consecrating the new partnership, and they gave Sally a spear and a thick copper bracelet.

People showed us their projects, speaking of Jean Gaston's leadership, of how he'd used his own money to lay the groundwork for a community-based reserve. As they guided us to a large hollowed area where they had cleared the trees and dug up a spring for their pisciculture project, Sally and I walked past a mamba, oblivious to the danger. Behind us, Mwanza saw it, just off the path, a few feet from our ankles. He jumped, spun, and ran. The snake apparently fled, too. Jean Gaston's people beat at the underbrush with sticks, but the snake didn't reappear. We learned that Jean Gaston's daughter had died the year before from a mamba bite.

After a final meal, we again headed toward the river. The boat had left Befori to meet us at the port nearest to Likongo. Again, the motorcycle ride took an hour, though in a different direction, with an additional forty minutes for the removal of a large fallen tree from the path. We then walked for an hour through forest toward the boat. In each village, we stopped and spoke to local leaders, Mwanza or Sally explaining BCI's work and its long-term vision, taking sips of *lotoko* and leaving small gifts of cash.

On the boat, whatever reticence I had about a six-day river haul, sleeping head to heel with nine others, dissolved, and soon I knew that the journey would be one of the most memorable of my life. Immense palms grew thick on the shores, a corridor of pale foliage beyond which the forest canopy rose. Every few hours we passed a solitary fisherman standing in a dugout as small as a surfboard. He paddled close and held up a fish that the team bought. At one point they purchased a large chunk of electric catfish, a creature that gave powerful shocks when alive but was delicious, its bright white meat handed over wrapped in a palm leaf. Landrine, BCI's field cook, had set up a kitchen in the front of the right pirogue, dirt spread over the wood, charcoal braziers made of battered cans. The left pirogue was loaded with bananas and plantains. A pole rose from the bow of the center pirogue so that the boatmen who steered the outboard motors from the back could sight their destination.

The inside was cozy, roof slats made from the center stems of palm leaves, a mosquito net above each bed, tucked into the slats during the day. So that we didn't have to crawl over Sally and Michael at the foremost beds, there was a space between the oil drums on the side, where we could squeeze out and sit, pee into the river, walk the pirogue's four-inch edge of hewn wood to the front, or relax on an empty fuel barrel in the sun.

Day two on the river, a Wednesday, Sally got word on the sat phone that Michael needed to be in Kinshasa by Monday for a meeting with the African Development Bank, and thus that he should ideally fly that Saturday from Mbandaka to Kinshasa. We had been on schedule to arrive late that Sunday, just in time for a conference BCI would be holding in Mbandaka.

Richard Eonga Esafuka, BCI's Mbandaka director and the boat's captain, a tall, light-brown man whose concerted gaze gave the impression that he was softly, almost sadly smiling, went to sit with Sally and Michael. Together, they estimated our distance from Mbandaka with the GPS and calculated that if we traveled constantly for the next two days and nights we might arrive by late Saturday morning, enabling Michael to catch a flight from Mbandaka to Kinshasa on Saturday afternoon. Though the river level had risen slightly with the storms, sandbanks remained a problem. There was also a flight Sunday. Though it wouldn't give Michael as much time to prepare for his meeting, it would be a last resort. We cruised through the first day, under thick groves of palms overhanging the water, or past high trees whose pale trunks stood ranked along the shore like bodies in the dusk.

The sun fell quickly at the equator, its light reflected on the river before us. As we rounded a bend, it vanished beyond the forest, a faint golden emanation from the treetops. Then at the next bend, it reappeared, a large yellow disk sinking through the mist, falling again behind the trees as we turned, and again reappearing, lower each time. Over the years, I'd read travelers' descriptions of this. Camille Habert in 1898: "There is no twilight in the tropical countries, and the night succeeds the day almost without transition." Or Beryl Markham, in 1942: "Night tramps on the heels of Day with little gallantry and takes the place she lately held, in severe and humorless silence." Coleridge referenced the equatorial sunset in "The Rime of the Ancient Mariner": "The Sun's rim dips; the stars rush out: / At one stride comes the dark." The phenomenon is due to the sun descending perpendicularly to the horizon at the equator, rather than diagonally closer to the poles, where the sunsets, far enough up, can seem to last forever.

The night sky was moonless, the wind cool as we gathered in the front of the pirogues, the deepest dark along the shores, where the shadows of trees appeared to fall far past the surface, sinking black ravines that carved the Maringa into a faint, starlit path.

Standing in a windbreaker, Richard pressed a button on his GPS and the screen lit up, showing the river snaking before us, looping side to side, its circuitous route doubling the distance we traveled. He aimed his spotlight ahead of us, the beam flickering through banks of mist. He moved it rapidly up and down, directing the boat, and the four men at the back adjusted the outboards. As we neared a bend, he raised and lowered the beam to his left so that we steered to the outside of the curve, where the water was usually deepest. He swept the light over the surface, looking for the faint froth that gathered on the slow deep water; the fast current over sandbars was always a dark glassy plate.

Eventually, one by one, we returned inside and lay on our beds. Shortly after I closed my eyes, the first sandbar grated against the bottom of the pirogues. Everyone was getting out as I put on my headlamp. I climbed from beneath the tarp, between two fuel drums, and looked down, my light shining through the rippling surface against red sand.

I stepped in. The river was ankle-deep. Each of us walked into the darkness in a different direction from the boat, the river so wide here that the shores were hardly visible in the beams of our headlamps. Wisps of mist rose from the surface and the sand creaked beneath my feet as I looked for a channel. With each step, the water turned a darker red, rusty silt and tannins clouding up and swept away.

The current rose to my thighs, and I called back, telling the others. Briefly, I had a sense of vertigo. Warm air blew over the river, and I turned and saw five other headlamps, each alone, moving across the gleaming dark surface, turning this way and that, mist in tendrils, distant forested shoreline in glimpses, and above us a few faint stars penetrating the haze. The susurrus of insects and frogs was as steady as silence.

I skirted the channel, trying to see where it passed closest to the boat, so that we knew in what direction we should push it. Another headlamp neared, briefly blinding me, and then a hand tilted it up, and Michael's pale hair appeared in the glow.

"This is what we do this for, this place," he told me, speaking softly as he turned and took in the breadth of the river, the spacious dark. "When a trip's been challenging, it's the river that makes up for it."

We stood side by side, at the edge of the deeper current, looking back at the boat. Lit in our headlamps, it appeared long and ancient, like a dhow on the Indian Ocean, the hand-hewn pirogues loaded with barrels and synthetic sisal bags.

We walked back and discussed with the others which way to push. We were all in the water, the four boatmen shoulder to shoulder with us, Dieudonné, Gabriel, Freddy, and Médard—Miracle Bonobo. Counting one, two, three, we shoved the boat a few feet at a time. Then we went to the front and pivoted it toward the center of the river, across the deeper current. With half its weight afloat, we easily slipped it from the sandbar. The boatmen fired up the outboards, and we coasted back across the dark.

That night, we hit two other sandbars, the second not long afterward, but the third hours later, after one in the morning. This was the shallowest. We pushed the boat in circle after circle, trying to pivot it above deeper water as small green moths fluttered about our headlamps, their wings waxy and transparent.

It took nearly an hour before we were afloat again. As the engines revved

Empty Hands, Open Arms

and we started to move, I lifted myself over the side, between the barrels, and changed into dry shorts. I lay on my bamboo bed and listened to the thrum, the rush of water in the narrow spaces between the three pirogues, and then I was asleep.

The next day, as Sally and I talked, she described the sites where BCI supported the local people, and their current project with Conservation International to create conservation concessions in much the same way that logging companies leased timber concessions for very little. BCI had proposed this project to the DRC government during the moratorium on new logging concessions, and President Joseph Kabila, the World Bank, and other multilateral donors supported it in the context of developing innovative approaches to long-term protection of the rainforest. The project would provide livelihoods for the local communities, as they would be the ones managing and zoning land, and the concessions would link up to other reserves and unofficial protected areas in the Bonobo Peace Forest. It was for this project that BCI advisor Dick Rice, who'd developed the concept during his time as chief economist with Conservation International, would soon be meeting Sally in Mbandaka, along with members of BCI's Kinshasa team, officials from the ICCN, the Ministry of the Environment, and CI.

Sally described other areas where BCI had done *sensibilisation,* where enthusiasm wasn't lacking, only funding. Among the most promising sites was Lilungu, on the Tschuapa River, midway between Kokolopori and Sankuru. The bonobos there had become so habituated that they would come into the trackers' camps. They were also feeding in the fields, and the village women had taken conservation into their own hands, growing buffer crops that the bonobos could eat instead of the people's food. Given that bonobos weren't destructive and harvested carefully, unlike monkeys and baboons, this approach worked.

As we talked, we sat just inside the tarpaulin shelter, in the shade as the sunlight beat down on Michael in the front of the boat, where he faced the widening river. After a pause, she told me how suited she felt for her life now, how much the aspects of the work that others might find intolerable had thrilled her, whether it was living in mud huts for months, being dirty and sweaty and surrounded by insects, spending as many as ten or twelve days in dugout canoes without privacy, or dealing with the turmoil of Kinshasa. She paused and added that during the hardest periods the relationships she had forged with the Congolese kept her going.

"I remember hearing people say," she told me, "that if you're depressed, help someone else and it will make you feel better on the simplest level. The suffering in this country is unbelievable. People have so little and yet are so resilient and hopeful in the face of what other people would see as hell on earth."

The next day, we read and talked, occasionally pushing the boat off a sandbar. A fisherman held up what looked like a thirty-pound carp from his tiny pirogue, eliciting shouts of surprise from everyone. Landrine bought it and cut it into chunks that she seared over the fire.

That afternoon, we stopped in Basankusu, a vision from another world, like a movie set from a film about space cowboys—a distant, dilapidated outpost, crowded with rusted relics of machines and the carcasses of old ships. One iron hulk, maybe a hundred feet long, sprawled on the shore, another half submerged just below. There was a barge so loaded with bags and boxes that it appeared as if it might capsize, already floating at an angle. At the top of the mountain of haphazardly lashed sacks, people had tied on red and blue plastic chairs, so many of them bundled together that they looked like the blossoms in a bouquet.

On shore, a ship's boiler with large iron rivets served as the wall of a building. Shirtless men with the bodies of athletes loaded the barge as women washed pots and clothes in the scummy water, the surface streaked with soapsuds and the rainbow sheen of oil. At least fifty pirogues clustered at the shore. Docking, we squeezed into a gap, our sides rubbing theirs. We had to step into an empty boat next to ours before we could reach the sand. Broken dugouts lay alongside smoldering refuse, wood and thatch and vines, scraps of plastic, though never soft drink or water bottles—these we saw for sale in the market, empty ones for 200 francs each. The rank smoke drifted over everything, and I held my breath as we walked through it.

The path veered up through small huts, broken red rock beneath our feet and fragments of cobbles from the city's Belgian days. Each hut and lean-to sold something: sugar, rice, cassava, or even phone cards, since Basankusu had a cell tower and provided an island of connectivity. Prices were written on pieces of wood, and farther up, the products were from China: plastic backpacks, thick foam flip-flops, hairbrushes, safety pins, children's underwear, and small hand mirrors, most of them cracked. There was a pharmacy and a shoe shop, the shoes used, scuffed and dark and battered, not a single pair alike, all set out neatly in rows—a rare precision that made their value clear. Clothing stores held a variety of cheap polyester pants with bright prints and the T-shirts that were common in the Congo, the ones Americans discarded without wearing. They were silkscreened for company fund-raisers and promotions, business and academic conferences, as well as high school sports teams and clubs: MISSOURI FFA, WALK FOR LIFE 2006, WILLIAMS HIGH BIBLE CLUB, SPRINGFIELD CROSS-COUNTRY 2008. Charity organizations in the United States collected and shipped these in tightly twined rectangular bales.

As we did at each airport earlier in our trip, we had to register our passports and explain our purpose in the region. We went to the Direction Générale de Migration, an old Belgian building with crumbling steps and bricks visible where cracks had appeared in the concrete walls. The DGM officer, a lean man with a dignified smile, introduced himself. He shook our hands and spoke with such courtesy that I had the impression of being on an important visit. He brought broken plastic chairs out so we could sit, though I couldn't put my full weight in mine without falling through it. Then he meticulously filled out forms, recording each *ordre de mission,* checking the dates, asking where we were from and what we were working on. When he finished, he told us that he couldn't demand anything, but that he was at the mercy of our generosity to live and do his job. Richard gave him 5,000 francs—five dollars—and the officer smiled brightly. He again shook our hands, thanking each of us by name.

Back at the boats, a man in a white button-down shirt came to tell us in French that he was from the tourist office and needed our passports. Dr. Mwanza was sitting on the side of the pirogue, eating peanuts.

"There are no tourists here," he grumbled and laughed.

The man smiled nervously. "There are three *mundele.*"

"They are not tourists," Mwanza told him. "They work here."

"But they are traveling in Équateur and need to register with me."

"Just because they are traveling doesn't mean they are tourists."

"They are required by law to register with me."

"If you want their money," Mwanza told him, "you should have been waiting at the DGM. You've missed your chance. You could have discussed this there and found out that they aren't tourists."

"I need their passports," the man insisted.

"And what about me?" Mwanza asked, then shook the peanuts in his hand like dice and tipped them into his mouth.

"What about you?" the man asked.

"Maybe I'm a tourist. Just because I'm Congolese doesn't mean I can't be a tourist in my own country."

"What do you mean?"

"A person can be a tourist in his own country. You can live somewhere and travel and be a tourist."

Médard had just returned from registering our pirogue with the naval authority, and our engines fired up. Sally was using her cell phone to speak to the Kinshasa office, and Landrine had come back from the market with vegetables. We pulled out, leaving the tourist officer on the smoking, littered shore. Men loaded boats, veins bulging in their arms, their lined, sun-weathered faces expressionless, their naked torsos cut by hunger and years of incessant labor.

By nightfall, clouds gathered on the horizon. The stars vanished, the river so dark that we came into each curve tentatively. Wind began to gust, flapping our tarp. Michael had told me how sudden storms could be, but tonight's rain came sporadically, tapping the tarps, brushing the water. I dozed and when I woke, the boat was silent, motors off, everyone asleep, even the boatmen. I crawled from beneath my mosquito net, between the barrels, then shone my headlamp over the edge. We had run aground on a sandbar, the shallowest yet, and with no light from the stars or moon, the others must have agreed to wait, dawn being only a few hours away.

I swung my legs down and walked out into the empty dark, the river wide, the sky a perfect black, distance falling away with each step I took. The sandbar went on for another forty feet, and finally I stopped and stood, watching mist gather from the surface and lift in tendrils. A few banks of reeds broke the surface between me and an island. We must have chosen to pass to the left of it and run aground. It seemed as if I could cross all the way to it, the water at times to my knees, almost to my thighs. But I didn't. I was already far enough from the boat.

In *Voyage au Congo,* when asked what he would be looking for in Africa, André Gide replied, "I am waiting to be there in order to know." There are details we have to feel: what it means to work in a place where the yellow lines of highways on maps denote mud paths that break axles; where white people have left a legacy of disempowerment and the Congolese blame their problems on outsiders; where a simple task requires a deep knowledge of tradition, and every tribal chief and official wants to be respected with a meeting and a gift. Though navigating this society can be challenging for a foreigner, the social protocols are evidence of the people's cultural stability. Their formalized relationships manage the territory and resources, and reveal that there is a foundation upon which conservation can be built, and from which outsiders like myself can learn, with a little patience.

And yet I hadn't foreseen the gravity of the conflicts. Over the last few weeks, I'd caught myself wishing that the path forward for conservation were less complicated. Before I'd come here, it was hard to feel the urgency of the problems and how long change takes, the constant attention to detail it requires, the endurance and patience.

I reached up and turned off my headlamp. The night was so dark I might as well have been standing on the bottom of the ocean. I became aware of the hum of frogs and insects, the water rushing loudly past my ankles. My eyes refused to adjust. I flicked my headlamp back on, and as I turned, its beam swept over a stretch of reeds. Two blue eyes shone at me from the river. I moved the lamp again over the same space, but this time there was nothing, just misty dark. I walked to the boat, scanning the river. The eyes did not reappear, and I sat on the hewn wood and turned the lamp off. Wind splashed the water against the side of the pirogue. I slipped back inside, under my mosquito net, and went to sleep.

Our last day, we couldn't make Michael's Saturday flight, so we took our time. We stopped at a stretch of white sunbaked sand where cormorants held their wings out, as if in flight, to dry them. We swam, and after cooling myself, I walked across the sand, sunlight refracted up from it, blinding. The clouds of the day before were gone, though cumuli gathered in the west, the sun illuminating them like mountains.

Later, back on the boat, Mwanza told us that we were nearing the Congo River and should keep our cameras out of sight. Even though we'd bought photo permits in Kinshasa, police and military still used photographic equipment as an excuse to extort money.

Mud-brick buildings and fishing shacks crowded the shore. Young women washed dishes and stacked them in blue plastic tubs that they balanced on their heads to carry up the slope, beneath a few scraggly trees, to houses with thatch roofs. Naked children, many with swollen bellies, waved, playing in the water. In a lean-to, new pirogues were stacked, ready for sale.

We were close to Mbandaka, a place of exchange, where the fragile lines of commerce link into the Congo River from its many tributaries. After Kokolopori and Djolu, the economy's relative strength showed itself in the variety and brightness of people's clothes, the occasional concrete building and corrugated roof. However, the mud houses remained dilapidated, many of the families appeared malnourished, and men in tattered pants still paddled across the current.

As Michael, Sally, and I talked, I realized that what I wanted to know—what I hadn't yet asked them—was how much of their success depended on their charisma, and what would happen without them. Would their achievements vanish once the two of them were gone?

"If there's anything we've done," Sally told me, "it's build a team. If we die tomorrow, the team is still there—Albert, André, Mwanza . . ."

The list went on, dozens of Congolese educated in conservation and passionate about their heritage. And from what I could see, she was right. I'd met a number of Congolese working with BCI and Vie Sauvage, each of whom deserved to have his or her story told.

Over the last decade, Sally had seen the growing awareness of the Congolese and how some local cultures were shifting to renew traditional concepts of conservation. They were increasingly valuing their land for what could be sustained rather than the material exploitation that had dominated their country for more than a century. In a sense, they were on the heels of the vision that underpinned the West's economy: thinking of wealth in terms of investment.

If we need a PhD in science in order to protect what little wildlife and few rainforests remain, then the numbers of those who can change the situation on the ground are severely limited. The hard science of animal behavior, as Dian Fossey herself realized after Digit's death, will not save wildlife from poachers. Even though the government has banned the hunting of many endangered species, it cannot enforce the laws. Only the local people and their leaders can.

Michael, Sally, and I stopped talking. The Congo River opened before us, two or three times as wide as the tributary we were on, and staring across it, I realized that the far shore was one long tear-shaped island after another. I had seen this stretch on a map, the river broken into as many as six or eight channels, two or three of them nearly a mile wide.

Just beyond the confluence, we stopped at a military checkpoint. A handful of scruffy men, apparently soldiers, commandeered some gasoline and demanded ten dollars. Richard disembarked to show them our passports, and we sat in the boat as the sun descended through the clouds that had been building on the horizon. Spokes of light shone up through layer after layer, the forest molten gold at the far shore. The river turned silver, tiny fish jumping for insects.

When we got our passports back and pulled out, a soldier leaped into a light pirogue and grabbed the rear of our boat, insisting that he hadn't been given enough money. The boatmen yelled at him in Lingala and accelerated as he shouted. There were no guns, no trappings I had expected of soldiers, though the stern faces of the men on shore seemed military enough. After ten seconds being pulled in our wake, the hanger-on let go.

Soon it was dark, and we were traveling along a much wider path. Every now and then we scraped over a sandbar, slowing but not stopping. The team sat near the outboards with Landrine, singing, her laughter occasionally ringing out over the drone of the engines.

Epilogue: The Red Queen

Michael and I left Mbandaka at dusk the next day, Sally staying for her meeting. Our CAA jet got held up, waiting on the tarmac until a regional football game finished and the team boarded. Kinshasa looked different to me now, the airport lit up, the parked vehicles gleaming despite their dents, as if in the time I'd been gone, the city had modernized. Construction was everywhere, roads being rebuilt, banks and hotels going up. There were new car dealerships and shopping centers, numerous Western Union and cyber café signs, and constant advertisements for Vodacom, Airtel, and Tigo.

It was hard not to wonder what the city would be like in a decade. The DRC's mineral reserves could make the country one of the most affluent in Africa, but most likely the wealth would be siphoned through its elite, enriching foreign investors. If Zaire was one of the continent's poorest nations and its largest importer of luxury automobiles under Mobutu, what should we expect from the boom that is likely coming? Will it resemble the excesses of gulf cities that I've passed through on trips, Doha or Dubai, with their Hummers and BMWs, their showcases of sleek skyscrapers, boutiques, luxury villas, and five-star hotels? Or will the city have the closed compounds of those nations where the divide between the rich and poor has grown so extreme it can be sustained only with walls and police?

My last week in Kinshasa, I spent most of my time with André Tusumba, and the world I saw, while run-down, with open sewers and potholes in streets, was that of a determined business class. I accompanied him to meetings with Congolese entrepreneurs and local NGOs, at which he discussed plans for schools, for clinics, for transportation to the reserve. He told me that he needed to unlock Sankuru, to free the people from their isolation, to create work and resources so as to take the pressure off the forest. He contacted Kinshasa artisans whom he hoped to bring to Sankuru, to have them teach people new trades. One of the men he met had brought images of airboats used in Louisiana and the Florida Everglades. While researching ways to take supplies upriver, the man had determined that airboats could pass over sandbars and arrive in good time, though he didn't know how feasible it would be to buy them or build them here.

In the afternoon, André's phone rang, and he listened silently. When he hung up, he told me that a baby bonobo had been brought to his main site in Sankuru and he needed to go and get it so that he could take it to the Lola ya Bonobo sanctuary. He dropped me off at the BCI offices, and we said good-bye.

The next morning, the day before I would leave for Brussels and then New York, I met with Albert Lokasola, and he told me how challenging the last years had been in terms of funding, that he was worried about losing momentum as well as the enthusiasm and trust of the people when there were so many politicians looking to undercut each other. He'd chosen to run for office for this reason, to influence conservation on a national level, and whenever parliament wasn't in session, he planned on returning to Kokolopori.

I told him that of the people I'd spoken with there, many believed he was the region's only hope, and the others thought he would become a typical politician and forget them. He promised me that the latter would not happen, and listening to him, I was struck by how much work both he and André had before them. As international funds trickle into the Congo, the local people want to see constant improvement. The wages that trackers and eco-guards enjoyed would seem less significant as industries moved back into these regions and brought people in contact with the national economy. The conservation values that were being instilled in them could quickly be forgotten for larger profits, for coffee and palm oil plantations.

Both André and Albert appeared to be at crossroads—the first, after a decade of work, finally having the funds to carry out his projects and earn back the confidence of his people, and the second, having established his reserve and gained power in the process, facing the temptations and burdens of all powerful men and politicians.

As for BCI, their challenges couldn't be clearer, but their achievements stand: the reserves and numerous unofficial community-protected areas that, though not recognized nationally, provide safe passage for endangered species; and the network of Congolese trained in conservation, and ready to be mobilized for new projects. A Bonobo Peace Forest, spanning tens of thousands of square miles, would be no small achievement in a time of accelerating climate change, and yet, as Kokolopori and Sankuru have shown, it is clearly attainable through partnerships between conservationists and local people. The Congolese, both those involved in conservation at the national level and those living in the rainforests, are unquestionably motivated to protect their natural heritage, and if the various conservation groups can put aside their differences and collaborate, the Bonobo Peace Forest could become a reality within this decade.

As for BCI's struggles, I would discuss them a month later, when I spoke with BCI advisor John Scherlis in Washington, DC. He told me that he wished Sally had the time to explain to people everything she knows, that doing so might draw far more support for BCI.

"It's almost a winningly humanizing aspect of her," he said, "her capacity to go mute, which has happened at certain moments, in meetings and so on, where, had she stated what she's capable of saying in the way she's capable of speaking it, it would have served her and BCI extremely well. Sometimes that's the result of the vicious cycle, of burning the candle at both ends, of being chronically exhausted, feeding everything that's needed in DC at the same time she's keeping Congo hours, because she's up at ridiculous hours on Skype, or on the phone to people in Kinshasa."

After a pause, he added, "So much of it for BCI is like the Red Queen in *Through the Looking-Glass*. The Red Queen has to run as fast as she can to stay in the same place. So how do you make progress when you're already running as fast as you can?"

John's words made me see my time with BCI in a different light. What better image could there be for the entire Congolese experience, not just conservation—attempting to protect nature even as it's being destroyed— but the entire country trying desperately not to fall behind?

A day before my departure from Kinshasa, Sally returned, accompanied by Dick Rice. We'd joined her in Mbandaka, and Dick was on the same flight to Brussels as I was. When our taxi arrived at the BCI office and we said good-bye to Sally and Michael, an evening storm was blowing in.

The taxi driver steered the Corolla through the traffic as Dick spoke of BCI's self-replicating model. After seventeen years as head economist at Conservation International, where he developed the conservation conces- sion model, he was convinced that money wasn't used well and that a lot more could be done for a lot less. He often found himself asking how the big NGOs could justify funding their corporate structures and high salaries in perpetuity when the fragile nature reserves depended on irregular and often insufficient cash flow.

The driver left the main road, attempting to take a shortcut, and we soon appeared to be lost in a shantytown, splashing through long mud puddles and over rubble that scraped the car's bottom so violently that the floorboards rolled against our feet like a wave. Lightning flickered in the distance, then shot across the sky, linking up one thunderhead after another. The filthy, narrow road snaked between clapboard shacks and buildings of rusted metal sheets.

Dick and I stopped speaking when we realized that our car was stuck on the other side of a train track from the main road. The driver weaved through weeds and trash, looking for a place to cross over, and finally did. There was construction ahead, the airborne dust creating a sudden night, wind swirling it up. Hundreds of people gathered along the shoulders, running for *les esprits des morts*. A white pickup slowed, its bed empty, and the crowd charged it, clambering into the back. A pretty young woman in a slim floral dress grabbed the tailgate just as a man, climbing up before her, accidentally kicked her in the face. She jerked her chin down but fought for a place, putting her bag inside and pulling herself in, then cupping her mouth. The truck sped up, into the fog of dust, and she vanished. Soon we could see only the vehicles directly around us, the bumpers of big trucks and the vans with their mismatched panels.

Even with the windows closed, I felt grit on my face and between my teeth. I stared out, no sense of space, as if in a vertiginous, underwater world. Oncoming vehicles appeared as dim headlights swimming toward us until the massive trucks materialized, loaded for the provinces, carrying every possible ounce of freight. We pulled up behind one that emerged from the darkness like a mammoth. The only light on the back was a single headlamp wired to the bumper and angled at the ground. Goods were heaped nearly two dozen feet high, covered with tarps and lashed down, and rows of jerry cans were tied to the sides like sequins on a dress. At the top, high above us, in the gusting dust and lit by flashes of distant lightning, seven or eight young men sat, holding the ropes that bound the cargo in place.

It was impossible not to feel that the country was in the throes of change, a violent, necessary process that the people had been waiting for and demanding. But in the frenzy, once highways cut across the country, opening the forests and linking them to markets, would the people know what they were losing before it was gone?

Our driver accelerated through a clear stretch and braked. As the car moved onto a section of road that had been gouged up, its floorboards scraped rubble once more. The storm was close now, the dust around us even darker as we passed the hulking, indiscernible machines churning it up, the driver hurrying, slowing, then racing again.

Empty Hands, Open Arms

Acronyms

ACOPRIK	Action Communautaire pour la Protection des Primates de Kasai
	Community Action for the Protection of the Primates of Kasai
AFDL	Alliance des Forces Démocratiques pour la Libération du Congo-Zaïre
	Alliance of Democratic Forces for the Liberation of Congo-Zaire
ANC	Armée Nationale Congolaise
	Congolese National Army
AWF	African Wildlife Foundation
BCI	Bonobo Conservation Initiative
BGAN	Broadband Global Area Network
BINGO	Big International Non-Governmental Organization (or) Business-Friendly International NGO
CARPE	Central Africa Regional Program for the Environment
CBFF	Congo Basin Forest Fund
CBFP	Congo Basin Forest Partnership
CDM	Clean Development Mechanism
CI	Conservation International
CNS	Conseil National de Sécurité
	National Security Council
CREF	Centre de Recherche en Écologie et Foresterie
	Center for Research in Ecology and Forestry
DGM	Direction Générale de Migration
	Directorate General of Migration
DRC	Democratic Republic of the Congo
GRASP	Great Apes Survival Partnership
ICCN	Institut Congolais pour la Conservation de la Nature
	Congolese Institute for the Conservation of Nature

ISDR	Institut Supérieur de Développement Rural
	Superior Institute for Rural Development
IUCN	International Union for the Conservation of Nature
MLC	Mouvement de Libération du Congo
	Movement for the Liberation of the Congo
MPR	Mouvement Populaire de la Révolution
	Popular Revolutionary Movement
NGO	Non-Governmental Organization
PERSE	Protection de l'Écosystème et des Espèces Rares du Sud-Est de Équateur
	Protection for the Ecosystem and Rare Species of Southeast Équateur
PNP	Partie Nationale du Peuple
	National People's Party
RCD	Rassemblement Congolais pour la Démocratie
	Rally for Congolese Democracy
REDD	Reducing Emissions from Deforestation and Forest Degradation
RPA	Rwandan Patriotic Army
RPF	Rwandan Patriotic Front
TL2	Tshuapa Lomami Lualaba
USAID	United States Agency for International Development
WCS	Wildlife Conservation Society
WWF	World Wildlife Fund

Notes

Prologue

x   *To make matters worse*   "Congo Volcano Devastation Mounts," CNN.com, January 18, 2002, http://archives.cnn.com/2002/WORLD/africa/01/18/drcongo.volcano/; Danna Harman, "Volcanic Eruption Devastates War-Weary Congo City," *National Geographic News,* January 22, 2002, news.nationalgeographic.com/news/2002/01/0122_020122_wirevolcano.html.

Naked Apes, Furry Apes, Godlike Apes

5   *In an age when*   Peter Sauer presents a compelling argument for including our bodies and habitats when we speak of the environment. "Reinhabiting Environmentalism," in *The Future of Nature,* ed. Barry Lopez (Minneapolis: Milkweed Editions, 2007), 5; essay originally published in *Orion Magazine* (Summer 1999).

5   *Two large community-based reserves*   Kay Prüfer et al., "The Bonobo Genome Compared with the Chimpanzee and Human Genomes," *Nature,* June 13, 2012, http://www.nature.com/nature/journal/vaop/ncurrent/full/nature11128.html; Elizabeth Pennisi, "A Little Gorilla in Us All," *Science,* March 7, 2012, http://news.sciencemag.org/sciencenow/2012/03/gorilla-genome-sequenced.html?ref=hp; Aylwyn Scally et al., "Insights into Hominid Evolution from the Gorilla Genome Sequence," *Nature,* March 7, 2012, http://www.nature.com/nature/journal/v483/n7388/full/nature10842.html.

7   *With their long, slender limbs*   Michael Nichols, *The Great Apes: Between Two Worlds* (Washington, DC: National Geographic Society, 1993), 42–43.

7   *It was difficult to imagine*   "Chimpanzee and Bonobo," EAZA Ape Campaign, 2013, http://www.apecampaign.org/apes/chimpanzee; Claudine André et al., "The Conservation Value of Lola ya Bonobo Sanctuary," in *The Bonobos: Behavior, Ecology, and Conservation,* ed. Takeshi Furuichi and Jo Thompson (New York: Springer, 2010), 303.

8   *Chimpanzees first appeared*   Takayoshi Kano, *The Last Ape: Pygmy Chimpanzee Behavior and Ecology,* trans. Evelyn Ono Vineberg (Stanford: Stanford University Press, 1992), 17.

8   *Though records since the 1880s show*   Carmen Lacambra et al., "Bonobo (*Pan paniscus*)," in *World Atlas of Great Apes and Their Conservation*, ed. Julian Caldecott and Lera Miles (Berkeley and Los Angeles: University of California Press, 2005), 83.

8   *He wrote:*   Robert Yerkes, *Almost Human* (London: Jonathan Cape, 1925), Chapter 13, quoted in Richard Wrangham and Dale Peterson, *Demonic Males: Apes and the Origins of Human Violence* (New York: Mariner, 1996), 203.

8   *"I shall never forget . . ."*   Harold J. Coolidge, "Historical Remarks Bearing on the Discovery of *Pan paniscus*," in *The Pygmy Chimpanzee*, ed. Randall L. Susman (New York: Springer, 1984), xii, quoted in Sue Savage-Rumbaugh and Roger Lewin, *Kanzi: The Ape at the Brink of the Human Mind* (New York: Wiley, 1996), 95.

8   *"He asked Schouteden . . ."*   Ibid., 95–96.

8   *But reasonably enough*   Ernst Schwarz, "Das Vorkommen des Schimpansen auf den Linken Congo-Ufer," *Revue de Zoologie et de Botanique Africaines* 16, no. 4 (1929): 425–26, referenced in Wrangham and Peterson, *Demonic Males*, 202.

8   *Having remarked the similarities*   Harold J. Coolidge, "*Pan paniscus*: Pigmy Chimpanzee from South of the Congo River," *American Journal of Physical Anthropology* 17 no. 1 (1933): 1–57, quoted in Savage-Rumbaugh and Lewin, *Kanzi*, 96.

9   *Though the word* bonobo   Wrangham and Peterson, *Demonic Males*, 293.

9   *While Tratz and Heck's classification*   H. Lyn White Miles, an anthropologist at the University of Tennessee, writes: "There are significant differences between humans and great apes, but we share 98–99 per cent of our genetic make-up with them. If we were to strictly follow our own taxonomic system of classification, scientists would place the great apes in one genus with hominids (humans and near-human ancestors). But, an anthropocentric (human-centred) view prevails and humans are conveniently placed in a different genus from apes." "Language and the Orang-utan: The Old 'Person' of the Forest," in *The Great Ape Project: Equality Beyond Humanity*, ed. Paola Cavalieri and Peter Singer (New York: St. Martin's Griffin, 1993), 44.

9   *Even Carl Linnaeus*   Mary G. Smith, "A History of Research," in Nichols, *The Great Apes: Between Two Worlds*, 36. Also see Jared Diamond's essay in *The Great Ape Project*: "Since our genus name *Homo* was proposed first, it takes priority, by the rules of zoological nomenclature, over the genus name *Pan* coined for the 'other' chimps. Thus, there are not one but three species of genus *Homo* on Earth today: the common chimpanzee, *Homo troglodytes*; the pygmy chimpanzee, *Homo paniscus*; and the third chimpanzee or human chimpanzee, *Homo sapiens*. Since the gorilla is only slightly more distinct, it has almost equal right to be considered a fourth species of *Homo*." "The Third Chimpanzee," in Cavalieri and Singer, *The Great Ape Project*, 97.

9   *It clarified that the term*   De Waal is responding to a *New Yorker* article by Ian Parker, in which Parker writes: "When I asked Hohmann about the bonobo sex at Lui Kotal, he said, 'It's nothing that really strikes me.' Certainly, he and his team observe female 'g-g rubbing,' which is not seen in chimpanzees, and needs to be explained. 'But does it have anything to do with sex?' Hohmann asked. 'Probably not. Of course, they use the genitals, but is it erotic behavior or a greeting gesture that is completely detached from sexual behavior?' A hug? 'A hug can be highly sexual or two leaders meeting at the airport. It's a gesture, nothing else. It depends on the context.'" Ian Parker, "Swingers," *New Yorker,* July 30, 2007, http://www.newyorker.com/reporting/2007/07/30/070730fa_fact_parker.

This question is an important one, and seeing Parker passed over it briefly in this way, I got the sense of a dismissal, an interest more in contradicting readers' expectations rather than in understanding bonobos. Like human sexuality, that of bonobos is nuanced and plays important roles in social bonding. Certainly Gottfried Hohmann, a research associate at the Max Planck Institute for Evolutionary Anthropology, knows this. He is a serious scientist, one of the prominent researchers in the field, and a reader can't help but wonder whether Hohmann is being described with the same nuance with which he might deliver his views.

Parker's article became a subject of some controversy after its publication. Frans de Waal critiqued his portrayal of bonobos on the website of *Skeptic* magazine, stating, "The impression that there are new discoveries is merely a product of creative writing." Here is de Waal's full quotation: "Fortunately, a United States court settled this monumental issue in the Paula Jones case against President Bill Clinton. It clarified that the term 'sex' includes any deliberate contact with the genitalia, anus, groin, breast, inner thigh, or buttocks. In short, when bonobos contact each other with their genitals (and squeal and show other signs of apparent orgasm), any sex therapist will tell you that they are 'doing it.'" (Here, he cites Susan Block, "Bonobo Bashing in the *New Yorker,*" *Counterpunch,* July 25, 2007, http://www.counterpunch.org/block07252007.html.) Frans de Waal, "Bonobos, Left & Right," *eSkeptic,* August 8, 2007, http://www.skeptic.com/eskeptic/07-08-08/.

9   *De Waal suggests*   Frans de Waal, *Bonobo: The Forgotten Ape* (Berkeley and Los Angeles: University of California Press, 1997), 100.

10   *As I began to gain*   Primatologist Sue Savage-Rumbaugh has suggested the possibility of a bonobo language, not unlike that of vervet monkeys who have a different cry for a python, a leopard, and an eagle, though all are predators. Vervets respond differently to each of the three cries. Dorothy L. Cheney and Robert M. Seyfarth, "Selective Forces Affecting the Predator Alarm Calls of Vervet Monkeys," *Behaviour* 76 no. 1/2 (1981), 25–61.

10 *The approach Savage-Rumbaugh developed*   Journalist Alexander Fiske-Harrison wrote that Savage-Rumbaugh's "holistic approach to the research, rearing the apes from birth and immersing them in a 'linguistic world,' seems the most sensible way forward given its success with Kanzi, Panbanisha and her eldest son, Nyota." "Talking with Apes," *Financial Times,* Weekend section, November 24–25, 2001.

10 *On a day when Matata*   Nichols, *The Great Apes: Between Two Worlds,* 127.

10 *She hadn't realized that*   "Kanzi," Bonobo Hope/Great Ape Trust, iowaprimatelearning.org/bonobos/bonobo_family/kanzi/.

10 *He can also understand*   Pär Segerdahl, William Fields, and Sue Savage-Rumbaugh, *Kanzi's Primal Language: The Cultural Initiation of Primates into Language* (New York: Palgrave Macmillan, 2005), 14.

13 *Though I'd read Japanese primatologist*   Takayoshi Kano, "A Pilot Study on the Ecology of Pygmy Chimpanzees *Pan paniscus,*" in *The Great Apes,* ed. D. A. Hamburg and E. R. McCown (Menlo Park: Benjamin Cummings, 1979), 123–36; also cited in Wrangham and Peterson, *Demonic Males,* 204.

15 *Watching, I recalled words*   Segerdahl, Fields, and Savage-Rumbaugh, *Kanzi's Primal Language,* 39.

15 *He reflects on French philosopher*   Raymond Corbey, "Ambiguous Apes," in Cavalieri and Singer, *The Great Ape Project,* 132–35.

15 *However, human attitudes are changing*   In *Eating Apes,* Karl Ammann and Dale Peterson critique conservation NGOs' portrayal of wildlife and their failure to educate people about the bushmeat crisis. Ammann's own photos of slaughtered or suffering apes have been instrumental in educating people about the problem. *Eating Apes,* California Studies in Food and Culture (Berkeley: University of California Press, 2004).

Kinshasa

17 *Over four hundred years ago*   Jason K. Stearns, *Dancing in the Glory of Monsters: The Collapse of the Congo and the Great War of Africa* (New York: PublicAffairs, 2011), 328–29.

18 *By 2011, the DRC*   United Nations Development Programme, *Human Development Report 2011: Sustainability and Equity; A Better Future for All* (New York: Palgrave Macmillan, 2011), http://www.undp.org/content/dam/undp/library/corporate/HDR/2011%20Global%20HDR/English/HDR_2011_EN_Complete.pdf. As of 2013, at the time I was finishing this book, the DRC had moved to second last, just before Niger, on the UNDP report: *Human Development Report 2013: The Rise of the South; Human Progress in a Diverse World,* http://www.undp.org/content/dam/undp/library/corporate/HDR/2013GlobalHDR/English/HDR2013%20Report%20English.pdf.

18 *However, conservation often requires*   There has been a trend in conservation

that reduces the value of nature to economic benefits for the development of rural communities. John F. Oates examines the worst manifestations of this trend in *Myth and Reality in the Rain Forest*. BCI and their partners argue strongly for the intrinsic value of the bonobos and nature, and they are clearly motivated by a desire to protect them. However, to make struggling communities amenable to reserves, conservationists have to engage in questions of building a local economy. *Myth and Reality in the Rain Forest: How Conservation Strategies Are Failing in West Africa* (Los Angeles: University of California Press, 1999), 45.

19 *Though DRC's security forces* "DR Congo Police 'Killed 24 Civilians' After Elections," BBC, December 21, 2011, www.bbc.co.uk/news/world-africa-16297258; "DR Congo: 24 Killed Since Election Results Announced," Human Rights Watch, December 22, 2011, hrw.org/news/2011/12/21/dr-congo-24-killed-election-results-announced. The story was told in Reuters ("World Has Little Stomach to Take on Congo Vote Row," December 14, 2011, http://www.reuters.com/article/2011/12/14/congo-democratic-idAFL1E7NE61T20111214).

20 *Humans have cut down much* The forest has numerous values for our civilization. One that is significant is the presence of chemical compounds that are still unknown to science and that could be useful in medicine. Guy Cowlishaw and Robin Dunbar, *Primate Conservation Biology* (Chicago: University of Chicago Press, 2000), 2. See also Felicity Barringer, "Fewer Rain Forests Mean Less Energy for Developing Nations, Study Finds," *New York Times,* May 13, 2013, http://www.nytimes.com/2013/05/14/science/earth/study-finds-loss-of-rain-forests-can-deplete-hydropower.html?ref=todayspaper&_r=1&.

20 *In Southeast Asia* "Indonesia still held most of its forests as late as 1950, but over the following 50 years forest cover declined from 1,620,000 km² to 980,000 km². The rate of forest loss is still accelerating, with lowland forests most at risk. At current rates, lowland forests will disappear entirely from Sumatra and Kalimantan (Indonesian Borneo) within 10–20 years and perhaps even sooner." Lera Miles, Julian Caldecott, and Christian Nellemann, "Challenges to Great Ape Survival" in Caldecott and Miles, *World Atlas of Great Apes and their Conservation,* 222.

"Supposedly 'protected' habitat for orangutans has been declining by 50 percent per decade in recent times, which suggests that the red-haired Asian ape could be the first of the four modern apes to go extinct." Peterson and Ammann, *Eating Apes,* 2.

20 *In Brazil, forests are* "Amazon Destruction: Why Is the Rainforest Being Destroyed in Brazil?" Mongabay.com, rainforests.mongabay.com/amazon/amazon_destruction.html.

21 *In the Congo* The wars may have slowed large-scale logging operations in many parts of the Congo rainforest even as famished, displaced people decimated the wildlife. It's hard to find a silver lining to any war, and this one,

however slight or debatable, at least raised the urgency of protecting what forest habitat was left. (Andrew Harding, "How Wars and Poverty Have Saved DR Congo's Forests," BBC, December 5, 2011, http://www.bbc.co.uk/news/world-africa-16037543.) However, illegal charcoal operations in the eastern Congo devastated numerous forests. Michela Wrong writes: "The denuded areas left as they felled woodland for charcoal were so large, they were visible on satellite photos." *In the Footsteps of Mr. Kurtz: Living on the Brink of Disaster in Mobutu's Congo* (New York: Harper Perennial, 2002), 245.

23 *BCI's goal, he explained*   Over a period of ten years, BCI had 13,650 square miles formally protected, with a number of other areas under development, while the other groups in the bonobo habitat had approximately four thousand square miles designated. BCI's annual budget only recently exceeded a million dollars and was tiny compared to larger NGOs with budgets that ranged from approximately $20 million to more than $230 million. Over a period of ten years, BCI gazetted more than three times the area for a fraction of the funding.

26 *The effect of all this*   There is no reliable census of Kinshasa. Kinshasa is possibly the most populous city in Africa. Cairo and Lagos are also rated among the largest, all of them having urban areas containing between nine and ten million people, two to four times the size of most major African cities.

26 *One in five adults*   Mike Davis, *Planet of Slums* (London: Verso, 2006), 192.

26 *In* Planet of Slums, *Mike Davis*   Ibid., 191. Davis's information regarding salaried Kinois is referenced from René Devisch, "Frenzy, Violence and Ethnic Renewal in Kinshasa," *Public Culture* 7 (1995), 603.

27 *Known as* kulunas   Alex Engwete offers a good description of *kulunas:* "Kuluna and Kuluneurs in Kinshasa: A Low-Intensity Urban Insurgency?" Alex Engwete Blogspot, February 2, 2010, http://alexengwete.blogspot.in/2010/02/kuluna-and-kuluneurs-in-kinshasa-low.html.

Also, as Michael Hurley wrote to me, the problems with *kulunas* are precisely the sort of detail donors don't take into consideration when making grants:

> While they do often have sections about possible constraints and assumptions, this is rarely given much weight and deliverables are still based on Western standards. Consideration of the difficulties of the daily life of local implementers is rarely given much weight. The Paris Declaration hints at this when it talks about time frames established in grants for deliverables that are based on Western schedules without considering problems on the ground. It is often considered easier to fund expatriates to do a lot of the work. This can assure timely and professional reporting on grants, etc. In this way, many of these local issues are avoided because step 1 is to assure that Western expats are provided with a base of operations comparable to Western standards . . . Yet it is hard for us to allocate a few extra dollars for safe transport for our staff to avoid *kulunas.*

In a later email, Michael described his own encounter with *kulunas*. He wrote that he didn't fully understand what the BCI staff were dealing with when they told him that they had to leave work early because of traffic and their fear of arriving home late, when the *kulunas* were out. He didn't take their concerns too seriously until he attended the wedding of Mwanza's daughter in Messina, a poor neighborhood in Kinshasa. Michael wrote:

> When you turn off the main road to go to Mwanza's place, you drive along roads as bad as at Yetee, but without the ambiance. Crummy shacks and beat-up walls, concrete, cinder-block houses with rusted iron bars in the windows. These are like little village enclaves, and you get the feeling that many folks never even make it to the main road. . . . We headed home around 2:30 a.m. We wove through little roads without much room to maneuver and hit an intersection. There was a kind of concrete block in its center and someone sitting on it with his back to us. As we tried to figure how to turn, I noticed about ten other shadowy figures moving in from all corners, kind of furtively hovering. Then the guy in the center turned slowly while still sitting—very dramatically. He stared at me as he stood (I was in the front seat). He was naked from the waist up and his face was covered with white powder giving a skull-like appearance. The powder extended down his torso. He started toward the car as he pulled out a machete. We turned and squeezed into another road, drove over trash and piles of broken stones and headed away as fast as we could.

Hurley references "The Paris Declaration on Aid Effectiveness," March 2, 2005, http://www.oecd.org/dac/effectiveness/34428351.pdf.

28 *Two days before we were to leave*   The names of rivers in the DRC can be confusing, given that they often change after each major confluence. For instance, at Basankusu, the Maringa and Lopori Rivers become the Lulonga River.

Équateur

29–30 *Relative to North America and Europe*   *The World Factbook*, Central Intelligence Agency website, https://www.cia.gov/library/publications/the-world-factbook/geos/cg.html.

30 *As of 2005*   "Congo Deforestation Statistics," Mongabay.com, http://rainforests.mongabay.com/congo/stats.html.

30 *Though little of it was logged*   Hampton Smith, Tim Merrill, and Sandra W. Meditz, "The Economy," in *Zaire: A Country Study*, ed. Meditz and Merrill (Washington, DC: Government Printing Office, 1994), 174–75. Describing the early 1990s, the authors write: "Eleven foreign-based companies or joint ventures accounted for 90 percent of the country's logging operations. One German subsidiary alone accounted for 40 percent of logging in Zaire."

30 *With the war now over* This is happening despite a moratorium on indus-
trial logging imposed by the Congolese government. Many logging companies
are in fact getting artisanal logging permits, as reported by Greenpeace.
"DRC's moratorium on industrial logging being bypassed," Greenpeace,
May 15, 2012, http://www.greenpeace.org/africa/en/Press-Centre-Hub/
Press-releases/Greenpeace-DRCs-moratorium-on-industrial-logging-
being-bypassed/. See also: Jeremy Hance, "Congo Legalized 15 Logging
Concessions, Prompting Concern That Moratorium Will Be Lifted Next,"
Mongabay.com, March 13, 2011, http://news.mongabay.com/2011/0313-
hance_drc_logging.html#.

The deforestation rate for 1990–2005, previous to the current economic
and political stability, was only 1.1 percent (according to Mongabay.com), or
1.84 percent (according to Observatoire des Forêts d'Afrique Centrale): http://
www.observatoire-comifac.net/docs/edf2010/EN/SOF_2010_EN_Chap_1.pdf)

30 *Already, global deforestation* Daniel Howden, "Deforestation: The Hidden
Cause of Global Warming," *Independent,* May 14, 2007. Howden writes:

> Figures from the [Global Canopy Programme], summarising the latest
> findings from the United Nations, and building on estimates contained
> in the Stern Report, show deforestation accounts for up to 25 per cent
> of global emissions of heat-trapping gases, while transport and industry
> account for 14 per cent each; and aviation makes up only 3 per cent of the
> total. . . . Scientists say one day's deforestation is equivalent to the carbon
> footprint of eight million people flying to New York. Reducing those
> catastrophic emissions can be achieved most quickly and most cheaply by
> halting the destruction in Brazil, Indonesia, the Congo and elsewhere.

30 *In the process* One study suggests that, for unknown reasons, Africa's tropical forests might sequester a disproportional amount of carbon. University of
Leeds, "One-Fifth of Fossil-Fuel Emissions Absorbed by Threatened Forests,"
ScienceDaily, February 19, 2009, http://www.sciencedaily.com/releases/2009/
02/090218135031.htm.

30 *Zoologists Guy Cowlishaw* Cowlishaw and Dunbar, *Primate Conservation
Biology,* 1.

30 *Humans have devastated* W. H. Freeman and Company, "The Current
Mass Extinction," PBS, 1992, http://www.pbs.org/wgbh/evolution/library/
03/2/l_032_04.html.

30 *Despite the severity* Cowlishaw and Dunbar, *Primate Conservation
Biology,* 1.

30 *and given our current rate* Michael Soulé, "Conservation Biology and the
'Real World,'" 1986, http://www.michaelsoule.com/resource_files/172/172_
resource_file1.pdf.

31 *Trees covered the earth* Christopher James Williams, "Reconstruction of

High-Latitude Tertiary Floodplain Forests in the Canadian Arctic." PhD diss.,
University of Pennsylvania, 2002. ProQuest (AAT 3055015); Jaelyn. J. Eberle
et al., "Seasonal Variability in Arctic Temperatures During Early Eocene Time,"
Earth and Planetary Science Letters 296 no. 3–4 (August 2010): 481–86.

31 *Palm trees grew*   Bruce Bower, "Wyoming Fossils Shake Up Views of Early
    Primate Migration," *Science News* 129 no. 5 (February 1986). The existence
    of simple primates previous to this timeframe is open to some speculation,
    molecular clock studies suggesting that they originated as early as eighty-five
    million years ago (Cowlishaw and Dunbar, *Primate Conservation Biology*, 18).

31 *But as the continents*   Cowlishaw and Dunbar, *Primate Conservation Biology*,
    18–19.

32 *It eventually covered*   Elizabeth A. Kellogg, "Evolutionary History of the
    Grasses," *Plant Physiology* 125 no. 3 (March 2001): 1198–1205, http://www
    plantphysiol.org/content/125/3/1198.full.

32 *This dry habitat*   Cowlishaw and Dunbar, *Primate Conservation Biology*, 20.

32 *And as rainforests shrank*   A number of other extinction events occurred
    during this period. The most notable and the one that appears to have eliminated
    primates from North America, Europe, and Asia was the Eocene-Oligocene
    extinction event 33.9 million years ago, also known as the Grande Coupure.

32 *One strong theory*   L. Alis Temerin and John G. H. Cant, "The Evolutionary
    Divergence of Old World Monkeys and Apes," *The American Naturalist* 122
    no. 3 (September 1983): 335–51.

32 *With an average body weight*   T. Geissmann, "Body Weight in Wild
    Gibbons (Hylobatidae)," in Abstracts, XVIIth Congress of the International
    Primatological Society, August 10–14, 1998, abstract no. 282, University of
    Antananarivo, Madagascar,.http://www.gibbons.de/main/congress/
    98madagascar.html.

32 *Such abilities no doubt*   Temerin and Cant, "The Evolutionary Divergence
    of Old World Monkeys and Apes," *The America Naturalist*.

32 *Gibbons also lack tails*   Takayoshi Kano explains: "Brachiation is a form of
    locomotion in which an animal hangs by its arms from a branch and moves by
    swinging or alternating the arms. A relatively heavy animal can move and feed
    in the trees because brachiation redistributes body weight. The complete lack
    of a tail in apes is related to the change in brachiation: monkeys use the tail
    for balance when leaping and running, whereas brachiation does not require
    one. The shoulder, elbow, and wrist joints of apes are flexible and can rotate
    to a high degree. From a hanging position, various courses of movement
    are possible" (*The Last Ape*, 9).

33 *With diversifying monkey species*   Masato Nakatsukasa and Yutaka
    Kunimatsu, "Nacholapithecus and Its Importance for Understanding Hominoid
    Evolution," *Evolutionary Anthropology* 18 no. 3 (May/June 2009): 103–19.

33 *Even today, unlike monkeys*   R. W. Wrangham and P. G. Waterman,

"Condensed Tannins in Fruits Eaten by Chimpanzees in Gombe National Park, Tanzania," *Biotropica* 15 no. 3 (1983): 217–22; R. W. Wrangham et al., "The Significance of Fibrous Foods for Kibale Forest Chimpanzees," *Philosophical Transactions of the Royal Society of London* 334 no. 1270 (November 1991): 171–78.

33 *Those who survive*   The theory that the disappearance of forests and the drying of much of the African continent was an important factor in the evolution of apes is under continuous evaluation. Current scientific drilling projects (which take core samples from ancient lakebeds and examine the pollen content and composition of the soil during the different geologic periods) aim to chart the environmental changes over millions of years of human evolution. See Andrew Cohen et al., "Understanding Paleoclimate and Human Evolution Through the Hominin Sites and Paleolakes Drilling Project," *Scientific Drilling* 8 (2009): 60–65, doi:10.2204.

33 *Of the great apes*   Justin R. Ahrens, "The Orangutan: 'Person of the Forest,'" BioWeb, April 2008, http://bioweb.uwlax.edu/bio203/s2008/ahrens_just/adaptation.htm.

33 *and on the ground*   Frans de Waal, *Bonobo: The Forgotten Ape,* 51; Takayoshi Kano, *The Last Ape,* 7–8.

34 *The practice may have led*   "It has been proffered that a major leap forward in the cognitive evolution of hominoids may first have occurred in the building of nests, and a second major step may have been the full transition to ground sleep. These two changes may have begun a modification of the quality and quantity of hominid sleep, which in turn may have enhanced waking survival skills through priming, promoted creativity and innovation, and aided the consolidation of procedural memories. Current dream research with children, adults, animals and the dreams of modern hunter-gatherers, appears to support the hypothesis that these changes in sleep may have been important to the cognitive evolution of hominids from *Homo habilis* to *Homo erectus*." Frederick L. Coolidge and Thomas Wynn, "The Effects of the Tree-to-Ground Sleep Transition in the Evolution of Cognition in Early *Homo*," abstract, *Before Farming* 2006 no. 4, article 11, http://www.uccs.edu/Documents/fcoolidg/Before%20Farming%202006%20Dream%20paper.pdf.

34 *One theory proposes that*   Referencing articles by Jeremy Cherfas and John Gribbin that appeared in *New Scientist* in 1981, Kano describes how ape lineages that were possibly coevolving with pre-humans on the savannah may have returned to the rainforest, abandoning their largely terrestrial lifestyles (*The Last Ape,* 11). See also Committee on the Earth System Context for Hominin Evolution and National Research Council, *Understanding Climate's Influence on Human Evolution* (Washington, DC: National Academies Press, 2010), http://www.nap.edu/openbook.php?record_id=12825.

34 *And some genetic studies*   Bjorn Carey, "Human and Chimp Ancestors Might Have Interbred," Live Science, May 17, 2006, http://www.livescience .com/783-human-chimp-ancestors-interbred.html.

34 *As for DNA*   Prüfer et al., "The Bonobo Genome Compared"; Pennisi, "A Little Gorilla in Us All"; Scally et al., "Insights into Hominid Evolution."

35 *Scientists have theorized*   Wrangham and Peterson, *Demonic Males*, 204.

35 *This theory, however*   Wrangham and Peterson, *Demonic Males*, 225, referencing Marc Colyn et al., "A Re-appraisal of Palaeoenvironmental History in Central Africa: Evidence for a Major Fluvial Refuge in the Zaïre Basin," *Journal of Biogeography* 18 (1991): 403–7.

35 *The glacials come in cycles*   Daniel A Livingstone, "A Geological Perspective on the Conservation of African Forests," in *African Rain Forest Ecology and Conservation: An Interdisciplinary Perspective,* ed. William Weber et al. (New Haven: Yale University Press, 2001), 51.

36 *If we continue our time-lapse*   Livingstone, "A Geological Perspective," 53. It is extremely difficult, based on existing evidence, to evaluate the size of forest refuges that existed during the last glacial, though it is certain that the rainforests were greatly reduced.

36 *Rivers would have hampered*   Wrangham and Peterson, *Demonic Males,* 225.

37 *However, the chimp-bonobo ancestor*   In explaining the bonobo diet, Wrangham and Peterson write: "They have evolved to take advantage of the more digestible parts of the gorilla diet—not the tough, low-quality stems that occur in patches around swamps, but the juicy, protein-rich growth buds and stem bases of young herbs. We even can see the marks of this evolution in their teeth: Bonobo teeth have longer shearing edges than those of chimpanzees, adapted for eating herbs in a way that surprised people when they first discovered it in 1984. Bonobos have evolved in a forest that is kindlier in its food supply, and that allows them to be kindly, too." *Demonic Males,* 223–24, referencing Kano, "A Pilot Study on the Ecology of Pygmy Chimpanzees *Pan paniscus,*" in Hamburg and McCown, *The Great Apes*; Richard K. Malenky and Richard W. Wrangham, "A Quantitative Comparison of Terrestrial Herbaceous Food Consumption by *Pan paniscus* in the Lomako Forest, Zaïre, and *Pan troglodytes* in the Kibale Forest, Uganda," *American Journal of Primatology* 32 (1994): 1–12; Richard K. Malenky et al., "The Significance of Terrestrial Herbaceous Foods for Bonobos, Chimpanzees and Gorillas," in *Chimpanzee Cultures,* ed. Richard W. Wrangham et al. (Cambridge: Harvard University Press, 1994): 59–75; W. G. Kinzey, "The Dentition of the Pygmy Chimpanzee, *Pan paniscus,*" in *The Pygmy Chimpanzee: Evolutionary Biology and Behavior,* ed. R. L. Susman (New York: Plenum, 1984): 65–88.

37 *With so many resources* Wrangham and Peterson, *Demonic Males*, 222–27.

38 *New research, however* Stuart Wolpert, "Last Time Carbon Dioxide Levels Were This High: 15 Million Years Ago, Scientists Report," *UCLA Newsroom*, October 8, 2009, http://newsroom.ucla.edu/portal/ucla/last-time-carbon-dioxide-levels-111074.aspx.

As I was in the final stages of writing this book, atmospheric carbon dioxide surpassed 400 parts per million. Sources stated that it was the highest level in at least three million years, as opposed to fifteen million years, as suggested by Tripati: Justin Gillis, "Heat-Trapping Gas Passes Milestone, Raising Fears," *New York Times*, May 10, 2013, http://www.nytimes.com/2013/05/11/science/earth/carbon-dioxide-level-passes-long-feared-milestone.html?pagewanted=all&_r=0.

38 *Historically, global temperatures* Justin Gillis, "Global Temperatures Highest in 4,000 Years," *New York Times*, March 7, 2013, http://www.nytimes.com/2013/03/08/science/earth/global-temperatures-highest-in-4000-years-study-says.html?_r=0.

38 *The DRC's population* Until the separation of South Sudan, the DRC was the continent's third largest country, though, as Thomas Turner points out, both Sudan and Algeria "include large swathes of uninhabited desert" (*The Congo Wars*, 24). This point is important because of the fertility and wealth of resources of the Congo's land. (The comparison of national populations is also drawn from Turner.)

See also Carmen Lacambra et al., "Bonobo (*Pan paniscus*)," in Caldecott and Miles, *World Atlas of Great Apes and Their Conservation*, 92: "DRC's human population is increasing almost 3 percent per year, the highest annual growth rate in Africa. In 1999, there were 60 million people; at current growth rates, this number is expected to double within 25 years. Conditions of life in DRC are very difficult and much of the population still relies on forest products for food, shelter, and fuel. Pressure on all forest resources is increasing rapidly."

See also Peterson and Ammann, *Eating Apes*, 123: "Central Africa human populations are growing by 2 to 3 percent a year, which means that by the year 2025 there could be twice the number of bushmeat consumers living in Central Africa."

See also Alden Almquist, "The Society and Its Environment," in Meditz and Merrill, *Zaire: A Country Study*, 70: "Zaire's population was estimated at 39.1 million in 1992, making the country among sub-Saharan Africa's most populous. This figure represents a substantial increase over the 29.7 million inhabitants recorded in the last official census, taken in July 1984, which in itself had indicated a near doubling of the 16.2 million population at independence in 1960."

Mbandaka to Djolu

39 *He explained that both*   For more details on the value of animal proteins, see M. Premalatha et al., "Energy-Efficient Food Production to Reduce Global Warming and Ecodegradation: The Use of Edible Insects," *Renewable and Sustainable Energy Reviews* 15 no. 9 (December 2011): 4357–60. See also R. A. Olowu et al., "Assessment of Proximate and Mineral Status of Rhinoceros Beetle Larva, *Oryctes rhinoceros* Linnaeus (1758) (Coleoptera: Scarabaeidae) from Itokin, Lagos State, Nigeria," *Research Journal of Environmental Sciences* 6 no. 3 (2012): 118–24, http://docsdrive.com/pdfs/academicjournals/rjes/2012/118-124.pdf.

40 *Now, Mbandaka, a city*   "Congo (Dem. Rep.): Largest Cities and Towns and Statistics of Their Population," *World Gazetteer,* http://www.world-gazetteer.com/wg.php?x=&men=gcis&lng=en&des=wg&geo=-46&srt=npan&col=abcdefghinoq&msz=1500&pt=c&va=&srt=pnan.

45 *The river begins south*   Almquist, "The Society and Its Environment," 69: "In the third of the country that lies north of the equator, the dry season (roughly early November to late March) corresponds to the rainy season in the southern two-thirds. There is a great deal of variation, however, and a number of places on either-side of the equator have two wet and two dry seasons. Rainfall averages range from about 1,000 millimeters to 2,200 millimeters."

47 *Though she wanted to run*   Not only is Sarah Pike Conger's life featured in *The Empress and Mrs. Conger,* but her diaries reside in the Boston's Museum of Fine Arts and Harvard's Peabody Museum, and she was mentioned in an exhibit about the empress at the Smithsonian. Grant Hayter-Menzies, *The Empress and Mrs. Conger: The Uncommon Friendship of Two Women and Two Worlds* (Hong Kong: Hong Kong University Press, 2011).

47 *It crashed, killing the pilot*   There are numerous accounts of this story. Here is MSNBC's version: "Crocodile Blamed for Congo Air Crash," NBCNews.com, updated October 21, 2010, http://www.msnbc.msn.com/id/39781214/ns/world_news-africa/t/crocodile-blamed-congo-air-crash/#.UJ7_tYdfCSo.

51 *Later, she told me that*   Josephine Mpanga's NGO is called Réseau des Femmes pour le Dévéloppement de Djolu (REFED).

A Sense of Place

54 *By 65 million years ago*   Kevin Burke, "The African Plate," Alex L. du Toit Memorial Lectures No. 24, *South African Journal of Geology* 99 no. 4 (1996): 3.

54 *The African plate ceased*   Ibid., 8–9.

54 *This large, flat expanse*   Ibid., 3.

54 *The gradual slope of the*   Ibid., 7.

55   *But at some point*   Adam Hochschild, *King Leopold's Ghost: A Story of Greed, Terror, and Heroism in Colonial Africa* (New York: Houghton Mifflin Harcourt, 1999), 20.

55   *Today, most of the DRC*   Almquist, "The Society and Its Environment," 64.

55   *Though great apes*   Caldecott and Miles, *World Atlas of Great Apes and their Conservation.* See also Jean Maley, "The Impact of Arid Phases on the African Rain Forest through Geological History" and Alan Hamilton, David Taylor, and Peter Howard, "Hotspots in Africa as Quaternary Refugia," in Weber et al., *African Rain Forest Ecology and Conservation,* 57–87.

55   *As early as six million years ago*   The longstanding theory that the spread of grasslands and disappearance of forests resulted in bipedalism has yet to be proven conclusively. For a more thorough examination of the questions, see Committee on the Earth System Context for Hominin Evolution and National Research Council, *Understanding Climate's Influence on Human Evolution,* 12.

56   *Supporting this theory*   K. D. Hunt, "Bipedalism," in *Encyclopedia of Anthropology,* ed. H. J. Birx (Thousand Oaks: Sage Publications, 2005), 372–77.

56   *Again, if the environmental*   One theory is that humans evolved as runners, the most successful of whom had little or no fur. They ran down their prey by hunting in groups that spread out in large circles, using their endurance to keep the animal moving until it overheated and collapsed and they could kill it, a practice still done by a few hunter-gatherer tribes in Africa. As evolution favored those who could cool their bodies by sweating, they became increasingly hairless over the millennia. They were also among the few animals comfortable with mouth breathing, allowing them to lower their temperature further while running long distances. See Daniel E. Lieberman et al., "Brains, Brawn, and the Evolution of Human Endurance Running Capabilities," in *The First Humans: Origin and Early Evolution of the Genus* Homo, ed. Frederick E. Grine, John G. Fleagle, and Richard E. Leakey (New York: Springer, 2009), 77–92. See also Dennis M. Bramble and Daniel E. Lieberman, "Endurance Running and the Evolution of Homo," *Nature* 432 no. 18 (November 2004): 345–52.

56   *Those human ancestors*   The speed at which evolution can take place is clearly illustrated with a very different sort of creature: Australia's invasive cane toad. In 1935, this non-native species was imported from Hawaii (though they are native to South and Central America) and released in Queensland as a means of pest control. Given its toxicity and the lack of natural predators there, few creatures can eat the cane toad, and most that try don't survive. Its population has grown to two hundred million and has been slowly spreading across Australia, expanding its range thirty miles a year. In his article "Restless Genes," David Dobbs writes: "The leading toads hop on legs that are 10 percent longer than those of their 1930s ancestors—and measurably longer than the legs of toads even a mile behind them. How so? Toads that

are both restless and long legged move to the front, bringing any restless, long-legged genes with them. There they meet and mate with other restless, long-legged toads." A similar scenario could hold true of primate radiations in a changing environment. A volcanic eruption or meteor strike or even a decade of severe winters can kill off numerous creatures and create a vacuum into which survivors spread. The survivors propagate the very genes that allowed them to endure, creating offspring who, within a few generations, look a little different from their ancestors. The example of the cane toad sheds light on how, in the great ape family, humans could have evolved to have significantly longer legs than our ape cousins. When early hominids had to travel on foot in search of food, those at the vanguard would have interbred, increasing the likelihood for offspring to have even longer legs. David Dobbs, "Restless Genes," *National Geographic* 223 no. 1 (January 2013): 44–57.

56   *They could also move*   note 1: Regarding the earliest fossils of prehuman bipedal ancestors, scientists debate whether they lived in woodlands or the landscape had already changed to savannah. In many cases, their long, curved fingers are suited for climbing trees and their leg and pelvic structures are adapted to walking, though not with our current ease. Wrangham and Peterson, *Demonic Males,* 227–28, referencing Elisabeth S. Vrba, "Late Pliocene Climatic Events and Hominid Evolution," in *Evolutionary History of the 'Robust' Australopithecenes,* ed. Frederick E. Grine (New York: Aldine, 2007), 405–26. See also Steven Stanley, "An Ecological Theory for the Origin of *Homo,*" *Paleobiology* 18 no. 3 (summer 1992): 237–57.

   note 2: Jim Foley, "Hominid Species," TalkOrigins Archive, April 30, 2010, http://www.talkorigins.org/faqs/homs/species.html; Winfried Henke and Ian Tattersall, eds., *Handbook of Paleoanthropology: Primate Evolution and Human Origins,* vol. 2 (New York: Springer, 2007), 1528–29.

56   *Imagine going to a sporting event*   Richard Wrangham, *Catching Fire: How Cooking Made Us Human* (New York: Basic Books, 2010), 2–3.

56   *As for all of the grandmothers*   For attendance at the University of Michigan stadium, see Associated Press, "Michigan Scores with 2 Seconds Left, Stuns Irish," ESPN, September 10, 2011, http://scores.espn.go.com/ncf/recap?gameId= 312530130.

   Richard Wrangham explained to me in an email: "If you use a date of 6,000,000 years for the LCA [Last Common Ancestor], and 25 years for generation time (as per Langergraber et al. *PNAS* 2012), then your scenario needs to house 240,000 generations. If you shift to grandmothers, you need 120,000 spots. So all you need is a stadium with 120,000 seats."

   Wrangham references Kevin E. Langergraber et al., "Generation Times in Wild Chimpanzees and Gorillas Suggest Earlier Divergence Times in Great Ape and Human Evolution," *PNAS* 109 no. 39 (September 25, 2013): 15716–21.

57   *In Richard Dawkins's essay*   Dawkins asks us to imagine a line of people. You would hold your mother's hand and she that of her own mother, and so on. Dawkins calculates that if we allow one yard per person, we would arrive at the common ancestor of humans and chimpanzees in less than three hundred miles. A similar line of the same length, starting with that ancestor and moving back, would lead to modern chimpanzees. Richard Dawkins, "Gaps in the Mind," in Cavalieri and Singer, *The Great Ape Project,* 84–85.

57   *The Neanderthals left*   There are a number of online genetic testing services. I used https://www.23andme.com/howitworks/.

57   *Numerous tribes of early*   Chris Stringer, *Lone Survivors: How We Came to Be the Only Humans on Earth* (New York: St. Martin's, 2013).

57   *Unlike in other parts*   Kano, *The Last Ape,* 3. Paleobiologist Bernard Wood takes issue with this theory: "In the past it has been 'explained' that because chimps lived in the forest, and because there is little chance of erosion in the forest, then there are no exposures, and thus no places where fossils could be uncovered by erosion. Others say that high levels of humic acid in the soils of forests dissolve bones before they can be fossilized. Neither of these explanations is wholly convincing. Fossils are difficult to find in forests, but they are there." *Human Evolution: A Very Short Introduction* (New York: Oxford University Press, 2006), 69.

57   *Before the arrival of*   There are a number of theories explaining pygmy size, among them lack of sunlight and low calcium intake, but a new study suggests that other factors might be in play, such as selection for genes that provide the strong immune systems necessary to live in the tropical forests and that have the secondary trait of small stature. Katherine Unger Baillie, "Penn Geneticist Researches What Makes Pygmies Short," *Penn Current,* May 3, 2012, http://www.upenn.edu/pennnews/current/2012-05-03/latest-news/penn-geneticist-researches-what-makes-pygmies-short.

57   *As Dale Peterson writes in*   Peterson and Ammann, *Eating Apes,* 124.

57–58   *The destruction of other creatures'*   In "State of the Species," Charles Mann makes an argument for the ability of humans to adapt and find solutions before we destroy our habitat. Mann, "State of the Species," *Orion Magazine* (Nov/Dec 2012).

61   *There were four working vehicles*   The census numbers for Djolu Territory date back to 2004 and are likely much higher now.

The Bonobos of Kokolopori

67   *But when he crossed east*   Peterson and Ammann, *Eating Apes,* 75.

67   *Bongandu literally means*   The words "Mongandu" and "Bongandu" are often mistakenly used interchangeably. Anthropologist Alden Almquist explained the following to me: "'Mongandu' means a Ngandu person, not

the culture. 'Bongandu' or 'Bongando' is the people. Mo/Ba are classic Bantu language prefixes designating person(s). The safest usage in print is to use the root as an adjective, as in 'Ngandu culture,' 'Ngandu territory' (but 'territory of the Bangandu/Bongandu'). The terminal 'u' or 'o' varies both in usage and in written reference."

67 *Kano established his first*   The Luo Scientific Reserve was gazetted in 1990. There is a mistaken notion that Wamba, in the Luo Scientific Reserve, is the only place where one can see habituated bonobos. Wamba was the first, but there have been other sites for years, and their numbers are growing.

67 *Recent studies theorize*   Brian Hare, Victoria Wobber, and Richard Wrangham, "The Self-Domestication Hypothesis: Evolution of Bonobo Psychology Is Due to Selection Against Aggression," *Animal Behaviour* 83 no. 3 (March 2012): 573–85.

68 *Not only are the statuses*   Whereas chimpanzee males form alliances to take power in their group and win both breeding rights and control over food sources, bonobo males do not. Wrangham and Peterson, *Demonic Males*, 211; Joroen M. G. Stevens, Hilde Vervaecke, and Linda Van Elsacker, "The Bonobo's Adaptive Potential: Social Relations under Captive Conditions," in Furuichi and Thompson, *The Bonobos: Behavior, Ecology, and Conservation*, 28.

68 *And, even if*   Frans de Waal, "Foreword, Behavioral Study Section," in Furuichi and Thompson, *The Bonobos: Behavior, Ecology, and Conservation*, 13; Kano, *The Last Ape: Pygmy Chimpanzee Behavior and Ecology*, 189.

68 *Their hip movements are fast*   Wrangham and Peterson, *Demonic Males*, 209–10.

68 *The result is that males*   Lacambra et al., "Bonobo (*Pan paniscus*)," in Caldecott and Miles, *World Atlas of Great Apes and Their Conservation*, 87.

68 *This strengthens the bond*   Wrangham and Peterson, *Demonic Males*, 212–27.

69 *When a leopard bit him*   Alan Root, *Ivory, Apes, and Peacocks: Animals, Adventure and Discovery in the Wild Places of Africa* (London: Chatto & Windus, 2012), 143.

71 *The seeds are mixed with*   Cowlishaw and Dunbar, *Primate Conservation Biology*, 89.

71 *Because the bonobos travel*   Zoologist and conservationist Ian Redmond explained this to me at Kokolopori. The process is also described in Frances White, "Seed Dispersal by Bonobos and the Survival of Rain Forest," in Caldecott and Miles, *World Atlas of Great Apes and Their Conservation*, 87.

71 *Without the bonobos*   Cowlishaw and Dunbar, *Primate Conservation Biology*, 2. Furthermore, many other species of animals are important for seed dispersal, and without them, numerous types of flora would vanish. One mistake in conservation is to focus on the protection of the forests but not of the wildlife, since without the latter, the survival of the forests becomes tenuous at best. The ideal approach is to highlight the inextricable relationship

between forests and wildlife. For more information on seed dispersal by animals, see "Roles of Animals in Tropical Rainforests," Rainforest Conservation Fund, http://www.rainforestconservation.org/rainforest-primer/ 2-biodiversity/f-animals/1-roles-of-animals-in-tropical-rainforests; Ellen Andresen and Douglas J. Levey, "Effects of Dung and Seed Size on Secondary Dispersal, Seed Predation, and Seedling Establishment of Rain Forest Trees," *Oecologia* 139 no. 1 (March 2004): 45–54, http://link.springer.com/article/ 10.1007%2Fs00442-003-1480-4; E.-D. Schulze, E. Beck, and K. Müller-Hohenstein, *Plant Ecology* (New York: Springer, 2005), 543. For the impact of loss of wildlife on seed dispersal, see Lund University, "Hunting for Meat Impacts on Rainforest, Fruit Tree Seed Dispersal," *ScienceDaily,* March 20, 2013, http://www.sciencedaily.com/releases/2013/03/130320094854.htm.

Yetee

76 *Guy Cowlishaw and Robin Dunbar*   Cowlishaw and Dunbar, *Primate Conservation Biology,* 2.

76 *With an estimated fourteen million*   Mark Dowie, "Conservation Refugees," in Lopez, ed., *The Future of Nature,* 70, referencing Charles Geisler, a sociologist at Cornell University; essay originally published in *Orion Magazine* (Nov/ Dec 2005).

76 *Community-based reserves*   Cowlishaw and Dunbar, *Primate Conservation Biology,* 6, 343–44. Cowlishaw and Dunbar offer an excellent overview of community-based conservation projects:

> Because the unsustainable exploitation of primate populations and their habitats by local communities is often believed to pose the greatest threat to their survival, a great deal of conservation action is now aimed at making these natural resources more valuable to local people in the long term. This goal is achieved by increasing the economic value of that resource, either by establishing new harvesting or tourism programs or by distributing more effectively the economic benefits of existing programs (e.g., the revenues from tourism that would previously have gone directly to the state are redirected to neighbors of the national parks). Such projects have the attraction that the improved economic benefits at the local level will bolster livelihoods and community development. This approach of emphasizing the link between biodiversity and the well-being of human populations has led to the emergence of Integrated Conservation and Development Projects (ICDPs).
>
> The wisdom of this approach is still hotly debated (see Spinage 1998, 1999; Colchester 1998; Martin 1999), not least because the accumulated evidence suggests that humans show little natural inclination for sustainable use: what conservation does occur seems to be epiphenomenal rather

than intentional. . . . Nonetheless, harsh economic realities dictate that conservation will reap substantial benefits if ways can be found to ensure that this approach succeeds.

Projects that involve local people in conservation are generally termed community-based conservation projects (CBC). There are three basic types of community-based schemes (Gibson and Marks 1995). First, there are direct benefit-sharing schemes: local people gain directly from state-controlled conservation activities in the form of either cash income (e.g., from the sale of meat from safari-killed game) or employment as game scouts or tour guides. Second, there are indirect benefit-sharing schemes: local people gain indirectly if a share of the profits of conservation income is used on local development projects, such as building hospitals and schools. Finally, there are local empowerment schemes: local people are given responsibility for managing the resource, so that they have a vested interest in ensuring its long-term existence.

76 *Benefiting from the conservation economy*   Cowlishaw and Dunbar, *Primate Conservation Biology*, 6.

76 *They rotate their fields*   The assessment here of the low level of deforestation as a result of traditional slash-and-burn is based on the assessment in Cowlishaw and Dunbar, *Primate Conservation Biology*, 192.

77 *Whether in Japan or Afghanistan*   For a few of the many critiques of NGOs, see:

Mac Chapin, "A Challenge to Conservationists," *World Watch* magazine, November/December 2004, http://watha.org/in-depth/EP176A.pdf.

Dan Brockington and Katherine Scholfield, "The Work of Conservation Organisations in Sub-Saharan Africa," *Journal of Modern African Studies*, 48, 1 (2010): 1–33, doi:10.1017/S0022278X09990206.

Rana Lehr-Lehnardt, "NGO Legitimacy: Reassessing Democracy, Accountability and Transparency," *Cornell Law School Inter-University Graduate Student Papers*, Paper 6 (2005), http://scholarship.law.cornell.edu/cgi/viewcontent.cgi?article=1020&context=lps_clacp.

Issa G. Shivji, *Silences in NGO Discourse: The Role and Future of NGOs in Africa* (Oxford: Fahamu, 2007), http://www.oozebap.org/biblio/pdf/2011/shivji_forweb.pdf.

77 *It was hard not to ask*   In *Myth and Reality in the Rain Forest,* John F. Oates writes: "I will also try to show how the conservation projects I am most familiar with in these countries often seem to have been designed more to improve the career and financial prospects of the consultants and administrators than to genuinely improve the survival prospects of the forests and their wildlife" (58). "I also learned . . . that foreign planners, consciously or not, had a strong tendency to design conservation plans likely to provide significant future benefits to themselves or their own

organizations—either job opportunities for themselves or a continuing role for their organization" (93).

77 *The conservationist Richard Leakey* *note 1:* Leakey quoted in Peterson and Ammann, *Eating Apes,* 219–20.

   note 2: In an *Outside* profile of conservationist Mike Fay, who, for his "MegaTransect," hiked two thousand miles across the Congo Basin, Michael McRae writes, "In his mind, global conservation was becoming all theory and no action." (Transects are surveys in which occurences of plants, animals, or other phenomena of interest are recorded along a path.) Michael McCrae, "How the Nomad Found Home," *Outside,* October 21, 2011, http://www .outsideonline.com/outdoor-adventure/nature/How-the-Nomad-Found-Home .html?page=all.

77 *He asserts that* Peterson and Ammann, *Eating Apes,* 220. Oates, in *Myth and Reality in the Rain Forest,* also addresses the financial question: "The material benefits that have trickled to ordinary rural people from integrated conservation and development projects have often been slight relative to those that have flowed to political leaders and bureaucrats in the countries where the projects have been put into practice, and to the consultant experts and conservation administrators (based mostly in North America and Europe) who have planned the projects" (xvi).

77 *By partnering with local leaders* In *Myth and Reality in the Rain Forest,* Oates examines "the origins of the current enthusiasm for 'community-based' conservation efforts" and discusses "the dangers of this approach, which appears to be based in part on the myth that, left to their own devices, poor rural people in the tropics will inevitably act as good wildlife conservationists" (44). However, he acknowledges the importance of working with the local people and that there is a need for outside support.

81 *Hearing him speak* Peterson and Ammann, *Eating Apes,* 221.

81 *BCI built their projects* For an analysis of how BCI built local partnerships in Kokolopori, see L. Alden Almquist et al., "Kokolopori and the Bonobo Peace Forest in the Democratic Republic of Congo: Prioritizing the Local in Conservation Practice," in *Indigenous Peoples and Conservation: From Rights to Resource Management,* ed. Kristen Walker Painemilla et al. (Arlington: Conservation International, 2010), 311–26.

Albert Lotana Lokasola

85 *A Belgian served as a godfather* *note 1:* In the 1920s and 1930s, Belgium had already begun experimenting with the class of *évolués,* demanding that such people conform to Belgian values and ways of living. But only in the years after World War II did education become dramatically more available and a

substantial middle class of *évolués* begin to form. Tödt writes: "In the 1920s and 1930s the term évolués already appeared in Belgian Congo to describe a highly heterogenic group of (mostly literate) Congolese that differed in occupational, regional and linguistic aspects but shared education and/or employment in colonial institutions and the urban lifeworld" (7).

note 2: With worldwide colonies increasingly achieving independence, Congolese rioted for their own. In 1955, Belgian professor Antoine van Bilsen published his *Thirty Year Plan for the Political Emancipation of Belgian Africa,* a treatise setting forth gradual emancipation in step with the creation of an educated elite. Whereas the Belgian government was skeptical of the plan, not willing to give up its lucrative colony, many Congolese *évolués* thought that thirty years was too long. When Ghana achieved autonomy in 1957 and de Gaulle, a year later, promised all French colonies that they could decide their futures, Congolese independence movements quickly gained support. Already established in 1956, the Mouvement National Congolais rallied the people, Patrice Lumumba among its founders. He became its president and attended the All-African Peoples' Conference, hosted by President Kwame Nkrumah in Ghana. Here, Lumumba became inspired to look beyond the paternalistic vision of the Congo's future that Belgium was proposing. Daniel Tödt, "Les Noirs Perfectionnés: Cultural Embourgeoisement in Belgian Congo During the 1940s and 1950s," Working Papers des Sonderforschungsbereiches 640 no. 4 (2012), http://edoc.hu-berlin.de/series/sfb-640-papers/2012-4/PDF/4 .pdf. See also Turner, *The Congo Wars,* 70.

86 *Only with riots in Léopoldville*   Thomas Turner and Sandra W. Meditz, "Introduction," in Meditz and Merrill, *Zaire: A Country Study,* xxxix.

87 *an ardent and idealistic fight*   Quoted in Suzanne McIntire, *Speeches in World History* (New York: Infobase Publishing, 2009), 438.

87 *The discontent exploded*   Turner and Meditz, "Introduction," in Meditz and Merrill, *Zaire: A Country Study,* xxxix.

87 *Janssens, refusing to allow*   Ch. Didier Gondola, *The History of Congo* (Westport: Greenwood, 2002), 118; Martin Meredith, *The Fate of Africa: A History of the Continent Since Independence* (New York: PublicAffairs, 2011), 102.

87 *The outraged soldiers began*   Stanley Meisler, *United Nations: The First Fifty Years* (New York: Atlantic Monthly, 1997), 117.

87 *But the chaos intensified*   As Thomas Turner writes in *The Congo Wars,* "Belgium's neo-colonial strategy had centered on Katanga, richest of the six provinces of Congo and the one where much of its investment was centered. That was not a viable long-term strategy, since Belgian firms had major interests in the other five provinces. The Belgian government and major companies apparently intended to reconstitute a loose federal structure, within which Katanga would continue to enjoy substantial autonomy. Lumumba, seen as

the principle obstacle to Belgium's neo-colonial plan, was demonized" (32). This situation is also described in Turner and Meditz, "Introduction," in Meditz and Merrill, *Zaire: A Country Study*, xxxix.

87 *These were the provinces*   Turner, *The Congo Wars*, 44.

88 *The Congolese saw this*   Turner and Meditz, "Introduction," in Meditz and Merrill, *Zaire: A Country Study*, xxxix.

88 *When the army began rioting*   Michela Wrong, in *In the Footsteps of Mr. Kurtz*, compares the story of Lumumba and Mobutu to that of Caesar and Brutus, and Macbeth and Banquo. (82)

88 *Larry Devlin, a CIA officer*   Devlin quoted in Wrong, *In the Footsteps of Mr. Kurtz*, 77. Wrong writes that Mobutu had been on the diplomatic radar since before independence, when the Americans hosted a reception at the US Embassy in Belgium in order to get a better sense of the Congolese delegation. Mobutu's name came up repeatedly, everyone remarking on the intelligence of Lumumba's aide, though some of Mobutu's contemporaries now claim that during the time he studied journalism in Belgium, he was won over to the Belgian cause and served as their spy.

88 *It was only later*   Wrong, *In the Footsteps of Mr. Kurtz*, 80–86. Mobutu worked to create peace, promising that he would eventually step down, and his government enjoyed a great deal of popularity: professors and students were in favor of the nationalization of universities; the people supported his curtailing of the politicians that they perceived as dishonest and self-interested; and the end of conflict as well as the international demand for copper boosted the Congolese economy. And yet Mobutu abolished the post of prime minister, ostensibly to prevent the rivalries that had been so damaging for the country. He banned other political parties and created a one-party state, gradually becoming obsessed with threats to his power. Thomas Turner writes, "At first, Mobutu served as president while a popular military man, General Léonard Mulamba, was prime minister. Then the constitution was amended, eliminating the duality that had led to so many rivalries: Kasavubu v. Lumumba, Kasavubu v. Tshombe, and so on." *The Congo Wars*, 34–35.

88 *Both then commanded Mobutu*   Wrong, *In the Footsteps of Mr. Kurtz*, 68.

88 *The Soviets left*   Wrong, *In the Footsteps of Mr. Kurtz*, 82.

88 *A month and a half*   Hochschild, *King Leopold's Ghost*, 302.

89 *In 1964, a four-part rebellion*   Richard Gott, "Introduction," in Ernesto "Che" Guevara, *The African Dream: The Diaries of the Revolutionary War in the Congo* (New York: Grove, 2001), xv–xvi.

89 *Tribesmen whose sorcerers*   In *The Congo Wars*, Thomas Turner writes that the Simbas "relied heavily on magical protection, 'Mai Mulele' (later, 'Mai Lumumba'). Rather than working in the countryside in a Maoist manner, they moved from town to town, in trucks" (33). "Mai" means "water"

and is formulated with the name of a powerful individual for protection, in this case the Congolese rebel Pierre Mulele or Patrice Lumumba.

90 *Believing that colonization*   Gott, "Introduction," in Guevara, *The African Dream,* xvii–xx.

90 *As the mercenaries*   In *The Congo Wars,* Thomas Turner writes, "The parachutist operation was necessitated by the threat of Christophe Gbenye, head of the People's Republic, to massacre the western hostages being held at Kisangani" (34). See also Robert Anthony Waters Jr., *Historical Dictionary of United States-Africa Relations* (Lanham: Scarecrow, 2009), 269.

93 *As for Albert's father*   Different sources list the number of graduates differently. In *The Congo: From Leopold to Kabila; A People's History* (London: Zed Books, 2002), Georges Nzongola-Ntalaja writes: "When medical assistants, Catholic priests and agricultural technicians, who had a university-level education, were excluded, the Congo had about twelve university graduates at independence" (173). Hochschild, in *King Leopold's Ghost,* writes that there were fewer than thirty (301). Jason Stearns, in *Dancing in the Glory of Monsters,* writes that there were "five pseudo-university graduates at independence" (7).

From Slave State to Failed State

95–96 *The Portuguese shipped millions*   Wyatt MacGaffey, "Kongo and the King of the Americans," *Journal of Modern African Studies* 6 no. 2 (August 1968): 171–81, referenced in Turner, *The Congo Wars,* 50.

96 *Illness and parasites*   Hochschild, *King Leopold's Ghost,* 231.

96 *Pictures that missionaries took*   Ibid., 215.

97 *Entire villages were enslaved*   Robert Harms, "The End of Red Rubber: A Reassessment," *Journal of African History* 16 no. 1 (1975): 73–88, referenced in Turner, *The Congo Wars,* 27.

97 *Roger Casement and Arthur Conan Doyle*   Mark Twain, *King Leopold's Soliloquy* (New Delhi: LeftWord Books, 2005), 57.

97 *The system had always been*   The *chicotte* was outlawed only in 1955. As for the iconic abuses of King Leopold's reign, they diminished but in no way stopped when, after a decade of pressure from the British and US press, Belgium annexed the Congo Free State. For the next fifty-two years, it ruled the colony with a markedly paternalistic approach, claiming to civilize a savage people while exporting massive quantities of rubber, cobalt, copper, gold, and diamonds, as well as cotton, coffee, and palm oil. René Lemarchand, "Historical Setting," in Meditz and Merrill, *Zaire: A Country Study,* 16.

97 *Writers have speculated*   Michela Wrong addresses the claim, made by some, that because the people have no memory or clear knowledge of the colonial period's abuses, there is no causal link between the abuses of the colonial

period and the later exploitation by Mobutu. Wrong responds by making a comparison with which I entirely agree: "But it wasn't necessary to be an expert on sexual abuse to know it was possible to be traumatised without knowing why; that, indeed, amnesia—whether individual or collective—could sometimes be the only way of dealing with horror, that human behaviour could be altered forever without the cause being openly acknowledged." Wrong, *In the Footsteps of Mr. Kurtz*, 59.

98 *Thomas Turner, a professor* Turner, *The Congo Wars*, x.

98 *In 1971, Mobutu changed* As Thomas Turner writes, "Mobutu ignored the fact that 'Zaire' was only a Portuguese mishearing of the Kikongo word *nzadi* (river). One imagines the scene. A Portuguese asks, using gestures, 'What is that called?' A Kongo answers, 'The river'." Turner also points out that, rather than being a rejection of colonial terms, it merely repeated one, given that "Zaire" was and remains the name of a northern Angolan province. Turner, *The Congo Wars*, 62.

98 *He even renamed himself* Michael G. Schatzberg, *Political Legitimacy in Middle Africa: Father, Family, Food* (Bloomington: Indiana University Press, 2001), 49. See also Howard W. French, "Mobutu Sese Seko, Zairian Ruler, Is Dead in Exile in Morocco at 66," *New York Times*, September 8, 1997, http://www.nytimes.com/1997/09/08/world/mobutu-sese-seko-zairian-ruler-is-dead-in-exile-in-morocco-at-66.html?pagewanted=all&src=pm.

99 *This was also the time* Ibid., 52; Turner and Meditz, "Introduction," in Meditz and Merrill, *Zaire: A Country Study*, xlii–xliii.

99 *The Congo is composed* *The World Factbook*, Central Intelligence Agency website, https://www.cia.gov/library/publications/the-world-factbook/geos/cg.html. Turner and Meditz offer the following estimates: Catholics (46–48 percent), Protestants (24–28 percent), the indigenous Kimbanguist Church (16.5 percent), Muslims (1 percent), and the remainder who practice traditional forms of African religion. Turner and Meditz, "Introduction," in Meditz and Merrill, *Zaire: A Country Study*, xxvii.

99 *Mobutu's popularity faded* Schatzberg, *Political Legitimacy in Middle Africa*, 172.

99 *"They chartered Boeings . . ."* Pierre Janssen quoted in Wrong, *In the Footsteps of Mr. Kurtz*, 227.

99 *What he didn't squander* William Reno, *Warlord Politics and African States,* (Boulder: Lynne Rienner, 1998), 35. Referenced in Turner, *The Congo Wars*, 44.

99 *The symbol of Mobutu* Hochschild, *King Leopold's Ghost*, 304.

99 *Mobutu presided over* Wrong, *In the Footsteps of Mr. Kurtz*, 98.

99 *The Congo's distribution networks* Turner, *The Congo Wars*, 35. Despite the Congo Crisis, the country's economy continued to grow by 7 percent a year, but this stopped with Mobutu's greatest blunder. In 1973, in the largest

nationalization of privately owned companies in the history of Africa, he confiscated $1 billion in foreign-owned farms and businesses, then shared them with his elite, keeping a large portion for his tribe and himself. Mismanagement and neglect drove businesses into the ground; many of them were simply liquidated, the new, wealthy Congolese owners never intending to run them and using their proceeds for luxury items. Foreign investors, having lost so much, subsequently refused to take even the smallest risk. Turner and Meditz, "Introduction," in Meditz and Merrill, *Zaire: A Country Study,* xliv–xlv; Wrong, *In the Footsteps of Mr. Kurtz,* 96–98.

100   *After the Congo Crisis*   Turner and Meditz, "Introduction," in Meditz and Merrill, *Zaire: A Country Study,* xxxi.

101   *But after an attempt at*   He became involved with an independent association in Kinshasa composed of people from Djolu, which then merged with a larger group that included people from the six territories surrounding Djolu. Four government ministers from that region chose advisors from this association, and in 1993, the minister of external affairs picked Albert. But as soon as he had, the minister was appointed governor of Orientale, the province to the east of Équateur. Though Albert moved with him to Kisangani, the tribalism in the minister's cabinet caused steady conflict. Kokolopori was just across the provincial border, and Albert worked to facilitate trade with it, but the minister's supporters contested his position, accusing him of not being aligned with Orientale's interests. To keep peace, the minister let him go.

101   *With the Cold War over*   "One of the most egregious instances occurred in Bandundu in 1978, when the security forces summarily executed about 500 people following a minor uprising set off by a self-proclaimed prophet. Another occurred in 1981, when perhaps 100 diamond miners were killed in Kasai-Oriental. The incident that gained the greatest international attention and that had the most serious repercussions for the Mobutu regime was the May 1990 massacre of students at the University of Lubumbashi. Up to 100 students were killed in the incident, ultimately prompting most multilateral and bilateral donors to terminate all but humanitarian aid to Zaire." Turner and Meditz, "Introduction," in Meditz and Merrill, *Zaire: A Country Study,* xlvii.

101   *Bureaucrats took similar measures*   Wrong, *In the Footsteps of Mr. Kurtz,* 99.

102   *Officials sold everything*   Hochschild writes, "During the Tokyo real estate boom, the Congo's ambassador to Japan sold the embassy and apparently pocketed the money." *King Leopold's Ghost,* 306.

102   *In 1993, when Mobutu*   Wrong, *In the Footsteps of Mr. Kurtz,* 128.

102   *In rural areas*   Turner and Meditz, "Introduction," in Meditz and Merrill, *Zaire: A Country Study,* liii; Alden Almquist, "The Society and Its Environment," in Meditz and Merrill, *Zaire: A Country Study,* 63.

104   *Even the army lootings*   In *In the Footsteps of Mr. Kurtz,* Michela Wrong

describes "two rounds of looting so terrible they have become historical land-
marks in people's minds, so that events are labelled as being 'avant le premier
pillage' or 'après le deuxième pillage', before and after the lootings" (20). In
Planet of Slums, Mike Davis refers to the same lootings, which took place in
1991 and 1993, and which were also called the *jacquerie* (194).

104 *The Kinois had been*   Turner and Meditz, "Introduction," in Meditz and
Merrill, *Zaire: A Country Study,* xlviii, l–li.

104 *For an invasion to topple*   Turner, *The Congo Wars,* 37. Jason Stearns, in
Dancing in the Glory of Monsters, 193–94.

104 *And yet the Congo Wars*   This tension was in part a result, as Thomas
Turner writes, of the Belgian colonial idea "that parts of Congo were under-
populated, especially by 'useful' Africans [i.e., supposedly racially superior
Tutsis]. This led to programmes to transfer families from Rwanda to eastern
Congo, with consequences that are still being felt." *The Congo Wars,* 29.

104 *Though ethnic division*   As for the roots of Rwandan conflict, they lie in
myth and conjecture, since no one has established a definitive history of the
Rwandan people. Though they speak the same language, the division between
Tutsis and Hutus traditionally functioned like a caste system, the Tutsis being
herders and the Hutus farmers. The Germans, whose colonization of Rwanda
lasted from 1885 to 1916, believed that the Tutsis were of Hamitic origin,
from Ethiopia or the Horn of Africa, though there was no archaeological or
historical evidence to back this up. Seeing the Tutsis' physical resemblance to
Europeans, the Germans had them rule over the Hutus in what was essentially a feudal system. The Hutus are a Bantu people who most likely first
spread along the coast, then migrated west, displacing the Twa, a Pygmy
people. Some historians view the Tutsis and Hutus as two social groups that
emerged from the same root, much as French aristocrats and peasants did.
However, others claim that the Tutsis migrated south, herding cattle, then lived
and interbred with the Hutus long enough to share a language and culture, and
that successful cattle-owning Hutus traditionally were able to join the Tutsis.
The ability of adult Tutsis to digest lactose is remarkably high in comparison to
other regional peoples like the Hutu and required millennia to develop, supporting this theory to some degree. Genetic tests also suggest that the Tutsis
may have Nilotic origins though they are quite similar genetically to the Hutu
as a result of centuries of intermarriage. See J. R. Luis et al., "The Levant
Versus the Horn of Africa: Evidence for Bidirectional Corridors of Human
Migrations," *American Journal of Human Genetics* 74 no. 3 (March 2004):
532–44, http://www.ncbi.nlm.nih.gov/pmc/articles/PMC1182266/; Razib Khan,
"Tutsi Probably Differ Genetically from the Hutu," *Discover,* August 29, 2011,
http://blogs.discovermagazine.com/gnxp/2011/08/tutsi-differ-genetically-from-
the-hutu/; Razib Khan, "Tutsi Genetics ii," *Discover,* August 31, 2011, http://
blogs.discovermagazine.com/gnxp/2011/08/tutsi-genetics-ii.

105 *Over two million citizens*   Kevin C. Dunn, *Imagining the Congo: The International Relations of Identity* (New York: Palgrave Macmillan, 2003), 143.

105 *Between thirty and forty thousand*   Gérard Prunier, *Africa's World War: Congo, the Rwandan Genocide, and the Making of a Continental Catastrophe* (New York: Oxford University Press, 2009), 25.

105 *Since the end of the Cold War*   In fact, for years, Mobutu's military units had been promoting ethnic violence in the Kivus against the Congolese Tutsis, the Banyarwanda, and "most observers" saw the violence there as "less historical than the result of deliberate government manipulation designed to divert popular resentment of the Mobutu regime." Turner and Meditz, "Introduction," in Meditz and Merrill, *Zaire: A Country Study,* l–li.

106 *Whereas the United States*   In *The Congo Wars,* Thomas Turner writes:

> The same community failed to act between 1994 and 1996 in response to the crisis generated by the flight of Hutu Rwandan authorities, troops and civilians to eastern Congo, even though the danger of international war was obvious. There were various reasons for this inaction, but a major one was the rivalry between France on the one hand, which was backing Mobutu, and the United States, which wanted to replace its former protégé. This relationship had shaped the catastrophes in the Great Lakes region at least since 1990, when the West began pressurizing the dictators Habyarimana [of Rwanda], Mobutu and their neighbours to democratize. As often as not the USA and France were pulling in opposite directions, preventing effective international intervention (150).

Turner references Michael Barnett, *Eyewitness to a Genocide: The United Nations and Rwanda* (Ithaca: Cornell University Press, 2000); Samantha Power, *"A Problem from Hell": America and the Age of Genocide* (New York: Basic Books, 2004); Linda Melvern, *A People Betrayed: The Role of the West in Rwanda's Genocide* (New York: Zed Books, 2000).

106 *At the time Zaire*   note 1: As per Turner and Meditz, "zinc, tin, manganese, gold, tungsten-bearing wolframite, niobium, and tantalum also are found in Zaire. In addition, the Atlantic coast contains important oil reserves, and the country also has some coal deposits." "Introduction," in Meditz and Merrill, *Zaire: A Country Study,* xxxv.

note 2: The RPF, furious that the UN proposed no political solution, only a largely ineffective humanitarian one, prepared for war. The RPA's decision to attack is thoroughly described in Prunier, *Africa's World War.*

note 3: Mobutu had numerous adversaries by now and was seen as an embarrassment and a dinosaur on the African continent. He had often harbored and supported the enemies of neighboring countries. As Jason Stearns writes in *Dancing in the Glory of Monsters*: "In his Machiavellian bid to become a regional power broker, Mobutu had come to host over ten different foreign

armed groups on his territory, which angered his neighbors to no end. By
1996, a regional coalition led by Angola, Uganda, and Rwanda had formed
to overthrow Mobutu."

106 *Che Guevara, who had*   Guevara, *The African Dream,* 244.

106 *Kabila had spent*   "Laurent Kabila," *Economist,* January 18, 2001, http://
www.economist.com/node/481974.

106 *He'd received international attention*   Brian C. Aronstam, "Out of Africa,"
Standford Magazine, July/August 1998, http://alumni.stanford.edu/get/page/
magazine/article/?article_id=42098.

106 *The primary casualties*   Gérard Prunier's *Africa's World War* offers a more
in-depth account of this event, explaining the role and fate of the refugees in
the Second Congo War over the course of a careful, several-hundred-page-
long analysis.

107 *Kongolo died two years afterward*   Wrong, *In the Footsteps of Mr. Kurtz,*
15–16.

107 *The economy and infrastructure*   Peterson and Ammann, *Eating Apes,* 133.
Peterson cites the word *eyama,* whereas in Kokolopori people said *nyama.*

Sally Jewell Coxe

112 *They were the remnants*   "Conflict in Congo," International Crisis Group,
updated January 27, 2011, http://www.crisisgroup.org/en/publication-type/
key-issues/country/conflict-in-congo.aspx.

114 *One of her assignments*   Michael Nichols, *The Great Apes: Between Two
Worlds* (Washington, DC: National Geographic Society, 1993).

114 *Fossey then gave up*   In her contribution to *The Great Apes: Between Two
Worlds,* National Geographic Society photo editor Mary G. Smith writes:

> I discussed this with George Schaller not long ago, and he sent me a review
> he had written about one of the numerous books on Fossey that appeared
> after her death.
>
> "She made several important new observations on gorilla behavior," he
> noted, "including the discovery of infanticide and the transfer of females
> out of old-established groups to new ones." But, he said, "after her favorite
> gorilla, Digit, was killed by poachers in 1977, she abandoned all pretense of
> scientific effort. . . . With singular devotion, Dian made the correct choice
> for herself: gorilla protection had to take precedence over research. . . . She
> helped this magnificent ape endure during a critical decade of its history."
> (28–29)

115 *She worked with him*   The description of this scene is based on the recollections of Sally Jewell Coxe.

116 *In focusing on attributes*   In a PBS interview, Frans de Waal supports this view:

If you look at human society, it is very easy, of course, to compare our warfare and territoriality with the chimpanzee. But that's only one side of what we do. We also trade, we intermarry, we allow each other to travel through our territory. There's an enormous amount of cooperation. Indeed, among hunter-gatherers, peace is common 90 percent of the time, and war takes place only a small part of the time. Chimps cannot tell us anything about peaceful relations, because chimps have only different degrees of hostility between communities, whereas bonobos do tell us something: they tell us about the possibility of having peaceful relationships.

From "The Bonobo in All of Us," *Nova*, PBS, January 1, 2007, http://www.pbs.org/wgbh/nova/nature/bonobo-all-us.html.

116 *Bonobos use eye-contact*   Gorillas have on rare occasions been seen mating in the missionary position.

117 *Savage-Rumbaugh pushed*   Many other primatologists and researchers have studied ape language among chimpanzees, orangutans, and gorillas. The essays in Cavalieri and Singer's *Great Ape Project* provide an overview of these studies.

117 *The difference between their species*   Carole Jahme, *Beauty and the Beasts: Woman, Ape and Evolution* (New York: Soho Press, 2001), 284, referenced in Frances Bartkowski, *Kissing Cousins: A New Kinship Beastiary* (New York: Columbia University Press, 2008), 114.

119 *During the hundred days*   Stearns, *Dancing in the Glory of Monsters,* 8.

120 *It recalled her childhood*   Sally's story reminds me of what David Sobel writes about how we learn to feel affinity for the natural world. "What's important is that children have an opportunity to bond with the natural world, to learn to love it and feel comfortable in it, before being asked to heal its wounds," he writes, citing studies showing that children given classroom lessons about the plight of nature are far less likely to develop an affinity for it than those who get to explore it in a carefree way, to enjoy being outdoors. It's hard not to wonder how successive generations of urbanized children will grow up—whether they will have a desire to see places like these, or to protect them. David Sobel, "Beyond Ecophobia," in Lopez, ed., *The Future of Nature,* 186; essay originally published in *Orion Magazine* (Autumn 1995). See also Richard Louv, *Last Child in the Woods: Saving Our Children From Nature-Deficit Disorder,* (Chapel Hill: Algonquin Books, 2008).

121 *"It was never my goal . . ."*   On the subject of the Jane Goodall syndrome, BCI advisor John Scherlis explained the following to me:

My impression around 2001 was that some other bonobo people, long-standing field researchers, believed that Sally sought to be regarded as the Jane Goodall of the bonobos, a status it seemed they wished for themselves. In fact, Sally's strongly held and overwhelming motivation was to facilitate effective conservation of bonobos by whoever could do the necessary work. Her time with the Bonobo Protection Fund, which was not allowed to engage in conservation work, reinforced her rightful conviction that another organization was needed, and that the best way to do this was by unifying the disparate bonobo people in an alliance that would speak on their behalf and foster their efforts. Only the emergent power of a coalition could improve the effectiveness of bonobo conservation activities, whether collaborative efforts or individual actions by members of the coalition. But the suspicion and needless vigilant territoriality of the others thwarted her original goal of creating the umbrella advocate. They wrongly projected onto BCI what one might assume to be their own motivations and goals and erroneous implicit assessment of it all being a zero sum game; that was tragic and incurred opportunity costs for bonobo conservation, but was explicable given that both resources and opportunities to do bonobo work were then very limited indeed, as were the opportunities for face-to-face communication between the bonobo people. Of course, none of the bonobo researchers could meet the criteria to be the "Jane Goodall" of bonobos, because circumstances have changed. This is nothing against them; they are intrepid people who have accomplished a great deal. But Jane Goodall and Dian Fossey and Birute Galdikas were each the first to publicly be the "man of the woods," the boundary-penetrating emissary from us to them, the then inscrutable great apes, returning to us with the first widely distributed (thanks to the National Geographic Society's gazillions of dollars worth of wonderful publicity) firsthand accounts of deep experience with the *other,* when such experiences were novel. That time, that opportunity, has passed, in part because we are now saturated with similar tales from many non-human realms, and because of the work at several sites by those bonobo researchers themselves and their more recent colleagues. BCI's original goal of creating an alliance for bonobo conservation has been taken on by the USFWS [United States Fish and Wildlife Service], Arcus Foundation, and IUCN [International Union for Conservation of Nature]/SSC [Species Survival Commission]/PSG [Primate Specialist Group]–backed Bonobo Working Group.

Africa's Great War

123 *He declared that the* Stearns, *Dancing in the Glory of Monsters,* 168–69.
123 *He explains that though Kabila* Stearns, in *Dancing in the Glory of Monsters,* notes that Kabila's position of power was in no way assured; an independent poll suggested that only 14 percent of Kinois would have voted for him (171). Thomas Turner writes in *The Congo Wars* that "Kabila was

supposed to be weak enough to obey his backers yet strong enough to secure their common borders" (37).

123 *When Kabila, needing a loyal army*   Stearns, *Dancing in the Glory of Monsters*, 183.

124 *Rwanda and Uganda sold*   In *Dancing in the Glory of Monsters*, Jason Stearns writes:

> The minerals were transported, processed, and consumed by companies and consumers elsewhere, especially in Europe, Asia, and the United States. In some cases, these companies had close relationships with rebel groups. For example, the Belgium-based company Cogecom bought tin and coltan directly from the RCD monopoly, sending money into RCD coffers. Another joint venture by American and Dutch businessmen, Eagle Wings Resources, engaged Paul Kagame's brother-in-law as its local representative, which gave it easier and cheaper access to the Congolese minerals. These companies then sold their minerals on to large processing companies, including U.S.-based Cabot Corporation, Chinese Ningxia, and German H. C. Starck. The transport was assured by multinational logistics companies such as the state airline of Belgium, Sabena, while financing was supplied by large regional banks and, in one case, by Citibank. (302–3)

124 *When Rwandan and Ugandan forces*   UN Security Council, *Report of the Inter-Agency Assessment Mission to Kisangani, S/2000/1153*, December 4, 2000, referenced in Stearns, *Dancing in the Glory of Monsters*, 285–90, 292.

124 *The Second Congo War*   Ian Bannon and Paul Collier eds., *Natural Resources and Violent Conflict: Options and Actions* (Washington, DC: World Bank, 2003); Léonce Ndikumana and Kisangani F. Emizet, "The Economics of Civil War: The Case of the Democratic Republic of Congo," in *Understanding Civil War: Evidence and Analysis* vol. 1, *Africa,* (Washington, DC: World Bank and Oxford University Press, 2005); both referenced in Turner, *The Congo Wars*, 2.

124 *The Congolese political scientist*   Nzongola, *The Congo from Leopold to Kabila*, 227.

124 *As Dena Montague writes*   UN Security Council, *Report of the Panel of Experts on the Illegal Exploitation of Natural Resources and Other Forms of Wealth of the Democratic Republic of the Congo*, April 12, 2001, 29, referenced in Dena Montague, "Stolen Goods: Coltan and Conflict in the Democratic Republic of Congo," *SAIS Review* 22 no. 1 (Winter/Spring 2002): 103–18, http://archive.niza.nl/docs/200207051622594404.pdf.

124 *"Between late 1999 . . ."*   Stearns, *Dancing in the Glory of Monsters*, 300.

124 *Agricultural produce, livestock*   Turner, *The Congo Wars*, 24.

124 *The price of tantalum*   Stearns, *Dancing in the Glory of Monsters*, 299.

125   *Copper prices increased*   Thomas Turner offers a detailed assessment of the pillage in the Second Congo War. *The Congo Wars,* 40–41, 46–47.

125   *Even as Kabila was*   Stearns, *Dancing in the Glory of Monsters,* 298–301. In *Africa's World War,* Gérard Prunier writes: "Today President Kagame does not try to control 'the Congo' anymore but simply to control enough *mining interests* in the Congo to help finance his great dreams of turning Rwanda into the Singapore of Africa. The money comes from a variety of nonferrous metals (niobium, cassiterite, not much coltan these days since the Australians got back into the market) extracted from mines controlled by local Congolese militias who export their product to Rwanda in light planes" (326).

125   *A committee of military leaders*   Stearns, *Dancing in the Glory of Monsters,* 308.

125   *In recent years, however*   Étienne Tshisekedi, Joseph Kabila's foremost opponent and a political figure since Mobutu's time, also claimed victory and had himself inaugurated at his residence. To the media, Kabila admitted that the elections hadn't been as efficient and reliable as they could have been, but he insisted that he had won. Despite the conflict, the violence that many feared didn't take place.

125   *The damage was long lasting*   The International Rescue Committee places the number at 5.4 million, based on an April 2007 study, though this does not include casualties from the First Congo War. "IRC Study Shows Congo's Neglected Crisis Leaves 5.4 Million Dead," International Rescue Committee, http://www.rescue.org/news/irc-study-shows-congos-neglected-crisis-leaves-54-million-dead-peace-deal-n-kivu-increased-aid—4331.

Jason Stearns, in *Dancing in the Glory of Monsters,* writes: "Over five million people have died, and hundreds of thousands of women have been raped" (327).

In *The Congo Wars,* Thomas Turner writes: "The International Rescue Committee estimated the total at 3.8 million deaths for the period 1998 to 2004. In contrast, the Sudan civil war produced 2 million deaths in twenty-two years. The Rwandan genocide and massacres of 1994 may have involved 1 million deaths. The Indian Ocean tsunami of 2004 killed around 300,000 people, and the terrorist attacks of '9/11' around 3,000" (2). Turner also writes:

> The International Rescue Committee (IRC) has conducted a series of epidemiological studies. The first of its reports was published in 2000. IRC concluded that 1.7 million people had died during the previous two years as a result of war in the eastern part of the Democratic Republic of the Congo. About 200,000 of those deaths were the direct result of violence. The vast majority of deaths were caused by the destruction of the country's health infrastructure and food supplies.

Two years later, the IRC estimated that at least 3.3 million Congolese died between August 1998, when the war began, and November 2002. Again, most deaths were attributable to easily treatable diseases and malnutrition, and were often linked to displacement and the collapse of the country's health services and economy. A third study, in 2004, raised the likely death total to 3.8 million. More than 31,000 civilians continued to die every month as a result of the conflict. (3)

The NGO Caritas writes that the number of deaths may be more than six million. "Six Million Dead in Congo's War," Caritas.org, http://www.caritas.org/activities/emergencies/SixMillionDeadInCongoWar.html.

126 *As Sally tried to understand*   The Bonobo Protection Fund had been organized under Georgia State University, whose statutes were such that BPF could only promote education and research. Furthermore, given the conflicts between researchers over strategy and the use of sites, Sally realized that the BPF didn't stand a chance of addressing the deeper issues of conservation, of working with community needs.

126 *In 1997, on a night*   Among the future members whom Sally met that night were Ted Green, an anthropologist who pioneered studies on HIV prevention in Africa and who joined BCI's board, as well as John Scherlis, a Harvard- and Cambridge-educated conservationist and zoologist who had spent years studying elephants in Tanzania.

126 *In 1998, they created*   Sue Savage-Rumbaugh and her husband, the scientist Duane Rumbaugh, encouraged Sally to start an independent non-profit organization.

126 *In 1999, Sally traveled*   In Europe, Sally spent time in Antwerp with bonobo researchers Linda Van Elsacker and Jef Dupain. Sally and Dupain got on well, appearing to be on the same page about the importance of cooperation as regards conservation, though a few years later, as BCI and Albert Lokasola worked to establish Kokolopori, they found themselves in conflict with Dupain, who was by then in charge of African Wildlife Foundation's projects in the area (a position for which, according to Sally, she had recommended him). In Germany, Sally visited Barbara Fruth and Gottfried Hohmann, scientists at the Max Planck Institute for Evolutionary Anthropology.

127 *The most important connection*   Kano's book on bonobos, *The Last Ape: Pygmy Chimpanzee Behavior and Ecology,* though released in Japanese in 1986, did not appear in English until 1992.

127 *She copied his notebooks*   Sally stayed at the Primate Research Institute in Inuyama (associated with Kyoto University) for a month that autumn. She also met with Takeshi Furuichi and Gen'ichi Idani, two researchers who would continue fieldwork at Wamba.

127 *The report cites BCI*   United States Agency for International Development,

The African Diaspora in the U.S. and Its Interaction with Biodiversity Conservation in Africa, June 2012, http://diasporaalliance.org/wp-content/uploads/2012/02/AFRDiasporaReport_14June2012.pdf. The text in the USAID study reads:

> One organization that has had tremendous success in working with the Diaspora is the Bonobo Conservation Initiative, founded in 1998, and active in the Democratic Republic of Congo (DRC) since 2001. BCI President Sally Coxe and other BCI founders partnered with the Congolese Diaspora in the U.S. from before the beginning of the program. On a personal quest to learn Lingala, one of the main languages in DRC, Ms. Coxe joined a Congolese evangelical church in the Washington, DC area and met individuals who were later instrumental in enabling her to set up a culturally appropriate and locally embedded and originated program on the ground. Some of the individuals she met in the church went on to play significant roles in BCI. One fellow church attendee served on the BCI Board of Directors and later returned to DRC to work in the government, and later, the private sector, facilitating support for BCI and its Congolese NGO partners. Congolese medical professionals in the Diaspora advised BCI on creating a health clinic in Kokolopori. Others helped translate documents. Ms. Coxe has managed to establish genuine and mutually respectful relationships with the Congolese Diaspora. From facilitating an innovative Sister City cooperation between Falls Church City, Virginia and Kokolopori in DRC (which hosts the community-based Kokolopori Bonobo Reserve), to sponsoring an individual to learn how to set up eco-villages, creating his own NGO, and facilitating relationships with faith-based communities in the DRC, her partnerships have had a transformative effect on the program. The Diaspora has many, varied relationships with BCI; this would merit a small case study of its own. (13–14)

127 *Sally's vision was* Peterson and Ammann, *Eating Apes,* 221.

127 *As the war raged on* When the Second Congo War broke out, Alison Mize coordinated an emergency fund-raising campaign to help conservationist Claudine André, who was then taking care of the orphaned bonobos and who would go on to found Lola ya Bonobo. Mize recalls that BCI got in touch with André through embassy staff and received a list of things that André needed for the zoo and the bonobos.

"People don't realize that during a war, zoos are the last thing on people's mind, because people are dying," Mize told me. "They're not going to worry about a leopard or something like that. Claudine sent us an email that basically said yes she needed help and she was trying to take care of the zoo animals, too."

Sally Jewell Coxe and Alison Mize contacted everyone they knew in the bonobo and zoo world, and raised $3,500. None of the banks in Kinshasa were working, so they wired the money via Western Union to a lieutenant colonel in Brazzaville. The woman got the cash in Congolese currency, put it in a backpack, took it over the river, and gave it to Claudine.

128 *Using the folktales* Sally did much of the work with Mupenda Bin Muzumbi, known as Pastor Bin, whom she'd met through the church in 1994. Pastor Bin's younger brother, Bienvenu (literally, "Welcome"), who lived in Kinshasa, would become one of BCI's senior staff. Two of Pastor Bin's daughters sang to the music of Wynne Paris.

128 *She was able to get* According to Sally, Karl Ammann, the wildlife photographer and conservationist cited on several occasions in this book, took a recording to the MLC Ugandan-occupied side, who agreed to broadcast it.

129 *In the DRC, Sally* Sally met Jean-Marie Benishay through Z, who had two NGOs, one for women's literacy and the second for conflict resolution. Jean-Marie Benishay had approached Sally after finishing his degree at the University of Kinshasa. He was from a poor family and had succeeded in his studies, having done a thesis on bonobo social structure. He later left BCI because he wanted to live in North America and pursue other work.

129 *Her primary Congolese partner* Among the many titles Mwanza has held are the following: secrétaire permanent du Conseil Scientifique National (CSN), directeur générale of CREF, and permanent secretary of the Center for Scientific Research. Now he is officially directeur général du Centre de Recherche Multidisciplinaire pour le Développement/Matadi (CRMD/Matadi).

130 *The two strongest influences* In *Zaire: A Country Study,* Thomas Turner and Sandra W. Meditz write: "State, church, and business thus constituted what was called, even by Belgian officials, the 'colonial trinity.' It was not simply a question of the state's taking care of administration, the church of evangelization, and the business community of economic development. Rather, the tasks of the three overlapped and reinforced one another" (xxxvii).

130 *The broadcasts also discussed* One BCI board member, Ted Green, had studied AIDS prevention in Africa, documenting the success of the ABC model (abstain, be faithful, and use condoms) when it was transmitted through what, inside the Beltway, people call FBOs—faith-based organizations. BCI has a similar vision in the Congo and continues to work on this, trying to fund further radio education that would involve musicians, religious figures, and other leaders speaking to the Congolese about conservation, environmental issues, and other subjects.

131 *As for the CIA* During this time, Mobutu swindled the IMF and World Bank repeatedly, bullying them into giving him loans. Michela Wrong gives an excellent account of his tactics in *In the Footsteps of Mr. Kurtz,* 196-216.

132 *When a new person comes* In *Facing the Congo,* Jeffrey Tayler describes his 1995 journey on the Congo River, during which he frequently encountered

people who believed that he was looking for diamonds or gold rather than simply adventure. See *Facing the Congo: A Modern-Day Journey into the Heart of Darkness* (New York: Three Rivers Press, 2000), 91.

135　*He and his researchers*　The center was established by the Institut de Recherche Scientifique pour Afrique Central (IRSAC). IRSAC's centers had been hugely productive during and after the colonial period, supplying Europe with much of what the scientific community knew about Central Africa.

135　*During their years*　Researchers knew that many bonobos had been slaughtered for the bushmeat trade, and there was little information as to where the surviving groups were living.

136　*But as she explained*　Furuichi may have been concerned about the possible effect of outsiders on his relationships with the people of Wamba, which were important to the continuity of the research. However, given that he has declined to be interviewed, I do not know his reasons.

136　*She also realized that*　A chapter on Mwanza could be as long as the one on Albert Lokasola. Mwanza has had a significant career in conservation, and his struggles convey much about the history of the Congo. BCI has had a number of local partners of this nature, though Mwanza is among the more important of them. However, the narratives that I have chosen to develop are those that create a sense of place for the reserves. The area that Mwanza sought to develop in Lac Tumba became the territory of the World Wildlife Fund under the Congo Basin Forest Partnership. According to both him and BCI, they were displaced and discouraged from working in this area.

136　*According to Mwanza and Sally*　In Furuichi's response, he referenced only his concerns about the creation of the Sankuru Nature Reserve, which will be discussed in the chapter, "Defending the Vocation."

137　*"I need to do something good . . ."*　The description of this scene is based on the recollections of Sally Jewell Coxe.

Michael Hurley

144　*His trips to Haiti and Easter Island*　Viewed from the sky, the line between Haiti and the Dominican Republic separated two similar mountain landscapes, though while the DR's was forested, Haiti's was without trees. The beginning of Haiti's deforestation dated back to the plantations of the 1700s, the most lucrative in the New World, importing more African slaves than the United States did in its entire history; but the country's situation further deteriorated after it won independence from France in 1804. Its impoverished people, marginalized in the international community and by the United States, which feared a similar slave rebellion, scavenged every piece of wood for building and cooking. Without trees, the landscape had become susceptible to erosion and landslides, each hurricane creating rivers of mud, erasing roads and villages. See Philippe Girard, *Haiti: The Tumultuous History—from Pearl of the Caribbean to Broken Nation* (New York: Palgrave Macmillan, 2010), 25.

Easter Island had a similar story. One of the world's most isolated islands, over two thousand miles from the coast of Chile, its sixty-three square miles was once fertile, covered with lush forests. Around 400 AD, Polynesians reached it, and the civilization that grew there expanded to as many as twenty thousand people. By 1400, they'd used up the trees, the soil had degraded, and the streams and springs had stopped flowing. Without wood to make fishing boats, approximately 90 percent of the population died. William P. Cunningham and Mary Ann Cunningham, "The Saga of Easter Island," in *Principles of Environmental Science*, 2nd ed. (New York: McGraw-Hill, 2003), http://highered.mcgraw-hill.com/sites/0072919833/student_viewo/chapter4/additional_case_studies.html.

147 *Effective and sustainable*   In their preface to *African Rain Forest Ecology and Conservation,* William Weber and Amy Vedder state that "current conservation theory has raced far ahead of real-world, on-the-ground experience" and argue for the importance of "the leap from an aggregated multidisciplinary information base to a truly integrated interdisciplinary foundation—analogous to the difference between a mixture and a true compound." Furthermore, they write that "human beliefs, behaviors, politics, and economies are seen as powerful forces shaping the forest ecosystem." This book shows an awareness of the underlying issues that BCI is addressing and affirms that people at the big conservation NGOs are conscious of their importance. Weber et al., eds, *African Rain Forest Ecology and Conservation,* xi.

147 *We often miss opportunities*   In "Why Didn't We Just Ask?"—the title of which perfectly sums up their conclusion—Erik Meijaard and Andrew Marshall explain the difficulty and cost of identifying orangutan populations with transects, and they explain the benefits of using local knowledge:

> If we optimistically assume that a particular transect system effectively monitors population fluctuations in some 100 km², a complete understanding of orangutan population trends would require more than 1,000 transect systems. Each transect requires monthly repeat surveys by 2–4 survey staff, at a cost of ca. US $1,500/month. An annual survey budget of some US $50,000,000 would be required to sustain such an effort. This is about the same as the total annual conservation investment in Indonesia, i.e. entirely unrealistic. The question is whether there are realistic alternatives.
>
> [The Nature Conservancy] are presently developing and testing a new orangutan census technique in East Kalimantan. It uses structured interview-based approaches, similar to rural surveys employed by the World Health Organization. In a set of 35 questions, randomly selected

interviewees in villages, logging camps, and plantation areas are asked about the work and frequency of forest travel. They are also asked about when and where they have last seen an orangutan. A combination of additional questions establishes the reliability of time-related questions and the interviewees' knowledge of different primate species. Preliminary tests in areas where orangutan densities are well known indicate that the interview surveys provide quantitative information about orangutan densities with relatively small standard errors. Integrated methods such as these are especially useful because the interviews provide multidimensional information, encompassing not only the density of the species in question but other information that is equally important to conserving orangutans, such as the intensity of local threats such as hunting, habitat conversion, and human attitudes towards orangutans.

Erik Meijaard and Andrew Marshall, "Why Didn't We Just Ask?" *Forest Science News* 4 no. 10 (October 2008): 4, http://anthropology.ucdavis.edu/people/ajmarsha/publications-1/Meijaard%20-%20Marshall%202008-Why%20didnt%20we%20just%20ask.pdf.

Economics around the Campfire

150 *The problems arise when*   David S. Wilkie and Julia F. Carpenter, "Bushmeat Hunting in the Congo Basin," *Biodiversity and Conservation* 8 (1999): 927–55, http://www.brookfieldzoo.org/pagegen/inc/acwilkie.pdf.

150 *River barges passing through*   Both Dale Peterson's *Eating Apes* and Jeffrey Tayler's *Facing the Congo* offer compelling portrayals of the bushmeat markets on the river.

150 *The hunters who enter*   Concerning Africa, Jane Goodall writes: "For hundreds of years, people have lived in harmony with nature, killing just those animals they needed to survive. Now the hunters kill everything they see and send the bodies out on the logging trucks into the town to cater to the popular taste for the flesh of wild animals. . . . It also threatens the indigenous forest people, for when the logging companies move on, they leave behind a forest where only the smallest creatures remain." Michael Nichols and Jane Goodall, *Brutal Kinship* (New York: Aperture, 2005), 70. Furthermore, in *Eating Apes,* Dale Peterson describes the work of hunters: "These people are very efficient hunters, who hunt as many as possible and then move to another place when the forest is 'empty'" (118).

150 *The proponents of logging claim*   Peterson, *Eating Apes,* 196.

150 *Some of the sapele trees*   Ibid., 166.

151 *White's point is that*   Lee J. T. White, "The African Rain Forest: Climate

and Vegetation," in Weber et al., *African Rain Forest Ecology and Conservation*, 4.

151 *Conservation is enriched when*   Caughley and Anthony R. E. Sinclair, *Wildlife Ecology and Management* (Oxford: Blackwell, 1994), referenced in Cowlishaw and Dunbar, *Primate Conservation Biology*, 2.

151 *However, while humans have*   Lacambra et al., "Bonobo (*Pan paniscus*)," in Caldecott and Miles, *World Atlas of Great Apes and Their Conservation*, 92–93.

151 *systematic logging of the oldest trees*   John Oates references Kent Redford's essay, "The Ecologically Noble Savage," writing: "Redford acknowledges that indigenous people have often had better and more sustainable ways of using tropical ecosystems than new settlers, but he argues that their techniques worked only because they had low population densities and limited involvement with market economies." Kent Redford, "The Ecologically Noble Savage," *Cultural Survival Quarterly* 15 no. 1 (spring 1991): 46–48, referenced in Oates, *Myth and Reality in the Rain Forest*, 56.

151 *As Dale Peterson writes*   In fact, it is far worse and spells the eventual end of the forest itself, given the role of animals in perpetuating plant life through pollen exchange and seed dispersal. Dale Peterson, in describing the cutting of the ancient sapele trees, enumerates the human impact, the loss of a tree prized by the local people for its "special strength, hardness, lightness, and water resistance that make it a favored source of wood for dugout canoes and roof beams, while the bark and outer trunk provide a number of local anti-inflammatory and analgesic medicines for treating headaches, eye infections, sore feet, and so on." And only the highest, most mature trees—the ones most likely to be logged—host a type of caterpillar, *Imbrasia oyemensis*, that "rains down abundantly . . . during the rainy season, when food from hunting and fishing can be scarce." *Eating Apes*. 196.

152 *If the much larger population*   Nichols and Goodall, *Brutal Kinship*, 34.

152 *For the first, local people*   *note 1:* Dowie, "Conservation Refugees," in Lopez, ed., *The Future of Nature*, 65–77; originally published in *Orion Magazine* (Nov/Dec 2005).

note 2: Recent research shows that population densities are on the rise around Africa's national parks more than in other rural areas, given the infrastructures and markets that parks create. The longterm impact of this on parks and people has yet to be fully evaluated. See also "Fertile Fringes: Population Growth at Protected-Area Edges," Wilson Center, Environmental Change and Security Program webcast 1:54:23, October 22, 2008, http://www.wilsoncenter.org/event/fertile-fringes-population-growth-protected-area-edges.

152 *National parks frequently lack*   Cowlishaw and Dunbar, *Primate Conservation Biology*, 332. In speaking of populations evicted from parks, Cowlishaw and Dunbar write:

These people, who had a tradition of using these resources, were now for-
bidden access to them and were rarely provided with any compensation for
their eviction. Moreover, the expanding wildlife populations in the parks
often imposed further costs on them through crop raiding. . . . Because
evicted people often have no alternative, they still use those resources
within the protected area, albeit illegally. This can lead to problems of
unsustainable hunting, forestry, and agriculture, if only because people
who have no legal right to the resources have little incentive to use them
sustainably. In addition, their treatment understandably generates resentment, with the consequence that local people may actively obstruct the
running of the park (Hough 1988).

Recent news sources echo the problem of poaching within national parks.
Here are just a few examples: "Tragic Elephant Poaching Incident In
Garamba," African Parks, March 27, 2012, http://www.african-parks
.org/News_24_Tragic+elephant+poaching+incident+in+Garamba.html;
Aislinn Laing, "Last Rhinos in Mozambique Killed by Poachers," *Telegraph,*
April 30, 2013, http://www.telegraph.co.uk/news/worldnews/africaand
indianocean/mozambique/10028738/Last-rhinos-in-Mozambique-killed-by-
poachers.html; Jon Herskovitz, "Despite Armed Guards, Africa's Rhinos
Losing Battle to Poachers," Reuters, April 11, 2013, http://www.reuters.com/
article/2013/04/11/us-safrica-rhinos-idUSBRE93A0WP20130411.

152 *And as a result*   Guy Cowlishaw and Robin Dunbar write, "Populations
have less genetic flexibility with which to respond to changes in environmental conditions, thus making extinction because of failure to cope more
likely. Second, it increases the risk of inbreeding depression: the phenotypic
expression of deleterious recessive genes. As population size gets smaller, the
impact of such recessives may become disproportionately severe." *Primate
Conservation Biology,* 166.

152 *Furthermore, as the habitat*   Cowlishaw and Dunbar, *Primate Conservation
Biology,* 208.

153 *As BCI's partner, Albert*   BCI advisor John Scherlis states in an interview:
"It is better for the ostensible and actual goal not to hire the best and the
brightest out of local organizations into the international organizations, but
to facilitate their own local efforts, if that is what they want. Otherwise,
you're creating a brain drain and removing precisely the sort of people who
are best adapted and most needed. The point is not to deny or limit options
or opportunities, but to facilitate or create them."

155 *National Geographic Society-funded photographer*   Jeffry Oonk's personal
website, http://www.jeffryoonk.com/Photo_Safari_Guide/Photo_Collection_
Great_Apes_1.html.

155 *Whenever he came into contact*   Corrugated roofs are seen as a sign of

status and affluence in the Congo, so people often want them despite the high cost of getting them into rural areas and the natural and renewable materials readily available to build roofs.

157 "Nous sommes arriérés"   Alden Almquist explained to me that the people in Kokolopori often referred to themselves as *des gens enclos,* "people closed in," or *des gens inutiles,* "useless people."

159 *Albert was already overloaded*   "New Conservation Groups Formed at World Wilderness Congress," *Environment News Service,* October 10, 2005, http://www.ens-newswire.com/ens/oct2005/2005-10-10-06.asp.

160 *During the war*   The African cassava mosaic virus is transmitted by white-flies and is one of the most economically devastating problems in the Central Africa, thought to cause losses of between 1.9 and 2.7 billion USD annually. B. L. Patil and C. M. Fauquet, "Cassava Mosaic Geminiviruses: Actual Knowledge and Perspectives," *Molecular Plant Pathology* 10 no. 5 (September 2009): 685–701.

   BCI formed a relationship with Robert Goodman, executive dean of agriculture and natural resources at Rutgers University, a microbial ecologist who did key early work on the African cassava mosaic virus.

160 *The community's productivity*   In *Myth and Reality in the Rain Forest: How Conservation Strategies Are Failing in West Africa,* John Oates states that "the emphasis on the close relationship between economic development and conservation has led to a view of wildlife conservation as predominantly an exercise in materialism, at local, national, and international levels; meanwhile, the ethical and aesthetic principles of conservation that strongly guided the founders of the World Wildlife Fund have been reduced to secondary considerations." Oates, *Myth and Reality in the Rain Forest,* xii–xiii.

161 *The way they spoke*   Peter Scott, *Animals in Africa* (New York: Clarkson Potter, 1962), quoted in Oates, *Myth and reality in the Rain Forest,* 41.

Human Cultures and Cultured Animals

163 *In Rwanda and Uganda*   Jessica Aldred, "Mountain Gorilla Numbers Rise by 10%," *Guardian,* November 13, 2012, http://www.guardian.co.uk/environment/2012/nov/13/mountain-gorilla-population-rises.

165 *One of BCI's cornerstones*   Information Exchange is a BCI variation on a standard methodology called Participatory Rural Appraisal (PRA). Michael, Mwanza, and Albert also participated in developing it. For more information on BCI's approach, see L. Alden Almquist et al., "Kokolopori and the Bonobo Peace Forest in the Democratic Republic of Congo," in Painemilla et al., *Indigenous Peoples and Conservation.*

167 *There's a saying*   Turner, *The Congo Wars,* vii.

167 *Gérard Prunier's meticulous account*   Prunier, *Africa's World War*, 214.

168 *The Congolese memorize his songs*   Young men who make an art of the way they dress are called *sapeurs*. For a disempowered society, this vision, modest as it might be, gives young people something for which they can be respected.

Michela Wrong offers an excellent account of *sapeurs* in *In the Footsteps of Mr. Kurtz*, 178–84. For an excellent photographic study of *sapeurs*, see also Daniele Tamagni, *Gentlemen of Bacongo* (London: Trolley, 2009).

169 *BCI's vision has always been*   Michael described a similar experience with a field researcher named David Mikwaya Yamba-Yamba, who was working for the Japanese when he contracted a severe gastrointestinal illness. He and his fellow CREF researcher, Norbert Mbangi Mulavwa, rode several dozen miles on their bicycles to Djolu, where the small hospital didn't have the right medicine for him. As his condition worsened, Mbangi contacted Sally in Kinshasa. She called Doctors without Borders, who had a plane scheduled to fly to Djolu from Mbandaka, and arranged for them to bring the medicine that would keep him alive for a while longer. Then Sally contacted Michael, who was in Kokolopori, and told him that a motorcycle would be bringing Yamba-Yamba to Befori's port. Michael quickly had the boats prepared and recalled, when he arrived, seeing Yamba-Yamba on the riverbank, lying under a mosquito net, skeletal and barely conscious. The boatmen broke their record and returned to Mbandaka in three and a half days, and were able to get him better medical attention.

"The medicine kept him alive," Sally told me, "because our team could mobilize. We had good communication between a number of different groups. Every person involved is necessary for things like this to work, from the guys on the ground in Djolu to the boatmen, to our people in Mbandaka and Kinshasa."

170 *In 1871, the British anthropologist*   Sir Edward Burnett Tylor, *Primitive Culture*. (London: John Murray, 1871).

171 *If we feel that culture*   Adriaan Kortlandt, "Spirits Dressed in Furs?" in Cavalieri and Singer, *The Great Ape Project*, 138.

171 *Dale Peterson and Richard Wrangham*   Peterson and Wrangham, *Demonic Males*, 256.

171 *They are right that*   Stevens, Vervaecke, and Elsacker, "The Bonobo's Adaptive Potential," in Furuichi and Thompson, *The Bonobos: Behavior, Ecology, and Conservation*, 33.

171 *When Sue Savage-Rumbaugh speaks*   In *Kanzi's Primal Language*, Segerdahl, Fields, and Savage-Rumbaugh write:

The seemingly unimportant fact that we did not develop the Pan/Homo culture by design will be a recurrent theme of this book. Spontaneity is expounded as a central mark of culture and language. . . . We began to interact more spontaneously with the apes, we did things that both humans and apes found exciting and we began to improvise the research on the basis of how our interactions actually developed. In some sense, we became ourselves the subjects of a research that no one controlled in advance. Gradually we discovered that we developed an *intermediary* culture with both human and bonobo features. . . .

The term 'culture' has two aspects. The first, increasingly emphasized in biology, is the transmission of information non-genetically from animal to animal and from one generation of animals to another. The second aspect of culture, which is more important for us, is the content of a culture: a shared way of living containing characteristic activities, tools, environments, communication means, social relations, personalities, games, gestures and so on. What is culturally transferred is itself a culture, or 'way of life', as Frans de Waal . . . says in his definition. [3–8, citing de Frans de Waal, *The Ape and the Sushi Master: Cultural Reflections of a Primatologist* (New York: Basic Books, 2001).]

171 *Their easy familiarity was unlike*   And yet we must acknowledge that the wild bonobos differentiate between types of human culture, observing our approach and attitudes, the way we share food or speak to each other, before deciding how close they will get to us and how much time they will spend nearby.

171 *For instance, in* Brutal Kinship   Nichols and Goodall, *Brutal Kinship,* 16.

172 *"Tai mothers teach . . ."*   Ibid.

172 *Similarly, Jane Goodall*   Ibid., 60

172 *Humans, Ryder explains*   Richard D. Ryder, "Sentientism," in Cavalieri and Singer, *The Great Ape Project,* 221.

172 *African hunters describe*   Peterson and Ammann, *Eating Apes,* 54.

172 *And Koko, a lowland gorilla*   Francine Patterson and Wendy Gordon, "The Case for the Personhood of Gorillas," in Cavalieri and Singer, *The Great Ape Project,* 59.

172 *Jane Goodall describes*   Nichols and Goodall, *Brutal Kinship,* 60.

172 *A series of photographs*   Sue Savage-Rumbaugh, Stuart G. Shanker, and Talbot J. Taylor, *Apes, Language, and the Human Mind* (New York: Oxford University Press, 1998), 5–6.

173 *And as for their altruism*   Sue Savage-Rumbaugh also describes how Kanzi, thinking a person injured, wanted to pour water on the part of the body that he took to be hurt. Ibid., 53.

173 *They recognize themselves*   Patterson and Gordon, "The Case for the Personhood of Gorillas," in Cavalieri and Singer, *The Great Ape Project,* 59. Patterson and Gordon write of Koko the gorilla: "Once, when she had been drinking water through a thick rubber straw from a pan on the floor after

repeatedly asking her companion for drinks of juice which were not forth-coming, she referred to herself as a 'sad elephant'" (65).

173   *The young chimp was almost surely*   Wrangham and Peterson, *Demonic Males,* 252–53.

173   *It would seem that*   Nichols and Goodall, *Brutal Kinship,* 58. Roger S. Fouts and Deborah H. Fouts also remark on this contradiction: "Unfortunately, much of the biomedical research on chimpanzees assumes a kind of schizo-phrenic position: it justifies the use of chimpanzees as a medical model because of Darwinian continuity, and yet at the same time it claims moral immunity with regard to the physical and mental damage done to the chimpanzees on the basis that humans are different from other animals." "Chimpanzees' Use of Sign Language," in Cavalieri and Singer, *The Great Ape Project,* 39.

     The National Institutes of Health have recently begun to take action in re-sponse to such criticism: Lisa Myers and Diane Beasley, "Goodall Praises NIH Decision to Remove Some Chimps from Research, but Controversy Erupts Over Their Next Home," NBCNews.com, October 17, 2002, http://usnews .nbcnews.com/_news/2012/10/17/14125394-goodall-praises-nih-decision-to-remove-some-chimps-from-research-but-controversy-erupts-over-their-next-home?lite.

173   *He points out that humans*   James Rachels, "Why Darwinians Should Support Equal Treatment for Other Great Apes," in Cavalieri and Singer, *The Great Ape Project,* 154–55 (italics his).

174   *Do humans, as several*   Several essays in Cavalieri and Singer's *The Great Ape Project* touch on the question of human superiority: Fouts and Fouts, "Chimpanzees' Use of Sign Language," 28; Miles, "Language and the Orang-utan: The Old 'Person' of the Forest," 42; Kortlandt, "Spirits Dressed in Furs?" 140; and Christophe Anstötz, "Profoundly Intellectually Disabled Humans and the Great Apes: A Comparison," 168.

174   *Some scientists even emphasize*   Jane Goodall writes: "The trouble is that many lab chimps have learned to distrust and even hate humans; they await the opportunity to spit, to throw feces, to bite." Nichols and Goodall, *Brutal Kinship,* 71. Vanessa Woods describes this well in *Bonobo Handshake,* 8–9.

174   *We don't put forth*   Quite recently in terms of human history, people have used disempowered groups for experiments, as with the Tuskegee Syphilis Experiment, conducted from 1932 to 1972. It is no surprise that, if we are only beginning to recognize each other's humanity, we still struggle to accord consciousnesses to the other apes.

174   *He goes on to enumerate*   The discovery of what isn't known may be what most excites us, and we often seek out what isn't yet understood about bonobos and attempt to inflate it, not so much to educate people as to make a name for ourselves, to put a stamp on little-known territory. Ian Parker's *New Yorker*

article, "Swingers," is representative of this mentality. It deserves scrutiny not only because of what it reveals about how research works in the Congo but because of the *New Yorker*'s reach in our culture and the way that it influences opinions.

In his response to Parker's article on *Skeptic* magazine's website, Frans de Waal explains that we must not conflate hunting with aggression:

> Perhaps the bonobo's peaceful image can be countered with descriptions of them catching and eating prey? Isn't this violent behavior? Not really: feeding has very little to do with aggression. Already in the 1960s, Konrad Lorenz explained the difference between a cat hissing at another cat and a cat stalking a mouse. The neural circuitry of the two patterns is different: the first expresses fear and aggression, the second is motivated by hunger. Thus, herbivores are not any less aggressive than carnivores—as anyone who has been chased by a bull can attest. The fact that bonobos run after duikers and kill squirrels—which has been seen many times—is therefore best kept out of debates about aggression.

Also regarding their alleged violence, de Waal writes:

> How much bonobos differ from chimpanzees was highlighted by a recent experiment on cooperation. Brian Hare and co-workers presented apes with a platform that they could pull close by working together. When food was placed on the platform, the bonobos clearly outperformed the chimpanzees in getting a hold of it. The presence of food normally induces rivalry, but the bonobos engaged in sexual contact, played together, and happily shared the food side by side. The chimpanzees, in contrast, were unable to overcome their competition. For two species to react so differently to the same experimental set-up leaves little doubt about a temperamental difference.
>
> In another illustration, at a forested sanctuary at Kinshasa it was recently decided to merge two groups of bonobos that had lived separately, just so as to induce some activity. No one would ever dream of doing this with chimpanzees as the only possible outcome would be a blood bath. The bonobos produced an orgy instead. [In this citation, he references Brian Hare et al., "Tolerance Allows Bonobos to Outperform Chimpanzees on a Cooperative Task," *Current Biology* 17 no. 7 (April 2007): 619–23.]

Frans de Waal, "Bonobos, Left & Right," *eSkeptic,* August 8, 2007, http://www.skeptic.com/eskeptic/07-08-08/.

174   *Though it's true that bonobos*   Richard W. Wrangham and Emily van Zinnicq Bergmann Riss, "Rates of Predation on Mammals by Gombe Chimpanzees, 1972–1975," *Primates* 31 no. 2 (April 1990): 157–70; Craig B.

Stanford et al., "Patterns of Predation by Chimpanzees on Red Colobus Monkeys in Gombe National Park, 1982–1991," *American Journal of Physical Anthropology* 94 no. 2 (June 1994): 213–28; Kano, *The Last Ape*, 106; all referenced in Wrangham and Peterson, *Demonic Males*, 216–17.

174   *"For years," he writes*   Frans de Waal, *The Bonobo and the Atheist: In Search of Humanism Among the Primates* (New York: W. W. Norton, 2013), 11.

174   *Over the centuries,*   Why should we, in light of our own worst traits, expect great apes to be angelic? For instance, the Lola ya Bonobo sanctuary was flooded with orphans during and after the war, and started a reintroduction program in Équateur. But several of the bonobos, shortly after being reintroduced, attacked and injured the trackers. In light of the resemblance between the bonobo and human nervous systems, bonobos who have been traumatized in their youths and who have seen human hunters kill their mothers and even their entire families might become as volatile as we would. How many of our novels and films are based on the violent actions of a human with PTSD, who, as a child, experienced brutality or witnessed murder? Kidnapped by traders, the bonobos of Lola ya Bonobo spent weeks or months tied up inside baskets or boxes, starved and covered with parasites. Then they found themselves in a sanctuary, raised by human "mothers" in a culture of similarly traumatized bonobos. Whether bonobo, gorilla, or chimpanzee, apes—once they have lived with humans—exhibit changes in their behavior, and whereas wild bonobos have never been witnessed attacking people, those raised in captivity, with human "mothers" to bottle-feed them, are more comfortable with humans and may do so. However, it is also possible that even without their trauma, the dramatic change in their environment and the release from the pressure of confinement after so many years into a freedom whose limits they did not yet understand could have led the bonobos to test their boundaries and behave atypically. Apes are significantly stronger than we are, and can injure or kill with blows that, directed at another bonobo, would simply express frustration. (In conversation, John Scherlis explained this view of the apes behaving differently after the pressure of confinement.)

    Michael "Nick" Nichols writes, "Former captives can never be truly wild, and may be dangerous to humans as they have lost the fear of man and know their own strength compared to his." Given their level of familiarity and pain in relation to humans, it is no wonder that an attack the likes of which has never been seen with wild bonobos, during centuries of humans and bonobos living side by side, could occur with those raised in a sanctuary. Nichols, *The Great Apes: Between Two Worlds*, 122.

174   *Male chimpanzees battle*   Wrangham and Peterson explain: "Chimpanzee males form alliances, as we have seen, which are crucial for their success in gaining and keeping high rank. Bonobo males don't. . . . But bonobo males are less aggressive with each other for another reason as well: They are much

less concerned about who mates with the females. Among chimpanzees, copulation attempts by low-ranking males are often stopped by high-ranking males, especially near ovulation time. This happens very rarely among bonobos." *Demonic Males,* 211–12, referencing Takeshi Furuichi and Hiroshi Ihobe, "Variation in Male Relationships in Bonobos and Chimpanzees," *Behaviour* 130 (1994): 211–28.

175 *Wrangham and Peterson describe*   Wrangham and Peterson, *Demonic Males,* 204–5.

175 *Even recent brain studies*   James K. Rilling et al., "Differences Between Chimpanzees and Bonobos in Neural Systems Supporting Social Cognition," *Social Cognitive and Affective Neuroscience* (2011), doi:10.1093.

175 *He goes on to explain*   note 1: Kano, *The Last Ape,* ix.

   note 2: Mary Smith, the *National Geographic* editor who specialized in great apes, remarks that, unlike Western scientists, the Japanese "attribute a reasoning mind" to their subjects and see them as composing "cultural groups." "A History of Research," in Nichols, *The Great Apes: Between Two Worlds,* 33.

175 *The flexible nature of*   note 1: Frans de Waal writes: "This makes gesture the better candidate for early language evolution. If our ancestors used gestures in the same flexible manner, this may have provided a stepping stone for the evolution of symbolic communication, which may have originated in the gestural rather than vocal domain (e.g. Corballis 2002)." "Foreword, Behavioral Study Section," in Furuichi and Thompson, *The Bonobos: Behavior, Ecology, and Conservation,* 13, referencing Michael C. Corballis, *From Hand to Mouth: The Origins of Language* (Princeton: Princeton University Press, 2002).

   note 2: "As our close kin," primatologist George B. Schaller writes, "apes are windows to our minds. They provide experimental models useful in highlighting issues on the evolution of intelligence." "An Epilogue," in Nichols, *The Great Apes: Between Two Worlds,* 191.

176 *Language is a funny thing*   Savage-Rumbaugh, Shanker, and Taylor, *Apes, Language, and the Human Mind,* 226–27.

Territory and Power

177 *CBFP's mandate emphasized*   "Sustainable Forest Management," United Nations Department of Economic and Social Affairs, http://www.un.org/en/development/desa/climate-change/reforestation.shtml.

177 *BCI's 2011 revenue reached*   2011 financial statements and auditor's report, submitted by Raffa, Inc. to the Board of Trustees of the African Wildlife Foundation, Inc., dated October 12, 2011, http://www.awf.org/sites/default/files/media/Resources/Financials/Financial%20Statement%202011.pdf; *2011*

Annual Report, World Wildlife Fund, http://assets.worldwildlife.org/financial_ reports/1/reports/original/Annual_Report_2011.pdf?1342667695.

178 *When BCI petitioned* All information offered here is according to BCI sources: Sally Coxe, Michael Hurley, Alden Almquist, and John Scherlis.

178 *Between 2002 and 2011 note 1:* Indirectly, BCI received $25,000 of Congo Basin Forest Partnership funds. They were channeled through Conservation International and given to BCI with only one week to spend it before the official project end date. They also received funds for a biodiesel project.

Furthermore, the conflict with the African Widlife Foundation illustrated the degree to which misguided actions can endure in the memories of the local people. One story that I heard several times from local people in Djolu and Kokolopori was about when AWF hired Vie Sauvage to do a survey. AWF let them use two bicycles and approximately a dozen flashlights. The Congolese working on the project were outraged when, after its completion, AWF requested the return of the bicycles and flashlights. Given the poverty of the region and the lack of any such tools, the Congolese refused, intending to use the equipment to do their own conservation work, in Kokolopori and the nearby conservation sites they were developing. Albert Lokasola interceded, explaining to AWF the importance of resource sharing. Negotiations revealed that AWF's USAID funding stipulated that all materials valuing less than $2000 should be left with local partners. But the damage had been done. It was the sort of information that villagers shared often, and clearly, the worth of such objects could in no way compete with the loyalty to be gained by letting people keep them.

note 2: The funds that USAID allocated to the CBFP are as follows: 2002–2005: $12 million annually dedicated to landscapes; 2006–2011: $10 million annually dedicated to landscapes, with a 100% match requirement. *Evaluation of the Central African Regional Program for the Environment—Phase II,* United States Agency for International Development (USAID), December 2010, http://carpe.umd.edu/Documents/2011/ECODIT_ CARPE_II_Evaluation_Final_Report_for_USAID.pdf.

178 *Even after the Kokolopori note 1:* This issue was only recently resolved by the cartographers at the University of Maryland, and the Kokolopori Bonobo Reserve is now on the map.

note 2: As of the writing of this book, AWF's website read: "At the request of local communities—who saw the success and economic benefits to the community that arose from the establishment of the nearby Lomako-Yokokala Faunal Reserve—AWF worked with local stakeholders and the Iyondji community to establish another protected area in which bonobos can live free of external threat.

"Iyondji is a priority conservation target, as it has a high concentration of bonobos and an intact forest. It is also situated on the periphery of the already-safeguarded Luo Scientific Reserve, allowing for an immediate expansion of core protected habitat."

    The website does not mention the Kokolopori Bonobo Reserve, which is contiguous with AWF's new Iyondji Reserve (created in 2012)—as close to it as the Luo Scientific Reserve and far closer than the Lomako-Yokokala Faunal Reserve (which is approximately one hundred miles away). Iyondji Community Bonobo Reserve, African Wildlife Foundation website, http:// www.awf.org/projects/iyondji-community-bonobo-reserve.

178 *Some of the employees were*   On another day, he shut the generator off shortly after Sally, Michael, and I showed up, and asked us to buy gas. Sally agreed, and only later, when I checked the price of gas on my way out, did I discover that he'd charged much more than the going rate. Of course, BCI struggled with skimming as well, with a culture that learned, over Mobutu's three decades in power, that the only way to survive was theft. And we were grateful to use the Internet. When their generator broke down, BCI brought their own, the man who had been skimming suddenly sheepish and their offices crowded as everyone there tried to get online.

178 *I got the sense that*   Phila Kasa Levo said that in their area, habituation was coming along well, though at AWF's other bonobo conservation site, Lomako, one of the oldest in the Congo, it was failing, the bonobos returning to their old habits of fleeing people. He explained that at Lomako, AWF had built modern accommodations, but that the work on the ground hadn't been very effective, and hearing him say this, I recalled my first impressions of Kokolopori, my feeling that I had expected more by way of construction—a modern eco-lodge, for instance. The idealist in us often wants to see a tangible achievement, an image of success that the mind can easily identify, rather than the daily management of rudimentary camps, the trackers, and the villagers' needs. (Lomako is one of the oldest bonobo research areas in the Congo, established in the mid-seventies by Noel and Alison Badrian. Francis White and Randall Susman, the first person to publish a book on bonobos [*The Pygmy Chimpanzee: Evolutionary Biology and Behavior,* Plenum Press, 1984], worked there as well. The Lomako site was used extensively by Max Planck Institute researcher Gottfried Hohmann from 1989 to 1998, his presence a source of contention among American researchers.)

180 *The feeling that everyone*   *note 1:* Despite this, BCI survived on the strength of its network. Sally had been in Kinshasa after the war, when few of the major NGOs were there, and she had created a broad network that made Congolese throughout the country aware of her goals. Increasingly, they would come to her looking for support. Her good relations with CREF and Dr. Mwanza led her to make contact with numerous community groups seeking to work in conservation.

    note 2: According to Dr. Mwanza, a similar though less dramatic story would unfold between BCI and the World Wildlife Fund, which had been put in charge of the "Lac Tele-Lac Tumba Swamp Forest Landscape." At a Congo Basin Forest Partnership meeting, where a number of NGOs gathered to make their cases for funding, Alden Almquist, a BCI board member, and Alison Mize, BCI's co-founder, made a case for funding BCI projects in the landscape. They explained that BCI had been supporting conservation at numerous locations in the DRC and had an established partnership with CREF's Congolese researchers, whom they were funding to do surveys in the area. In conversation, Alden told me, "Alison and I were the ones who got BCI on the CBFP. . . . They were under a mandate, and the Smithsonian moderator enforced it to include whoever was working on the ground. They went through all of the areas where the assembled groups could have a role. They said, 'How about community development?' Alison said, 'We do that.' They said, 'How about research?' 'Yeah,' I'd say, 'we do that.' We got our name put into spreadsheets. Many years later now, I'm not sure that Alison and I did the organization a favor. We've spent so many hours writing reports to these people to get our work at Lac Tumba funded for three years, but then WWF cut us out."

Alden describes WWF's people in the Congo as actively non-collaborative at the time, his emails ignored or redirected, and Sally tells me that WWF had no presence on the ground for the first year of that phase and that they never convened a meeting of all partners until the project was nearly over. As she recalls it, halfway into the first phase, which lasted from 2003 to 2006, WWF began scrambling to figure out how to work in the area. By then, BCI had thirty-seven community accords and had already drawn up plans for three community-based reserves, even laying out boundaries. They had done education, Information Exchange, and numerous surveys, as well as cassava projects. They had also been developing the capacity of the CREF researchers based in the region, although, according to BCI, WWF never paid out all of the funds originally designated for this purpose.

As the second phase of CBFP was about to begin, Sally repeatedly contacted WWF, asking if BCI would be included so she could negotiate the terms. WWF said that they would, but two weeks before the proposals were due for the second phase, WWF cut them out, notifying them by email. The funding for numerous bonobo projects in the landscape suddenly halted.

"Getting relationships started and beginning projects and raising expectations and having no follow-through is almost worse than nothing," Sally tells me, explaining that it severely damages social capital and hurts conservation in general. Of equal importance, WWF's decision raises the question of how conservation funds are used. Cutting off funding and not finishing projects already begun is tantamount to wasting three years of funds. Lastly, WWF's decision brings up the question as to whether CBFP's mandate ("to promote the sustainable management of the Congo Basin's forests and wildlife by improving communication, cooperation, and collaboration among all the partners") was being honored.

Alden explained to me that in his experience this behavior is typical of the big NGOs: "They'd play with you until they could establish their own beachhead with their own interests. That's what WWF did in Lac Tumba. And it's easy to do. If we are the subcontractor, and they're getting the money, all they have to do is make vague complaints. They don't have to substantiate anything. 'At this stage in the development, we need a different set of skills,' was the verbiage for dumping us after three years. 'We're at a different phase in the development process.' 'We need a different set of skills.' All so vague, which to me is the killer."

I contacted WWF to get more information on their reasoning, and despite my questions, I received only very brief answers. Their first email said, "BCI was not included in the second phase as our consortium thought they were not the right fit at that phase moving forward." I replied: "I asked the question to get insight into how WWF's decision-making worked in that particular instance. Saying that an organization was 'not the right fit' can mean anything. Can you be more specific? Why were they not the right fit? And also, given that BCI had been working on the ground in that landscape for the first phase, what happened to the projects that they started under WWF? Did WWF have a stake in that work and continue it in any way?" Here is WWF's one-line response: "Work on bonobo conservation continues in the landscape, as part of our larger conservation goal."

180 *They had hoped to*   In *Myth and Reality in the Rain Forest,* John Oates explains that reserves shouldn't require great expenses, though recurrent expenditures for guards, vehicles, buildings, and education are necessary. He explains that such projects can be indefinitely sustainable if the costs remain low. "Individuals or organizations helping to plan for conservation in developing countries should therefore consider the *least* expensive ways to meet management goals. This is the opposite of the way in which many such conservation projects are currently planned." Oates, *Myth and Reality in the Rain Forest,* 248.

180 *Instead of dictating*   He believes that the only reason BCI has survived so long with so little funding is that its staff worked well with the Congolese. Locals saw reserve villages transformed and those they knew rise to prominence through conservation. They realized that this was available to them, that their efforts would be respected and not supplanted by outsiders. Cosmas said that BCI spent months in villages, learning how people thought, but that AWF's staff didn't have the same level of closeness. But what I heard in Cosmas's words wasn't that one system should replace the other, only that they should reinforce each other, so that each could excel at what it did best.

181 *Scherlis explained that communication*   John Scherlis wrote to me that Sally

and Michael "are open to other perspectives, rather than being constrained by a priori concepts. . . . But that isn't unique to BCI. Africa Biodiversity Collaborative Group, supported by USAID, has become increasingle innovative, and that helps cajole its member NGOs into new endeavors. This too may be a matter of scale. It's harder to shift approach in a big organization. WWF, for example, is constrained by being part of a world wide network, with coordinated policy."

181 *but that Sally and Michael*   John Scherlis stated: "I'd like to see BCI with a really serious, heavy-weight, grizzled professional, a hard-headed but enlightened administrator taking on a lot of the work that Sally and Michael do, to free them up to do other things."

181 *But each person I asked*   John Scherlis pointed out to me that the situation was a vicious cycle: "The struggle for funding has been caused in part by the perception of problems that are in part the result of lack of funding. There is a discrepancy between BCI's assets, the opportunities represented by social capital and commitments for community-based protected areas in the DRC, and BCI's capacity to pursue them. There would be a significant payoff for conservation from ending the vicious cycle by investing in BCI's management and administrative capacity."

181 *Many cited their corporate structure*   This isn't to say that there's not a great deal of investment in small partner organizations and that the big conservation NGOs haven't done good work throughout the world. But the question remains as to how much of the massive funding that the BINGOs receive should go directly to the field, and how much should be used for self-promotion so that they can remain competitive for fund raising and do advocacy for their programs.

181 *And if BINGO employees*   Others have leveled similar critiques of BINGOs. John Oates offers his view that "conservation policymakers and senior managers tend to be motivated more by the material rewards that they or their organizations may obtain from a project than by a deep concern for the future of threatened nature." Oates, *Myth and Reality in the Rain Forest,* 197–98.

182 *In* Political Legitimacy in Middle Africa   Schatzberg, *Political Legitimacy in Middle Africa,* 3. Here is the full quotation: "Attention to these apparently nonpolitical spheres is also important because large numbers of middle Africans do not necessarily share Western assumptions concerning the normative and empirical relationships between politics and the larger social environment. Furthermore, as we shall see, the inclusion of these sources becomes all the more critical because middle Africans inhabit a political realm whose boundaries can differ substantially from those prevalent in parts of the West." Schatzberg references Ilunga Kabongo, "Déroutante Afrique ou la Syncope d'un Discours," *Canadian Journal of African Studies* 18 no. 1 (1984): 13–22.

182 *The "big man"*   Schatzberg, *Political Legitimacy in Middle Africa,* 2, 10–11,

131; Turner and Meditz, "Introduction," in Meditz and Merrill, *Zaire: A Country Study*, xlii.

182 *Mobutu ruled Zaire*   Thomas Turner and Sandra W. Meditz write: "Indeed, the term *presidential monarch* has been used, appropriately, to describe Mobutu. Acting as 'Father of the Nation,' his self-awarded title, Mobutu presided over a political system that had the formal trappings of a republic but was in reality the personal fiefdom of the president, who used the national treasury as his personal checkbook and disbursed both rewards and punishments at will." "Introduction," in Meditz and Merrill, *Zaire: A Country Study*, xlii.

182 *Contrary to the historically*   Schatzberg, *Political Legitimacy in Middle Africa*, 58, referencing Johannes Fabian, *Power and Performance: Ethnographic Explorations Through Proverbial Wisdom and Theater in Shaba, Zaire* (Madison: University of Wisconsin Press, 1990), 25.

182 *Though the notion of*   Robert B. Edgerton, *The Troubled Heart of Africa: A History of the Congo* (New York: St. Martin's Press, 2002), 136; Crawford Young and Thomas Turner, *The Rise and Decline of the Zairian State* (Madison: University of Wisconsin Press, 1985), 30–31, referenced in Turner, *The Congo Wars*, 50. "The post-colonial state still refers to itself as Bula Matari, in radio broadcasts in national languages," writes Turner.

182 *or the Belgian Congo's paternalism*   Turner and Meditz, "Introduction," in Meditz and Merrill, *Zaire: A Country Study*, xxxvii.

182 *Unfortunately, in their dealings*   For instance, the local big man likely expects money and gifts to pass through him so that he himself can distribute them. A gift being given independently of him questions his power, for he, as the father, is the provider. However, the big man is not without responsibilities. Albert, in his rise to prominence in Kokolopori, found himself accosted constantly for material support. The people accorded him a role of power, and he had to follow through by offering what that role required. In this sense, colonialism could not have been sustained under the Bantu system, for it did not dispense in relation to what it took, and the same was true of Mobutu, who, though seen as a good leader and father of his people early in his presidency, later presided over "the pillage of national resources, as well as the widening gulf between the vast majority of the population and the very privileged minority resulting from it"—a state of affairs that a Congolese columnist in 1983 described as "worse than colonization." N'Zinga N'Singi, "Fait du Jour: Les Mains Sales," *Elima*, February 18, 1983, 2, referenced in Schatzberg, *Political Legitimacy in Middle Africa*, 169.

As Schatzberg explains it—and this is advice that conservationists should heed—"Put briefly, the father-chief may eat, and eat well, but not while his political children go hungry." Schatzberg, *Political Legitimacy in Middle Africa*, 168.

182 *The men of Lompole*   Parker, "Swingers," *New Yorker*.

183   *This is a disturbing scene*   Frans de Waal points out in his critique of
Parker's article, "The impression that there are new discoveries is merely a
product of creative writing." De Waal is speaking of discoveries relating to
bonobos; however, given the snide tone of the article and the degree to which
Parker's credibility is questionable, his portrayal of Hohmann, while instru-
mental for an examination of power dynamics between foreigners and local
Congolese, may also be a product of creative writing. De Waal, "Bonobos,
Left & Right," *eSkeptic,* h ttp://www.skeptic.com/eskeptic/07-08-08/#note01.

183   *It may not be a social*   The message is that power has a price. From listening
to villagers speak, I sensed that there is a sort of grace period—usually after
the big man has distributed the first gifts—when they would allow him to take
his place, to begin his work and get established, before they expected him to
honor his responsibility and begin sharing. He must then sustain a complex
chain of relations, supporting village chiefs and local leaders who themselves
risk appearing to have lost power with the ascent of the new big man. Gifts
must also pass through them to others and reaffirm their roles in society. No
one should lose face or go hungry.

In Kokolopori, I often saw BCI's members negotiating the subtleties of
this power structure. They faced it in their interactions with traditional leaders
and government officials, using ceremony and small gifts to show the people
that BCI respected their leaders. They even worked with these notions of power
within the organization of the reserve. On the day that BCI took Alan Root
to the river, to explore the possibilities of ecotourism and get a sense of the
landscape, Prosper Bafosimo Losaila, the man Albert had put in charge of the
reserve in his absence, behaved in a way that would make sense to me only later.

Though Prosper was responsible for facilitating the day's activities, he let
BCI do the organizing and simply enjoyed the activities himself. When the
dugout canoe was brought to the shore, he immediately relaxed into one of
the few chairs, and I suddenly realized the degree to which he perceived his
position as a symbol of power. Even people in Yetee, near the camp, explained
their frustration with him, that though they liked him, he was new to power
and increasingly behaving like a "big man," without realizing the responsibilities that came with that. At the river, however, Sally diplomatically explained
to him that BCI very much needed his help in organizing the people and that
without him they would have a hard time.

Albert told me that he had struggled with this before, that abuses in the
country had taught many young people to see power without the responsibilities that it entails. He pointed out that BCI had supported him, never
undercutting his work but allowing him to operate in a way that the people
respected. The Congolese, however, had been starved of opportunity, and
some leaders were quick to undercut him each time he lacked financing or had
a small failure.

184　*"What makes humans . . ."*　Parker, "Swingers," *New Yorker*. I confirmed this quotation with Hohmann by email, and he said that he stood by his words.

184–185　*The forest's value beyond*　In an article authored by five Japanese researchers and to which Dr. Mwanza contributed data, the discontent of the Congolese villagers in Wamba, near Kokolopori, is a central theme, how they constantly complain and want more. Sally and Michael once told me that BCI's conservation work has made Kokolopori's neighbors realize that they could be getting more and thus has, unintentionally, created some discord. But there is no voice of the local people in either of the articles, Parker's or the one by the Japanese researchers (Mwanza contributed only scientific calculations and isn't from Wamba or Équateur). In both cases, the people's discontent is shown only as an impediment to research, and there is no examination of the villagers' point of view or context, with the goal of understanding why they are complaining. While in Kokolopori, I heard from the local Bongandu that Wamba's villagers felt that the Japanese had been very slow to make good on their promises to invest in the community and had done so only when there was enough social pressure. Might this conflict never have come about had conservation and research worked in a more unified way and had the concern for territorial control not been so strong?

　　　　Gen'ichi Idani et al., "Changes in the Status of Bonobos, Their Habitat, and the Situation of Humans at Wamba in the Luo Scientific Reserve, Democratic Republic of Congo," in Furuichi and Thompson, *The Bonobos: Behavior, Ecology, and Conservation.*

185　*NGOs and researchers may*　As John Scherlis, who studied elephants for years in Tanzania, and was involved in early efforts to reconcile conservation and development, pointed out to me, as a general rule, scientific research and conservation have better circumstances and outcomes when there is a commitment to stewardship and partnership with local people.

186　*If we are cursed*　Wrangham and Peterson, *Demonic Males*, 258.

André Tusumba

192　*Already in his first year*　As Mobutu once said, *"Ondimi, ondimi te, ozali MPR"*—"You agree, you disagree, you are MPR anyway." Alden Almquist gave me this information in an interview in Washington, DC, in October 2012.

196　*Whereas Kabila followed*　Prunier, *Africa's World War*, 124.

196　*Some accounts state that*　Prunier, *Africa's World War*, 130–31. Prunier writes:

　　　　Four days later the AFDL military leader Kisase was killed by the RPA. He had always been a thorn in the side of the Rwandese because of his openly nationalistic attitude, which often brought him into conflict with his RPA minders. There was a famous occasion when he stopped the RPA from taking a large electric generator from Goma Airport to Rwanda, saying that it belonged to the Congolese state and that he was accountable to that state and not to Kigali. And there were numerous occurrences of public speeches when he had voiced his defiance of the overbearing Rwandese. The RPA had never managed to keep him under control, while Kabila accepted the nonstop day-and-night presence of six to ten Tutsi "guardian angels" around him. After the AFDL "consolidation" everything went very quickly: since he was "a nationalist" the Rwandese asked him with some irony to go and take care of this newly developing Mayi Mayi problem. At the last moment, as he was heading to Butembo, his bodyguards were removed and replaced by some of Kabila's. Kisase was careless enough to go anyway, and they killed him.

197 *But the decay of*   In *The Congo from Leopold to Kabila*, Georges Nzongola-Ntalaja writes: "For it is this decay that made it possible for Lilliputian states the size of Congo's smallest province, such as Uganda, or even that of a district, such as Rwanda, to take it upon themselves to impose rulers in Kinshasa and to invade, occupy, and loot the territory of their giant neighbour" (214).

197 *They gave him further*   Stearns, *Dancing in the Glory of Monsters*, 201.

197 *They believe that*   Turner, *The Congo Wars*, 10, 12. In building his argument for the Congolese distrust of outsiders, Turner cites Kevin C. Dunn, *Imagining the Congo*, 172.

198 *Today, given the Congolese's*   Prunier, *Africa's World War*, 153–54.

198 *suspending political parties*   Stearns, *Dancing in the Glory of Monsters*, 167–69, 176.

198 *The RDC massacred*   Ibid., 212.

201 *Park guards were equipped*   Paul Raffaele discusses the military situation in the Virungas in *Among the Great Apes: Adventures on the Trail of Our Closest Relatives* (New York: Harper Collins, 2010) 62–67.

201 *But as he argued with*   As much as from the bushmeat markets, André learned about the wildlife because of the gifts that villages gave him when he protected them from military predation. This was how he discovered the presence of okapis, which, like bonobos, were not thought to live in the area. That he'd received okapi skins as gifts made the job of asking the villagers not to hunt them extremely delicate. He spent time with local leaders, gradually introducing them to the idea of endangered species. After a number of meetings, several villages agreed to sign accords against hunting okapis, elephants, and bonobos. He knew that the population was poor, that they had no other resources, so he asked them only to limit the number of animals of other species that they hunted. Gradually, the villagers even began

reporting to him when soldiers hunted the protected species so that he could stop them.

Defending the Vocation

204 *He focused on bonobos*   Research supports the theory that humans can contract diseases from eating primates. In *Eating Apes,* Dale Peterson writes: "The notion that chimpanzee SIV was the origin of HIV-1 has today become more or less accepted dogma, increasingly confirmed as the viral examination of wild chimpanzees continues and the evidence expands. The news alerted medical professionals about the importance of bushmeat as a potential route of viral transmission" (102). See also Nathan D. Wolfe et al., "Naturally Acquired Simian Retrovirus Infections in Central African Hunters," *Lancet* 363 (March 20, 2004): 932–37, http://www.jhsph.edu/research/affiliated-programs/walter-reed-johns-hopkins-cameroon-program/documents/Papers/Wolfe2.pdf; Nathan Wolfe, "Where Will the Next Pandemic Come From?" *Wall Street Journal,* October 8, 2011, http://online.wsj.com/article/SB100014 24052970203476804576615133333388072.html?KEYWORDS=Where+Will+The+Next+Pandemic+Come+From; Anne W. Rimoin et al., "Major Increase in Human Monkeypox Incidence 30 Years After Smallpox Vaccination Campaigns Cease in the Democratic Republic of Congo," *Proceedings of the National Academy of Sciences of the United States of America* 107 no. 37 (September 14, 2010): 16262–67, http://www.pnas.org/content/107/37/16262.full; HaoQiang Zheng et al., "Emergence of a Novel and Highly Divergent HTLV-3 in a Primate Hunter in Cameroon," *Virology* 401 no. 2 (June 5, 2010): 137–45, http://www.ncbi.nlm.nih.gov/pubmed/20353873.

206 *As soon as Jean-Marie*   The funding came through the US Fish and Wildlife Service from the Great Ape Conservation Fund and was allocated to Sankuru as part of the Bonobo Peace Forest.

208 *They discussed the RCD*   Speaking of this now, Michel sees both points of view: "André understands that Kabila was doing the same thing as Mobutu, so they had to act quickly to get rid of him. [André] represented Lodja and restored control to the people, and everyone there speaks well of him. . . . He helped the population get back to work and form committees and make peace. He met with local authorities to discuss democracy and helped people increase production. Given that André was from the village of Lumumba, from the same bloodline, people respected him. The father's bloodline mattered and you were always home if you came from that region."

210 *These populations are expected*   Peterson and Ammann, *Eating Apes,* 135.

210 *or, as Dale Peterson writes*   Ibid., 116.

210 *In 2000, the bushmeat trade*   Miles, Caldecott, and Nellemann, "Challenges

to Great Ape Survival," in Caldecott and Miles, *World Atlas of Great Apes and Their Conservation,* 226.

210 *Pregnancies produce only one*   Lacambra et al., "Bonobo *(Pan paniscus),*" in Caldecott and Miles, *World Atlas of Great Apes and Their Conservation,* 88.

210 *Parents must invest a great deal*   Peterson and Ammann, *Eating Apes,* 136.

210 *Like humans, bonobos develop*   In *Primate Conservation Biology,* Cowlishaw and Dunbar write: "Brain tissue is one of the most energetically expensive tissues in the body (in humans it consumes eight to ten times as much energy as would be expected based on its mass alone: Aiello and Wheeler 1995). . . . This finding suggests that one of the reasons large-brained species have slow growth rates is that neural tissue is laid down at a fixed rate: developing a large brain simply takes longer." [32–33, referencing Leslie C. Aiello and Peter Wheeler, "The Expensive-Tissue Hypothesis: The Brain and the Digestive System in Human and Primate Evolution," *Current Anthropology* 36 no. 2 (April 1995): 199–221.]

210 *In the typical life span*   Lacambra et al., "Bonobo *(Pan paniscus),*" in Caldecott and Myles, *World Atlas of Great Apes and Their Conservation,* 88.

210 *He knew the classic scenario*   Peterson and Ammann, *Eating Apes,* 118.

210 *The villagers said they*   In developing a community model for the Sankuru Nature Reserve, BCI looked to the Tayna Gorilla Project in the east of the country, which, though only 270 square miles, was the first community-based reserve in the Congo to be legally designated as a new form of protected area: *réserve naturelle.* The World Conservation Union has different designations for the various types of protected areas, and the Congo adapted their own names for one of those categories. This reserve was to be multi-zoned and managed by the locals for sustainable development of the forest. There were also integral zones where there was no hunting or use of the forest's resources.

211 *Instead, she asks rhetorically*   Terese Hart, "Something Went Wrong in the Middle of Congo," Searching for Bonobo in Congo, July 29, 2008, http://www.bonoboincongo.com/2008/07/29/something-went-wrong-in-the-middle-of-congo/. The full text of this part of the blog reads:

> **But what did ACOPRIK do?**
> - Did they steal chickens or goats from someone in the village? NO
> - Did they make off with village women? NO
>
> **It was something more subtle . . .** something that I had a lot of trouble understanding. This is what the villagers said:
> - ACOPRIK had been well received by the village on several visits between 2005 and 2007.
> - ACOPRIK came to get the Djonga chiefs to sign documents saying they would not hunt bonobo or okapi.

- ACOPRIK deceived Djonga by using these signatures on a different document in distant Kinshasa, with the result that
- ACOPRIK "sold" their own Djonga forest and officially lost their traditional rights.
- Word of this fundamental deception swept like wildfire over radio and word of mouth from the capital of Kinshasa.

She goes on to state that though André did "push through a decree creating the Sankuru Reserve," it didn't take away the villagers' rights. She explains that "limits are drawn on a map but there are in fact no restrictions inside the Sankuru Reserve at all: not on hunting, fishing, farming nor even logging." However, just afterward, she posts a copy of the reserve legal documents, which, as they are in French, most readers of her English-language blog will not understand. The proclamation in fact states that in the reserve's zones that are dedicated to conservation, firearms, traps, hunting equipment, the exploitation of valuable materials and hunting are banned. The formulation is standard for community-based reserves, allowing people areas for farming and hunting animals that are not endangered or legally protected, and others strictly for conservation.

The full text of the proclamation can be seen at "second page of Sankuru Reserve statute," Flickr, July 29, 2008, http://www.flickr.com/photos/teresehart/2715289566/. It forbids the following:

1. to introduce any kind of animal or plant, firearms, traps or all hunting equipment, to capture or transport living or dead wild animals, skins or trophies, their meat or all other byproducts of the fauna;
2. to chase, to hunt, to capture, to destroy, to frighten or to trouble in any way all types of wild animals, even those thought to be harmful, except in the case of legitimate defense;
3. to exploit valuable material or to carry out all activities likely to alter the animals' habitats or the natural character of the reserve.

212 *While community reserves allow* I contacted Pierre Kakule, director of the Tayna Gorilla Reserve and the Tayna Centre for Conservation Biology, who defended André's character and work. I also met with Lambert Mende, who represented the Sankuru region and was the DRC's presidential spokesman.

"André," Mende told me, "is the only person who brought us a real project. He's the only one who follows that project daily. He's in the villages. He explains. He speaks to the people. And I support him entirely. So who in the forest doesn't support him? Who is it? . . . There is serious environmental deterioration. We saw how the nature was being destroyed by the local populations, and André is the first person who brought us a clear project, who told us how we can stop this deterioration. Here's how we can lead people to have a different view of nature, to tell them that the forests aren't inexhaustible. We have to turn toward other sources. . . . We need to use the people to protect their own environment and give them reasons and explain what they can do so that they won't die of hunger while protecting their environment. These notions, we didn't have them. He was the first person who talked to us about them."

212 *Hart presents one other*   Hart references Isidore Ndaywel è Nziem, *Histoire Générale du Congo: De l'Héritage Ancien à la République Démocratique* (Paris and Brussels: De Boeck and Larcier s.a., 1998), 955.

213 *"I remember when André . . ."*   Everyone I interviewed insisted the Harts would have known that BCI and ACOPRIK had already been working in that region, and had nonetheless started their project without mentioning it to them or offering to collaborate. Furthermore, a 2007 grant proposal by the Harts emphasizes the uncertainty regarding which parts of that area might comprise bonobo habitat. BCI advisor John Scherlis told me, "ACOPRIK and BCI were involved in this before TL2 (the Hart's future park, named for the area's rivers). They were actually unaware of Terese and John's program in the TL2 area, whereas I believe that John and Terese would have been very aware of what was going on at Sankuru."

Grant application to U.S. Fish & Wildlife Service's Great Ape Conservation Fund for project entitled "A New Conservation Landscape for Bonobo: Discovery and Conservation of the Tshuapa-Lomami-Lualaba Landscape, Democratic Republic of Congo," submitted by Terese Hart (project manager) and Jo Thompson (grant administrator), dated July 20, 2007, signed by Jo Thompson, Executive Director, Lukuru Wildlife Research Foundation.

213 *And yet the idea that*   For instance, the Wildlife Conservation Society (WCS), in one of its reports, writes the following:

> Most of the SNR [Sankuru Nature Reserve] contains no bonobos at all, and what bonobos there are were found outside the Reserve to the southeast. We conclude that any further funding should be targeted at areas with much greater bonobo conservation potential. Salonga National Park, to the west of Sankuru, contains several areas with high bonobo densities . . .

Innocent Liengola et al., *Conserving Bonobos in the Last Unexplored Forest of the Democratic Republic of Congo: The Tshuapa-Lomami-Lualaba Landscape,* Wildlife Conservation Society, June 2009.

The first line of the quote above is false based on CREF and ICCN surveys; at least half of Sankuru contains bonobos. Conveniently for WCS, this scientific report suggests that funding should go to Salonga, where WCS has its sites, or that new protected areas should be created. Furthermore, one of the report's authors works with the Harts on the TL2 project (See http://lomami .wildlifedirect.org/2007/05/21/bout-ash/), and the map included in the report shows the TL2 project boundaries taking up nearly half of the Sankuru Nature Reserve. However, if we look at a grant report by the Harts from 2009, we see a contradiction emerging:

> The first phase of our TL2 project is closing with our strong presence in the southern forests where we have been able to document that the bonobos are not only present, but reach their highest density in central Congo.

Terese Hart and John Hart, *A New Range Extension for Bonobo, Pan paniscus, in D.R. Congo,* http://www.bonoboincongo.com/wp-content/uploads/2011/03/Wallace-Report_juillet09.pdf.

Reading this, one could easily assume that the TL2 area to which Terese Hart refers is far outside Sankuru. The name TL2, the location for the Harts' projected park, refers to the three rivers that frame it: the Tshuapa, the Lomami, and the Lualaba, the last of which is the name for the Congo River in this region. I spent some time looking at maps of TL2 that the Harts composed for their reports, and in them, the boundary of the Sankuru Nature Reserve is drawn in a pale mauve that is hard to follow alongside all of the dark blue rivers and the green and red lines of boundaries for the Harts' proposed park and conservation zone. Sankuru's eastern border is largely invisible, hidden beneath a river, and yet we see that, in the Harts' map of bonobo occurrence, some of the highest concentrations are in the eastern portion of Sankuru. Lastly, in their map of "conservation villages" for the development of their future national park and community conservation zone, the mauve line of Sankuru has vanished entirely, its eastern territory taken up within the Harts' project. It is easy to speculate that they removed the line of Sankuru so as not to draw attention to the fact that one of their "conservation villages" appears to be directly on its border. Terese B. Hart, *A New Conservation Landscape for Bonobo: Discovery and Conservation of the Tshuapa-Lomami-Lualaba Landscape, in the Democratic Republic of Congo,* Lukuru Wildlife Research Foundation, June 29, 2009, http://www.bonoboincongo.com/wp-content/uploads/2011/03/TL2-Final-Report-to-USFWS_June-2009.pdf.

"The natural thing," Sally tells me, "would have been for the Harts to work in partnership with Sankuru. They were in the area that we originally proposed for a bonobo reserve. The DRC's Ministry of the Environment and the ICCN wanted to enlarge it to protect the entire watershed, and to include the entire administrative territory, for better governance. We respected [the ministry and ICCN's] decision and wanted to work with them on creating sustainable livelihoods in the larger area. . . . We invited the Harts to work with us, but instead they attacked. The only possibility for them was their project or nothing, and they were ready to destroy Sankuru to have their way, rather than to acknowledge and honor different conservation approaches."

213 *None of the people   note 1:* I have found that one common theme at BCI is a

consistently high degree of respect for the Harts' scientific work in Ituri, in the DRC. BCI funded trainings of Vie Sauvage staff and CREF researchers with John Hart when he worked for the Wildlife Conservation Society. Sally recalls meeting him at a conference years before and asking him to help with bonobo conservation. She insists on the need to cooperate for a common goal, to be bonobo-like about conservation, pointing out that there is a huge challenge just saving the bonobos and very few people available to work on it. And despite the conflict, even Alden Almquist and John Scherlis, both of whom have been with BCI since its founding, still have respect for the Harts, offering similar reasoning.

"I respect anybody," Alden tells me, "who in the most successful material civilization that the planet earth has ever seen—ours—can manage to sustain idealism over a lifetime, and they have. And I apply that to missionaries. I apply that to conservationists. I apply that to health workers. Teachers. Across the board. If you can live and work in the middle of highly stressful physical circumstances for a lifetime out of dedication to an ideal, you have my respect, and the Harts do, because they've done that. And it doesn't mean that I agree with them. I disagree with them strongly on quite a lot of things. They're very weak in their understanding of local culture. . . . I've been to meetings and in workshops with these people. They're not bad people. They're bad to BCI. They're unfair to BCI."

note 2: A number of the people I interviewed said that the Harts were originally working within the Sankuru Nature Reserve, but that they moved their programs just to the east of it, allegedly under pressure from the ICCN and the Ministry of the Environment, though I have not been able to confirm this. (The reserve is based in the Sankuru administrative region, and any conservationist working within it would normally be required to go through its administration.) André Tusumba, Michel Kitoko, and Benoît Kisuke have said that the Harts first worked in the east of Sankuru without permission from the reserve's administration and then moved just outside of it to the east. What is certain from the biodiversity maps that the Harts created is that they did work in eastern Sankuru without permission and recorded high levels of bonobos there.

213   *As conservation biologist*   Soulé, "Conservation Biology and the 'Real World,'" 1986, http://www.michaelsoule.com/resource_files/172/172_resource_file1.pdf.

214   *The authors go on to state*   *World Atlas of Great Apes and Their Conservation* also states, "The other area of absence falls between the Tshuapa and Lomami Rivers"—a statement that appears to reflect the belief that Sankuru has no bonobos even though the Harts' survey maps show high concentrations in this very area. Lacambra et al., "Bonobo (*Pan paniscus*)," in Caldecott and Miles, *World Atlas,* 84–85, 93.

214 *The East Coast of the United States* Environmentalist Bill McKibben describes the return of forest to the northeast. In 1850, he notes, only 35 percent of Vermont was covered with woods, whereas 80 percent of the state is forested today, and animals not seen in generations are making a comeback. By the 1960s and 1970s, he writes, the pattern of forest and field in Vermont was similar to the pattern before 1800, "its appearance much like it must have been prior to the American Revolution." *Hope, Human and Wild: True Stories of Living Lightly on the Earth* (Minneapolis: Milkweed Editions, 2007), 14–15.

214 *This would create a buffer* We must remind ourselves that if the people have no reliable source of livelihood, they will travel the distance to the high biodiversity areas and hunt, even if those areas are protected as a reserve or a park.

215 *"If you look at the eastern . . ."* *note 1:* Michael goes on to say: "It's true that to the west of the Tshuapa River, the biodiversity decreases. There are still bonobos, okapi, elephants, and a great deal of primates, among them an unknown species that the CREF researchers noticed. But we lacked the funds to help them do the necessary tests and research to identify it. Since then the Harts have announced it as a new species. There's nothing wrong with that, but we should be working with them. As for the rest of Sankuru, it is an important watershed, and our goal was never to make small, fenced-in protected areas. Everyone knows what happens to the biodiversity in places like that. We are aiming for long-term restoration."

note 2: The Harts recently announced this monkey. In an interview on NPR, John Hart states, "As we talked to the local hunters . . . we realized that this animal was well known to the locals." This statement supports Michael's claim that CREF and ACOPRIK were well aware of the monkey's presence. Scott Neuman, "Monkey, New to Science, Found in Central Africa," NPR, September 13, 2012, http://www.npr.org/blogs/thetwo-way/2012/09/13/161097374/monkey-new-to-science-found-in-central-africa. See also Becky Crew, "Lesula: New Species of African Monkey Discovered," *Scientific American,* September 15, 2012, http://blogs.scientificamerican.com/running-ponies/2012/09/15/new-species-of-african-monkey-discovered/.

215 *Was it scientific jealousy* Sally, Michael, André, and Benoît Kisuke all believe that the Harts saw that they had no justification for the funding they had taken; they should have known that a local NGO was already working in the area, and that the ICCN was informed of the work going on there before the Harts began their own project. Benoît states that the Harts' frustration at having someone else make a scientific discovery "was translated by a reaction of disdain towards those who were able to do something before them, who weren't scientists." (Benoît is referring to Sally and Michael here, given that the CREF researchers and ICCN staff are scientists.)

215 *Michael believed they wanted* Another line of attack, which I have heard

mentioned in Kinshasa by people who did not wish to go on the record, but who claimed that the argument originated with the Harts, was that Sankuru should not have been made a protected area because there was still the hunting of bonobos, elephants, and okapi there. The people said that it shouldn't have been made a reserve until that hunting stopped. However, where would the funding to stop the hunting come from? There has been hunting in many of the DRC's national parks, including Salonga—indeed, in national parks across Africa. A realistic evaluation of the socioeconomic situation in Sankuru and most of the Congo would suggest that in the creation of a reserve, laws are set in place that allow NGOs and the government to procure funding to protect the species and reeducate the people. In an interview with Lilly Ajarova, executive director of the Ngamba Island Chimpanzee Sanctuary and Wildlife Conservation Trust in Uganda, I asked her what the most important aspect of conservation is, and she replied that it is creating laws that can be enforced, that give conservationists a concrete basis for their programs.

215 *Terese Hart's blog* Hart, "After Two Years in the Forests of Central Congo," Searching for Bonobo in Congo, August 25, 2009, http://www.bonoboincongo .com/2009/08/25/after-two-years-in-the-forests-of-central-congo/.

216 *Even the title of* Grant application to U.S. Fish & Wildlife Service's Great Ape Conservation Fund for project entitled "A New Conservation Landscape for Bonobo: Discovery and Conservation of the Tshuapa-Lomami-Lualaba Landscape, Democratic Republic of Congo," dated July 20, 2007.

216 *In* Primate Conservation Biology Katrina Eadie Brandon and Michael Wells, "Planning for People and Parks: Design Dilemmas," *World Development* 20 no. 4 (April 1992): 557–70; Christopher B. Barrett and Peter Arcese, "Are Integrated Conservation-Development Projects (ICDPs) Sustainable? On the Conservation of Large Mammals in Sub-Saharan Africa," *World Development* 23 no. 7 (July 1995): 1073–84; Clark C. Gibson and Stuart A. Marks, "Transforming Rural Hunters into Conservationists: An Assessment of Community-Based Wildlife Management Programs in Africa," *World Development* 23 no. 6 (June 1995), 941–57; all referenced in Cowlishaw and Dunbar, *Primate Conservation Biology,* 343–44.

216 *The public nature of the Sankuru* This assessment is based on Sally, Michael, and André's description. They believe that the conflict with the Harts led to difficulty in finding funding. Michael states: "While the Harts led an effective campaign to indicate to the major donors that there were no bonobos in Sankuru, that it was also weak in overall biodiversity—and this significantly contributed to Sankuru being cut off from great ape conservation funding—their own survey reports clearly show survey results with important bonobo populations, okapis, and even the newly discovered monkey species in Sankuru."

216 *However, shortly after an* An email to a number of people working in

bonobo conservation, written in December 2008 by an official at the IUCN Netherlands, cites "an apparent lack of synergy amongst at least some of the principle actors involved" in bonobo conservation. He states that "within the 'Bonobo conservation community' we found out that quite some people do not get along, or do not work very well together."

217 *Some village leaders sided*   The way the conflict caused the local people to break into camps is described by André Tusumba, Benoît Kisuke, Michel Kitoko, Michael Hurley, and Sally Coxe.

217 *In one year alone*   Claudine André et al. mention the influx of bonobos to the sanctuary but do not explain where they came from in "The Conservation Value of Lola ya Bonobo Sanctuary," in Furuichi and Thompson, *The Bonobos: Behavior, Ecology, and Conservation,* 303–22.

217 *In Kokolopori, BCI*   The goal of CDM is to "earn saleable certified emission reduction (CER) credits, each equivalent to one tonne of CO_2, which can be counted toward meeting Kyoto targets," according to the website of the United Nations Framework Convention on Climate Change, http://unfccc.int/kyoto_protocol/mechanisms/clean_development_mechanism/items/2718.php. According to Sally and Michael, Gian Claudio Faussone, the first designated national authority (DNA) for the Congo for the Kyoto Protocol, chose the Bonobo Peace Forest as the number one project in the country that the Kyoto Protocol wanted to support.

219 *There is a growing need*   Sheila Jasanoff, *Science and Public Reason* (New York: Routledge, 2012), 169–70.

219 *She described Sankuru*   "World's Largest 'Avoided Deforestation' Project Helps Save Endangered Great Ape in Congo," PR Newswire, http://www.prnewswire.com/news-releases/worlds-largest-avoided-deforestation-project-helps-save-endangered-great-ape-in-congo-79296412.html.

Viral Conservation

230 *He continued the degree*   Alden Almquist, "Society and Its Environment," in Meditz and Merrill, *Zaire: A Country Study,* 61–133; Alden Almquist, "Horticulture and Hunting in the Congo Basin," in Weber et al., *African Rain Forest Ecology and Conservation,* 334–43.

231 *He also told me that*   Alden cites Igor Kopytoff, "The Ancestors as Elders," *Africa* 41 no. 2 (April 1971): 129–42.

231 *Even at the national level*   "Confession Publique d'un Ancien Baron du Président Mobutu," *Elima,* April 22, 1992, 9; referenced in Schatzberg, *Political Legitimacy in Middle Africa,* 13.

231 *Some have attested that*   Emmanuel Dungia, *Mobutu et l'Argent du Zaïre: Révélations d'un Diplomate, Ex-Agent des Services Secrets* (Paris: L'Harmattan, 1993), 42–49; Emmanuel Dungia, *La Pieuvre Tropicale: Les Tentacules de*

Mobutu (Brussels: Emmanuel Dungia, n.d.); both referenced in Schatzberg, *Political Legitimacy in Middle Africa,* 136–37.

231 *During the 1974 World Cup*   "Soccer—Democratic Congo Warns of Magic Ahead of Key Match," *Reuters,* February 24, 1998; referenced in Schatzberg, *Political Legitimacy in Middle Africa,* 123.

231 *and in other situations*   Thassinda uba Thassinda H., *Zaïre: Les Princes de l'Invisible: L'Afrique Noire Bâillonnée Par le Parti Unique* (Caen: Editions C'est à Dire, 1992), 211–12; Kitemona N'Silu, "Les Léopards Exorcisés par les Chefs Coutumiers Batékés," *Elima,* April 2, 1987, 11; both referenced in Schatzberg, *Political Legitimacy in Middle Africa,* 55–56.

232 *Schatzberg writes that*   Simon Bockie, *Death and the Invisible Powers: The World of Kongo Belief* (Bloomington, Indiana University Press, 1993); Suzanne Preston Blier, *African Vodun: Art, Psychology, and Power* (Chicago: University of Chicago Press, 1995); both referenced in Schatzberg, *Political Legitimacy in Middle Africa,* 134.

232 *With regard to conservation*   Alden defined *pomoli* as the form of magic used to exchange the lives in one's lineage for kills in the forest. The people who live in the rainforest know what normal is, that a balance of life must be maintained, and they can see when the balance is off and someone is using sorcery.

232 *They only hunted during*   Alden points out that the exception to hunting rules was often for funerals: "They mostly trapped, but there were some exceptions. If there was a death and you needed to feed villagers, they would still do the communal net hunt. That was something I loved. They would still go out and spread the nets. . . . People would come out as a whole village, kids included. And the adults would tell the kids, 'Stop talking village talk,' and before they went to sleep, they would say, 'Dream of animals, because if you dream of them, you will kill them the next day.' And this was a group thing. They would spread the nets, and then the women and the kids with the dogs would bang on pots and take the leaves out from the dogs' collars and let them out in the horseshoe of nets and flush the duikers and antelopes into the nets." (The *basenji,* a breed of Congolese dog that can't bark, wear collars with wooden clappers. This way the hunters can keep them silent when necessary and follow their movements otherwise.)

233 *Even BCI's scientific surveys*   Ecologists Christiaan A. van der Hoeven, Willem F. de Boer, and Herbert H. T. Prins describe an approach similar to that used by BCI:

> Methods currently used for assessing wildlife density in rainforests are time and money consuming. The precision of the most commonly used methods is disputed, but accepted because more exact methods are not available. In this study a new method of wildlife density estimation is

explained. The new method is less time and money consuming, but yields comparable results with classical methods. The method was tested in the field in Cameroon and compared with transect surveys in the area and with relevant literature. The Pooled Local Expert Opinion (PLEO) method is based on the knowledge of local experts. A number of hunters were asked to estimate wildlife abundance in a specified area, after which the density/ km^2 was calculated for 33 wildlife species. These estimates were pooled and extrapolated for the whole study area. Elephant (*Loxodonta africana*) density outside the National Park was estimated to be 0.06 animals/km², and 0.3 inside. Buffalo (*Syncerus caffer*) density for the study area was estimated at 0.2 animals/km² and gorilla (*Gorilla gorilla*) density at 1.05 per km². Transect surveys carried out at the same time for considerably more money, taking far more time, produced too few data to calculate densities. The evaluation of the PLEO method was favourable and the method offers a substitute for conventional methods of estimating wildlife density in rainforests. The methodology is simple and it can be incorporated in many tropical biodiversity and conservation projects. It can also be used for long-term monitoring of wildlife status in a given area. In contrast with classical methods, the PLEO method is low in cost and assures local ownership of the results.

Van der Hoeven, de Boer, and Prins, "Pooling Local Expert Opinions for Estimating Mammal Densities in Tropical Rainforests," abstract, *Journal for Nature Conservation* 12 no. 4 (December 2004): 193–204.

See also Meijaard and Marshall, "Why Didn't We Just Ask?" *Forest Science News*.

234 *Blinded by the old*   Joseph Conrad's voyage in 1890 was the worst experience of his life, from which neither his health nor his spirit recovered. He went so far as to say that before going to the Congo, "I was a perfect animal," and that since, "I see everything with such despondency." In *In the Footsteps of Mr. Kurtz,* Michela Wrong writes: "Conrad was more preoccupied with rotten Western values, the white man's inhumanity to the black man, than, as is almost always assumed today, black savagery" (184, 210).

234 *In* Dancing in the Glory   Stearns, *Dancing in the Glory of Monsters*, 328.

234 *Neither Albert Lokasola*   John Oates, in *Myth and Reality in the Rain Forest,* contests the notion that "rural people will tend to be more protective of wildlife if they are given greater control over it." He describes the presumption of such people living harmoniously on ancestral land as "an alternative romantic myth that has become even more pervasive than the myth of Africa as a primeval wilderness." Oates, *Myth and Reality in the Rain Forest,* xii.

Others have pointed out that conservation theory can be wed with traditional practices for sustainability. In *Eating Apes,* Dale Peterson writes:

Marcellin Agnagna, who grew up in a village called Kouyougandza in northern Congo, informs me that thirty years ago, before European "development" arrived, village hunting worked the old way. "Each village used to have a delimited area for survival activities purposes: a piece of forest. No activity was allowed in the village forest without previous authorization of the clan leader or the chief. Each village had a limited number of hunters and they used to hunt for the entire community, not for themselves. When a hunter killed a big prey (buffalo, sitatunga, or bushpig), he was supposed to give a leg or the head and neck to the village or clan leader, a piece for each family, and the rest was for himself. He was allowed to sell part of his extra meat, but he was more likely to exchange it for something he could not afford (such as cassava, salt, soap, et cetera). There was no bushmeat trade. And as everyone was attached to the tradition, the rules were respected—so the concept of 'sustainable use' is not new for the forest people." (64–65)

235 *Later I read one*　Ian Redmond, "Where Are the Great Apes and Whose Job Is It to Save Them?" in Caldecott and Miles, *World Atlas of Great Apes and Their Conservation*, 290.

The River

241 *Over the years, I'd read*　note 1: In *Au Soudan: Excursion dans l'Ouest Africain*, Camille Habert wrote, "Il n'y a pas de crépuscule dans les pays tropicaux, et que la nuit succède au jour presque sans transition." Habert, *Au Soudan* (Paris: Delagrave, 1898), 100, http://archive.org/stream/ausoudanexcursiooohabe#page/n5/mode/2up.

　　note 2: Beryl Markham, *West with the Night* (New York: North Point Press, 1982), 45–46. The book was first published in 1942.

　　note 3: Samuel Taylor Coleridge's *The Rime of the Ancient Mariner* was first published in 1798.

243 *The next day, as Sally*　The workshop with the DRC's government and Conservation International was part of a project that BCI initiated ten years ago and invested heavily in to start the first conservation concessions in all of Central Africa. BCI attracted the attention of the World Bank after having proposed conservation concessions in the DRC logging review, in which many logging concessions were nullified for not qualifying. Before then, a significant portion (24–55 percent) of the bonobo habitat was carved up into logging concessions. The World Bank contacted BCI because they saw that BCI had put in a dossier. BCI contacted CI, which had invented and first implemented (in Guyana) the conservation concession model. Sally presented the concept as applied to the bonobo habitat at a meeting in Belgium about the DRC's forests

(CONFOR DRC), hosted by the King of Belgium. This led to BCI and CI deciding that CI would take the lead on the conservation concessions, applying for the grant from the Congo Basin Forest Fund, newly created by the UK and Norway, with the agreement that BCI would be the implementing partner. (Mehlman, P., Rice, D., Niesten, E., Coxe, S., Hurley, M., Scherlis, J. and F. Hawkins. 2008. *A Pilot Conservation Agreement: The Bonobo Conservation Concession Project Équateur, Democratic Republic of Congo.* Concept piece submitted by Conservation International to the Chatham House Roundtable Review of Innovative Management and Financing Mechanisms for the Forests of the Democratic Republic of Congo.) The estimates for the percentage of bonobo range designated as logging concessions are taken from Miles, Caldecott, and Nellemann, "Challenges to Great Ape Survival," in Miles and Caldecott, *World Atlas of Great Apes and Their Conservation,* 223–24.

243 *The project would provide* The concessions would provide income to the national government, paying them in the same way that a logging company would. Furthermore, the concession project would provide *"cahiers de charge"* similar to what logging companies are supposed to provide. This is a benefit package that would most likely include health clinics, infrastructure, schools, and sustainable livelihood programs and assistance. The government normally should receive concession fees annually, to offset the loss from not having the land be logged.

An explanatory footnote from CIFOR, The World Bank, and CIRAD, *Forests in Post-conflict Democratic Republic of the Congo: Analysis of a Priority Agenda* (Indonesia: Center for International Forestry Research, 2007) explains conservation concessions:

> Although many of the details for implementing this approach have yet to be worked out, the general idea of a conservation concession as provided for in the Forest Code is clear: by providing compensation, a conservation concession agreement would make the absence of logging economically attractive to the government and to the local communities. It would offer reliable and steady compensation calibrated to offset the economic impact of foregone timber industry, in exchange for the right to manage the area as a protected site. This would be a legally binding agreement. The specific commitments of the parties would be negotiated between the biodiversity investors, local communities and the government. In essence, such an agreement would stipulate that the government will not open the forest for logging as long as payments, support to local development, and conservation activities are delivered, and vice versa, based on agreed-upon indicators and performance standards.
>
> Conservation concessions would come in addition to the country's commitment to establish formal protected areas such as parks and reserves.

They would be established in areas that could otherwise be allocated for logging. At the time this study was being finalized, conservation groups had expressed an interest in establishing such a conservation concession in the DRC. This would be a pilot project for the Congo Basin. It should be noted however that, since 2000, the Government of Cameroon has set aside about 800,000 hectares of production forests with a view to establishing such conservation concessions, but has not received any concrete proposals so far. (76)

Epilogue: The Red Queen

251 *If Zaire was one of*   In *Political Legitimacy in Middle Africa,* Michael Schatzberg writes:

> A decade later, during Mobutu's partial liberalization, the CNS set up a Committee on Stolen Property. The committee's final report noted that although Zaïre was one of the poorest states in sub-Saharan Africa, it was also one of the continent's largest importers of luxury automobiles. In addition, the report also noted that in 1989 the budgetary rubric "purchase of vehicles" represented 10 percent of the total national budget and that the sums expended on the health and education sectors did not even receive 3 percent of the total. (170–71)

Schatzberg cites Lambert Mende Omalanga (rapporteur) and Tshilengi wa Kabamba (président) et al., "Rapport de la Commission des Biens Mal Acquis" (République du Zaïre, Conférence Nationale Souveraine, Commission des Biens Mal Acquis, Palais du Peuple, September 1992), 118 (CEDAF, Brussels, 2492—III).

Author's Note

When I set out to write this book, my goal was to examine BCI's model for conservation and to see what I could learn from it. I had no knowledge of conflicts between conservationists in the bonobo habitat and no interest in writing about them. Only when I realized the degree to which those conflicts were part of the story and were weakening conservation efforts did I decide that they needed to be addressed.

The conflicts between conservation NGOs and bonobo researchers, as described in this book, are based on the accounts of the people I have interviewed, among them, Sally Jewell Coxe, Michael Hurley, Nicolas Mwanza, John Scherlis, Alden Almquist, Albert Lokasola, and André Tusumba. There are at least two perspectives on every story, and I attempted to contact and interview the principal individuals who have been in conflict with BCI. However, I was not able to get responses, or sufficient responses, to understand how they would explain their positions.

This book does not in any way attempt to describe the totality of the contributions to conservation made by the above-mentioned people and organizations; it simply tries to address, with the information available, specific cases of conflict, in order to highlight ways that conservationists might be impeding the work of other conservationists. The scientists and organizations mentioned in this book—AWF, WWF, Dr. Furuichi, and the Harts—have made significant contributions to research and conservation over the years. Conservation organizations consist of numerous individuals who may or may not represent the organization's policy, and policy is constantly evolving. Furthermore, individuals move on to new positions or NGOs though the names of the organizations under which they worked remain the same. It is important to remember that the book is presenting a snapshot built around my research and the views of the people to whom I had access. It does not strive to denigrate the careers of others but to show the damaging effects that result from the competition for funding, prestige, and territory, as well as from the inability of groups to work together despite their having divergent visions.

Acknowledgments

My goal was to illustrate an approach to conservation while examining the institutional cultural that created it; however, due to narrative constraints, I could not mention or describe in detail the contributions of every person or organization involved with the Bonobo Conservation Initiative. Many have contributed to BCI's success: Alison Mize (co-founder of BCI), Ingrid Schulze, the Kokolopori-Falls Church Sister City Partnership, John Waugh, Jean-Marie Benishay, Edward Green, Suzanne Litner, Amy Clanin, Russ Mittermeier, Maryll Kleibrink Moon, Richard Ruggiero, Joanne Cipolla Moore, Abbé Jean Claude Atusameso, Jatukik Providence Foundation, Linsey Hurley, Salvadore Alonzo, Jane J. Coxe, Wynne Paris, Sue-Savage Rumbaugh, Richard Wrangham, Laurie Timmerman, BCI-Australia, Angus Gemmell, Martin Bendeler, Philip Strickland, Luke Bennett, BCI-France, Charles Duke, BCI-UK, Tallulah Bygraves, Tom Brady, Philip Bonn, Malcolm Jones, Jane Mansour Solomon, Daniel Solomon, Jerry Litner, Gene Mosby Blackwell Nash, Ted Turner, Israel Eiss, Don Capoccia, Elaine Broadhead, Athena Buchanan, Steve Hamblin, Mark Johnson, William Meade, Norman Rosen, Sue Ann Taylor, Mulegwa Zihindula, Anthony Rickert, DLA Piper, LLP, Alan Lewine, Takayoshi Kano, Karl Ammann, Douglas G. Cogan, Corneille Ewango, Michael Fay, Donald Goldberg, Ursula Goodenough, John King, Mbangi Mulavwa Habari, Mark Leighton, Honorable Tidal W. McCoy, Lucrecia Myers, Amy Parish, Erik R. Patel, Richard Rice, Tony Rose, Duane Rumbaugh, Gerald Seligman, Gurucharan Singh-Khalsa, Wayne Skipper, Andrew Sparkes, Steven Stone, Michael Sweatman, Gabriel Thoumi, Theodore Trefon, Pierre Kakule Vwirasihikya, Chip Comins, Sally Ranney, Jan Hartke, Mupenda Bin Muzumbi, Susie Wellington, Jeff Wellington, Billy Duggan, William Garvelink, Linda Garvelink, Bernardo Issel, Geoffrey Kent, Alex Georgiev, Jeffry Oonk, Arne Schiotz, Don Tuttle, Tim Roman, Ceres Bainbridge, Annie Neal Corkill, Annie Goeke, Leanne Hankey, Paku Tshambu, Magdelena Bermejo, Celeste Maia, Protecyo Gran Simio, Rebecca Bossen McHugh, Faida Mitifu, Cosmas Wilungela, Didace Mpembe, José Ndundo, Essylot Lubala, Mbangi Mulavwa,

Yangozene Kumugo, Yamba Yamba Mikwaya, Motema Salo, Mola Ihomi, Veronique Lilima Lokasola, José Ikongo, Anatole Bekoma, Jean Robert Iyeya, trackers from the Kokolopori Bonobo Reserve (Ekalakala, Nkokoalongo, Hali-Hali, Bongima, Yotemankele, Iyondje groups), trackers in Lac Tumba (Botwali and Mbie-Mokele).

Lastly, during the writing of this book, two members of BCI passed away due to illness, Charles Malu "LeBlanc" and Aimée Nsongo, as did Panbanisha, at the Great Ape Trust (now known as the Iowa Primate Learning Sanctuary).

I would personally like to thank the following people: Austin Lin, Leza Lowitz, Ray Klein, Kevin Hunt, Richard Wrangham, Robert Hedin, Ann Gibbons, John Waugh, John Hayes, Bonnie Huang, Bob Engels, Amy Clanin, Alison Mize, Arthur Moore, Graham Moore, Heather Faris, Kevin Lin, Mark Anderson, Dorothy Hearst, Joel Hernandez, Frank Bures, Judith Landry, Audrée Wilhelmy, Yael Goldstein Love, Sue Savage-Rumbaugh, Suzanne Kamata, Elizabeth McKenzie, Tricia Theis Rogalski, Amber Dermont, Joanne Cipolla Moore, Susan Hradil, Kermit Blackwood, Michael Khadavi, Martha Marin, Corey Redekop, Mary Purdey, Kelsey Davis, Jennifer Ailles, Claire Bidwell-Smith, Laura Ciccone, Lisa Morales, Charity Oetgen, Patrick Thomas, Daniel Abrams, Maria Turner, Nithin Coca, Wendy Grossman, Walter Krumholz, Dean Klinger, Louis-Philippe Ouimet, Linsey Hurley, Brian O'Leary, Louise Doire, Helen Amiri, Llana Barber, Brian Clopp, Cheryl Annie Doucette, Michelle Soucie, Jess McCormick, Jenn Rowland, Sandi Liu, Simone Allmen, Tracy Motz, Mireille Granger, Nathalie Bergeron, Barbara Potvin, Renee Morel, Sal Alonzo, Michael Berryhill, Joanna Cockerline, George Grinnell, Mélanie Gauthier, Mal Jones, Stephen Hunt, Myriam Fehmiu, Mark Preston, Catherine Lefebvre, Vanessa Green, Éditions Alto, Antoine Tanguay, Tristan Malavoy-Racine, Amber Compton, Julianne Lange, Alden Almquist, Richard Rice, Hjalmar Kuehl, Hollis Melton, Geoffrey Byrd, Beth Hanson, Nick Counts, Hannah Ehlenfeldt, Christianna Fritz, Kalie Caetano, Greg Foster, and Bonnie Ellis. I would like to thank everyone at BCI, ACPORIK, and Vie Sauvage for taking the time to share their knowledge and resources with me, especially Sally Jewell Coxe, Michael Hurley, André Tusumba, Albert Lokasola, Nicolas Mwanza, and John Scherlis. The Writers Room offered me a much needed space for work in Manhattan, and the Canada Council for the Arts provided a grant that covered a portion of the funding necessary to research and write this project. Lastly, I would like to thank everyone at Milkweed Editions, especially Allison Wigen, for her continual support, and Daniel Slager, for his editorial guidance and for making this book possible.

Empty Hands, Open Arms

Deni Béchard is the author of a memoir, *Cures for Hunger,* and a novel, *Vandal Love,* which won the 2007 Commonwealth Writers' Prize. He has traveled in over fifty countries and reported from India, Rwanda, Afghanistan, and Northern Iraq. He has written for a wide range of publications, including the *Los Angeles Times, Outside,* and *Salon.com.* When not abroad, he lives in New York.

Interior design by Ann Sudmeier
Typeset in Sabon Pro
by BookMobile Design and Digital Publishing Services